"Dan Berger gives us a highly readable person... ... ...
master historian and storyteller who manages to reveal and illustrate what the
lived experience of the sixties was like for a group of militant idealists who
wanted to make a difference."
—HERNÁN VERA, author of *White Racism*

"Meticulously researched, *Outlaws of America* demolishes prominent myths of
the Sixties, especially the notion of the Two Sixties, one Good and the other
Bad. Dan Berger's loving recounting of the movement's later phase provides us
with fresh insight into our history. Unafraid to be critical, Berger's recounting
of the Weather Underground's evolution gives us the inside story. We have
waited a long time for a book like this. It will be essential reading for activists
wishing to rekindle popular insurgencies and radical action."
—GEORGE KATSIAFICAS, author of *The Imagination of the New Left*

"With each transition in the life of the organization, Weather activists reckoned
with a compelling question: if you had to choose, would it be immortality without knowledge or mortality with freedom? This question was the wellspring for
strategy through the late 1960s and early 1970s, when revolution was a word of
celebration, on the tip of activists' consciousness across the United States and
beyond. By drawing upon the voice of compassion offered by activist and political prisoner David Gilbert as the touchstone throughout the book, Berger treats
us to a deep understanding of why commitments taken up by the Black Power
and anti-imperialist struggle thirty years ago continue to accompany us now.
This book is welcome company for all those who want their history straight up,
who seek to honor the vulnerable, circuitous, imperfect and brave struggle for
racial justice in U.S. history."
—BECKY THOMPSON, author of *A Promise and a Way of Life*

"The book is essential to understanding the history of the 1960s, as well as the
present movements against racism and imperialist war.... Even more than the
previous works about Weatherman/WUO, *Outlaws of America* brings it home,
especially to the US reader, that people do make choices (life-changing choices)
based on their politics. This in itself is revelatory in a culture that thinks politics
begins with the Republicans and ends with the Democrats."
—RON JACOBS, *CounterPunch*

OUTLAWS
of
AMERICA

...a single spark can start a prairie fire...

We are outlaws, free and high—a youth guerrilla underground in the heart of Babylon.

—Weather Underground communiqué (1970)

OUTLAWS

of

AMERICA

THE WEATHER UNDERGROUND AND THE POLITICS OF SOLIDARITY

BY DAN BERGER

AK PRESS

·EDINBURGH, WEST VIRGINIA, OAKLAND·

1990   15 YEARS   2005

Outlaws of America: The Weather Underground and the Politics of Solidarity
© Dan Berger 2006

ISBN 1 904859 41 0
ISBN13 9781904859413

Library of Congress Control Number 2005938412

AK Press
674-A 23rd St
Oakland CA
94612 USA
www.akpress.org

AK Press
PO Box 12766
Edinburgh, Scotland
EH8 9YE
www.akuk.com

Layout and design by Josh Warren-White
Cover photograph by David Fenton

IN LOVING MEMORY OF MY GRANDMOTHER, ROSALIA Benau, and for David Gilbert—compassionate souls, learned teachers, and lovers of life.

And for all who make it their life's work to build a world in which justice, peace, liberation, and freedom are not the rhetoric of the ruthless but the reality for all people—in hopes that we learn from history to create a better future.

★ CONTENTS ★

ACKNOWLEDGEMENTS

T HIS BOOK HAS BEEN MY HOPE AND FEAR, MY DREAM and nightmare, my love and frustration—but ultimately my pride and joy—for four years. In that process, I've met many people who have helped in the project. To be sure, below is but a partial listing.

First and foremost, a heartfelt thank you to my interviewees, whose open and honest discussions with me form the backbone of the book: Vicente "Panama" Alba, Ashanti Alston, Bill Ayers, Terry Bisson, Scott Braley, Lyndon Comstock, Bernardine Dohrn, Herb Dreyer, David Gilbert, Naomi Jaffe, Jeff Jones, Claude Marks, Esperanza Martell, Rob McBride, Judith Mirkinson, Michael Novick, Susan Rosenberg, Suzanne Ross, Robert Roth, Mark Rudd, Judy Siff, Michael W. Tarif Warren, Laura Whitehorn, Cathy Wilkerson, and Donna Willmott. (In the interest of eliminating superfluous documentation, I have not footnoted in the text comments from the interviews, a listing of which can be found in the bibliography.)

Sundiata Acoli, Marilyn Buck, Kathleen Cleaver, Helen Garvy, Ray Luc Levasseur, Robert Pardun, J. Sakai, Zoharah Simmons, Susan Tipograph, Jeremy Varon, and Victor Wallis all offered helpful comments about some facet of this project, providing informed perspectives on some of the ideas presented here. Thanks to those who didn't get interviewed but who participated in lengthy, repeated conversations with me that helped shape my thinking for the project: Max Elbaum, Bob Feldman, Sharon Martinas, Matt Meyer, Jalil Muntaqim, Roz Payne, and Meg Starr. John Mage read the manuscript with a careful legal eye and provided useful edits.

This book would not be what it is without Bob Feldman's generosity in sharing resources—as well as his willingness and availability to discuss many issues relating to this project. Sam Green, director of the documentary *The Weather Underground*, was also very open in sharing resources, including complete transcripts of several interviews conducted for his film and pictures he had discovered in the course of his research, for which I'm most grateful. To the extent many people pick up this book, the prodigious efforts of Sam and his co-director, Bill Siegel, deserve some of the credit for sparking renewed interest in the group. Naomi Jaffe and Roz Payne (www.newsreel.us) not only opened up their personal archives to me, but also let me stay at their respective houses when I was doing research with them.

This book started as a 40-page senior thesis at the University of Florida. My undergraduate advisors there, professors Louise Newman and Kurt Kent, went above and beyond the call of duty in assisting me, academically and personally. Above all else, they helped me develop a "life of the mind" at the University of Florida, which I would not have otherwise been able to do. I thank them with all my heart. Louise also read and commented on a penultimate draft of the manuscript, for which I am most grateful. Although they are too numerous to name here, I'm immensely thankful to all who offered comments on my senior thesis or other sample chapters.

Thanks are also due to the libraries and the librarians. The Tamiment Collection at NYU's Bobst Library proved particularly useful in finding archival material. (My first trip there was funded by a University Scholar's grant from the University of Florida.) The Columbia Oral History Project, especially Mary Marshall Clark and Ron Grele, was especially generous in sharing three interviews they did, including a rather lengthy one. Matt Meyer deserves all the credit for alerting me to the office.

A hearty and loving thank you to Josh Warren-White and all at AK Press, who understood the importance of this project from the beginning and were nothing but encouraging throughout, despite dealing with an occasionally temperamental author. AK Press continues to meet the challenges of being an independent and social justice publisher with great skill. Thanks also to Palgrave Macmillan for sharing with me an anonymous review of the manuscript, and to them and Rowman & Littlefield for their understanding.

In addition to providing the inspiration of his impressive writing career—not to mention his long activist history—Terry Bisson rescued the rather unwieldy first draft of this manuscript. His careful editing throughout greatly improved the quality and clarity of this book, and it was a great pleasure to work with someone so knowledgeable, good-humored, and talented. Claire McGuire, besides being a good friend, did an excellent job preparing the index. Suzy Subways copyedited the book with acumen and good timing. For putting up with last-minute requests to read near-final drafts of certain chapters—and then giving immensely useful comments in a short time period—I want to give special thanks to Walidah Imarisha, Sharon Martinas, Matt Meyer, Judith Mirkinson, Robert Roth, and Meg Starr.

Despite any political differences we may have, my family was very encouraging in the writing process. My dad, Alan, predicted years ago that I would write a book and gave me scholarly advice throughout; my mom, Naomi, reminded me to keep my eyes on the prize. My brothers, Ariel and Michael, and my sister-in-law, Carrie, have been supportive and gracious from day one.

Several friends offered invaluable political guidance, moral support, and good humor throughout this project. Thanks especially to Clare Bayard, Chesa Boudin, Inja Coates, Andy Cornell, Chris Crass, Lula Dawit, Chris Dixon, Patrick Dunn, Mike Erwin, Zoë Erwin, Kenyon Farrow, Jeff Frank, Guillermo Rebollo-Gil, Jessica Hardy, Jethro Heiko, Walidah Imarisha, Naomi Jaffe, Eugene Koveos, Heather La Capria, elana levy, B. Loewe, Matthew Lyons, Molly McClure, Claire McGuire, Matt Meyer, Moira O'Keeffe, Debbie Sanford and Greg Schirm (House of Our Own Bookstore), gabriel sayegh, Dara Silverman, Nicole Solomon, Meg Starr, Suzy Subways, Tom Thomson, Emily Thuma, and Josh Warren-White. I'm also grateful to the friends, comrades, and colleagues in the various social justice organizations I've been a part of over the years, especially Resistance in Brooklyn (RnB).

Scott Braley and Mickey Ellinger came along at the right time to read several drafts of the manuscript, offering detailed comments that greatly strengthened the final product and earned them my endless gratitude. Same for David Gilbert, who gave 30 pages of feedback on a draft he read quickly amidst the confines of prison life. More than that, David has been a close friend and a good example of what it means to be someone who lives life with dignity and principle. elana levy housed me several times during trips to Attica, read and commented on numerous drafts of several chapters with great precision and care, and invited me to give my first public talk about the Weather Underground. She was a tireless source of encouragement, humor, and good ideas. Matt Meyer immediately understood what this book would need to do to be of any value, and he knew better than I initially did the risks involved with writing such a book. I thank him for his political clarity and for his friendship. Heather La Capria, Eugene Koveos, Andy Cornell, B. Loewe, and gabriel sayegh were all smart, steadfast, and supportive friends throughout the course of this project in ways too detailed to mention here. While they never ceased to remind me of the world beyond my computer screen, all were more than encouraging when I had to disappear from the world to finish. Much love and respect.

ABBREVIATIONS

AIM	American Indian Movement
BLA	Black Liberation Army
BPP	Black Panther Party
COINTELPRO	Counterintelligence Program (FBI)
CORE	Congress of Racial Equality
ERAP	Economic Research and Action Project
FALN	Fuerzas Armadas de Liberación Nacional Puertorriqueña (Puerto Rican Armed Forces for National Liberation)
MFDP	Mississippi Freedom Democratic Party
NLF	Vietnam National Liberation Front
NLN	*New Left Notes* (SDS newspaper)
PFDC	Prairie Fire Distributing Committee
PFOC	Prairie Fire Organizing Committee
PL	Progressive Labor Party

PSP	Puerto Rican Socialist Party
RC	Revolutionary Committee of the Weather Underground
REP	Radical Education Project
RNA	Republic of New Afrika
RYM	Revolutionary Youth Movement
SDS	Students for a Democratic Society
SLA	Symbionese Liberation Army
SNCC	Student Nonviolent Coordinating Committee
VVAW	Vietnam Veterans Against the War
WUO	Weather Underground Organization

INTRODUCTION

*We study history not for the purposes of nostalgia
or exotica but rather to learn the lessons to enable
us to make history, to fight for a future that affords
all people the conditions for survival and the
opportunity to make a positive contribution.*
— *David Gilbert* [1]

MY JOURNEY FROM MY CHILDHOOD HOME IN suburban Syracuse, New York, to the state's most infamous prison is remarkably easy. After a brief visit to my old stomping grounds during summer break from the University of Florida, I drive for about two hours, first on the New York State Thruway and then on small highways that cut through mostly white, rural towns seemingly trapped in the 1950s. Near the village of Attica, a confederate flag flies from the front porch of a house. My destination, Attica Correctional Facility, is the area's major employer and a place that imprisons mostly Black and Latino people, as do other prisons across the country. The flag serves as an example of the link between racism and incarceration in the United States. It is a sobering reminder of who is being guarded and who is doing the guarding.

An eerie quiet permeates the car once I enter the town. The village of Attica lies, almost literally, in the shadow of the maximum security prison made famous by the 1971 prisoner revolt—and the ensuing tragic, brutal attack by the state of New York that left twenty-nine prisoners and ten guards dead. [2]

The gray castle walls of the prison seem to stretch for miles. Well-armed guard towers complete with cameras, searchlights, and heavily armed men appear every thirty feet, the only conspicuous sign of high technology on the otherwise medieval exterior. I pull into the second driveway, park, and get out.

"You can't park there," yells a voice from the guard tower.

After following the guard's instructions and moving to the opposite end of the parking lot, where a small but helpful sign is marked "Visitors," I head toward the only visible opening, a mouse hole in the prison walls.

Feeling like a mouse, I enter. Two uniformed cats seated at a battered desk direct me around the corner to fill out forms: name, address, and the name and number of the prisoner being visited.

David Gilbert

83-A-6158

A guard types my information into his computer and examines my ID. Dismissed, I go and sit on the bleacher seats with the other visitors, mostly Black, mostly female. In the bulletproof booth in front of us, an officer sits underneath half a dozen empty gun belts. This guard controls the gate leading to the visiting room. A Latino prisoner is led out, I imagine to court, with his hands cuffed and legs shackled. Several Black prisoners doing yard work are led in, talking softly in the sterile atmosphere. It's calm, almost peaceful—but eerie.

I'm so nervous I have to pee.

After a quick trip to the paint-peeled bathroom, I wait on the bleachers for at least twenty minutes, easing the tension by repeatedly reading the posted dress code. I'm cool, since it apparently applies only to women: short skirts and strapless tops are the major apparel offenses (punishable by being denied your visit). Guards periodically call out the last names of prisoners, to which visitors respond by submitting themselves to the security checkpoint.

When the bleachers are nearly empty, a guard yells, "Gilbert!"

I rise, as if responding to the scolding tone in his voice, and approach the metal detector. The guard doesn't have to tell me to remove my belt and shoes; I know the drill from the airport. The only difference here is the small bag of quarters for the vending machines that David told me to bring, and a pen and paper I brought to take notes. Instead of a boarding pass, I hand the guard the visiting paperwork along with my ID. The metal detector seems especially strong—more sensitive than those at the airport—as some women visitors have had to take off their bras to pass through because the underwire set off the flat beep of the detector and the angry stare of the guard.

I make it through unscathed, and an unsmiling guard stamps my hand with invisible ink. After more than half an hour, I've made it through the first room. I wait by the barred gate until the guard in the booth hits a switch and it slowly opens. I walk through, about seven feet, to another gate with the cold, white, metal bars I imagined this place would have. I have to show my invisible ink stamp to the guard.

While waiting for the gate to open, I study the bulletin board through the bars: Corrections Officers Golf Team get-together (an award-winning team, apparently); karaoke night at a nearby bar; someone's retirement party; and advertisements for vacation cruises. Not even the quasi-waiting room of a prison is safe from advertisements.

The gate opens and I am "outside" inside the walls, on a sidewalk surrounded by grass and little flowers. The big, gray outer wall is at my back. Images of helicopters dropping tear gas while state police fire down from the walls fill my mind as I walk fifty feet toward the red brick inner building, studying the flowers by the sidewalk. Is that the yard the prisoners seized, over there, behind the wire fence? Do people cultivate these flowers by the sidewalk or do they grow on their own? Life and death compete for space in my mind as I walk toward visiting a political prisoner in Attica.

Another door opens. I stick my hand under another black light to show my invisible stamp. Through another automatic gate. A little sign with an arrow directs me down a long hall to the VISITING ROOM. I'm not sure what I expected the room to be like, but this isn't it. It looks like a school cafeteria—complete with bad murals, small tables, and junk-food vending machines. I hand my form to a duo of guards sitting at a high table overlooking the room. They copy the information down, although I don't get the form back. One dispassionately says, "three, five," and nods toward the tables.

I start walking before I really understand the directions. But I figure it out and proceed to row three, table five. There are four chairs at each visiting table. I look around the room and notice that all of the prisoners sit in the chair facing the guards. It's going to be a long day, I assure myself. Little do I know how fast the time will fly.

The pseudo-Disney murals adorning the walls are mildly disturbing: a blonde-haired, blue-eyed man in Native regalia holds an eagle, while dolphins, sea horses, and pandas play poker. The visiting room is loud. About half the tables are occupied by men in green, mostly Black. They are playing cards or gossiping or necking (not allowed but tolerated) with their wives or girlfriends, or bouncing their kids on their knees. It's almost cheerful until you look up and see the dirty barred windows looking out on nothing at all and realize that half of the people here can't leave.

At last, a door at the back of the room groans open, and in walks a 50ish white man in green pants, just another prisoner. He looks like the pictures I'd seen of him, only with glasses—thick glasses with big frames, almost like the kind my father used to wear. After he checks in with the guards and greets some other prisoners, he joins me. We hug briefly; he's a few inches shorter than me and clean-shaven. He has an air of compassion and a tender, unassuming smile.

"How was the trip?" he asks, in his heavy Boston accent, as we meet for the first time.

Three years before this 2002 visit, I had found David Gilbert's name and a brief personal statement in a book about political prisoners and prisoners of war in the United States.[3] I was a young activist, a senior in high school, and something about his essay appealed to me—probably the gentleness with which he wrote and certain similarities in our identities. We are both white Jewish men from middle class backgrounds, both activists for social justice. David was also a revolutionary, and that interested me, although I couldn't fully articulate why at the time. Coming of age in the 1960s, he had been a member of Students for a Democratic Society (SDS) and the Weather Underground, one of the most controversial of 1960s-era radical groups.

He answered my letter and we began to correspond. His letters were thoughtful, honest, and often wryly funny. Through several wars, my entering college, global anti-capitalist movements on the upsurge, the radical newspaper I started, the September 11 attacks, and my father's bout with lymphoma, among many other notable events—joys and heartbreaks both personal and global—I stayed in steady communication with David through letters, plying him with questions about movement history and current events.

And now this: our first meeting. The food (from machines) is terrible and the coffee is weak, but who cares? The conversation shines. Everything is fair game: the global justice movement, summer plans, racism, family (mine and his; I'm the last visitor he has before a two-day visit with his son, who is a year older than me and was raised by two of David's lifelong friends and comrades). And of course, the Sixties, that mythological period of protest that predated and outlasted the decade after which it is named. In the first of several visits and a running series of letters and phone calls, David and I discuss his forty-year political history: the organizing he did, the groups he was a part of, and the lessons he takes from these experiences.

The feelings of unease, of somberness, that overtook me as I entered the village of Attica, and even more so, when I entered the prison, are disappearing as we sit laughing and talking. David is very honest about his experiences—what was good, what he learned, mistakes made, possibilities for the future. He is also very interested in me—how I am doing, what I think about various issues, my summer plans. This is, I think, what noted Brazilian educator Paulo Freire had in mind when he spoke of the importance of dialogue, a mutual exchange between people in the interests of education, reflection and action.[4] In talking with David, I can't help but think of Assata Shakur's description of Sundiata Acoli, a Black political prisoner and longtime activist, as having such strong love for people and for social justice that "you can almost hold it in your hands."[5] Despite the stringent conditions of his incarceration—including the real prospect that he may never get out—I am struck by how much David embodies the late feminist thinker Gloria Anzaldúa's assertion that, "To live is to struggle," and Che Guevara's dictum that true revolutionaries are guided by love.[6]

In a way, it's ironic to be sitting in Attica with a former member of the Weather Underground. One of the group's targets was the New York Department of Corrections, after the state's brutal response to the 1971 Attica rebellion. Like other actions by the Weather Underground, the bombing of the Department of Corrections office was carefully planned to avoid injuring anyone; the action was done to draw attention to the prisoners' grievances—and the dead and mangled bodies that defined the state's response. Now here's David, locked down in Attica for life times three.

The Weather Underground, initially the Weatherman and eventually the Weather Underground Organization, took its name from a popular Bob Dylan song and grew out of Students for a Democratic Society, the biggest and most organized representation of radical white youth of the 1960s. SDS was against the Vietnam War and opposed to racism, but Weather went further, emulating Third World revolutionaries—Cuba and Vietnam were especially the models—by going underground and undertaking armed actions. Weather was heavily inspired by the Civil Rights and Black Power Movements as well. The Black Panthers were its heroes, and Weather viewed the underground as a way to express its solidarity with the Third World, within and outside the United States. Guided by staunch support for these "national liberation" struggles, the Weather Underground saw clandestinity as part of creating a broad culture of resistance.

And David Gilbert was in the thick of it. The man sitting next to me, his brown hair salted with gray, co-wrote the first SDS pamphlet describing "the system" as imperialism.[7] During the 1960s, David was just one of many "young soldiers for the revolution," as Angela Davis would later call activists of the time period.[8] His organizing at Columbia in the early and mid-1960s earned him the title "father of Columbia's New Left"—an impressive accomplishment given how central activism at that university became to an ever-more radical movement among white youth.[9] Known as a movement theorist and intellectual, Gilbert was no stranger to action. In 1968, he played a role in the historic Columbia University strike, and joined Weatherman when SDS split in 1969, drawn to the group's emphasis on militant anti-racism. David was underground for more than ten years, until he was finally captured in the course of a political "expropriation" (armed robbery) that went terribly wrong. Two cops and a Brink's guard were killed in an action by the Black Liberation Army, a clandestine outgrowth of the Panthers. David drove a getaway car that didn't get away. And though he never fired a gun, he is serving three consecutive life terms for first-degree murder. He has been in prison ever since October 20, 1981—five weeks before I was born, and when his own son was just fourteen months old.

Though most activists of his generation did not end up with life in prison, Gilbert's trajectory from a liberal pacifist student to a member of a revolutionary anti-imperialist organization committed to armed struggle mirrors that of many Sixties-era activists. Hundreds of thousands of people committed their lives to the movement in some way, convinced that another world was not just possible but on its way. In this way, David Gilbert's story (in terms of his politicization and radicalization) is a quintessential one of the white Left in the Sixties. Thus, this book uses Gilbert as a narrative thread through which to explore how white activists became increasingly radical in relation to the Black freedom movement and the Vietnamese struggle, leading some to go underground and build clandestine resistance against the state. Based on two dozen oral histories and research into both primary and secondary materials, *Outlaws of America* seeks to uncover what spurred the Weather Underground to action. In so doing, I will situate the group in the context of its times and critically examine its politics and practice.

"THE BEST OF TIMES, THE WORST OF TIMES"
MOVING BEYOND THE TALE OF TWO SIXTIES

THE WEATHER UNDERGROUND was not an aberration, but rather one expression of the rising revolutionary fervor of the late 1960s that saw people going underground; establishing feminist collectives; heading to the factories to "organize the workers"; building lesbian, gay, and transgender communities; and generally breaking from the U.S. establishment.[10] The Weather Underground was one among several clandestine groups, including those organized by Black nationalists, Puerto Rican *independentistas*, multiracial anti-capitalists, Catholic antiwar pacifists, clandestine abortion providers, draft resisters, and others. It was part of "a parallel universe" of burgeoning movements against what seemed to be a decaying imperialist system in its last throes.[11] Even before people were building an underground, militancy was on the increase; a radical magazine listed 236 acts of "sabotage and terrorism" in the United States in 1968 alone, a figure that would rise in years to come as protests routinely turned into street fights and bombings, sabotage, and armed struggle became commonplace.[12]

The "Sixties," then, was not the imagined neat ten-year period of nonviolent protest that ended in a quick, misguided burst of nihilistic violence. Instead, it was a dynamic period starting with the first waves of civil rights activism domestically (and national liberation movements globally) in the 1950s and stretching to the antiwar, feminist, working class, queer, and anti-racist organizing that lasted well into the 1970s.[13] No one tactic circumscribed the era, and political perspectives were constantly shifting in response to global events. The Weather Underground emerged from a cauldron of Black Power and state repression, of national liberation and cultural shifts, of revolutionary hope and steadfast determination.

In much of the history written so far, however, the Weather Underground becomes the poster child for the "bad Sixties," the symbol of a dream deferred if not destroyed. Even sympathetic histories sometimes define the first, more liberal half of the decade as the "good Sixties" and the second, more radical half as the "bad Sixties."[14] The "good Sixties," according to participant-scholars like Todd Gitlin, author of *The Sixties: Years of Hope, Days of Rage*, were characterized by a youthful optimism heavily influenced by liberal ideals. The "bad Sixties" saw the "death of the dream," an allusion to Dr. Martin Luther King Jr.'s famous vision of integration—a dream that no longer defined even King's politics in the late 1960s.[15] This "death of the dream" was marked particularly by the rise in Black Power and a more radical view of U.S. society. In that context, the Weather Underground is seen at best as a naïve distraction, at worst as a willful destruction of what was good about the Sixties.

But the dream did not simply die; like scores of radicals in the 1960s and '70s, the "dream" was killed, mostly by the state or by those acting in its interest. Martin Luther King, who had gone from a liberal civil rights preacher to an outspoken critic of U.S. foreign policy, was murdered in 1968 while in Memphis supporting striking garbage workers.[16] Police and FBI agents murdered dozens of Black activists, particularly from the Black Panther Party, as well as Native American, Latino, and, to a much lesser extent, white radicals, in Chicago, New York, Los Angeles, New Orleans, Pine Ridge, Attica, San Quentin, and elsewhere.[17] At the same time, cities across the country rose up in rebellion after rebellion. Therein lies one of the greatest fallacies of the Tale of Two Sixties: it obscures *why* people embraced radicalism and militancy. Without understanding the impact of state repression, radical movements don't make sense. The rationality and motivations underscoring the rise of groups such as the Weather Underground and the Black Liberation Army—as well as revolutionary aboveground groups—is apparent only in the context of dozens of murdered Black radicals, from Malcolm X to Martin Luther King, Bobby Hutton to Sandra Pratt and beyond, as well as those Latino (e.g., Rubén Salazar) and Native American (e.g., Anna Mae Aquash) radicals murdered as the 1960s became the 1970s and the government conducted an expanded, and often secret, war against all forms of dissent. In its own words, the FBI was attempting to "expose, disrupt, misdirect, discredit, or otherwise neutralize" political opposition, particularly among insurgent people of color.[18]

The Tale of Two Sixties also misses the other side of the turn to radicalism: the sense of possibility, the very real and logical belief that revolution was not only feasible but likely. Dividing the decade into good and evil halves misses the continuity of resistance, as well as the magnificent accomplishments of the revolutionary movements of the period. People had a sense that their actions made a difference. Lyndon Johnson's refusal to run for re-election in 1968 showed that the ruling elite could be impacted by protest. The Vietnamese, unified against U.S. occupation, were showing that even a militarily superior superpower could be defeated; after the National Liberation Front's 1968 Tet Offensive, many activists became convinced not only that the United States was losing but *that it should lose*, in Vietnam and anywhere else it tried to dominate. It was time to choose sides, and it seemed that lines were clearly drawn between socialism and imperialism. As former Black Panther and current political prisoner Mumia Abu-Jamal put it, "Revolution seemed as inevitable as tomorrow's newspaper."[19]

Young people played an especially prominent role in this burgeoning movement. The SDS National Office in Chicago summed this up with a Cuban poster that read "Youth will make the revolution."[20] A *Fortune* magazine poll in the fall of 1968 found that 368,000 university students considered themselves revolutionaries.[21] A similar poll of college students by Gallup in 1970 found that 44 percent felt violence on behalf of social change was justified, and more than a third described themselves as Left or "far Left."[22] A few months after the U.S. invaded Cambodia, the *New York Times* reported that "four out of ten college students—nearly three million people—thought a revolution was necessary" in the United States.[23] By 1971, a *Playboy* survey found that 1.17 million university students considered themselves revolutionaries.[24] Resistance was also growing in the armed forces. In May 1970, the *Wall Street Journal* reported that "at least 500 GIs deserted every day of May." Many of the Black antiwar soldiers were joining radical organizations like the Black Panthers when they returned, and soldiers in Vietnam began to "frag" their officers as part of their opposition to the war and to U.S. imperialism.[25]

In the spring of 1970, following the murders of four students (and the wounding of nine) at Kent State by the National Guard during a protest against the U.S. invasion of Cambodia, a Harris poll "reported demonstrations on 80 percent of U.S. university and college campuses" as more and more students "agreed that social progress was most likely to come through 'radical pressures outside the system.'"[26] Radicals on and off college campuses were being met with increasing violence. Within ten days of the Kent State murders, police killed six (wounding twenty) Black people at a protest against police brutality in Augusta, Georgia, and state and local police killed two (and wounded twelve) Black students in demonstrations at Jackson State University in Mississippi.[27] Also that month, police bayoneted eleven students at the University of New Mexico, wounded twenty people with shotgun fire at Ohio State, and wounded another twelve with birdshot in Buffalo.[28]

Student strikes and sabotage of government buildings exploded across the country. By May 10, 1970, Max Elbaum writes, "a National Strike

Information Center at Brandeis announced that 448 campuses were either striking or shut down: some four million students and 350,000 faculty were taking part in what amounted to a campus general strike." Also during this time, "thirty ROTC buildings were burned or bombed and National Guard units were mobilized on twenty-one campuses in sixteen states."[29] Considering the leading role community-based struggles by people of color played, it is all the more significant that predominantly white campuses were in such open revolt, building in part off the ubiquity of Black ghetto rebellions—of which there were approximately 300 between 1964 and 1968 alone.[30] These rebellions, along with the rising belief in self-defense work pioneered by people such as Robert Williams and advocated by many revolutionary nationalist groups in this country, were blunt arguments against a strictly pacifist approach to activism.[31]

A rising militancy buttressed increased identification with struggles outside this country, where movements against colonialism were achieving success, often as the result of armed struggle led by Marxist-Leninist movements. In addition to the ongoing struggle in Vietnam, the Cuban revolution triumphed in 1959, when the Algerians were in the final stages of a long and bloody war (which was ultimately successful) to kick out French colonialism. Ten formerly colonized African nations received independence in 1960 alone, and revolutionary movements in Bolivia, Brazil, Pakistan, and elsewhere challenged the power structure, both globally and locally.[32] Students and workers in Paris effectively shut down the city in May 1968, and youth were active in grand anti-imperialist protest movements in Czechoslovakia, Germany, Greece, Japan, Mexico, Yugoslavia, and throughout the world. Domestically, the various manifestations of the Black freedom struggle—from Malcolm X to Black Power groups—were at the cutting edge of forging solidarity with liberation movements in the Third World.[33] While the two main Communist countries at the time (the Soviet Union and China) often supported national liberation movements elsewhere, the world Left generally opted for independence from either power. This was a New Left.

The call for Black Power, made popular in 1966 first by the Student Nonviolent Coordinating Committee (SNCC) and then by the Black Panther Party, challenged white anti-racists to organize other whites against racism rather than organize in Black communities. Black Power also raised the importance of analyzing the world through a lens that accounted for political power: who had it, what they did with it, and why. Rather than "bad ideas" being the problem and reform the solution, Black Power said that the "system" itself was to blame—and needed to be overthrown. Black Power identified people of color in the United States as being "internal colonies," citizens of the Third World. In a rising tide of national liberation and anti-colonial struggles, defining the system as imperialism and in need of a total, if violent, overhaul became the discourse of the day. The U.S. government was seen as the primary enabler and beneficiary of imperialism, and as such came under attack by a burgeoning radical Left movement.

The Black Panther Party was at the heart of the radical turn in the mid-1960s. Formed in Oakland, California, in 1966, the group became the "greatest threat to the internal security of the United States" by 1969, according to then-FBI director J. Edgar Hoover.[34] The Panthers, followed by the American Indian Movement (AIM), achieved such recognition by virtue of their insurgent community programs, most famously the community self-defense program. Far from a militaristic organization, however, the Black Panther Party instituted a range of community programs—what it called "survival pending revolution" programs—to meet the needs of Black communities while providing a direct challenge to the state. These initiatives included free breakfast for kids programs, free clothing giveaway programs, free schools, and free healthcare clinics.[35] These community programs inspired other radical groups, including El Comité and the Young Lords (both Puerto Rican), the Brown Berets and the Crusade for Justice (both Chicano/a), SDS and the Young Patriots (both white), the Red Guards and Yellow Peril (both Asian American), and the American Indian Movement—in addition to the women's liberation movement and the movement for lesbian, gay, bisexual, and transgender liberation, which also drew inspiration from the Panthers (groups such as The Feminists, the Gay Liberation Front, Radical Women, Redstockings, Street Transvestite Action Revolutionaries, WITCH, and others).[36]

THE WEATHER UNDERGROUND, MYTH AND REALITY

RECENT YEARS HAVE seen a spike in interest about the Sixties in general and the Weather Underground in particular, as scholars and activists alike seek to evaluate the last period of political, social, and cultural upheaval. Memoirs, scholarly texts, documentaries, and historical novels dot the landscape of both the academy and popular culture, and the Weather

Underground appears as a reference point in many of them.[37] Whether people love it, hate it, or don't understand it, the Weather Underground is a defining organization in Sixties history and mythology.

Indeed, it is hard to pick up a book about the period and *not* find a reference to the group. And yet, in becoming a fixture of Sixties history, the real Weather Underground is often lost in the process. The group becomes a symbol, a reference point for the "end of the Sixties," held up as the smoking gun that explains why the movements of the period failed, or dismissed as not meriting the attention it has received.[38] In some instances, the Weather Underground achieves near mythic status, so that any of the thousands of clandestine or illegal acts in the United States by white people in that time period is attributed to the group.[39] As a result, one organization stands in for a much broader set of circumstances or is even treated as the sum of what it, in reality, was just one part. And the group's frenetic first nine months are regularly taken to define the entire seven-year period in which it was active.

Given this widespread attention to the group, it is worth exploring who the Weather Underground was, how it came to be, what it saw itself as doing, and why. The group needs to be rescued from myths and symbols, and instead dealt with at the real level. And what, exactly, was it? The Weather Underground comprised, at its height, a few hundred people, mainly SDS organizers, though its reach extended far beyond its membership. Anti-racism and support for the Third World were its guiding principles. It was a group of white North Americans who defined struggles against colonialism and white supremacy as central to any social justice movement. The group sought to use the white privilege and largely middle-class background of its members in the service of revolutionary change. It attacked government and corporate buildings with bombs, as is well known, but also through its media-savvy. The group released dozens of communiqués; wrote and published a book, a regular newsmagazine, and strategic pamphlets; and was featured in a documentary while still on the run. It was, in short, part of a "culture of resistance," a vibrant and dynamic revolutionary movement dedicated to fundamental and progressive social change. Racial oppression and war were key questions animating its actions. In so doing, the group's legacy raises lasting questions about white supremacy, global U.S. power, and social justice endeavors.

Seeing the United States as an imperial power engaged in a real war against Third World people globally, the Weather Underground's emergence directly correlates to what seemed like an urgent need for some kind of retaliatory capacity, a force to try and block or at least respond to the state in its continuing war of attrition—whether in Vietnam or in Watts, Angola or Attica. As such, the group sought to respond to the leading issues of the day, in a context established by Third World people. And yet, some have suggested that the WUO was instead motivated out of "guilt," a psychological deviation emerging because people felt bad about being white.[40] Viewing white opposition to racism and imperialism as guilt-driven ignores the continued need for whites to address racial oppression in the United States and around the world. Indeed, dismissing the movement (or segments of it) as guilt-ridden misses the driving force that made the Sixties what it was: the glimpse of the liberating power of solidarity, of allying with the oppressed in building a better world, of recognizing that the most oppressed would be at the forefront of creating such change.

As outlaws of and in America, the Weather Underground attempted to actualize poet Langston Hughes' call to make the United States be what it has never yet been. *Outlaws of America* is an attempt to explain what drove the Weather Underground and why—to trace the group's rise through SDS and in relation to Black Power and national liberation movements, to describe what it did underground, to examine what led to its implosion, and to create space for a dialogue of what the Weather Underground means for today. The issues that made the Sixties so vibrant, turbulent, active, and important—disparity between the powerful and the powerless, U.S. power and military aggression ravaging the Third World, systemic oppression of nonwhite people, threats to dissent—are all the more with us today. By understanding what the Weather Underground was—how it came to be, what it tried to do, why, and to what effect—we can, perhaps, better understand the issues facing us today.

The Weather Underground has a legacy that can be felt today; its militant anti-racism and internationalism remains a potent challenge to the status quo. It serves as the backdrop to today's generation of activists, which is just beginning to cope with the issues of race and empire, revolution and social change. And I can see the threat its legacy poses in the icy stares of the guards at Attica, where I sit talking and laughing with David Gilbert. In the back of my mind, I know that I will be leaving here soon—and that he will not. How could an academic, an intellectual, a seasoned organizer end up in prison with a life sentence?

PART ONE

STUDENTS FOR A DEMOCRATIC SOCIETY AND GLOBAL REVOLUTION

A National Liberation Front fighter in Vietnam.

SHAKING AMERICA'S MORAL CONSCIENCE
THE RISE OF STUDENTS FOR A DEMOCRATIC SOCIETY

1

> *Reality burst into my consciousness when I was 15, with the Greensboro sit-ins of February 1960. I guess I had been unusually naïve in that I fervently believed in America's rhetoric about democracy and equality. This promise was totally belied by the patent racism, as well as by the U.S. practice of imposing brutal dictators on Third World nations around the globe. The Civil Rights Movement also showed me more of a sense of humanity and nobility of purpose than I found in the white suburbs where I had grown up.*
>
> —*David Gilbert* [1]

IN THE FALL OF 1962, A 17-YEAR-OLD FORMER EAGLE Scout from Brookline, Massachusetts, entered Columbia University. Like many freshmen, David Gilbert was excited to be in the Big Apple and attending an elite school. Having supported the civil rights movement during his high school years, Gilbert was eager to find ways to become more of an activist. And unlike many of his peers (and professors) at Columbia, he was lucky enough to have known since 1961 about the struggles taking place in a faraway place called Vietnam, where the United States had already began supporting (with money and "military advisors") an unpopular anti-communist regime against a popular communist movement.

Gilbert's knowledge of Vietnam, its struggle for national sovereignty, and the U.S. involvement there came from a Vietnamese exchange student. In the early 1960s, this student informed her U.S. friends of what the anti-war movement would come to understand only later in the decade: that the Vietnamese revered communist leader Ho Chi Minh the way Americans viewed George Washington, as a great leader and liberator.[2] After learning this, Gilbert wrote an article in his high school newspaper saying that the

17

United States was supporting a right-wing dictator and meddling on be-half of the wrong side in a civil war. The article didn't win him any friends in high school, though he still was respected for his good grades, research skills, and inquisitive spirit.

A kid from a middle class Jewish suburb of Boston, Gilbert was an ardent believer in the promise of U.S. freedom and democracy. But even before hearing of the burgeoning war in Vietnam, his faith in the American dream had been shaken by the civil rights movement. When he read about the sit-in at a segregated lunch counter in North Carolina on February 1, 1960, the 15-year-old Gilbert began to question his assumption that "every-one had access to good housing, nutrition, medical care, and education as a matter of course." It was around this time that he went on his first picket line to support the Southern desegregation protests.

The Greensboro sit-in helped launch a broader sit-in movement, and soon images of Black people and anti-racist Northern whites being attacked at lunch counters and in the streets of the South filled television screens and newspaper front pages nationwide. The sit-in movement also sparked the creation of the Student Nonviolent Coordinating Committee. SNCC (pronounced "snick") was made up of students, predominantly Black, from across the country working on community organizing projects against white supremacy in the South; it would serve as a powerful inspiration to count-less people in this country about the structure of power and the strength of morally grounded action.

While there were only four Black kids in his high school of 2,000 people, Gilbert was nonetheless an early supporter of civil rights, thanks in part to the influence of his older sister.[3] A headmaster at his high school branded Gilbert a "troublemaker" for his support for civil rights and his ear-ly but rather mild criticisms of U.S. involvement in Vietnam.[4] Denied entry at Harvard, Gilbert settled on his second choice: Columbia University.

Shortly after his arrival at Columbia, Gilbert joined the Congress of Racial Equality (CORE), a multiracial anti-racist group engaged in voter registration and direct action work in the South. In particular, CORE had organized the Freedom Rides, multiracial interstate bus journeys beginning in 1961 that challenged segregation laws in the South. The Freedom Rid-ers faced brutal attacks by local police, the Klan, and impromptu mobs of white Southerners.

Gilbert didn't go South as some civil rights activists did; in retrospect, he says he lacked the courage and the level of commitment (two inseparable criteria, he now says) to join the Freedom Rides.[5] He supported the movement from New York, where his academic studies of foreign policy, combined with seeing racial oppression in Harlem, contributed to a rising anger that the United States was not living up to its promise of democracy.[6] He was learning that you didn't have to look South to see racial oppression— nor did you have to head South to fight it. He joined with the students supporting the Black and Puerto Rican cafeteria workers at Columbia who were trying to unionize, an early example of what would become axiomatic by the end of the decade: the racism, class exploitation, and lack of democracy characterizing the university system.

"There's this majestic library [at Columbia] with Plato, Socrates, all these names on it and in the hallowed halls, ivory. All this represents this pretense of humanism, of the pinnacle humanism, of knowledge and concern and all this stuff, and then people who are serving the food and mopping the halls are getting treated like shit," he said in a 1985 interview. "So it was quite a contrast."[7]

While the movement in the South grew in numbers and national stature (culminating in the massive 1963 March on Washington) and the union struggle at Columbia brought home the interconnections between race and class in the North, the situation in Vietnam was also intensifying, with more U.S. "advisors" being sent to aid the unpopular Diem regime in South Vietnam. Then the country was shocked when James Chaney, Andrew Goodman, and Michael Schwerner—three civil rights activists, two white and one Black—were murdered in Mississippi. Although countless Black people had been murdered in the Deep South (searches for the three men's bodies in the river banks yielded the bodies of several other murdered Black people), the deaths of two white Northerners during a Student Nonviolent Coordinating Committee campaign in Mississippi focused more intense national scrutiny on the South and on the movement.[8]

The three had gone South as part of SNCC's Mississippi Freedom Summer, an audacious 1964 project melding voter registration, community organizing, and direct challenges to the openly racist Mississippi Democratic Party as a way of challenging the party nationally to stand up for civil rights. SNCC and affiliated organizations recruited and trained hundreds of white students from the North as part of the campaign, believing that the presence of whites would focus national attention on the state (and hopefully prevent high levels of violence against the movement). The crescendo for the campaign came later in the summer, when the Mississippi Freedom

Democratic Party (MFDP) attempted to unseat the state's Democratic Party delegates at the national convention in Atlantic City.[9] The MFDP said it was more democratic than the state party, basing its argument on the widespread Black community support it had and the fact that the state party was openly hostile to Black needs. But the MFDP was unable to convince the national Democratic Party to seat it instead of the traditional Mississippi Democratic Party delegation. "By pledging their unwavering loyalty to the national slate, which the 'regular' [i.e., Mississippi] delegation did not, the MFDP dissidents believed they could secure the ouster of the racist state delegation and, thereby, record a victory for the democratic process," Robert Allen reports. "But the national party, seeking support in the South, decided to employ the vicious weapon of racism once again and rebuffed the challengers."[10]

A MOVEMENT EDUCATION

DURING HIS JUNIOR year, Gilbert received an education he wouldn't forget. It didn't come from his formal schooling, which he found largely boring, even though he enrolled in graduate classes to find a more challenging curriculum (first in political science, then in philosophy). Like so many of his generation, Gilbert's most impressive and lasting education came from the movement—in his case, from a woman in Harlem, from Malcolm X, and, in a circuitous way, from the New York Police Department.

Particularly inspired by the Black freedom movement, Gilbert, like many young whites at this time, grew increasingly radical in his political outlook. Beginning in 1964, he participated in a tutoring program through Columbia that took him to surrounding Harlem to tutor poor Black and Puerto Rican children. He chose this program over the other ones that brought the children to the university. "We used to joke—with incipient consciousness that something was seriously wrong—that the programs were designed to mold Harlem Blacks to think like Brooklyn Jews. However, one of the projects had the position that learning best took place in the child's own environment. That's the one I chose."[11]

Shocked by the level of oppression he saw in Harlem—especially from the police, who began to look to him not like peace keepers but like the occupying army for white supremacy, as well as from the daily constraints associated with living in poverty—Gilbert also found that complaining to the Human Rights Commission and other government or social service agencies was getting him and the Harlem residents nowhere. He was angry at the social violence he saw, frustrated by his growing realization that the establishment offered little in the way of meaningful change.

But there was another side to the story; amidst the "strains from oppression," Gilbert also found "a strength from the resistance to oppression and a basic humanism" that left a lasting impact. "There was a much greater sense of community, of the extended family, of helping each other out, of openness and expression of human feelings than anything I had experienced in Brookline or Columbia."[12] He began to see that Black people could run their own lives—and that the barriers to doing so were embedded deep in U.S. society.

In the few blocks between Harlem and Columbia, Gilbert's politics changed dramatically.[13] This transformation led him and other whites to think in terms of radical change, where oppressed people were "the arbiters of their own destiny" and where allying with "the Black struggle for human rights was a key to achieving a more humane society for white people also." Gilbert identifies this experience in Harlem as what made him a revolutionary, because it was the beginning of seeing that "people who are oppressed not only are downtrodden, but they actually could run their own lives, whatever their weaknesses, better than anybody from the outside, even a nice, well meaning liberal like myself could run it for them."[14]

He also found that the people of Harlem had a "much more advanced" understanding of U.S. society than his professors in the political science department at Columbia. After the sustained bombing of Vietnam started in February 1965, he learned a valuable lesson from a Harlem resident, the mother of one of the kids he tutored. Having read of the new bombings in Vietnam on the train into Harlem, Gilbert arrived at the house quite upset. "I can't believe it, our government is bombing people on the other side of the globe for no good reason," he remembers telling the mother of his student when she asked what was troubling him. Although the woman had never heard of Vietnam and, like the other families he worked with, was not especially active, her response was immediate: "Bombing people for no good reason, huh? Must be colored people who live there." Her comment connected the dots for Gilbert. "She made the connection in a very direct way that I had had trouble seeing, even though I had been working on both fronts (civil rights and peace) for some four years," he says. "I was still blinded by defining our system as a 'democracy' (with some faults) while she understood it as, in its essence, a racist and exploitative system."[15]

This conversation, along with his knowledge of Vietnam and combined with his experiences in Harlem and support for the civil rights movement, led him to "catch the wink" that "America is a democracy for some but not for others."[16]

Two other experiences around this time also helped transform David's consciousness about the nature of the entrenched and oppressive power structure. On February 18, 1965, David went to hear Malcolm X, the fiery Black leader, speak at the Audubon Ballroom. Malcolm was arguably the most influential African American leader at the time, on a par with if not more famous than the pacifist leader Martin Luther King. Unlike King, who had an impressive following among the Black Southern middle class and the white Northern liberal establishment, Malcolm's base was much more in the Black working class Northern ghettoes.[17]

A former prisoner who converted to Islam while incarcerated and was recruited into the Nation of Islam (NOI), Malcolm was the most famous leader of the NOI until he split with the group in 1963 as a result of corruption within the NOI leadership and his growing emphasis on building a political rather than a religious movement. Like no other figure until that point, Malcolm made popular the idea of Black nationalism and examined the problem of racism from a human rights, rather than a civil rights, perspective. The difference, as Malcolm underscored in his talks, is that civil rights are given or taken by the state, whereas human rights are those that every person is born with.[18] Malcolm also located racial oppression in a global perspective of ongoing Western colonialism that impacted African Americans as well as Africans, Asians, and other non-white peoples worldwide. This perspective asserted that the struggle was between oppressed and oppressor, and that the racially oppressed were not "minorities" (as they were and are still thought to be in the United States) but were a world majority. This paradigm shifted the terms of the debate and challenged the anti-racist movement to confront the U.S. power structure in its entirety and to do so in concert with revolutionary nationalist movements the world over.

Following his split with the Nation of Islam, Malcolm traveled to Africa and met liberation leaders from across the continent, which at the time was engulfed in a tidal wave of anti-colonial national liberation movements.

He returned to this country an outspoken proponent of Black Power and Black nationalism. Indeed, he started a group called the Organization of Afro-American Unity, modeled on the Organization of African Unity he had learned of and met with in Africa. The OAAU was an attempt to build a Black nationalist organization inside the United States, uniting African Americans with Africans and the world's "colored" majority.[19] Malcolm's theories provoked discussion and spurred action across the country, from working class ghettoes to Southern civil rights marchers to Student Non-violent Coordinating Committee militants, to two young men in California who would form a group called the Black Panther Party, an organization built largely on Malcolm's philosophies. In addition to Black nationalism, Malcolm also pioneered a philosophy of self-defense against aggression, which would be of particular interest to Black Panther founders Huey P. Newton and Bobby Seale. Self-defense philosophy had been made popular in the late 1950s by Monroe, North Carolina, NAACP head Robert Williams, and was institutionalized in the 1960s (especially in Louisiana and Mississippi) by Southern Black people in an armed organization called the Deacons for Defense and Justice, as well as through less politically cohesive armed units.[20]

For white activists, Malcolm's ideas were both exciting and challenging. Upset at the deep entrenchment of racism in both foreign and domestic life, David Gilbert was eager to hear the famous Black militant. He was also anxious about how he, as a white person, would be viewed. Where did he fit into a Black nationalist paradigm? Would he be shunned or welcomed? Did he have anything to contribute to the emerging revolutionary struggle? Gilbert found Malcolm's talk to be one of the defining moments of his young adult life, academically as well as politically. Malcolm's political clarity and eloquence was even more surprising given that his home had been fire-bombed four nights before the talk. "What really hit me about the speech was ... he said [that] the key division in the world is between oppressed and oppressor," Gilbert remembers. "That's how to look at the world. I remember I had been studying all this philosophy and political science, and seeing injustice, but not knowing quite how to sum it up, and he said, 'The key division is between oppressed and oppressor.'" The talk secured once and for all for Gilbert that the issue "wasn't a problem of uplifting Blacks as much as breaking a structure of oppression," in the United States and globally.[21]

Three days later, Malcolm X was assassinated, shot and killed by Nation of Islam members.

The final defining experience for Gilbert in this period happened just three months later, one month after SDS organized the first anti-Vietnam War march in Washington, D.C., on April 17, 1965, with more than 25,000 participants (650 of them from Columbia, thanks in part to Gilbert's organizing). In May of 1965, the nascent Columbia SDS and the Independent Committee on Vietnam (two organizations Gilbert was instrumental in starting) joined in a demonstration initiated by the Columbia CORE chapter. The intention was to block the doorway to an ROTC ceremony on campus in a symbolic act of non-violent civil disobedience against military recruiting and the Vietnam War in general.[22]

Gilbert led the march up to the building, wearing the respectable jacket and tie he always wore to demonstrations. As the police cleared the approximately two hundred people from the doorway, one officer tried to hit Gilbert in the groin with a nightstick while another officer began twisting his tie until it broke. ("Clip-ons are better," he jokes today.) They threw him on the ground, began kicking him, and an officer again tried to hit him in the crotch. Beyond learning not to wear a Windsor knot to a protest, Gilbert was angry at the violent police response to such a non-violent demonstration. Although he remained a committed pacifist until 1967, this event, along with a systematic study he began that summer of U.S. economic and military aggression overseas, helped catapult him to a more radical analysis of U.S. society and the stakes for social change: Maybe the government *does* know about the terror it is causing and using in the Third World. Maybe the government *does* know about the terror it is allowing in the South. Maybe the government doesn't care. Maybe the government even plans to cause terror.

CAMPUS ORGANIZING, NATIONAL ORGANIZING

IN BETWEEN MALCOLM'S speech in February and the ROTC protest in May, Gilbert was instrumental in helping start two groups on campus.

President Lyndon Johnson announced in February 1965 that the United States was going to war in Vietnam to uphold the Geneva Accords of 1954, which he claimed made North and South Vietnam two separate countries. Therefore, Johnson said, the United States must go to war against the communist government of North Vietnam because it was acting as a foreign aggressor against South Vietnam. Gilbert was furious; he knew from his early study of Vietnam that the accords did not permanently divide Vietnam, which meant that Johnson's whole rationale for the war was based on a complete fabrication. Indeed, historian Stanley Karnow notes in no uncertain terms, the accords "provided for the *temporary* division of Vietnam pending a nationwide election to be held in the summer of 1956" (emphasis added).[23] Given the widespread popularity of communist leader Ho Chi Minh and the movement for unified national sovereignty, the accords called for a temporary division of what would soon be one country. But, with anti-communism as its rationale, the Eisenhower administration poured money, resources, and military training into the unpopular (and temporary) Diem regime of South Vietnam, which nullified the 1956 elections.[24] Fighting—and U.S. involvement—intensified from that point forward.

Nevertheless, the accords were clear: Vietnam was one country, not two. Furious with Johnson's willful distortion of the Geneva Accords (and the lack of response from the media), Gilbert formed the Independent Committee on Vietnam (ICV) at Columbia University in March 1965—one month after the intensification of bombings in Vietnam went public. ICV was an education group, hoping to teach fellow students about the situation in Southeast Asia. One of the first things the committee did was set up literature tables on campus. Gilbert remembers being "out there for hours and hours each day debating the war—debating, rather than discussing, because most students opposed us. But there was definitely a burgeoning antiwar sector, and events themselves were changing people rapidly. By 1968, more than two-thirds of the students at Columbia University opposed the war."[25]

Later in 1965, under the tutelage of Gilbert and others, ICV would help spawn the Columbia University chapter of Students for a Democratic Society. (The two would merge in the fall of 1966.) While there was already an SDS chapter at Columbia prior to 1965, it was small, poorly organized, and less active than most other SDS chapters in this period. It faded into obscurity; the one Gilbert co-founded was the Columbia SDS that would become world-famous before the end of the decade.[26]

SDS began in 1960 as a national organization, though it was initially based primarily in the Northeast (with a sizable presence in Michigan) among liberal/social democratic intelligentsia. It was the student wing of the Cold War liberal (and anti-communist) League for Industrial Democracy (LID). The young students laid out their vision of better society in 1962, in a document known as the Port Huron Statement. Written in Michigan by Tom Hayden (who would go on to become a California State Senator), the statement expressed the students' support for civil rights, disdain for nuclear proliferation, and hope for a progressive realignment of the Democratic Party. The statement rejected both the greed of the West and the authoritarianism of the East. By not categorically condemning communism, Port Huron broke with the Cold War paradigm—including that of LID—even though SDS as an organization would not embrace a communist analysis for several years.[27]

SDS moved too fast for the cautious League; the two were at odds from day one, when SDS refused to adopt a communist exclusion clause, believing that anyone should be able to freely participate in the group. The child would soon separate from the parent, especially after SDS refused to prohibit communists from attending and speaking at the landmark April 1965 antiwar march.[28] Calling itself a New Left, SDS believed itself to be charting new waters—by refusing to ban communists, the group separated itself from the liberal Left and its zealous anti-communism. Yet SDS was also unwilling to fall into the traps of the Old Left; it did not look to the Soviet Union for inspiration, nor did it view union organizing as the epitome of what it meant to be on the Left. Instead, SDS committed itself to community organizing.

The issue of communism was central to the relationship of SDS to the LID—and would prove to be a defining issue for SDS throughout its existence. While the non-exclusion clause was an important deviation from Cold War policies of liberals and conservatives alike, SDS also neglected to establish guidelines to prevent the abuse of its participatory democratic structure. As a result, the organization had no institutional safeguards against infiltration by dogmatic communist organizations that saw SDS mainly as an opportunity to recruit cadre or push their own agendas.[29]

The main group to attempt control of SDS was the Progressive Labor Party (PL), a spin-off of the Communist Party of the United States. PL was a Maoist organization that, by the mid-1960s, thought organizing the (monolithically defined) industrial working class was the primary, if not only, task for student radicals. PL started a militant antiwar group called the May 2nd Movement (M2M) in the early 1960s, which circulated strongly worded petitions against the war (calling for U.S. withdrawal when the fledgling antiwar movement was only pushing for negotiations) and held demonstrations. When SDS became the dominant antiwar force—at least among youth—the PL hierarchy dissolved the M2M and instructed its members to join SDS. There they voted the PL line without respecting the internal dynamics of SDS, which valued open debate. Problems arose at the outset; at the December 1966 National Council meeting, when an attempt was made to limit PL's voting rights, the desire for openness and to break from anti-communism won out.[30] The attempt was defeated and PL stayed on, unrestrained.

After that, PL's presence in SDS grew, and the group increasingly tried to use SDS as a recruiting ground while simultaneously working to control the organization's political direction. At national meetings, and in local chapters where they had a presence, PL members routinely cut off discussion through rhetorical regurgitations of Marxist theory and voted in blocs to exert a bigger power in the organization than their numbers otherwise would have allowed.[31] Although PL's insistence on taking politics seriously was a positive addition to the loose and not necessarily theoretical SDS, PL's organizing style and disrespect for SDS's internal process proved divisive for the organization during national meetings and in those regions where PL had a strong presence.

From the outset, SDS was a group with a multi-issue approach. One of its initial projects was known as the Economic Research and Action Project (ERAP). This endeavor sent earnest white students to poor, often Black, urban areas throughout the Northeast and Midwest in an effort to build "an interracial movement of the poor." Though the program built off lessons learned from the civil rights movement—especially SNCC—it tended to minimize race in its attempts to organize "around economic and political grievances" based solely on the "natural alliance among all poor people."[32] Still, it was a sincere effort that taught many SDSers a lot about organizing and built solid friendships among many early members in SDS. And it taught many SDS activists that the "natural alliance" would not materialize without attention to combating white racism.

Overall, SDS was on the upswing. Following its organizing of the first national antiwar march in 1965, SDS staff grew tremendously. Regional offices sprang up across the country, and soon the organization was no longer one where everyone knew one another. After that first national antiwar march on Washington D.C., the organization came under attack by the mass media as "subversive" and "unpatriotic." Cool! American youth responded eagerly: SDS membership grew from 3,000 people in June 1964 to 15,000 in June 1966.[33]

The rapid influx of new members after 1965 also brought a stronger sense of decentralized and participatory decision making. With the intensification of the war, SDS's membership grew exponentially, adding more class diversity as students (and others) from outside the Northeast began to join. This new influx included many people from the Midwest; hence, it was dubbed "Prairie Power."[34] Prairie Power activists brought with them an emphasis on merging politics with counterculture values (long hair, rock 'n' roll, and marijuana), as well as a healthy distrust of authority. Ever obstinate, Prairie Power SDSers distrusted the organization's leadership, which it called the Old Guard—those early members of the group resistant to the organizational changes offered by the new members. Prairie Power activists often came from less privileged backgrounds than the Old Guard, had less history of political involvement, and were more likely to be the first in their families to go to college. These new SDSers helped turn the organization's focus from ERAP projects to include a significant amount of antiwar work while embracing elements of the emerging counterculture.[35]

Though David Gilbert was from the Northeast and an intellectual, he was not a part of the Old Guard. Indeed, he didn't join SDS until after the April 1965 march on Washington. He was attracted to the group because of its multi-issue approach, combining antiwar, anti-racist, and community organizing initiatives with a vague sense of socialism. At the first SDS convention he attended (1965), he was among those pushing for more long-term antiwar work. "I felt that ERAP, in a way, was a more basic program because it got at the structure of things here, but I had the sense that everything was about to take off around Vietnam," Gilbert says. He hoped that the two strains then characterizing SDS—antiwar activism and community organizing—could complement each other. Among his allies at that SDS conference, also pushing for continued attention to Vietnam, were, interestingly enough, the PL cadres from the May 2nd Movement.[36]

In those heady early days, Gilbert also traveled the country in a project initiated by an older leftist. The older activist provided Gilbert with travel money so that he could visit the disparate Vietnam committees on college campuses to exchange experiences, ideas, and perhaps coordinate antiwar efforts. This idea would later be applied on a much grander and organized scale with the Vietnam Summer initiative in 1967, which built on the model put forth by SNCC and its Mississippi Freedom Democratic Party.

During his 1965 travels, Gilbert began a systematic study of Latin America, as part of a broader study of how the United States moved in the world. He found that his country had a long history of intervening in almost every country in Latin America, crushing popular insurgencies and imposing or supporting right-wing dictators who could be depended on to support the U.S. corporations in their countries.[37] Indeed, in late April of that year, the United States invaded the Dominican Republic with 40,000 troops to quell a popular insurgency against the (pro-U.S.) military dictatorship.[38] The one exception he found in his 1965 study was socialist Cuba, "the only country in Latin America that eliminated illiteracy, where all the children had shoes on their feet so they didn't get hookworm anymore. Food was rationed, they were poor, but it meant there was no super-rich and no one was starving. I saw that [it] was the only place where that ever happened was where there was actually a revolution, and the U.S. did everything they could to stop that."[39] It wasn't a pretty picture: revolutions were needed for systematic change, to eliminate poverty and oppression. What did that mean in the United States? SDS as an organization was trying to answer that very question.

FROM SHAKING THE CONSCIENCE TO SHAKING THE SYSTEM

IN THE EARLY to mid-1960s, SDS felt that the public was uninformed, especially about the war in Vietnam and racism in the South. Once the public and the government were made aware of these issues, SDS members felt, things would surely change. There was faith that the government would not knowingly participate in or tolerate illegal, unethical acts. This faith was coupled with a tremendous optimism concerning the people of the United States and their ability to make change, along with an assumption that the government would be receptive to change. It was thought that just by calling attention to atrocities in the South and in Vietnam, people would be moved to act and pressure the government to make change.

Six years after its quiet beginning in 1960, SDS was shifting its analysis as a result of dramatic world events. The group began to identify the problem as one of the use and control of power in society. In other words, the structure of society needed a total overhaul; the legitimacy of the United States itself was called into question. As this process occurred across the country, fueled by the emerging radicalism of the Black liberation movement and the deepening crisis in Vietnam, a revolutionary movement began to materialize nationwide.

"Our movement had begun with the hope that we could 'shake the moral conscience of America,'" Gilbert says. "But painful experience had taught us that there was an entrenched power structure which profited from and systematically enforced oppression. We could not make a dent in the overwhelming social violence of the status quo without coming up against that power structure."[40]

Central to this radical shift beginning in 1966 was the cry for Black Power, raised first that year by the Student Nonviolent Coordinating Committee. SNCC was the vanguard civil rights movement in the South, a major source of inspiration to the movement at large. Most SNCC members (and leaders) were Black, but liberal whites had been allowed to join. Now they were being "asked" to leave; some would say thrown out. SNCC's logic was simple, even unassailable. It demanded that whites leave the group to organize in their own communities, because that was where the system of racial oppression was *based*, not in the Black communities where they had been organizing. Black Power went even further. It defined the central task for oppressed people as achieving power, not just "justice" or "equality." It even suggested, indirectly, that African Americans were not just an "underprivileged" American "minority," but an oppressed and colonized part of the world's majority. It was Malcolm's vision come home: racism was a white problem, not a Black one. White people needed to confront white supremacy in their own communities, and Black people needed to organize for self-determination.[41]

Black Power created a ripple effect throughout the movement by raising self-definition and self-determination as central components to radical political struggle; it connected demands for an end to racial apartheid in the South with the struggles of Black people in the North and elsewhere in the country. The more cutting edge elements of this movement also made connections between the Black struggle here and struggles by other Third World people throughout the world. Black Power was an acknowledgement that racism was not a Southern problem but was fundamental to the structure of the United States. Whether they supported it or not, other Black groups now had to define themselves in relation to Black Power, and white activists were challenged to think about politics in an entirely new way.

Michael Tarif Warren was a student at Central State University in Ohio, where he worked with a Northern activist group affiliated with SNCC. For him Black Power was a necessary, almost inevitable, development, one that built off the years of struggle that had gone on until that point. "Black Power was an important element in terms of allowing Black people to recognize the importance of empowering themselves within the overall movement," he says today. "In other words, to create an individual power base that would relate to the governing of our affairs so that we would be able to, with some degree of prominence, interact with other groups who had their own power base." These separate groupings, in his view, allowed for *better* working relationships with white groups than the multiracial style prevalent prior to the rise of Black Power, when whites often assumed leadership positions (or were presumed to be in charge) at the expense of Black leadership. The rise of revolutionary nationalism, in the context of successful revolutionary struggles around the globe, enabled the different communities in this country to come together in a way previously made difficult by the presumption that all parties stood on an equal footing. "It's OK to be separate in terms of the organization, as long as you're working for the same fundamental ideas in terms of uplifting the position of the affected masses in society," Warren concludes.

Kathleen Cleaver, a former SNCC activist who would go on to become the first woman to serve on the Black Panther's Central Committee, identified the possibilities for cooperation that could flow from separate organizations. "[W]e did not see that we had the same relationship to the state [as white people], so we didn't have to be in the same organization," Cleaver says. The relationship she wanted was "one of coalition, collaboration, working together, sharing resources, supporting each other on specific projects, but not being members of the same organization." By having racially separate organizations, these groups hoped to exert their own push for economic, political, and social power more effectively without also having to deal with racism within organizations. "If whites are in an organization," Cleaver said, "there was a belief that they were going to dominate. ... So in order for people who were subordinated, who were historically excluded, historically oppressed, historically colonized, how do you liberate yourself from that kind of domination?"[42]

Black Power advocates argued that the roots of the problem were to be found not in individual white racism but in systematic white supremacy—the exclusion of Black people (and other people of color) from meaningful participation in the political and social realms, accomplished through economic domination and, when necessary, brute force.

The theoretical implications of viewing Black people as a colonized nation were made clear by the violent urban riots sweeping the country, the most famous of which occurred in the Watts section of Los Angeles in 1965; it lasted for six days, involved more than 30,000 people, and caused an estimated $200 million of damage. Thirty-five people were killed and more than 4,000 were arrested.[43] Two years later, forty-one people were killed in a Detroit riot. The Black ghettoes of the United States were rising up, seemingly in concert with those violent rebellions in Africa, Asia, and Latin America. In cities large and small, the riots found people fighting police and the National Guard, the armed enforcers of a racist state.

Ashanti Alston was one of many Black youths impacted by the urban rebellions. When his hometown of Plainfield, New Jersey (population 60,000), erupted in rebellion in 1967, the thirteen-year-old Alston was inspired by seeing armed Black people take over the city—and kick the local police out of town, if temporarily. Even in 1967, Alston remembers the harsh treatment he received at school or out in the street from white people, who owned almost the entire town. "The only things that weren't owned by white people were the barber shop, the funeral parlor, and the churches," he recalls, despite the town's sizable Black population. "That rebellion was my entry into what I considered the revolution. From there I really put a lot of effort into trying to read Malcolm X's autobiography. [He and] Stokely Charmichael and H. Rap Brown were shaping a far more radical consciousness, or at least a more radical approach to Black liberation."

From July to October of 1966, rebellions occurred in Omaha, Nebraska; Chicago; Cleveland; Brooklyn; Milwaukee; Dayton, Ohio; Waukegan and Benton Harbor, Michigan; Jackson, Mississippi; San Francisco; Oakland; and more than twenty-five other cities.[44] The following year, riots erupted in 128 cities, and there were 131 such uprisings in the first six months of 1968 alone. The country was exploding.

The turn from civil rights to Black Power also had a big impact on SDS, causing the organization to raise solidarity with the Black movement as a cutting edge issue. "Even though at that point we were primarily an antiwar group, more and more the situation of Black people in the U.S. became a focus," says Scott Braley, a Prairie Power SDSer from all-white and deeply conservative Midland, Michigan. The challenge Black Power raised for white organizers was a difficult one: organize other whites *against racism*. It was a challenge to the history of the white Left, in which struggles by people of color have largely been ignored, co-opted, or sold out.[45] This was quite a challenge, Braley recalls, because it gave white activists a much more defined role and responsibility. "It is hard enough to organize white people around general progressive ideals, let alone an antiwar program, or an anti-racism program. An anti-racism program was much harder to organize white people into, rather than just being part of some general 'movement.'"

Although SNCC was instrumental in its ascendancy, the cutting edge of the Black Power movement soon became the Oakland-based Black Panther Party for Self-Defense. Formed in 1966 by Merritt College students Huey Newton and Bobby Seale, the Panthers would become the most famous, the most controversial, and ultimately the most targeted organization of the 1960s. As an organization, the Black Panther Party organized among poor, unemployed, and incarcerated Black people; elucidated a clear ten-point program of demands and political platform; and instituted wide-ranging community programs, from self-defense to political education and free healthcare and food programs.[46] The Panthers, from the outset, were very much in the tradition of Malcolm X and the philosophies he espoused. "It seemed like they were putting Malcolm's philosophy into practice," Alston says, explaining what drew him to establish a chapter of the Black Panther party in Plainfield at age seventeen.

The Black Panther Party received national, then international, attention as it engaged in grassroots community work, pilloried institutional oppression, and publicly identified with global struggles for socialism and national liberation. As a result of their militant and empowering programs, FBI Director J. Edgar Hoover declared them the "greatest threat to the internal security of the United States," opening the way for a vicious attack on the group by police forces at every level, through overt and covert, legal and illegal means. This repression would soon lead to the destruction of the group, the murder of some key leaders, and the incarceration of many Panthers (some of whom still remain behind bars).

Meanwhile, SNCC was still on the scene and helping lead antiwar organizing.[47] The civil rights group publicly criticized the federal government for making war across the world without providing for the safety and well-being of civil rights workers in the South. SNCC leader Robert Moses, among others in the group, was also involved in antiwar work and pushed the organization to include it as part of its program. When Navy veteran and SNCC organizer Sammy Younge was murdered in Tuskegee, Alabama, on January 3, 1966, for trying to use a "white" restroom, the organization responded quickly with a statement. In it, SNCC asserted that it had a "right and a responsibility to dissent with the United States foreign policy on any issue ... the United States government [has] been deceptive in its claims of concern for the freedom of the Vietnamese people, just as the government has been deceptive in claiming concern for the freedom of colored people in such countries as the Dominican Republic, the Congo, South Africa, Rhodesia, and in the United States itself."

SNCC went right to the heart of the matter, connecting the murders of Black people with those of Vietnamese and other Third World people— all emanating from this country's refusal to respect human rights and abide by the law. As the SNCC statement said, "Younge was murdered because United States law is not being enforced ... Vietnamese are mudered because the United States is pursuing an aggressive policy in violation of international law. The United States is no respecter of persons or law when such persons or laws run counter to its needs and desires." SNCC urged people to work in the movement rather than accept the draft.[48] SNCC, the Panthers, and other revolutionary Third World groups in the United States connected anti-racist struggle domestically with the war in Vietnam as emanating from the same system of white supremacy and capitalism—of imperialism. This political articulation pushed SDS forward with a more radical antiwar (and specifically anti-draft) program.

With this political radicalization came an increasing turn to confrontational tactics. In one of the major protests of 1966, Harvard and Radcliffe students confronted Secretary of Defense Robert McNamara when he went to the Ivy League school to talk to a pre-selected group of fifty students. Harvard/Radcliffe SDS demanded that McNamara have a public debate about the war, or at least speak to a larger crowd; first this demand was made by SDS alone, and then the group presented a petition with 1,600 names on it, all supporting a public debate. Harvard and McNamara refused. Almost 1,000 SDSers surrounded the building where the "architect" of the Vietnam War was speaking. When he emerged in a police car, student radicals conducted a sit-in, preventing it from moving. McNamara stood atop the car to field questions. Not surprisingly, the questions focused on U.S. involvement in Vietnam and support for the military dictatorship in South Vietnam. The confrontation ended with police carrying the defense secretary over their heads out of the area.[49] It was a sign of things to come.

"[T]here became this realization that we weren't just going to shake up their consciousness and change things, that there was actually a power structure that was determined to keep up the current relationships and was quite willing and capable of using force and violence," Gilbert recalls. "I think that that realization created a crisis in the movement."[50]

Black Panthers rally outside a courthouse in New York City in support of the Panther 21 defendants. Photo by Roz Payne (www.newsreel.us).

In retrospect, 1966 and 1968 are pretty close, but at the time they seemed like light years away in terms of the politics, issues, crises and key players involved. I mean, in 1966 we were still in, or just coming out of, "shake the moral conscience of America," and by 1968 many folks were talking about revolution and guerrilla warfare.

—David Gilbert[1]

STARTING WITH THE GROUNDBREAKING APRIL 1965 antiwar march in Washington D.C., SDS began to feel the need to "name the system." At that demonstration, SDS leader Paul Potter denounced in his talk what SDSers (and millions of others around the world) would later call *imperialism* and *capitalism*, while intentionally avoiding those terms, which he believed had been rendered meaningless by Cold War politics and sectarian Communists of the 1930s.[2] Thus, although Potter's talk was a call for people to name the system, he avoided offering any name himself.

Seven months later, SDS head Carl Oglesby offered "corporate liberalism" as the system's name during the November 1965 antiwar march on Washington.[3] In his speech, Oglesby pointed out that all those responsible for the Vietnam conflagration, from John F. Kennedy and Lyndon Johnson to Robert McNamara and McGeorge Bundy, were "honorable men...all liberals"[4] who were brutally opposing a genuine revolutionary struggle in Vietnam.[5] Oglesby went on to describe other areas where the United States, particularly through the CIA, had intervened against popular democratic struggles under the cover of anti-communism. "Corporate liberalism," then, was the systematic relationship between U.S. investments, military interventions to maintain U.S. economic hegemony, and the "civilizing" of conquered people of color—all of which was beginning to seem more and more like official U.S. policy by 1965. Like Potter, Oglesby said later that his goal was to describe capitalism and imperialism without using the terms.

Not everyone thought it prudent to avoid those seemingly loaded words. Two articles David Gilbert co-wrote in 1967 display not only his willingness to grapple with theory, but also a burgeoning movement radicalism. Then a graduate student at the New School for Social Research, Gilbert saw *New Left Notes* (*NLN*), SDS's weekly newspaper, not just as a venue for chapter updates and activity reports, but a place to explore and build the movement's theory. Already aligned with the "praxis axis" group within Columbia SDS, Gilbert became part of a seven-person committee that worked on *Praxis*, a new monthly section of *NLN*.[6] Columbia SDSer Bob Feldman writes that the term praxis was "used by National SDS people to describe political theorizing and strategizing which related to daily radical activism."[7] In a preface to the first *Praxis* supplement, *NLN* editor Cathy Wilkerson explained: "with the current staff of *NLN* (1 person) it has been impossible to do justice to the large number of longer, more 'theoretical' articles which come in.... *Praxis* has been created in order to give more attention and consideration to these pieces."[8] *Praxis* fit nicely with what Wilkerson now describes as one of the paper's strengths. "*NLN* helped many of us understand what it meant to say 'all the issues are connected.'"[9]

The first issue of *Praxis* appeared on February 13, 1967. It included an article by Gilbert, Bob Gottlieb, and Gerry Tenney entitled "Praxis and the New Left." The article was part of a longer position paper by the three called the "Port Authority Statement," a humorous reference to SDS's founding document, the Port Huron Statement. Whereas the Port Huron Statement offered a political vision, no matter how progressive, still rooted in dominant U.S. institutions, the Port Authority Statement (named after a Manhattan bus terminal) was rooted in Marxism—beginning from its very premise, which accepted the notion of the working class, Marx's "proletariat," as agents of revolutionary change, rather than looking to a progressive realignment of the Democratic Party as the means to achieve more modest goals.

The Port Authority Statement developed what its authors called the "New Working Class theory," which identified students as "an emerging and increasingly important sector of the working class" by virtue of the technical and scientific jobs they were being trained to fill.[10] This concept was a precursor to the "revolutionary youth movement" theories that led to the founding of both the Weather Underground and the New Communist Movement of the 1970s and beyond.[11] "Port Authority" argued that classic

Marxist conceptions of the working class did not include the reality of the modern university, where students were being trained to be mid- to low-level workers. Further, it argued, students were important as a potential proletarian force because they were most responsive to civil rights and human rights struggles; simply put, they were not yet fully invested in the smooth functioning of the system, as many older people—with careers and families and mortgages—were.[12]

The New Working Class argument blurred class differences between the predominantly white students in SDS and their out-of-school peers, proportionally more people of color and including many GIs who could not get student deferments from the draft. But Gilbert et al. weren't the first theorists on students' political role to equivocate on racial and class distinctions. Responding to Berkeley Free Speech Movement leader Mario Savio's claim in 1964 that the student movement was fighting for the same rights as the Civil Rights Movement, Becky Thompson notes that "the same rights were not at stake. In the South people were fighting for the right to vote; the right to a quality pre-college education, let alone a college education; and the right to walk down the street without fear of being indiscriminately shot by a white person (police or private citizen). The rights white college students were fighting for assumed access to rights not yet secured for most Blacks and Latinos."[13]

Nevertheless, New Working Class struck a popular and timely chord within SDS, even though it was later disavowed by at least one of its authors. ("All these years of anti-imperialist struggle, and that's all I am remembered for [in SDS histories]," Gilbert complained with a smile at our first visit.)[14] It was part of the movement's theoretical experimentation and development, as activists were looking to make sense of the world and understand the political significance of the various populations in motion. "New Working Class is not a chapter of his intellectual development that David's proud of," says Naomi Jaffe, a lifelong friend and fellow New School SDSer. "But we were really thinking analytically, which doesn't always happen in a movement. I think that's one of the strengths our movement had over today's activists—we really studied."

The "Port Authority" article was part of an emerging class (specifically Marxist) consciousness within SDS. Gilbert later said the article was "trying to bring a Marxist analysis of imperialism into SDS, and we were also trying to look at class."[15] Indeed, the Port Authority Statement borrowed heavily from European intellectuals such as socialist theorist Andre

Gorz.[16] It was more academic in tone than other, cruder attempts at analyzing class, such as Jerry Farber's "Student as a Nigger" essay that NY SDS released as a pamphlet.[17] In his book *Democracy from the Heart*, former SDS national officer Greg Calvert, a New Working Class theorist in his own right, calls the Port Authority excerpt in Praxis "sophisticated…incomprehensible to most SDSers…abstruse, abstract, and stultifying."[18] The statement was one of many articles appearing in 1967 that adopted Marxist language and themes, even if the entirety of SDS (now with some 30,000 members) was not at the same political level.[19] In fact, Gilbert says, "tension soon developed between those pushing work on theory and those who felt it was elitist-intellectual and a diversion from militancy. As with many movement debates, both sides of that debate had elements of the truth and both were inadequate, but in the context of the times the emphasis on action did more to push things forward."[20]

Less notorious but arguably more important, at least to his later political trajectory, is the pamphlet Gilbert wrote with David Loud that would help end, at least within SDS, Potter's and Oglesby's awkward circumlocutions about "naming the system." *U.S. Imperialism* looked systematically at the relationship between the United States and Third World countries—particularly Vietnam, Guatemala, and Venezuela—and called it what it was. Gilbert and Loud labeled as *imperialism* the system of "U.S. military and non-military [i.e., economic] involvement in the internal affairs of other nations."[21] Even though Third World people, from Frantz Fanon in Algeria to Ho Chi Minh in Vietnam to Malcolm X in the United States, had defined "the system" as imperialism and colonialism, it was a significant break for white students (and economically privileged ones at that) in this country to identify their enemy as the system and the system as imperialism. The Gilbert/Loud pamphlet was used by SDSers across the country as a study guide and as a brief introduction to U.S. policies abroad; Gilbert remembers meeting people who used the pamphlet to argue against CIA recruiting on campus.[22]

 U.S. Imperialism went through at least three printings, and Gilbert's later article on domestic imperialism was widely distributed by SDS and the Movement for a Democratic Society, a post-grad spin-off of SDS.[23] Though Gilbert now thinks the article gives insufficient focus to racial oppression in defining imperialism, both pamphlets are nonetheless important documents of the time. Indeed, former Columbia SDSer Robert Roth says that Gilbert "helped a generation of people understand imperialism."

Shortly after the *U.S. Imperialism* pamphlet was published, Gilbert received a direct lesson in U.S. imperialism, specifically concerning the force the state was willing to use against peaceful dissent. On April 4, 1968 (the day Martin Luther King was assassinated in Memphis), an assassin shot and nearly killed Rudi Dutschke, a popular student leftist in Germany. New York activists called an emergency demonstration against the local office of *Der Spiegel*, the German news outlet, because of the role the German press had played in fostering anti-Left hysteria. Before meeting his father for lunch, Gilbert stopped by the demonstration to show his support.

He walked into a police riot.

"I saw one kid, I didn't know him [but he] had about four policemen beating him," Gilbert recalls. When another squad of six police officers ran out of an alley to join the attack on this demonstrator, Gilbert stopped short. "I just couldn't bring myself to step out of the way and let them vamp on this kid. So I just stood there, and they piled onto me." He looked up and saw a nightstick descending. "I rolled, and it missed my head and hit the sidewalk…. The cops started to kick [me]. Then a flashbulb went off, and a sergeant shouted, 'Cool it—press.'"[24]

This was Gilbert's first arrest. He was charged with assaulting a police officer—the cop who'd tried to club him had evidently scraped his hand when he missed Gilbert's head. Because a trial would put the word of six police officers against his, Gilbert took the advice of his lawyer and plea bargained: guilty of disorderly conduct and a fine of $50.

MOVEMENT SPLITS AND RISING MILITANCY

THE ANALYSIS OF the United States as an imperialist system gained currency in 1967, bolstered by both domestic and international developments. The war in Vietnam was increasing with ferocious intensity—so much so that civil rights leader Martin Luther King went against his cautious advisors and spoke out against the war in a speech one year before his assassination, calling the United States "the greatest purveyor of violence in the world today."[25]

World events would also split the antiwar and civil rights movements. On June 5, 1967, Israel launched a pre-emptive attack on Syria and Egypt while being attacked by Jordan. The Six-Day War brought under Israeli control the Golan Heights, the West Bank, the Gaza Strip, and the Sinai Peninsula (returned to Egypt in 1982).[26] To many activists, Israel's occupation seemed to be an act of open and racist hostility against its Arab neighbors. (An analysis seemingly confirmed a decade later by Israeli Defense Minister Moshe Dayan, who admitted that Syria posed no threat and that the idea was to "grab a piece of land and keep it, until the enemy gets tired and gives it to us.")[27] From the beginning of the 1967 war, there was fear that taking a position critical of Israel would be seen as anti-Semitic. This fear was especially pronounced in the United States, where Jews across the political spectrum supported the Six-Day War and subsequent occupation and were pushing the United States to do more to aid Israel.[28]

Both SNCC and SDS were criticized for taking positions in solidarity with the Arab countries and critical of Israel's war effort. Greater hostility, however, was directed against SNCC, already in white America's disfavor because of the group's Black Power position. While SNCC's position was at times naïvely simplistic—e.g., equating the Gaza Strip occupation with a Nazi death camp—the main problem was that it was a *Black* organization criticizing Israel. Jewish liberals denounced SNCC's "betrayal" and donations to SNCC dropped dramatically as talk of "Black anti-Semitism" increased.[29]

SDS had many Jewish members, and though the organization as a whole took a public stand against Israel's occupation, there was fierce internal dissension over the issue. Gilbert recalls that many people, including some of his close friends, "seemingly overnight" turned against the Black movement for its stance on this issue. But there was another side: Jews who connected their criticism of Israel (and support for Palestinians) to their Jewish heritage—just as surely as those who said being Jewish mandated supporting Israel, each side claiming to have learned its lesson from the Holocaust. "For myself and many other Jews in the movement," Gilbert has since written, "the bedrock lesson from the Holocaust was to passionately oppose all forms of racism; we could never join in the oppressing of another people."[30] For those Jewish activists who aligned with the radical wings of the Black movement and, especially, with the Palestinians, it was often a difficult and deeply personal split from family and friends. But it was a political decision many felt compelled to make.

That year also saw several important battles within the United States underscoring the movement's rising militancy—and the matching intransigence of the state. Ongoing demonstrations at Texas Southern University in Houston (a historically Black school) were brutally squashed in May 1967, when 600 police officers fired more than 6,000 rounds of ammunition into campus dormitories and then proceeded to "search" (i.e., trash) the rooms and possessions of students. Five students and SNCC activists were charged with the murder of a police officer. (Charges against the five were later dropped, when it turned out that the officer was killed by "friendly fire"—although no police were charged in the death of the *student* who died from police gunfire.)[31]

Later in the month, members of the Black Panther Party marched on the California State Capitol, openly displaying weapons to affirm the Black community's right to self-defense against police violence. (The lawmakers, in direct response to the Panthers, were meeting to discuss new restrictions on gun possession.) The Panthers were arrested for their audacious action, and cofounder Bobby Seale was jailed for seven months. In August the FBI officially initiated its counterintelligence program (COINTELPRO) against the Panthers and other Black militants. While the effects of this repression could be immediately seen, the full depths of COINTELPRO wouldn't become public knowledge for several more years.[32] In late October, Black Panther leader Huey Newton was stopped by police while driving in Oakland. A shootout erupted, during which officer John Frey was killed and Newton and another officer were both wounded. No gun was found on Newton, and he claimed that he passed out after being shot, not knowing who shot either officer. Newton's jailing launched a national "Free Huey" campaign, an initiative that became a widespread rallying cry among the U.S. Left.[33]

Meanwhile a number of vets, many of them decorated soldiers, were returning to this country and telling the truth about the horrors and cruelty of the imperial project in Vietnam. In June 1967, the antiwar movement gained perhaps its most valuable members with the launching of Vietnam Veterans Against the War (VVAW). The veterans had more public legitimacy than antiwar students because they had seen and participated in the horrors of which they spoke. VVAW also brought their military training to the movement, engaging in student strikes, militant demonstrations, and nonviolent street theater. It was VVAW that created one of the more dramatic images of the antiwar movement: the April 23, 1971, demonstration at which nearly 1,000 vets threw their medals over the Capitol steps.[34]

The fall of 1967 saw antiwar demonstrations across the country. In Madison, Wisconsin, student militants tried to prevent napalm-maker Dow Chemical from recruiting on campus. When six activists were put in a paddy wagon after police charged the demonstration, Kirkpatrick Sale writes, the students "began pounding on it with their fists, let the air out of the tires, and finally lay down in front of it; the police, stymied, took the names of their captives and let them free. More shoving, hitting, taunting, and then, tear gas—tear gas for the first time on a major college campus." Students responded with rocks, bricks and a two-day boycott of classes.[35]

In California, a week of anti-draft protests brought 10,000 people into the streets to shut down the Oakland induction center, one of the nation's busiest. Stop the Draft Week quickly became a battle not just against the war but against police power and the state itself. The week started with sit-ins and symbolic arrests; a spontaneous confrontation on day two ended poorly for the activists, and peaceful picketing on day three seemed pointless, since the demonstrators could see the draftees, protected by lines of police, still entering the induction center. Things changed on the final day, as protestors came prepared with helmets, shields, and the realization that they outnumbered the police. As *New Left Notes* described it: "trash cans and newspaper racks were pulled into the streets. Writing [graffiti] appeared on walls, on sidewalks.... Soon, unlocked cars were pushed into the intersections, along with potted trees and movable benches. The sanctity of private property, which had held white students back from this kind of defensive action before, gave way to a new evaluation." The protest, Karen Wald wrote in *NLN*, shattered the illusions that private property was sacrosanct, the police invincible.[36] SDS quickly took these realizations to heart.

Just one month later, the tactical lessons from Oakland were applied in New York City when the Foreign Policy Association hosted Secretary of State Dean Rusk as its featured speaker. Ten thousand demonstrators filled midtown Manhattan on November 14 in protest. Many came ready to do battle and prevent Rusk from speaking. Police arrested protesters trying to break through the barricades. "Then one group—New York police say it was Columbia SDSers—started throwing bottles, bags of red paint and cow's blood, and any available trash at the police and arriving limousines," Sale wrote in *SDS*. Taking lessons from their Oakland comrades, the New

York activists didn't wait to be attacked by police, but instead skirmished, retreated, and attacked again, depending on the situation.[37] Protesters were beginning to look, talk, and act like urban guerrillas.

While the tactical lessons would be employed in antiwar and other demos for the next few years, the overarching political lesson was even more salient. The political lesson from Madison, Oakland, and New York, was the same lesson SNCC had learned in Laurel, Greenwood, Selma, and elsewhere in the South—that it would take more than moral suasion, more than being right, even more than steadfast devotion, to change the system. Within a year of its founding, *New Left Notes* was printing articles written by self-identified Marxists and using words like *revolution* without a sense of hyperbole. SDS reading lists included Frantz Fanon's anti-colonial classic *The Wretched of the Earth*, Wilhelm Reich's *The Mass Psychology of Fascism*, and Régis Debray's insurrectionary primer, *Revolution in the Revolution?*[38] Between late 1967 and 1970, former Weatherman Scott Braley recalls, "We had gone from being slightly involved people to saying we were going to become full-time revolutionaries and overthrow the state…. It seemed like it went on forever, when in fact it was a really short period."

There was a growing feeling that pushing the envelope tactically could be used to overthrow imperialism and build socialism. Radicals in this country began to think of themselves as acting in concert with the guerrillas in Vietnam, Angola, Cuba, and elsewhere. The mood shifted from one of favoring negotiations with the Vietnamese National Liberation Front to one of wishing the NLF victory. With the analysis of U.S. imperialism—and the United States as the leading imperial power—came a strategy and a call to action for defeating it. The same year that the Gilbert-Loud pamphlet was published, so too was an essay by guerrilla war theorist and practitioner Ernesto "Che" Guevara. Born in 1928 in Argentina, Che became one of the most inspiring and revered figures on the world stage in the 1960s. Traveling through Central and South America in the early 1950s, the young medical student came into contact with indigenous and working class struggles. He was in Guatemala in 1954 when the CIA helped overthrow the country's democratically elected socialist government. From there, he moved to Mexico, where he met a young Cuban named Fidel Castro and began his studies of Marx and Mao Zedong. No mere theorist, Guevara went to Cuba to help build the armed struggle against the Batista regime, a struggle that successfully obtained state power in January 1959. After the Cuban victory, Che pledged his life to building revolutionary armed struggle for national liberation in the entire Third World.[39]

The Che Guevara essay, his only public statement between leaving Cuba in 1965 and his death in Bolivia in 1967, was published by the *Prensa Latina* news service on April 16, 1967—only six months before his murder. Guevara's message was directed to the Organization of Solidarity of the Peoples of Africa, Asia, and Latin America, also known as the Tricontinental. "To wish the victims [of imperialism, especially in Vietnam] success is not enough; the thing is to share their fate, to join them in death or victory," he wrote.[40] Noting the fierce struggles between national liberation and imperial aggression then taking place throughout Africa, Asia, the Middle East, and Latin America, Che said that the first step in defeating imperialism is "to identify its head, which is none other than the United States of North America." Guevara called for an expansion of struggle worldwide, thus engaging the United States "in a difficult struggle outside of his terrain" and "liquidating his bases of support, that is, his dependent territories," while at the same time intensifying "the class struggle inside its own territory." This struggle was already happening in Southeast Asia and could be replicated elsewhere. Guevara famously called for the creation of "two, three, many Vietnams, flowered on the face of the globe."[41] That is, Vietnam was a costly and consuming battle for the United States against socialism—and socialism was winning. By replicating such struggles elsewhere in the Third World, Guevara said, Goliath could be defeated. Che's call for "many Vietnams" was a hopeful one for the Left because it pointed the way toward a socialist future. He offered a strategy for the world Left.

Guevara's analysis put forward two military and political models for helping overextend and defeat imperialism. One was the strategy of People's War: mass-based guerrilla warfare of the kind that was happening in Vietnam and elsewhere in Asia and Africa. The second model, which Che also advocated, was based on the military success of the Cuban Revolution. Called the *foco* theory, it was popularized by French journalist Régis Debray in his book, *Revolution in the Revolution?* Debray's premise was that the victory in Cuba was not won by a mass movement under the direction of a communist party, but was the work of a small band of guerrillas attacking the enemy and inspiring the people, who ultimately rose up in rebellion. A small armed group could, it seemed, speak for the masses and contribute to toppling imperialism. It didn't replace People's War, but the *foco* theory argued that armed struggle could be beneficial well before the stage of People's War.

Debray's *foco* theory would not gain currency in the United States for a couple of years, but Guevara's strategy for defeating imperialism through overextending it would be tested in the United States at, of all places, Columbia University.

BRINGING THE WAR HOME, TO THE IVY LEAGUES:
THE COLUMBIA REBELLION AS CATALYST FOR WHITE RADICALS

BEGINNING ON JANUARY 31, 1968, the Tet Offensive laid bare the futility of U.S. efforts in Vietnam, a country unified in opposition to U.S. invasion and occupation. On the third day of the Vietnamese New Year, "synchronized attacks were launched from within almost every major city and town" in South Vietnam, against almost all of the U.S. military bases there.[42] Less than a month later, legendary news anchor Walter Cronkite declared on national television that the United States could not win in Vietnam.[43] For many in the movement, Tet not only showed that the United States *wouldn't* win, but that it *shouldn't* win—that it had no right to be in Vietnam to begin with.[44] A week after Tet began, peaceful student protests at South Carolina State College in Orangeburg were drowned in blood when police opened fire on unarmed Black students, wounding thirty-three and killing three.[45] In early April, Martin Luther King was assassinated, sparking rebellions in more than 100 cities and towns across the country. Two days after King's murder, the first and youngest member of the Black Panther Party, sixteen-year-old Bobby Hutton, was killed by police after surrendering to them following a shootout. Hutton was the first of many Panthers to be killed in the coming years.[46] And before the tumult at Columbia subsided, a worker-student alliance in France brought Paris to a standstill, inspiring radicals around the globe.[47] The surrealist and anarchist currents of the Paris rebellion—and the fact that it was the staid Communist Party of France that betrayed the insurgents—led to a widening worldwide chasm between New and Old Lefts, as well as an increased emphasis on militancy among many in the New Left.[48]

Two issues defined the Columbia strike, just as they defined the movement: the Vietnam War and racism. Columbia was involved in both, through Defense Department research and through the building of a de facto segregated gym in Harlem. Although the strike at Columbia began on April 23, 1968, its immediate roots reach back a month earlier, to a demonstration inside the administration building against the university's ties to the Institute for Defense Analysis, or IDA, a Defense Department research project in counterinsurgency located at twelve universities, including Columbia. "This research included evaluating counterinsurgency methods used in Vietnam for possible use in American cities," SDS leader Robert Pardun wrote in his memoir.[49] IDA had long been a target of Columbia SDS; six students faced disciplinary charges for their role in the demonstration, which was just the latest in an ongoing campaign against university complicity in the war.

The next round in the buildup to the strike came on April 12, during a university memorial service for Martin Luther King, assassinated the week before. SDS leader Mark Rudd grabbed the microphone from Columbia president Grayson Kirk and accused the university of hypocrisy for mourning a Black leader while refusing to let its Black and Puerto Rican cafeteria workers unionize and for building an essentially segregated gym in Harlem.[50] The gym, according to an SDS pamphlet, would have a back entrance allowing Harlem residents (those not displaced by the gym's construction) access to about 15 percent of the facility. The pamphlet referred to the project as "gym crow."[51] Resistance to the gym had been ongoing from Harlem residents and some students, culminating with the arrest of twelve protestors trying to block bulldozers at the proposed gym site two months before the strike.[52]

All these issues came to a head the third week of April, when a demonstration in support of the "IDA six" turned into the occupation of one the nation's top universities. After a rally in the center of campus, the 500 demonstrators tried to get into the administration building (Low Library) to demand an open hearing on the discipline of the six students. Finding Low locked, the protesters led an impromptu march to the site of the gym, where construction had already begun. One person was arrested as the crowd tried to tear down the fence surrounding the construction site.

Unable to get into the gym site, the protesters returned to the university. Inspired by more incendiary speeches, SDS and the Student Afro-American Society seized another building, Hamilton Hall, and with it, Dean Henry Coleman, who was inside his office. "Within hours," Mark Rudd writes in his unpublished memoir, "representatives from SDS, SNCC, CORE, and other civil rights, black power, and peace organizations were in the building; food and money donations streamed in, as did individuals from around the city."[53] The anti-racism and Black militancy underlying the strike's demands led to an outpouring of support from the Harlem community, which had hitherto kept its distance from the elite school. When right-wing students surrounded one of the occupied buildings in an attempt to block food deliveries, Harlem activists broke through and brought food, water, and supplies to the striking students.[54]

Once the marching was over and the building was seized, the talking began—passionate, round-the-clock political meetings that led to more building occupations and more meetings. In the early morning hours of April 24, the Black students decided that it was crucial for them to hold Hamilton Hall by themselves, in a show of self-determination and Black Power. Whites were asked to leave Hamilton. The SDSers then seized Low Library, to hold their own building and carry on the strike in solidarity with the Black militants, although it wasn't clear at the outset how long they would be able to last. At one point early in the occupation of Low, all but twelve students fled, fearing an immediate bust. But when the administration hesitated to send in the police, students quickly re-entered the building, rejoining the dozen militants who had never left. More students climbed in through the windows. Strikers rifled the university president's files, discovering more links between the school and the military-industrial complex, proving what SDS had been saying all along. Students—undergrad and grad, SDSers and unaffiliated progressives—seized three other buildings on campus. In total, student militants held five Columbia University buildings throughout the five-day strike. Politics and culture became intertwined during the strike, as the occupied buildings were turned into co-ed "communes"; one couple even held their wedding inside an occupied building.[55]

From beginning to end, six demands guided the strike:

1. That construction of the gymnasium be stopped.
2. That the university cut all connection to IDA.
3. That the ban on indoor demonstrations be rescinded.
4. That criminal charges arising out of protests at the gym site be dropped.
5. That probation for the IDA 6 be rescinded.
6. That amnesty be granted for the present protest.[56]

The final demand, amnesty for the strikers, proved the most controversial; even some of the strikers (mainly those who were not part of any political group) had a hard time holding fast to that demand.[57] Many in SDS felt that amnesty was needed, both because they were right about the university's war connections and in order to protect political speech on campus.

The university refused even to consider amnesty, and Columbia's administration finally called in the police in the early morning hours of April 28. New York's finest acted with brutal enthusiasm, arresting more than 700 and beating everyone in sight, including many students, faculty, and area residents who were not involved in the strike but were just trying to keep the peace.

Internationalism was a central component of the Columbia strike, even though the demands appeared, at least on the surface, to be specific to the university. In a rally preceding the building occupations, Columbia Student Afro-American Society (SAS) leader Bill Sales told the crowd: "If you're talking about revolution, if you're talking about identifying with the Vietnamese struggle...you don't need to go marching downtown. There's one oppressor—in the White House, in Low Library, in Albany, New York. You strike a blow at the gym, you strike a blow for the Vietnamese people. You strike a blow at the gym and you strike a blow against the assassin of Dr. Martin Luther King Jr. You strike a blow at Low Library and you strike a blow for the freedom fighters in Angola, Mozambique, Portuguese Guinea, Zimbabwe, [and] South Africa."[58]

Similarly, strike leader Mark Rudd remembers going to about seventy-five college campuses in the months following the strike. "In all cases, the issues reflected the same concerns at Columbia—Vietnam and racism."[59] The ripple effect created by the rebellion was bolstered by the ubiquity of the strike targets: connections to the war and white supremacy could be found in cities and on campuses everywhere. "Everyone was inspired by Columbia," says Bernardine Dohrn, who became head of SDS a few months after the strike. "Everyone wanted to seize their administration building." Following Guevara's lead, student militants across the country raised the rallying cry to create "two, three, many Columbias." ROTC, war research, and other university-military connections increasingly became targets of student unrest.

Just as the demands were conceived of in an international context, so too were the police seen to be wielding the nightsticks of imperialism, the brute force and terror of a decaying system. "As so many Third World countries bear the scars of U.S. imperialism, the dried bloodstains on the grounds of Columbia are the cruel testimony to Columbia's administrative justice," claimed an SDS pamphlet after the strike.[60] Some of the student radicals not arrested on April 28 went out to attack nearby banks, expressing, as Rudd recalls, "anger and disgust with Columbia, the police, [and] the war."[61] Imperialism was the enemy: the school, the police, the banks were all part of the same brutal system.

Three weeks later, Columbia was re-seized temporarily in a strike on May 21. This time strikers built barricades on the campus, spurred to militancy by the worker-student uprising in Paris in early May and hoping (in vain) to at least slow the inevitable police onslaught.[62] Beleaguered Columbia University president Grayson Kirk quickly ordered the campus cleared; police violence again ensued, resulting in 120 arrests, with dozens injured. More than four hundred students walked out of the commencement ceremony held shortly thereafter, and Kirk resigned that August. Radicals organized an alternative commencement, inviting renowned psychologist Erich Fromm, who quoted Nietzsche in his address, saying it was a time when "anyone who does not lose his mind has no mind to lose" and praising the students for their "revolution of life" in a "society of zombies."[63]

A PASSION FOR DEMOCRACY

THE ANTI-DEMOCRATIC NATURE of the university system—and, by extension, the U.S. system as a whole—had been made all too clear by the vicious police response to the strikers, in one of the first times police were called onto a predominantly white college campus in the United States. That the academy is not a democracy comes as no surprise to those who have spent any time there. But the combination of an anti-democratic university with the brutal police response was a major reason student radicals across the country stepped up the militancy in their activism. This combination of factors also reinvigorated a desire to build a democratic society at all levels, although more and more people were convinced that nothing short of revolution would achieve such a change.[64] Shortly before police descended on the campus during the April strike, Gilbert addressed a mass meeting of the strikers. "The original six demands [of the strike] are no longer sufficient," he told them. "In addition to winning political demands, we must begin to create a new university."[65]

Reflecting on the strike twenty years later, Gilbert summed up the events by saying that the strikers "demanded Columbia stand on the side of humanity."[66] The strike was an important turning point for the white Left as a whole, because it marked the beginning of SDS grappling with the meaning and functioning of power in society—and in the movement's own goals—in a new way. SDSers now had the battle scars to prove that which the Black Liberation Movement already knew—they were "in confrontation with an entrenched and ruthless power."[67]

This increasing commitment to revolution and to a neo-Marxism that broke with traditional dogmatic Marxism only strengthened SDS's dedication to building an anti-racist, democratic society, "by any means necessary." First, this meant breaking with the rigidity of the Old Left. SDS activists were more inspired by anti-racist and anti-colonial struggles than by traditional working class organizing. They placed much greater emphasis on youth culture (especially rock music and drugs), and were far more democratic in their internal group processes. In an April 28, 1968, statement, the day of the police riot against the strike, the Columbia strikers affirmed their belief "in the right of all people to participate in the decisions that affect their lives.... The people who are affected by an illegitimate institution have the right to change it.... Our goal is to create a functioning participatory democracy to replace the repressive rule of the Administration and Trustees of this University."[68]

The university tried to use the strikers' commitment to democracy to break the strike. As part of the strike team and someone who had good relations with many faculty members, Gilbert was called in as a negotiator, even though he was by then a graduate student at the New School for Social Research. (He was, he says now, acting as a "concerned alumnus.") The faculty asked Gilbert if the strikers would abide by a vote of the university on whether to end the strike. "They had surveys showing that, while about two-thirds of the students supported us on the issues, a comparable majority would vote against the strike as a tactic," he says. So how to respond? "Torn between their definition of 'democracy' and the fundamental principles of the strike, I stammered out an answer: 'We believe in democracy; we will abide by the results of a vote…uh, as long as the people of Vietnam and Harlem can vote too, since it is their lives that are most affected by these decisions.'" Gilbert's response was later quoted in the alumni magazine to show how unreasonable the strikers were. [69]

The Columbia strike and other events to come in 1968 had a tremendous impact on the size of SDS. As Max Elbaum reported, "SDS expanded from roughly 30,000 members and 250 chapters in the fall of 1967 to

80,000 to 100,000 members and 350 to 400 chapters in November 1968."[70] That summer proved a tumultuous and life-changing one for many, both individually and for the movement at large.

POLICE RIOTS, MOVEMENT RIOTS:
SUMMER 1968, U.S. NATIONAL LIBERATION MOVEMENTS, AND STATE VIOLENCE

TWO AND A half months after the second strike at Columbia came the Democratic and Republican conventions—with massive protests at both. In a decadent Miami convention hall, Richard Nixon was selected as the Republican nominee, running on a peace platform, while six Black people were killed in the melee outside.[71] Three weeks later, thousands of Yippies, antiwar activists, SDSers, Panthers, and others descended on Chicago to express their disgust with the Vietnam War. The focus of much antiwar opposition, President Johnson had announced in March that he would not seek re-election, leading many to believe that the war's end was within reach if the movement continued to apply pressure. But when Robert F. Kennedy, who had criticized the war, was assassinated in early June, and with openly antiwar candidate Eugene McCarthy running second to Vice President Hubert Humphrey for the party bid, the antiwar movement had to ensure that the Democratic candidate would not follow in the footsteps of his predecessor when it came to Vietnam. "Our battle in Chicago was not with the Democrats," wrote Abbie Hoffman, who would be tried for "conspiracy" as a result of his involvement in the protests. "Our battle was with those responsible for the Vietnam War."[72]

As is now well known, the Chicago Police, at the direction of Mayor Richard Daley, went on a rampage against the demonstrators, refusing protest permits and revoking those granted—preferring instead some good, old-fashioned beatings. The cops waded through the crowds chanting, "kill, kill, kill."[73] As George Katsiaficas recounted in his *The Imagination of the New Left*, "The events of Chicago revealed how far the new hard-line within the Establishment had reached. Non-violent sitting protesters were mercilessly and bloodily clubbed in front of television cameras, and even network anchorpeople were not immune from what was later characterized as a 'police riot' by the official Walker Commission report."[74] The images of police mercilessly beating demonstrators were broadcast globally. When Senator Abraham Ribicoff complained on the convention hall floor about the violence outside, the mayor responded, "Fuck you, you Jew son of a bitch, you lousy motherfucker, go home!"[75]

The force used at Chicago and at Columbia was a much more publicized replay of the violence carried out against Black communities in ghetto rebellions throughout the decade (more than 300 by the time of the Chicago protests).[76] What Watts and other rebellions did for the Black movement, Chicago and Columbia did for the white Left: pushed many to see the limits of nonviolence, the entrenched brutality of the power structure, and the need for a revolutionary movement. "As the system exposed its own viciousness in the violence it exported to Indochina, the brutality it brought to the nation's inner cities, and the force it used in Chicago in 1968 at the Democratic National Convention, millions of people came to see the U.S. government as an enemy of freedom and democracy," Katsiaficas wrote.[77] For Scott Braley, Chicago "was the point where it became much clearer that you have to decide whether or not to fight back."

At its annual summer convention, a newly vitalized and radicalized SDS elected a woman for the first time as national leader—and she came out with a bang. Bernardine Dohrn, a 25-year-old Chicago native and assistant executive secretary for the National Lawyers Guild, described herself on the convention floor as a "revolutionary communist."[78] SDS had come a long way from its social democratic beginnings. There was a growing recognition that the movement was changing and that new forms of struggle would be required to combat the powers SDS now found itself facing. "The core of our common ideology was about empire and race," Dohrn says of SDS in 1968. "In my view white supremacy and anti-imperialism were at the core of what we understood and were right about."

The more difficult part was race. Black Power had by now become a popular ideology in the U.S. Left. Taking inspiration from the Black Panthers, a plethora of organizations based in communities of color in the United States were rising up en masse, often with a specifically nationalist framework (or at least one that benefited from nationalism) that was at the same time strongly connected to international developments and usually incorporated some Marxist or Marxist-Leninist analysis. The Republic of New Afrika, a Black group with the goal of establishing an independent, sovereign Black Nation in the South, began in March 1968, with a specific presence in Mississippi.[79] The American Indian Movement formed in July 1968, asserting indigenous sovereignty as a defining issue with the slogan "U.S. out of North America." (Although AIM was inspired by the Panthers and attentive to global liberation struggles, it had a different relationship to Marxism from that of other liberation movements, due to its emphasis on Native spirituality.)[80] Among Latinos, groups such as the Brown Berets (1968), the Young Lords Party (1969), and El Comité (1970) were on the rise. And in Asian and Asian-American communities, groups such as the Red Guard and I Wor Kuen attracted younger militants.[81] What all these groups shared was a radical critique of U.S. imperialism at home and abroad, community programs, a belief in the need for revolution, and support for armed self-defense.

People of color within this country also began to speak of being colonized, applying many of the same standards used for discussing colonization overseas. These standards included: the occupying of low- and lowest-level jobs at a disproportionate level for lower wages than even the white working class; the denial of access to land, whether because of theft of indigenous land or white ownership of ghetto and barrio properties; occupation of communities by military or police; and attacks on culture, language, and customs by the colonial (i.e., white) population.[82] This analysis defining people of color "captive nations" and "internal colonies" within the United States, when joined with an internationalist sensibility, led many to identify themselves as Third World. Rather than a purely racial identification, the Third World label was a political designation denoting the social, political, economic, and cultural location of colonized people relative to the ruling order. These movements deemed it important to organize with other Third World people around a specifically anti-colonial platform.

These movements suggested a role and responsibility for white radicals that had never before been articulated in so strong and widespread a way. With the advent of Black Power, SNCC had raised the call for white radicals to "organize their own community." That demand was now being echoed by other groups as well. Thus, the Panthers, AIM, the Brown Berets, the Young Lords, and countless other Third World groupings in the United States asserted that the role of white people was to work in solidarity with them.

SDS set out to build an empathic response with the emerging nationalist movements in this country. As head of SDS, Dohrn tried to strike a balance by encouraging SDS chapters to build political relationships with the rapidly emerging Black Student Unions, and to respond to the strategic courses being charted by the BSU and Panther chapters—with campaigns such as open enrollment, Black studies, access for the communities of color surrounding universities, and unionization of campus workers—but without compromising SDS's independent character or turning it into a mere support group. "What we tried to do," she says now, "was to bridge the moment of separatism at the same time as trying to take seriously the mandate to organize among white people outside of the comfortable pockets of white supremacy.... Part of our job was to shake white people, and ourselves, of all the baggage that goes with seeing the world from a place of privilege."

THE LIMITS OF NONVIOLENCE

A S PEOPLE IN SDS looked at their world, they found two common threads to any successful revolutionary struggle: the ideology of Marxism, and armed struggle (whether the People's War model found in Vietnam or the small and focused version of Cuba). As a result, many in and around the student movement followed the path taken by many in the domestic Third World liberation movements—abandoning strict adherence to nonviolence and increasing support for the use of violence in political struggle. That the Panthers and other groups were under constant attack made it easier to at least support armed self-defense.

David Gilbert had begun to question doctrinaire pacifism in 1965, as a result of his study of Latin America and U.S. interventions on the continent. Though he remained philosophically a pacifist for two more years, the process beginning in 1965 was one he found life-altering—and deeply troubling. "It was a traumatic experience for me," he says, "because being a pacifist gave me a certain moral certitude as an individual.... But what had motivated me was the conditions of life of most people, and to turn [away from] social violence, and not be willing to fight against the forces who actively use force and violence to maintain those social conditions, was acquiescing to more violence." It was a difficult choice, but ultimately one he felt he had to make. "After seven years of activism and analysis, I reluctantly concluded that there wasn't a chance against the forces of repression without developing a capacity for armed struggle." [83]

For Scott Braley, then a Midwest regional SDS organizer, it was Martin Luther King's opposition to the war and the rising tide of liberation struggles that convinced him that the struggle needed to move to a higher level. He had already dropped out of school and was helping organize SDS chapters throughout the area. "It became clear to me in 1967 that the U.S. was, as MLK said, 'the greatest purveyor of violence in the world.' A year later, I realized that national liberation and social justice movements were the alternative to imperialism. It seemed like a pretty clear choice—to be on the immoral and historically losing side of white supremacy, or to join a vibrant struggle for liberation around the world." From there, it was a small step to the summer of 1969, when Braley and his comrade and then-partner, Linda Evans, each took a vow to follow their convictions. "We said, 'OK, it looks like we're going to do this [go underground]. We're probably going to end up dead or in prison for the rest of our lives. Maybe we'll win. But we know that's what we're doing."[84]

THE RISE OF THE WOMEN'S MOVEMENT

THE YEAR 1967 was not just marked by the naming of the system as imperialism, and "many Vietnams" as the strategy for defeating it. That year also saw the emergence of the feminist movement. The women's movement was bubbling to the surface at all levels, with groups such as Redstockings and Women's International Terrorist Conspiracy from Hell (WITCH) taking the stage. Many women activists left mixed-gender groups to build all-women formations, while others tried to inject new consciousness into existing organizations.[85]

One of the first stirrings of consciousness around gender oppression came in 1965, when women at a civil rights workshop demanded that SNCC "confront the issue of sexual discrimination" within the group. Casey Hayden and Mary King drafted "a kind of memo" called "Sex and Caste." The memo, which was widely distributed (and published the following year) described some of the ways in which male supremacy manifested itself in SNCC, denying women's potential and abilities by relegating them to menial tasks and chores.[86] Within a few years, women would also begin criticizing the sexual abuse and objectification of activist women at the hands of activist men.[87]

Although SDS had passed a resolution in fall 1965 affirming the full participation of women, it had not been put into practice.[88] By 1967, women activists were bringing feminist politics to bear inside SDS, in concert with the burgeoning feminist movement, targeting not only sexist group dynamics but a broader structure of male supremacy. Bernardine Dohrn and Naomi Jaffe wrote an article that year, printed in *New Left Notes* under the title "The Look Is You," but elsewhere called "Two Tits and No Head," in reference to an image of a woman's chest (sans head) that had graced a recent cover of the radical magazine *Ramparts*.[89] The article attempted to analyze the role of women as consumers and women's unpaid labor in the family. "The Look Is You," an attempt to relate women's liberation to a broader system of imperialism, arose from a women's study group, one of the first of its kind. "The idea that there was any reason for women to be together in a room other than to be the ladies auxiliary was totally new," Jaffe says. Similar formations started to emerge, including a women's dance collective and a women's theory collective of SDS activists.

The emerging women's movement took lessons from the revolutionary nationalist movements when it came to organizational forms: independent organizing was viewed as a necessary step. Also taking their cue from Third World movements, many early women's liberation activists spoke of women's oppression as being a kind of colonial domination.[90] Even in progressive SDS, women's independence was seen as threatening. The first all-women's workshop at the 1967 SDS National Convention—chaired by Marilyn Buck, now a political prisoner in California—was greeted with catcalls such as "I'll liberate you with my cock!" Gilbert recalled the incident in an essay about Buck and her contributions to the movement. "SDS was supposed to be an organization defined by siding with the oppressed against the oppressor; even with little previous struggle, one would have hoped for at least an initial openness to and support for women's issues. Clearly there was a lot of struggle yet to go."[91]

A federal government presentation in 1968 on the leadership structure of SDS.

> *Black nationalism was the spearhead for revolutionary development within the United States. The government recognized this and intensified its attacks with the then-secret but now infamous COINTELPRO (Counter-Intelligence Program).* —*David Gilbert* [1]

I N ONE OF THE MORE SUBDUED BUT NEVERTHELESS telling examples of state repression in the 1960s, a member of the Independent Committee on Vietnam at Columbia University approached David Gilbert with a list she claimed to have found while working at a government agency. The list named five ICV members who were, she said, undercover police agents. But it didn't add up; Gilbert knew the individuals involved too well to believe it. "If I had gone for this faked information and accused these people or tried to kick them out, at the very least we would have lost five fine activists; more likely we would have had a major and bitter split in the ICV," he says. [2]

Although the ICV's primary activism was education, along with some nonviolent demonstrations, it nevertheless captured the government's attention. And the government was clever enough to know that the way to stir up group dissension was not through questioning members' patriotism or attacking them for having long hair. As the movements of the 1960s grew, and grew more radical, the state abandoned the "repressive tolerance" that Marxist scholar Herbert Marcuse said was at the heart of liberal democracies such as the United States. In his 1965 essay, Marcuse said governments tolerated opposition as long as it didn't challenge the status quo. [3] When movements began to directly challenge the state, however, the tolerance gave way to repression, pure and simple. Given the history of white supremacy and the fact that movements for self-determination were playing a leading role, this repression was concentrated most heavily on people of color.

The vanguard of state repression was the Federal Bureau of Investigation, led by the utterly paranoid, rabidly anti-communist, and vehemently bigoted J. Edgar Hoover. To be sure, the FBI didn't act alone. A multitude of government agencies were involved, from the CIA (in violation of the 1947 National Security Act) to the Army to the IRS to local and state police agencies (especially through their communist investigation units called Red Squads).[4] Indeed, as we shall see, even the mainstream media participated in the attempts to shut down the Left. But the FBI, through its COunterINTELligence PROgram (COINTELPRO), was the primary force attempting to destroy the Left.

The movement organizations had their own weaknesses and flaws, to be sure; the state cannot and should not be solely blamed for all their problems. But COINTELPRO and similar repressive programs had a deep and lasting impact on how organizations and activists operated: on the tactical and strategic decisions they made; on how they spent their time and money; and on their rise, fall, and mutations. As a result, state repression is at the heart of any discussion of movements of that period.

One could argue, of course, that it's not surprising that the state attacked the movements. Radicals did, after all, openly advocate resistance, rebellion, and, increasingly, revolution. When told that he had made the government's "shit list," radical publisher (*The Realist*) Paul Krassner replied, "That's a coincidence…. The government is on my shit list."[5] But the difference between the way radical movements and the government attacked each other is as stark as night and day. Radicals used moral suasion, polemics, creativity, and humor. The state used intimidation, harassment, censorship, and live ammunition. The playing field was far from level, not just in terms of the weapons (literal and figurative) each side had at its disposal, but also in terms of how far each side was willing to go in attacking its enemy. Even when the Civil Rights and Black Power Movements used arms—as did Robert Williams's NAACP chapter in the mid-1950s, the Deacons for Defense in the early to mid-1960s, the Black Panther Party in the late 1960s—the emphasis was on self-defense. When the militancy of the white Left was on the ascendancy, it was focused more on property than people. Even with the turn to armed struggle, tactics differed.

What were the state's tactics? Attorney Brian Glick identified four main methods by which COINTELPRO operated: *infiltration, psychological warfare, harassment through the legal system,* and *extralegal force and violence.*[6] These methods took different forms depending on the situation.

Surveillance was an obvious feature, whether by telephone taps, opening mail, or physically following people. Infiltration was another popular tactic, whereby agents or paid informants would join an organization and report back to the FBI—and frequently disrupt the group's activities. Other tactics of COINTELPRO included spreading false rumors that activists were agents or liars ("bad-jacketing"), spreading lies via the mainstream press (which the FBI called "gray propaganda" and Glick called "psychological warfare from the outside"), petty arrests meant to waste time and money, and, in some cases, assassinations.[7] Not surprisingly these tactics were deployed most thoroughly and brutally against Black and Native American dissidents. COINTELPRO researcher Ward Churchill counts at least twenty-seven Black Panthers and sixty-nine American Indian Movement activists murdered between 1968 and 1976.[8]

The Black Panther Party suffered every weapon in the COINTELPRO arsenal. In an attempt to sabotage working relationships between Black Nationalist groups, FBI agents sent fake letters between the Panthers and the United Slaves (US), a California-based cultural nationalist organization. The letters created such a climate of acrimony that three members of US murdered Panthers Bunchy Carter and John Huggins on January 17, 1969.[9] The Carter-Huggins murders took place against a backdrop of police murders of Black Panthers, starting with sixteen-year-old Bobby Hutton— the first member to join the Black Panthers—on April 6, 1968.[10]

Although it was the most dramatic, murder was not the most widely utilized tactic. Character assassinations were more widespread, and fomenting splits became a primary task for COINTELPRO operatives. Infiltration of radical organizations was a classic technique. Police agents, informants, and provocateurs gained high rank in chapters of the Black Panthers, SDS, and other radical groups across the country. In this capacity, agents not only spied on radical organizations but also tried to divert their energies and discredit them. An agent in the Northern Illinois University SDS chapter attacked the university president and threw him off a stage, "creating a pretext for official action against the chapter."[11] In Seattle, an FBI informant offered disaffected Vietnam veteran Larry Ward $75 to do a bombing. When Ward agreed, the informant gave him the bomb, drove him to the site—and alerted the police, who shot and killed Ward as he tried to flee. "The police wanted a bomber, and I got them one," the informant later boasted.[12]

One group destroyed by COINTELPRO was the Revolutionary Action Movement (RAM), a Black Nationalist organization headquartered in

Philadelphia. Starting with surveillance, the FBI quickly moved to detaining RAM members and arresting them for passing out literature, *suspected* drug use, and graffiti. Address books were then confiscated, providing police with more suspects to harass and arrest. Members were arrested with such frequency that they could no longer afford bail money, and anyone with previous convictions was sent to prison for parole violations. RAM ran out of people and resources, and was quickly destroyed.[13]

While it was the radical movements in Black and indigenous communities that most attracted the FBI's enmity, a central goal of COINTELPRO was to prevent or break any attempts at multiracial solidarity. An FBI memo noted that the "creation of factionalism is a potent weapon which must not be overlooked."[14] With that in mind, FBI agents sent false letters to break up a progressive multiracial coalition in Chicago between the Black Panthers, radical white and Puerto Rican organizations, and local street gangs.[15] Similarly, numerous attempts were made to stave off relationships between SDS and the Panthers, including phony letters sent to the Panthers supposedly by an SDS chapter.[16] Indeed, the bureau's one-two punch of attempting to destroy organizations such as the Panthers while also working to cut off any white solidarity with Third World groups led ex-Panther Mumia Abu-Jamal to say that the "FBI functioned as political and race police—agents for the preservation of white supremacy."[17]

Although the bureau's files on the Civil Rights Movement and Martin Luther King date back to the 1950s, the official start of an FBI counterintelligence program against the Black movement came in 1967.[18] An internal memo drafted on August 25 of that year described it as a national program designed "to expose, disrupt, misdirect, discredit, or otherwise neutralize the activities of black nationalist, hate-type [*sic*] organizations and groupings, their leadership, spokesmen, membership, and supporters, and to counter their propensity for violence and civil disorder."[19] The memo went on to say that "no opportunity should be missed" to weaken the movement. Specific groups mentioned include SNCC, Martin Luther King's Southern Christian Leadership Conference (SCLC), and the Congress of Racial Equality. Not long after the memo appeared, however, J. Edgar Hoover announced that the Black Panther Party was "the greatest threat to the internal security of the United States."[20]

Less than a year later—and three weeks after the Columbia rebellion—the FBI directed COINTELPRO against the predominantly white New Left. A May 9, 1968, FBI memo committed the bureau "to expose, disrupt and otherwise neutralize the activities of [the New Left] and persons connected with it."[21] A memo drafted later in May strategized "that they must be destroyed or neutralized from the inside."[22] Two months later, the bureau developed a twelve-point plan of action, recommending that the "hostility among SDS…and the Progressive Labor Party…should be exploited wherever possible."[23]

Other government entities used similar tactics to undercut the Left. The CIA instituted Operation CHAOS (named for what it hoped to create) in response to a story in *Ramparts* magazine that exposed the National Student Association as a CIA-controlled entity. CHAOS particularly looked for "foreign connections" (real or presumed) between the U.S. Left and communist governments.[24] The Army, meanwhile, conducted its own investigations of radical individuals and organizations; in particular, the U.S. Army Intelligence Command used court-martials, censorship, and demotions to hinder antiwar activism by GIs.[25] And at the request of the CIA and the FBI, the IRS handed over confidential tax information on more than 100 prominent radicals.[26]

COINTELPRO and similar programs recognized and went after the strongest links of leftist opposition: the domestic national liberation movements (the Civil Rights and Black Power Movements, the Puerto Rican independence movement, the American Indian Movement) and the radical media. The first were targeted because they directly challenged the foundations of white supremacy; the second because it was how the movement communicated.

In going after the Left, the government proved itself adroit at using the movement's ideals—of anti-racism, of solidarity, of democracy—against itself. CIA and FBI infiltrators exploited the movement's participatory democratic structures as a way to insert themselves in leadership positions and divert attention and funds away from the real tasks. Panther infiltrators and provocateurs accused white radicals of racism, or made real issues of racism insurmountable so as to sabotage coalition work. *New Left Notes* editor Cathy Wilkerson recalls instances when the Chicago Panthers would receive phone calls allegedly from the SDS National Office (but really from the FBI or local police), informing them that SDS was "too busy" to follow through on agreements to print Panther literature.[27] Speaking of this trend generally, Gilbert remarks that those carrying out the repression "were sophisticated enough to see racism in us, and to be able to play on that and have their infiltrators…raise issues that were real sore points."[28]

There were difficulties, of course. How can you attack longhairs for having long hair, or criticize Marxist-Leninists for being communists? An FBI memo sagely observed: "It is believed that the nonconformism [sic] in dress and speech, neglect of personal cleanliness, use of obscenities (printed and uttered), publicized sexual promiscuity, experimenting with and the use of drugs, filthy clothes, shaggy hair, wearing of sandals, beads, and unusual jewelry tend to negate any attempt to hold these people up to ridicule. The American press has been doing this with no apparent effect or curtailment of 'new left' activities."[29] Recognizing the limited utility of attacking the movement for being itself, the FBI instead opted for the "creating of impressions that certain New Left leaders are informants for the Bureau or other law enforcement agencies."[30] Adopting the movement's rhetoric, the FBI proposed to attack key radicals for "selling out."[31]

At the same time as it used the movement's ideals against itself, the FBI used the movement's own rhetoric to discredit it with the mainstream. In its plan of action, the FBI proposed using articles from radical papers "to show the depravity of New Left leaders and members. In this connection, articles showing advocation [sic] of the use of narcotics and free sex are ideal to send to university officials, wealthy donors, members of the legislature and parents of students who are active in New Left matters."[32] The FBI's powers were enhanced with new repressive laws. After SNCC leaders such as H. Rap Brown spoke to outraged Black communities, some of which later erupted in rebellion, Congress passed laws in 1967 prohibiting the crossing of state lines to "promote rioting." These laws were also used against other radicals, such as the eight antiwar activists indicted for the protests against the 1968 Democratic National Convention in Chicago.[33]

"The paranoia was everywhere," says Chip Berlet, who was a radical journalist in the 1960s. "You expected that your office was being broken into, and it turns out that it was. You expected that people were spying on you, and indeed sometimes you could see them—they would be out in cars looking at you."[34] Aware of the growing repression it was facing, SDS organized a workshop on "sabotage and explosives" at its 1968 national convention. The workshop, wrote former SDS leader Robert Pardun, was "specifically designed for the agents who we knew were spying on us."[35] The workshop succeeded in attracting a few presumed police agents, who were stuck in a phony session while the real conference continued without them.

The more serious and widespread result, however, was an atmosphere of mistrust. The FBI paid special attention to fomenting fighting and isolating important leaders within an organization. As COINTELPRO researcher Ward Churchill has shown, this created a situation "that allowed the successful fabrication of cases through which to bring about the lengthy imprisonment of targets or, in some instances, their selective assassination by police."[36] Thus, when Black Panther leader Geronimo Pratt was framed for a murder that police *knew* from their own surveillance records that he did not commit, he received minimal support because of FBI-created Panther infighting. In the *Black Panther* newspaper released on January 23, 1971, readers found an announcement by Huey Newton expelling Pratt from the Black Panther Party and forbidding members from communicating with him. Isolated from what would have been his base of support, Pratt was arrested, tried and convicted. He spent twenty-seven years (of a life sentence) in prison before being released when his false conviction was overturned.[37] Former Panthers Mondo we Langwa and Ed Poindexter remain in prison under similar circumstances.[38]

KILLING THE MESSENGER:
STATE REPRESSION AND RADICAL MEDIA

RADICAL MEDIA CAME under attack not just because it was the voice and, according to former radical journalist Angus Mackenzie, the "spinal column" of the movement, but because it was successful.[39] By 1970, the underground press had a readership as high as 6 million, and studies showed that 70 percent of people in the United States did not believe what they read in the mainstream media.[40] Radical media was an important way in which social movements communicated with one another, discussed strategic questions, negotiated complex political ideas, and organized new people into the growing social upheaval. Radical papers ran the gamut from organizational publications (the *Black Panther*, *New Left Notes*) to general movement papers (the *Guardian*, the *Movement*, *RAT*) to countercultural publications (the *Berkeley Barb, East Village Other, Kudzu*). All of them were united, if loosely, in a culture of opposition. Ex-*Washington Free Press* staffer William Blum writes that his paper, like other radical media outlets, "was merely a vehicle for the antiwar movement, the civil rights movement, and all the other burgeoning anti-authoritarian and social change tendencies that convinced the good burghers of America that society's fabric was rapidly unraveling."[41]

And so, the movement's media came under attack. Tom Forcade, head of the radical media consortium, Underground Press Syndicate, once summed up the many levels of the state's harassment campaign: "With obscenity busts, they get your money; with drug busts, they get your people; with intimidation, they get your printer; and if you still manage somehow to get out a sheet, their distribution monopolies and rousts keep it from ever getting to the people."[42] The government harassed street vendors; pressured advertisers to withdraw support from alternative and radical papers; pressured printers to "clear" advance copies of publications with authorities or stop printing them altogether; destroyed papers; and attacked media offices. In one incident, a warehouse containing back issues of the *Black Panther* was burned to the ground.[43]

While the harassment against SDS was less severe, it was nonetheless extreme (and, of course, illegal). "The government repeatedly and consistently harassed *New Left Notes*," says former editor Wilkerson. "At first, it went to the printer and made the printer show the advanced copy every week. Then it began to pressure the printer not to print it, but we were its major account, so they weren't successful for a long while. Finally, they did convince the printer to stop printing the paper. For a while we printed it ourselves in the office, and then managed to find another printer."[44] Still, *New Left Notes* managed to enlarge its print run from about 5,000 copies a week in 1967 to 12,000 copies in 1969.[45]

In the internal memo announcing COINTELPRO operations against radical media, the FBI brass instructed agents to create a "detailed survey concerning New Left-type publications being printed and circulated." The survey was to include information on staff, printer, circulation, finances, and advertisers, as well as any "subversive connections" or "foreign ramifications"—all in an effort to force papers to "fold and cease publication."[46] Not surprisingly, *The Black Panther* got special attention; the FBI noted that the publication was "the voice of the BPP and if it could be effectively hindered, it would result in helping to cripple the BPP."[47] Similarly, the FBI targeted SDS's Radical Education Project (REP) because it was, as the FBI described it, a "full-time publishing outfit of the New Left."[48]

Free speech can be expensive. Radical papers and radio stations in at least six cities (Atlanta, Houston, Los Angeles, Milwaukee, Phoenix, and Seattle) were firebombed.[49] The FBI convinced a shipper to overcharge the

Black Panthers, and then made plans (which were never carried out) to stink-bomb their offices.[50] Army Intelligence, together with the FBI, burglarized the office of the *Washington Free Press* before Nixon's inauguration in 1969. They stole several hundred pre-addressed postcards the paper planned to give out in an effort to find housing for demonstrators during the inaugural protests. The FBI and army filled out the postcards and mailed them back, trying to confuse those coordinating housing efforts.[51]

With the dramatic examples came the more mundane. A major strategy to shut down radical newspapers involved trying to scare advertisers, real and potential. The FBI sent phony letters from "disgusted patrons" to companies that advertised in radical and counterculture papers. Forged letters written by "concerned parents" asked university administrations to ban radical publications from campuses or, at least in one case, to stop professors from donating money to such papers. These forgeries were largely successful.[52]

The FBI even went so far as to establish mock alternative papers as a divide-and-conquer ploy. The *Armageddon News* of Bloomington, Indiana, was formed at Indiana University in the fall of 1968 while the editor of the legitimate local radical paper was on trial for draft resistance. *Armageddon* proclaimed: "As students, we feel the war in Vietnam is a political and military travesty.... This situation we can and should deal with at the polls.... The truth of the situation here at IU, however, is that this dissatisfaction with national policy is being used by a few to seize the university and to strike at the heart of the democratic system."[53] The *Longhorn Tale* in San Antonio and the *Rational Observer* in Washington, D.C., voiced similar FBI-generated "opinions." The government also established pseudo-radical news networks, including the Pacific International News Service and the New York Press Service.[54]

Infiltration was also used in the campaign against Left media. Under the guise of looking for "foreign connections," more than sixty CIA agents worked on the radical press. One of the agency's specialties was the years-long infiltration of radical newspapers; *Ramparts* was infiltrated after exposing CIA control of the National Student Association, and agent Sal Ferrera infiltrated both *Quicksilver* and the *Washington Free Press*.[55] Ferrera published dozens of articles and helped build the infrastructure of a variety of movement publications over the years. He was such a valuable part of *Quicksilver* that FBI operatives assigned to the paper were also spying on him, unaware of his true identity.[56]

Given the widespread use of recreational drugs in the movement, drug busts became an easy way for the state to harass radicals. Indeed, the fifth point on the FBI's 12-point program to neutralize the New Left suggested drug busts as a potent weapon.[57] Marijuana possession was used to arrest and in some cases incarcerate radical journalists in St. Louis, Ann Arbor, and Detroit. In Ann Arbor, the state arrested the entire staff of the *Argus*, forcing the publication to fold. For possession of two joints, Detroit *Sun* editor John Sinclair was given ten years in prison—the longest sentence at the time in Michigan for such an offense.[58] In a report on repression against radical media, Underground Press Syndicate director Tom Forcade wrote that radical journalists were arrested for drugs at a rate 100 times that of the mainstream society. In 1969, UPS estimated that 60 percent of radical papers were "experiencing major [government] repression."[59]

Where it could, the government also used "official channels" to shut down radical publications. High school radical papers were particularly susceptible to disruption, and their editors to suspension or expulsion.[60] Prison officials, bestowed with nearly supreme powers over those in captivity, denied prisoners access to publications sent to them, especially radical ones. Army Intelligence Command had a desk dealing specifically with underground newspapers, wiping out those papers on or near military bases (including publications by soldiers).[61]

MAINSTREAM MEDIA AS A WEAPON OF STATE REPRESSION

MALCOLM X WARNED his audience in a 1964 talk to be wary of the media. "If you aren't careful, the newspapers will have you hating the people who are being oppressed and loving the people who are doing the oppressing."[62] The argument could be made that the mainstream media did exactly that in the 1960s and '70s. The mainstream media was used, both with and without its knowledge, by the state in its campaign against the Left. Of course, the movement (especially the more radical sectors) expected to receive negative press, but there is a difference between hostile coverage and an orchestrated campaign of state repression. The mainstream media provided both.

In the August 25, 1967, FBI internal memorandum marking the official start of COINTELPRO against the Black Liberation Movement, the FBI made provisions for using the mass media in its repressive attempts. According to this historic document, "when an opportunity is apparent to disrupt or neutralize black nationalist, hate-type [*sic*] organizations through the cooperation of established local news media contacts" careful attention must be given to "insure the targeted group is disrupted, ridiculed, or discredited through the publicity and not merely publicized."[63]

The FBI's goal was to use the mainstream media to build public sentiment against Black radicals, and even the Black community at large, without allowing them to reply. And by and large, it worked. A 1976 senate committee investigation of COINTELPRO revealed that the FBI "attempted covertly to influence the public's perception of persons and organizations by disseminating derogatory information to the press, either anonymously or through 'friendly' news contacts."[64] Chip Berlet, an activist and researcher with Political Research Associates, found that the FBI spent considerable effort cultivating press contacts. "FBI offices in 16 cities were requested to compile lists of cooperative and reliable reporters for COINTELPRO use. The New Haven, Connecticut, office alone submitted a list of 28 media contacts. Media operations were carried out by agents in an additional seven cities. The FBI media program was especially active in New York, Chicago, Los Angeles and Milwaukee."[65] Three of the four cities where the FBI's media program was most active were also cities where the Black Panthers, SDS, and Puerto Rican and Chicano/a organizations were most active. Major frame-up trials aimed at neutralizing the Panthers occurred in both New Haven and New York, each starting in 1969. Chicago, headquarters for SDS and, later, early Weatherman, was also the home of one of the more active Black Panther chapters (under the direction of Fred Hampton) and the birthplace of the Young Lords.

Of course, the use of "friendly" media wasn't limited to just these cities. In the nation's capital, the FBI asked a reporter from the Scripps-Howard News Service to write a "special visual feature story" on nine Weatherman fugitives to aid in the Bureau's intensive search for the radicals. The story appeared on May 7, 1970. As historian Jeremy Varon notes, "[FBI Director J. Edgar] Hoover personally thanked [the reporter] for his 'excellent article,' and the FBI noted with satisfaction that a congressman—unaware of the story's origin—had placed it in the *Congressional Record*."[66]

An FBI memo suggesting points of action for neutralizing the New Left explicitly called for (and anticipated) mainstream media cooperation. "Whenever New Left groups engage in disruptive activities on college campuses, cooperative press contacts should be encouraged to emphasize that the disruptive elements constitute a minority of the students and do not represent the conviction of the majority. The press should demand an immediate student referendum on the issue in question.... It is felt that this technique...could put an end to lengthy demonstrations and could cause embarrassment to New Left elements."[67] The FBI found a firm counterinsurgency ally in the mainstream media, praising its "reliability and discreetness."[68]

The FBI used mainstream newspapers not just to build public opposition to the movement, but also to foster splits between revolutionary groups.[69] In one particularly telling example, a *New York Times* headline on October 7, 1968, proclaimed: "SNCC in decline after 8 years in lead; Pace-setter in civil rights displaced by Panthers." The article quoted unnamed "federal authorities" recalling a previously undisclosed "incident" in which unnamed "Black Panthers" tried to intimidate SNCC leader James Forman by placing an unloaded gun in his mouth and pulling the trigger. It never happened. Forman cites the incident in his memoir as one of many government-initiated public fabrications to smear the Black movement.[70] Because it was only his word against that of the unnamed "authorities," Forman had no chance of getting a retraction. Besides, who reads the "Corrections" page? As Todd Gitlin notes in *The Whole World is Watching*, "the 'story' is more newsworthy when it is fresh and false than when it is 'old' and true."[71]

In addition to what the mainstream media said about the movement and what it called the "outhouse press" and the "seedier media,"[72] it is also worth noting what the mainstream media *didn't* say. The mass media rarely spoke out in defense of the Left or its media. In a letter to the Commission on Obscenity and Pornography in May 1970, Underground Press Syndicate head Tom Forcade indicted the media for being complicit with the crimes of the state. "The straight media is equally responsible, for they bear the guilt of the *crime of silence*, the *crime of inaction* as they watch and cheer while their media brothers in the underground press go down the drain of lost freedom of the press. They mouth empty words and they are total hypocrites."[73]

In the heat of the moment, of course, the level of misdeeds and malfeasances against the movement was not fully known. But as the decade of the 1960s drew to a close, activists were keenly aware that something was wrong: political arrests and trials were on the increase, militants were being murdered, people were under constant surveillance, and the organizations leading the movement were beginning to splinter and fall apart. The stakes increased, lines were drawn. What was to be done?

The triumphant Weathermen, now in charge of SDS, at the podium of the 1969 SDS convention. Dorhn is in the center, and Mark Rudd is to the right.
Photo by David Fenton

TWO, THREE, MANY SDSes
THE END OF SDS, THE BEGINNING OF NEW GROUPS

4

> *We were too overwhelmed by the stark life-and-death challenges, combined with our own inexperience and weaknesses.... SDS splintered apart in 1969–1970.*   —*David Gilbert*[1]

I F THE PERIOD OF 1965 TO 1967 WAS ONE IN WHICH SDS tried to move, as its slogan went, "from protest to resistance," the period from 1967 to 1969 was one in which they tried to move from resistance to revolution.[2] This shift accompanied the rising tide of liberation movements and the growing ferocity of the state. With the election of Richard Nixon in November 1968, repression took a turn for the worse. One of the Nixon administration's first acts was the indictment of eight organizers for "conspiracy to incite riot" at the Democratic National Convention in Chicago in August 1968. Ramsey Clark, the attorney general under Johnson, had refused to convene a grand jury against activists for events that even a government commission had deemed "a police riot." But Nixon's attorney general, John Mitchell, had no such problem.

Rennie Davis, Dave Dellinger, John Froines, Tom Hayden, Abbie Hoffman, Jerry Rubin, Bobby Seale, and Lee Weiner were indicted on March 20, 1969. All had long histories of activism. Hayden was a founder of SDS, and Davis and Froines were also SDSers (with Davis being a prominent antiwar leader). Although Hoffman and Rubin had achieved notoriety as Yippie pranksters, the two had been politically active for years—Hoffman with civil rights and antiwar work, and Rubin with groups challenging the communist witch-hunters calling themselves the House Un-American Activities Committee. And the Yippies were not just hippies; they worked to support the Panthers and others, to inject a cultural frivolity into the antiwar movement as well as a political analysis into the hippie counter-culture.[3] Not as well known as his comrades, Weiner was also a Yippie. An activist since World War II, Dellinger was a tested anti-racist and antiwar pacifist. The only Black person in the group (and the least involved in the Chicago demonstrations), Seale was leader and cofounder of the Black Panther Party. Quite deliberately, Mitchell and company had picked some of the best-known activists in the country.[4]

In the coming years, the trial would become a battleground. Most infamously, Judge Julius Hoffman had Bobby Seale bound and gagged because he repeatedly demanded his right to serve as his own attorney. The white defendants tried to turn the trial into political theater (although Dave Dellinger, the oldest and least rowdy of the bunch, was the only one to respond when bailiffs beat and gagged Seale; Dellinger, a pacifist, tried to put his body between Seale and the police).[5] Everyone but Froines and Weiner would be convicted—including the defense attorneys, cited several times for contempt. All the convictions would be overturned because of prosecutorial misconduct, but that would take years.[6] In the spring and summer of 1969, the movement knew only that the state was gearing up for the biggest conspiracy trial of the decade in an attempt to crush antiwar organizing.

The new president—elected by a margin of less than one percent—had more than the movement on his mind. Nixon was also responsible for a brutal escalation of the war in Southeast Asia. After campaigning as a peace candidate, Nixon expanded the war beyond Vietnam into neighboring Cambodia and Laos, causing the deaths of millions. There were also heavy casualties for U.S. soldiers. "Of the nearly 58,184 American deaths in Vietnam, 23,957 were killed after Nixon was elected," SDSer Robert Pardun writes in his memoir. "This is the level of power and morality we were up against."[7]

The conspiracy trials, the stark repression of domestic movements, the unending war, the courageous examples of Third World liberation struggles—all these infused SDS with a sense of urgency at a time when problems within the organization were becoming more dominant and people were looking to expand the movement's focus and effectiveness. Whereas the early SDS was characterized by a small group of people who all knew one another, the SDS of 1969 was a geographically dispersed mass organization. In addition, SDS's commitment to participatory democracy was being taken advantage of by the Progressive Labor Party (PL), a Maoist sect with a significant presence in SDS. PL members of SDS brought with them a political platform determined by the PL hierarchy (with accompanying Marx quotes to prove their point) and thus disrespected the decision-making process SDS had established. Although other such entities had been a part of SDS, PL was the largest and therefore commanded the most influence. Different blocs emerged within SDS in response to PL's proposed strategy and its undemocratic approach.

The largest anti-PL bloc, the Revolutionary Youth Movement (RYM, pronounced "rim"), had its roots in a resolution of the same name passed at the December 1968 SDS convention. The RYM resolution pledged solidarity with Black and other Third World struggles, making anti-racism a defining political principle for white youth. This proposal stood in contrast to PL's perennial Worker-Student Alliance initiatives, which saw race as divisive and promoted a staid and conservative view of "the working class." For PL, politics began and ended at the point of production; student radicalism and autonomous organizing by people of color was a distraction.

Not so for RYM. "In order to fight racism, we must recognize that there is a struggle being fought right now for black liberation in America with which we must ally," the resolution stated. "This fight for black liberation is at once an anti-colonial struggle against racism and the racist imperialist power structure, as well as being part of the class struggle because black workers are among the most oppressed." These statements were a far cry from PL's approach, which rejected autonomous Black organizing. RYM's insistence on solidarity with the Vietnamese flew in the face of PL's assertions that the NLF was "selling out" to U.S. imperialism by negotiating.[8] Although the PL-controlled May 2nd Movement had been an early supporter of the NLF, the group's position had changed by the late 1960s—leading many in SDS to quip that "PL would fight to the last drop of Vietnamese blood."[9]

Equally if not more destructive was PL's insistence that "all nationalism was reactionary." This position was a direct argument against the Black Panthers, whom many in SDS viewed as their inspiration—as well as the most potent revolutionary force in the country. "That meant, for example, as relations were developing with the Panthers, PL was against it," says Robert Roth, of Columbia SDS. "Those [disagreements] became very difficult and divisive, for work on a local level and around the country." And it wasn't just the Panthers that PL decried as reactionary; as the Michigan-based Radical Education Project of SDS reported, PL worked against Black organizing on several campuses where fierce struggles around open admissions and Black studies programs were taking place, as well as opposing organizing campaigns by Black workers in Detroit.[10] PL's position contradicted the most inspiring activism of the period, movements with which SDS was trying to unite. Decrying nationalism at a time when most movements were in some way nationalistic not only sabotaged relationship-building but was an insult to those movements; it was a position that said that PL knew what was better for the struggles of oppressed people than did the people themselves.

This amalgamation of PL's frustratingly hierarchical structure and politically retrograde stance played out in a student strike at San Francisco State University during the 1968–1969 school year. The four-and-a-half-month strike by students of color, via both the Black Student Union and a multiracial group of people of color calling itself the Third World Liberation Front, put forth a host of demands relating to both academic and administrative aspects of the university.[11] PL activists in the Bay Area played a vital role in supporting the strike, until the PL hierarchy (and thus, membership) denounced the strike for displaying "bourgeois nationalism" rather than "proletarian internationalism." As Kirkpatrick Sale wrote: "Right in the middle of a lengthy strike for which it had provided influential support, and after weeks of denouncing people who were against the black demands as 'racist,' all of a sudden [PL began] attacking these demands as 'racist' and trying to enlist students to their own cause of working-class solidarity."[12] Such behavior was evidence to many that PL was preventing SDS from doing anti-racist and antiwar organizing.

For many in SDS, especially those who would go on to form the Weather Underground, PL's position on revolutionary nationalism was proof of its irrelevance, its unwillingness to look at the current world reality—and proof that PL was an obstacle to SDS becoming the revolutionary organization that many felt it needed to be. Though its members tended to be young, PL's hostility to anti-racism and national liberation showed that the organization was part of the Old Left. In the words of Scott Braley, PL expressed "a worldview that did not encompass any reality that I understood. It was something left over from a hundred years before." As a result of PL's obstinate behavior, SDS was stuck, nationally and in several local chapters. "You couldn't do any actions on campus while you had this debate going on because everything was objected to," says Robert Roth. PL was causing "constant disruption" by "hammering away" at SDS and insisting that the only revolutionary role for students was supporting the struggles of factory workers.

The fight against PL was a political one, but the Maoist group's culture also stood in opposition to the growing youth culture. "PL felt that the only way that you could be radical or revolutionary," Roth remembers, "was to abandon your position on campuses or in youth communities and go into the factories. We saw that as a dead-end, sacrificing the strengths of a youth resistance in a somewhat illusory attempt to 'reach the working class.'" RYM championed the counterculture—men with long hair; dope smoking; the alternative approaches to gender, sexuality, and families—whereas PL's stereotypical view of what working class people were like led them to dress conservatively and condemn marijuana as anti-working class (an "insane" move at the time, in Roth's view). PL's puritanical ideas and "superstraight" ways created the impression that its members were, in Bernardine Dohrn's words, "cultural aliens." And they were aliens with an agenda that was anathema to most of the local SDS chapters as well as the national leadership.

The 1968 RYM resolution yielded a RYM bloc, a loose coalition of activists who were concerned about PL's domineering presence in SDS, and who wanted to push the organization in a more explicitly revolutionary direction. Mark Rudd, who had made a name for himself in the Columbia strike of April 1968, was part of a group within the RYM bloc calling itself the National Collective. "We would get together at least once a month those first six months of 1969 to discuss strategy for combating the growing influence of PL and for pushing RYM politics in the organization," Rudd writes.[13] Although the National Collective, along with the RYM bloc itself, would soon splinter (some going on to build Weatherman; and others, first calling themselves RYM II, eventually forming various Communist parties), RYM was a potent force against PL going into the 1969 SDS National Convention.

What particularly raised the ire of those in RYM was PL's calling the Black Panther Party "bourgeois" and "reactionary," at a time when the government was engaged in a brutal campaign against the Black militants. In January 1969, Panther leaders Alprentice "Bunchy" Carter and John Huggins were murdered in California.[14] On April 2 of that year, two weeks after the Chicago 8 were indicted, fifteen Black Panthers in New York City were arrested in a pre-dawn raid as part of what would become known as the Panther 21 conspiracy case, a transparent attempt to destroy the radical Black group in the city. The state laid into twenty-one Panther organizers with 156 bogus charges, including "conspiracy to commit murder," "arson," "reckless endangerment," and "possession of explosive substances" with the intention of bombing a variety of public places ranging from the Bronx Botanical Gardens to police stations to the subway system.[15] A few of those who managed to avoid arrest went underground, fearing for their lives—and helped build the growing movement beneath the surface. Some even made their way to Algeria, where the Panthers had established an international chapter of the Party.[16] (Ultimately, only thirteen of the Panther 21 actually stood trial, as three were never apprehended, and five were severed from the case for various reasons. After what was the longest trial in New York history up until that point, the thirteen were found innocent in about an hour's time in 1971.)[17]

For Robert Roth, 1968 and 1969 felt "almost like you were in a vortex," with an "intensifying fight against empire" happening worldwide. "It was not enough for us to register our opposition," he says. "The crimes were too great, and also the possibility of change was too great. We thought we could do something, we could stop the war, we could give real material aid to the Black movement." Certainly, many felt that the stakes were too high for conventional protest politics or PL's recycled leftism.

Thus, many issues were in motion, from the seeming imminence of global revolution to the growing repression within the United States, when SDS met for what turned out to be its final convention in Chicago in June 1969. To set the tone for the coming battles, RYM distributed a packet to the delegates prior to the conference containing works by Lenin on imperialism and by Chinese communist Lin Piao on People's War.[18] And the special convention issue of *New Left Notes* contained a 10,000-word article, signed by eleven people, with a lengthy but memorable title swiped from Bob Dylan's "Subterranean Homesick Blues." The manifesto was called "You Don't Need a Weatherman to Know Which Way the Wind Blows."

The founding position paper for what became the Weather Underground Organization came complete with drawings of silhouetted soldiers that grew bigger with each page. This article called for a "white fighting force" in alliance with anti-colonial struggles, especially the Black Liberation Movement in the United States, and focused heavily on white working class youth as agents for change, when aligned in solidarity with the national liberation movements. The statement's support for the Black Panthers and the Vietnamese, as well as its critique of white workers as being corrupted by imperialism, put it at odds with the politics of PL.[19] Which was, of course, the idea. The counterculture swagger of the title made that clear from the beginning (though some of the authors claim today that it only meant that the song was playing when they were picking a title). The medium was the message, and the message was, "You don't get it, PL."

More generally, the "Weatherman" statement brazenly asserted that revolution was clearly on the horizon and was being led by national liberation movements. It was a roll call: white revolutionaries needed to support those movements by making their own revolution in the United States. For Scott Braley, the statement was "a solid attempt to deal with talking about the situation of the world in a different way, not just accepting the parameters of the old Marxism." Rather than saying "students are really the working class," the statement built off the RYM proposal in urging students to become revolutionaries. It built off Marxism as well as Leninism, but there was also something fresh, even cutting edge, about it.

From the outset, the statement asserted that the "main struggle going on in the world today is between U.S. imperialism and the national liberation struggles against it."[20] Friends and enemies were to be decided "according to whether [people] help U.S. imperialism or fight to defeat it." Indeed, "Weatherman" said that "any conception of 'socialist revolution' simply in terms of the working people of the United States" is a "very dangerous ideology" because it ignores most of the world's people who are oppressed by U.S. imperialism. The statement examined U.S. power and prestige relative to oppressed and colonized people in the world—both within and outside this country—and noted the "vanguard role" of both the Vietnamese and the Black liberation struggle. Living in the heart of the empire, the statement said, meant privileges at the expense of others. "The relative affluence existing in the United States is directly dependent upon the labor and natural resources of the Vietnamese, the Angolans, the Bolivians and the rest of the peoples of the Third World. All of the United Airlines Astrojets, all of the Holiday Inns, all of Hertz's automobiles, your television set, car and wardrobe already belong, to a large degree, to the people of the rest of the world."

The "Weatherman" statement especially concerned itself with the struggle of Black people in the United States—both as a counter to PL's notion that Black people were just "superexploited" members of the working class, and also, more significantly, to affirm their role as the cutting edge of political struggle within this country. In describing the situation of African Americans as a colonial one, the statement upheld autonomous organizing by Black groups as part of "struggle for socialist self-determination." Given the centuries of anti-Black oppression and the level of unity among

Black communities, "Weatherman" said, it was they who were leading the struggle inside this country. White activists had a lot of catching up to do. "Blacks could do it [make revolution] alone if necessary because of their centralness [*sic*] to the system, economically and geo-militarily, and because of the level of unity, commitment, and initiative which will be developed in waging a people's war for survival and national liberation." Therefore it was necessary to "build a white movement...so that white revolutionaries share the cost and the blacks don't have to do the whole thing alone."[21]

Noting that youth were hard hit by the "contradictions of decaying imperialism," and less invested in the system, the statement said that a revolutionary movement among young white people in the United States could contribute to building a humane socialist future—by allying with national liberation struggles. Thus, "Weatherman" argued for neighborhood-based, citywide organizing projects to "raise anti-imperialist and anti-racist consciousness and tie the struggles of [white] working-class youth (and all working people) to the struggles of Third World people."

For all its stilted language, "Weatherman" was a call to arms, both literally and figuratively; a call to build a revolutionary movement among (working class and/or white) youth in the belly of the beast. It was Che-meets-Malcolm in a militant call for solidarity.

CONVENTION TROUBLES

AT THE TIME of its June 1969 national convention, SDS claimed approximately 100,000 members across the United States, of whom between 1,500 and 2,000 attended the conference at the Chicago Coliseum. The convention was delayed a week, because fifty universities had refused to let SDS hold their convention on campus.[22] Most in attendance knew that this convention would not be just a place to debate policy for the next year; it would be a showdown over the future of SDS. PL had especially mobilized, even chartering buses and a plane, so that the disciplined Maoists accounted for about 500 of those present—a number far greater in proportion than their presence in SDS as a whole.[23] Although the RYM bloc hadn't worked as diligently to bring out its forces, about 100 people from what would become the Weatherman faction of RYM (mostly from Michigan, New York, and Ohio) met the night before the opening session in Hyde Park to discuss the "Weatherman" statement and make plans for the convention. A larger meeting of the RYM bloc also took place in preparation for the battles to come.[24]

June 18: The RYM bloc coordinated security at the convention, the first time an SDS convention had taken such measures, to prevent weapons from coming into the Coliseum. "It was our version of getting on the airplane," says Scott Braley, an SDSer from the Weatherman stronghold of Michigan (and Ohio) who was helping lead security efforts. "We knew there was going to be a split, and we wanted to make sure that there weren't a lot of guns and knives or whatever else coming into the building." The security team collected hundreds of knives.

Although registration occupied much of the first day—with the actual convention not beginning until after 2 p.m.—arguments characterized the event from the beginning, with PL and RYM delegates clashing over seemingly minor procedural issues. The first battle took place over the mainstream media. RYM wanted to allow reporters in only if they paid a $25 registration fee and "agreed not to testify against SDS before Congressional committees," (as a *New York Times* reporter had done following the previous year's convention). Scorning such a "soft" position, PL put forth a resolution that mainstream media be barred completely from the convention. It passed due to activists' distrust of corporate media, and PL was "up one."[25]

Later in the day, RYM proposed having a speaker from the Revolutionary Union (part of the emerging RYM II bloc) report on his experiences with the Red Guard in China. The Maoist PL opposed this talk because it distrusted anyone associated with the RYM bloc. In response, about fifty people from the Michigan and Ohio collectives stood up, waving copies of the "little red book," *Quotations from Chairman Mao Tse-Tung*, and began chanting "Mao, Mao, Mao Tse-Tung, Dare to Struggle, Dare to Win!" (in parody of PL's hero worship) and "Ho Ho Ho Chi Minh, the NLF is Gonna Win!" (because PL opposed the NLF leader). The chanting continued until the SDSers collapsed "in riotous self-applause."[26] The evening ended with a women-only workshop on women's liberation and patriarchy.[27]

June 19: Early in the day, the RYM II bloc officially emerged, after a morning workshop in which the larger RYM coalition split over disagreements with the Weatherman paper. Still, everyone agreed that a united front against PL was needed; other differences could be worked out later.[28]

In an obvious swipe at PL politics, the RYM-controlled SDS National Office had invited representatives from some of the leading liberation struggles in the United States—the Young Lords, the Brown Berets (a Chicana/o organization modeled on the Panthers), and of course the Black Panther

Party. The Young Lords and Brown Berets criticized the intense factional-ism of the conference, and then went on to challenge "those who say all nationalism is reactionary."[29] But the anti-PL front was severely embarrassed when the Minister of Information for the Illinois Black Panthers spoke. After attacking the "armchair Marxists" in PL, Chaka Walls managed to offend most in the room by criticizing women's liberation as "pussy power." PL members, eager for any reason to dismiss the Panthers, began chanting "Smash Male Chauvinism!" The cries only grew louder when another male Panther stepped to the microphone and said the proper position for women in the movement was "prone." Naomi Jaffe, an SDSer from New York and one of the group's leading feminists (she was also a member of the feminist group WITCH), stood up and said, "We refuse to have women's liberation used as a political football!" Although Jaffe was identified with the anti-PL forces, her comment was a criticism of both sides' opportunism regarding women's liberation.[30]

The evening ended with a fistfight; the battle had begun.

Unsure of how PL would respond to the growing faction fight, RYM wanted to secure its power base in the National Headquarters. Scott Braley was among those sent across town to guard the SDS National Office. Al-though PL never made a move on the office, RYM didn't want to risk losing control of the membership database or other organizational resources held there. Braley and the others stayed there for the rest of the convention.

June 20: The Panthers returned to the convention in the evening with an ultimatum co-signed by the Brown Berets and the Young Lords, de-manding that PL "change its position on the right to self-determination." What's more, SDS "will be judged by the company they keep and the ef-ficiency and effectiveness with which they deal with bourgeois factions in their organization."[31] SDS was being told, in no uncertain terms, to dump PL. While the Panthers read the statement, PL tried to drown them out with cries of "Read Mao!", "Power to the Workers!" (which they juxtaposed against the Panther slogan of "Power to the People"), and "Smash Redbait-ing!" More fistfights followed.[32]

Mark Rudd moved for a recess, but Bernardine Dohrn grabbed the microphone and led the RYM bloc in a walkout from the plenary session, saying that the organization needed to decide if it could allow in its ranks those who denied the right of self-determination for oppressed people. PL chanted, "No Split!" and "Stay and Fight!" while RYM responded with

"Two, Three, Many Vietnams!" and urged the confused, non-aligned conventioneers to join the walkout. Many did. Hundreds of delegates jammed the hallway as the RYM caucus moved into the adjoining room (with security at the door)—while inside, PL stopped chanting and began debating and passing proposals as if nothing had happened.[33]

But something had happened. Something historic. Beyond the messy process of faction fights was the reality that a sizable sector of white American radicals had broken with white supremacy and deliberately, consciously, and proudly allied themselves with people of color and national liberation struggles. Just as the Port Huron Statement had broken from the anti-communist liberal Left, SDS in 1969 felt the need to break completely with the Old Left of the Communist Party/Maoist variant (even the good components) in a search for anti-racist solidarity. As bizarre as they can be—and this one certainly was—organizational splits can also clarify things. The RYM split from PL clarified that there were thousands of white youth in the United States insisting on the centrality of anti-racism and solidarity with movements fighting U.S. imperialism. They did not intend to be next in a string of white accomplices with racism; they did not want the New Left to fall victim to the same fate as all the major social justice movements in the United States, from populism to unionism to women's suffrage.[34] Writing in the *Guardian* a month later, Carl Davidson of RYM II said that the SDS convention was significant in being the first time since Reconstruction that a predominantly white organization had split over questions of racism and white supremacy.[35]

In its historic impromptu caucus, the RYM bloc (including both RYM I/Weatherman and RYM II) tried to decide what to do next. Go back into the convention hall and fight it out with PL—or declare themselves the real SDS and expel PL? Most in the leadership, Weatherman and RYM II alike, wanted to expel PL immediately, but others thought the RYM bloc needed to win over the non-aligned delegates (and maybe even some PL cadre) through political argument. The discussion lasted all night, in both a full caucus and regional meetings, and resumed early the next day.

June 21: As the discussion resumed and continued, it became clear that the expulsion of PL was inevitable. Their fate was sealed by what radical journalist Andrew Kopkind called "obviously the outstanding political speech of the whole week."[36] Pacing back and forth on stage, Bernardine Dohrn chronicled the history of SDS, particularly in relation to the Black movement as well as Third World struggles in places such as Vietnam and Cuba. She reminded delegates of how they had been inspired to action by the concrete organizing strategies of the Black freedom movement, resistance to the Vietnam War and South African apartheid, the draft, GI organizing, exposing university complicity with the war, the struggle for a meaningful education, and peace and justice campaigns. With this legacy, she argued, SDS could not permit itself to become an organization that denounced the Vietnamese liberation movement for negotiating with the United States at the Paris peace talks and attacked the Black Panther Party and other radical Black Nationalist forces for "narrow nationalism" while under murderous attacks by law enforcement. SDS was not simply an opposition force, she said; not the Left wing of the Democratic Party or a union auxiliary. It was becoming a revolutionary movement; and as such, it could not allow a group such as PL in its ranks, she said, because PL opposed what was best about the movement.

At the end, Dohrn proclaimed "We are *not* a caucus. *We are SDS.*" As Kopkind reported, "suddenly it all became true to the crowds in the bleachers, and they knew that there was no going back."[37] (Because he was doing security at the time, Scott Braley now jokes that he "missed one of the great speeches of Western civilization!") A statement of principles was drawn up, pledging SDS support for revolutionary movements within the United States and across the world, and explaining that PL "has attacked every revolutionary nationalist struggle."[38] Dohrn then led the RYM bloc back into the main convention room, where she officially expelled the Progressive Labor Party from Students for a Democratic Society.

A volley of factional chants began, with RYM adherents chanting "Ho, Ho, Ho Chi Minh!" and PLers answering with "Shame!"[39] But although they controlled a third of the delegates at the final SDS convention, PL had a presence in only a handful of the locations where SDS was active, and everyone knew it. It was over.[40]

June 22: Excised as it may have been, PL continued to meet at the Coliseum, proclaiming itself the true SDS, electing its own national officers, and voting to set up its own SDS National Office in Cambridge. The PL version of SDS, however, would quickly fade following the convention.[41] Meanwhile, at a church across town, the RYM bloc met to elect officers and chart a course for the revolutionary SDS. The RYM I slate of candidates easily defeated those running from RYM II. Twenty-two-year-old Columbia strike leader Mark Rudd, a native of New Jersey, became the national secretary; Bill Ayers, a twenty-four-year-old from the suburbs of Chicago and a militant organizer at the University of Michigan, was elected education secretary. The final position of national leadership—the inter-organizational secretary—went to Jeff Jones, twenty-two, a surfer-type from California who had worked in the New York SDS Regional Office. Jones was the only one of the three who ran unopposed. All three of the new leaders were signatories of the "Weatherman" statement.

The RYM bloc still exhibited a measure of unity. A mixture of people aligned with both RYM I and RYM II were elected to serve on the eight-member National Interim Committee, a collection of national officers. Also in this meeting, SDS began planning demonstrations and local organizing projects, on principles supported by RYM as a whole.[42]

Kicking PL out was, in the eyes of many, a good thing. Although he recalls being "mind blown" at the split, David Gilbert still says that "expelling PL represented what the core of SDS was, and what the principles were."[43] For Ann Arbor delegate Lyndon Comstock, "PL had certainly brought it on themselves." As a result of helping lead an attempt at another Columbia strike in 1969, Robert Roth was serving thirty days in jail in New York City when SDS was splintering apart in Chicago. He remembers thinking that PL's expulsion was "fabulous" when he heard about it.

But, having removed the main enemy from their midst, the two factions within RYM began setting their sights upon each other. Those in RYM II felt that the politics presented in the "Weatherman" statement neglected to account for class, especially the revolutionary potential of white workers. Although RYM II's founding statement championed an anti-imperialist politics overlapping with parts of "Weatherman," it also argued for organizing U.S. workers into class struggle and moving much more immediately toward the creation of a Communist party.[44] Weatherman/SDS argued that RYM II was operating from the same flawed and dated Communist party model as PL, engaging more in intellectual discussion than much-needed action. It was a split over class and race, over aboveground versus underground, Communist party versus armed revolutionary movement—and more than a few strong egos were involved. As summer turned into fall, the shrill rhetoric increased on both sides: Weatherman/SDS became "ultraleft adventurists" and RYM II became "running dogs," lackeys, for imperialism.[45] Each side denounced the other until, as Cathy Wilkerson says, the "struggle for reality got lost and defeated."[46]

After the convention, both Weatherman/SDS and PL/SDS published their own version of *New Left Notes*, each claiming authenticity, not to mention moral and political authority. PL's *Convention Report*, its first attempt at *NLN*, criticized Weatherman/SDS for "anti-working class" politics and, with surprising clarity, predicted that SDS would continue to fracture into oblivion. But with typical absurdity, the paper also suggested that SDS had split in part over the "Albania question" (i.e., how to respond to the Communist government of Albania).[47]

Weatherman/SDS published a rival *New Left Notes*, but soon changed its name to *The Fire Next Time*, or *Fire!* for short. The new title, taken from a popular James Baldwin book of essays, signified a new role for the journal. *New Left Notes* was, as the title suggested, a theoretical journal and forum for organization updates. *Fire!*, on the other hand, was an alarm, or at least a wake-up call. Regardless, the paper was short-lived. As the Weatherman faction began to prepare to move underground and SDS ceased to exist as an organization, it died.[48]

More important than the competing newspapers was the competition at the local level, as SDS chapters tended to split in four ways: those supporting PL, those supporting RYM I/ Weatherman, those supporting RYM II, and those favoring (or at least joining) none of the above. The final group was the biggest. Still, "Weatherman" created waves in the movement; the statement was as exciting as it was challenging and, for more than a few, frustrating. Former head of SDS Carl Oglesby said that a "close reading of the RYM's Weatherman statement will drive you blind."[49] Andrew Kopkind perhaps summarized it best: "the paper was both too short and too long, too rambling as an action guide and too sketchy for a coherent work of political philosophy. It was assertive in places where reasoned explanation was needed, and obtuse in other places where definition and delineation were required. A viscous rhetoric suffused the whole. But despite all those disabilities, Weatherman produced a valuable and honest set of notes for a native American revolutionary youth movement, in a setting of worldwide liberation struggles."[50]

Naomi Jaffe remembers the paper's position on Black revolution as being particularly attractive. "One of the reasons I joined the Weather Underground was this concept, that people of color could do it alone, was very liberating," she says. "It took white people out of the center of world revolution." Recognizing that white people had to choose to join in on the side of the revolution, rather than naturally serve at the center of it was, she says, a step forward. "It wasn't like everything depended on white people in this country figuring out that their ultimate self-interest lay with the people of the world," says Jaffe. The revolution was already happening—and it was being led by people of color. "It wasn't complex enough, but historically at that time it was a real advance and an advance along the lines of [following] the leadership of Malcolm X. White people are not at the center of history."

Michigan SDSer Lyndon Comstock was excited by the statement's internationalist focus, its emphasis on anti-racism—and its countercultural title. More than that, though, he was glad to have proof that his politics existed. "We were happy to have the paper to wave around, because you were nothing in the New Left until you had a position paper setting forth your position," he says, adding that he knew few people who were "masochistic" enough to read the 10,000-word treatise in its entirety. Because New York had been one of the centers for the political discussions that led to the "Weatherman" statement, Robert Roth had been aware of its development and felt favorably toward it. "I supported it, but I can't say I had a full understanding either of what it meant or of what I was getting myself into," he says.

BEYOND THE BLAME GAME:
THE DEATH OF SDS, NOT THE "END OF THE SIXTIES"

DOMINANT HISTORIES OF SDS posit one of two entities as bearing the brunt of, if not the sole, responsibility for the organization's demise. In the more egregious instances, the death of SDS is then presented as the end of the social movements of the Sixties overall.[51] Either the Progressive Labor Party or the Weatherman faction of SDS is to blame. The first critique has more substance than the second (although it's less cited), so we'll turn there first.

PL was, in fact, a formidable force in the dissolution of SDS. Jared Israel, a PL leader with a major presence in SDS, has said that if anyone was to blame for the organization's death, it was PL, not Weatherman.[52] Although

---

PL had its strengths—emphasizing (albeit dogmatically) that class was an important subject and that activists needed to prioritize political study—the group's politics and culture became increasingly contradictory to the direction in which much of SDS was moving.[53] To blame the organization *completely* for SDS's downfall, however, misses some of the nuances of the period. Many chapters had little or no contact with the small Communist sect, reflecting the increasing disconnect between SDS as a national organization, whose leaders had constant battles with PL, and the various local chapters of the group—many of whom, especially in the South or the Midwest, had little relationship with the Maoist group.[54] With its rigid style and dogmatic approach, PL surely contributed to the polarization in SDS—but it was not the only polarizing force, nor was polarization the sole factor in the downfall of the organization.

More common than charging PL is blaming Weatherman for the dissolution of SDS. Leading the charge in this regard is former SDSer turned professor and self-styled Sixties expert Todd Gitlin. In the documentary *The Weather Underground*, Gitlin accuses Weatherman of "organizational piracy," because it "ran off with" and killed the student movement.[55] While Gitlin is excessive with his anti-Weather vitriol, he is not alone in suggesting that the group was responsible for the death of SDS. Other, more progressive, historians criticize Weatherman for going underground at a time when—as George Katsaificas puts it in his excellent book *The Imagination of the New Left*—the mass movement was looking to SDS for leadership.[56]

But is it productive or necessary to place blame? It is unlikely that SDS as an organization could have continued in the same manner for much longer.[57] It was 100,000 people, most of them young and inexperienced, taking on, in David Gilbert's words, "the most powerful government in world history."[58] Internal contradictions, rapidly changing world conditions, and increased government repression tore apart other famous groups of the time, including SNCC in the late 1960s and the Black Panthers in the early 1970s. Though the two Black militant organizations were under much more pressure from the state, the point is that this was a time period marked by rapid change, and it is naïve to blame the end of an entire movement—much less an entire time period—on the dissolution of SDS, let alone to blame the death of SDS on one faction within it. Across the globe, splits with Maoist, Trotskyist, and democratic-socialist factions were endemic. They reflect divergent political perspectives and worldviews, not just brutal factionalism. "You look around and think, what *didn't* come into light, have its flowering, and break up?" Bernardine Dohrn asks in reflecting on the late 1960s.

It seems that, regardless of the sectarianism of PL or the arrogance of Weatherman (or the vanguardism of RYM II), SDS lacked the structure and strategy to continue amidst all that was going on as the 1960s drew to a close. While united around opposition to the war and to racism, SDS chapters in places like New York City, Madison, Chicago, and San Francisco were in a very different place politically from those in Charlotte, Duluth, Des Moines, and other small cities with less of an activist infrastructure or lacking direct connection to the Black movement and other struggles by people of color. Heightened repression, coupled with the turn to revolutionary analysis, led many to become enamored of Leninism.[59] The result, as evidenced in the fracture of RYM, was a move toward building vanguard Communist parties or an armed movement, both ultimately relying on small, cadre-based groups rather than mass organizations.

Others left SDS to build "back-to-the-land" communes or pursue spiritual enlightenment.[60] Many continued working in anti-racist and antiwar groups, as evidenced by the massive flowering of activism following the Cambodian invasion and the killings at Kent State.[61] And more than a few left SDS to build the emerging movements for women's and gay liberation. Indeed, less than a week after the final SDS convention, Black and Puerto Rican drag queens led a massive rebellion against police violence at the Stonewall Inn in New York City's Greenwich Village, launching the modern lesbian, gay, bisexual, and transgender liberation movement.[62] With all these outbreaks and changes, can it be said that one sector of SDS killed the mass movement? "Everything got amped up," Braley says. "Police came down harder [on the movement]. The war came down harder." And people found solutions in a multitude of areas.

SDS, however, did die. It was fatally wounded in the summer of 1969, and died in the winter of that year, as Weatherman/SDS began to dismantle the national infrastructure and build what David Gilbert calls "an unprecedented, if seriously flawed group that carried out six years of armed actions in solidarity with national liberation struggles."[63] In June '69, though, those who had assumed control of SDS weren't quite sure what direction they would go in—or at least, how far they would go. But they were excited, even optimistic about what lay ahead. The Weatherman faction left the convention with a specific organizing task in mind—to galvanize white working class youth in battle against the state, through community organizing projects that summer and through a mass action in Chicago that fall.

Members of the Weatherman "Women's Militia" march during the Days of Rage demonstration in Chicago, October 9, 1969. Linda Evans is in the front right, Cathy Wilkerson in the front left. Photo by David Fenton.

PART TWO

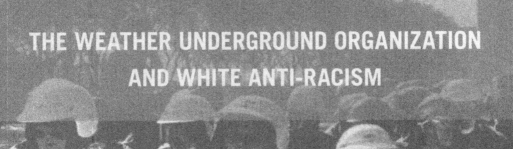

**THE WEATHER UNDERGROUND ORGANIZATION
AND WHITE ANTI-RACISM**

JJ, the principal author of the "Weatherman" statement, marching with other Weathermen at the Days of Rage demonstration in Chicago, October 1969.
Photo by David Fenton

A LINE IN THE SAND
WEATHERMAN AND MILITANT ANTI-RACISM

> *Weather's exciting breakthroughs coexisted with costly mistakes. The earliest and most visible came during the first six months (late '69 to early '70), while we were still aboveground...we psyched ourselves up by glorifying violence and with macho challenges about individual courage. This frenzy was accompanied by...scathing contempt for all who wouldn't directly assist armed struggle....*
> —*David Gilbert*[1]

THE WEATHERMAN FACTION OF SDS LEFT THE JUNE 1969 convention convinced of its leadership, of its correct position—and of the imminence of revolution. Collectives were established in cities in the East, the West, and the Midwest. These collectives held militant demonstrations, tried to organize working class whites against imperialism (generally in a macho way), did minor acts of property destruction (largely graffiti), and built an organization ready and willing to act as the "white fighting force" of the revolution—to challenge the state directly in solidarity with Third World liberation movements, particularly the Black movement here and the Vietnamese in Southeast Asia.

Weatherman/SDS from the beginning was committed to building an all-white organization that would "bring the war home" in solidarity with Third World struggles (although there was at least one Asian American, Shin'ya Ono, associated with the group in its early months).[2] The notion of all-white formations was not new; it was at least implicit in SNCC's 1966 Black Power directive, along with the message of Black Nationalist groups, to "organize your own people." And the range of revolutionary nationalist organizations that were intentionally all Puerto Rican, all Chicano/a, and so on, echoed the Black Power call. While others in SDS (RYM II in particular) endeavored to build multiracial groups with internal leadership by

people of color, Weatherman embraced the Black Power ideology by building an all-white group to fight racism. Indeed, as significant as the national
liberation struggle in Vietnam was, it would be hard to overstate the importance of the Black freedom movement in the formation of the Weather
Underground. Given the Panthers' all-Black orientation, Weather felt that
building a corollary revolutionary movement among white youth would be
the most help to the Panthers, thus hastening the revolution.

The Midwest National Action conference (August 29–September 1),
held in Cleveland just two months after the final SDS convention, provides an insight into Weatherman's developing thinking. The conference
was essentially Weather's first appearance as a national entity and not just
a bloc. In a speech, Bill Ayers spoke of "fighting the people," embracing a
phrase detractors had used to ridicule Weatherman politics. It was, to be
sure, part of the group's early hyperbole, but a closer reading reveals it to be
a more complex view of confronting white supremacy. "What's true about
it [the slogan] is that we've never been in a struggle where we didn't have
to fight some of the people," Ayers said, referencing the campus struggles,
where physical confrontations with jocks had expanded SDS's sense of its
own power and, in some cases, even "won over a number of these jocks."
But Fight the People was a commentary on white America, not on jocks.
Because people in the United States (including Weatherpeople) were in-
fected by the "white privilege, racism, [and] male supremacy" endemic to
this society, Ayers said, Weather had to combat these ideas wherever they
were manifest—in themselves and in others. The result may be polarization,
Ayers said, but it was a polarization that could prove useful in building a
revolutionary movement. Fight the People was an attempt to split the white
working class in an anti-racist way, to directly confront the privilege and oppression central to American life. Although the practical expression of this
slogan was needlessly sectarian and elitist, the principle behind it acknowledged the uphill battle of organizing whites against a system that gives them
material advantages.

Ayers also spent considerable time in his talk challenging "defeatism" in white people's view of Third World liberation movements. "It's
no longer [enough to] make posters about Vietnam with an old man and
a little kid who are burned by napalm," he said, calling instead for "the
symbol of a woman with a gun, or the picture of Nguyen Van Troi, the
hero who was captured and later shot for attempting to assassinate [U.S.
Secretary of Defense and Vietnam War architect Robert] McNamara in

1964."[3] The National Action that Weatherman had called for October, he said, was a way to "stamp out" such defeatism and build a sense of the movement's own power in confronting U.S. imperialism. The speech challenged the paternalistic view of Third World people only as victims, thereby highlighting the hope embodied in revolutionary movements and not just the repression facing them. Che Guevara's call for "Two, three, many Vietnams" affirmed that they were winning. Because of the successes being gained by liberation struggles globally, Ayers urged activism not just for "moral reasons" but because there was a "strategy to win."

The highfalutin' oratory notwithstanding, Ayers's words corresponded to a revolutionary reality. To speak of revolution in 1969 was not hyperbolic. "It was what was going on in the world," says Judy Siff. "What today we would call rhetoric corresponded [then] to reality. There were revolutions going on. If you talk about revolution when there aren't any, it's rhetoric. But when there are, it's just reality." Indeed, she says, revolutions in Cuba, Algeria, Vietnam, and other places were new or emerging, no matter how old or outdated the revolution in the Soviet Union seemed. In that context, having "a strategy to win" was an urgent necessity. It was a need felt by more than just the white Left. "It was a moment here and around the world where you could breathe the revolution, taste the revolution, smell the revolution," says former Young Lord Panama Alba. "It gave us the false sense that revolution—the conflict between liberation forces and the state and the takeover of state power—was imminent. That dictates a lot of what you do and don't do." Indeed, Alba remembers that some of the Young Lords seriously joked about the "five-year revolutionary plan" that promised that they would be free, dead, or in jail in five years.

The Cleveland conference proved the stepping-off point for some into nearly a decade of clandestine living. Naomi Jaffe, a graduate of Brandeis and the New School from rural New York, doesn't remember much of what was actually said at the conference, but she attended, convinced by another Weatherwoman that the event would be significant. On her way back from the conference, Jaffe joined with seventy-five other Weatherwomen in a militant protest at a Pittsburgh high school. She was arrested there—and again weeks later in a Weather action in Chicago, serving two months in Cook County Jail. When she came out of jail in December 1969, the organization was already moving underground, a process that would be completed with haste in March 1970, and she quickly joined the fray.

Robert Roth also attended the Cleveland conference, having withdrawn from Columbia University after his junior year. He dropped out of school to avoid disciplinary charges for his role in a 1969 university building occupation—and because he wanted to commit himself to revolutionary organizing. "That was a choice I think many activists at a local level were beginning to make as we saw ourselves as part of a broader movement," he says. "But it was a big step.... You were wrenching yourself away from a path that was heading toward career and the norm." After spending the summer working in an SDS community organizing project in the Inwood section of New York City, Roth went to the Cleveland conference because the Weatherpeople he knew were the ones he felt closest to when SDS splintered. Hearing about the "heavy-duty action" Weather collectives were planning in the Midwest was both enticing and scary. "I had mixed feelings about it, but I also knew that our project [in Inwood] wasn't going very far, and the moment demanded more."

Such was the frantic tenor of the times, when one conference people can scarcely remember today changed the course of their lives for the next nine years.

Now for the hard part—organizing other whites. Although some in the organization were already looking toward the underground, Weatherman/SDS was still a mass organization, committed to building a mass movement. Following Régis Debray's *foco* theory, Weatherman collectives tried to use exemplary militant action as a way to recruit working class white youth. The idea was that youth would be inspired by seeing them take action against the state. "We don't have to say to people what's wrong," Bill Ayers said at the Cleveland conference. "We have to say to people, what do you do about it, and what you do about it is fight."[4] Andrew Kopkind, a radical journalist critical of but sympathetic to Weatherman, noted that this strategy had been successful at Kent State, Ohio, in the spring of 1969. There, "a small group of SDS activists [led by future Weatherman Terry Robbins] broke first through a line of 'jocks' and then a phalanx of police to occupy a building where a hearing was being conducted on disciplinary and student-power issues. The attack so galvanized the campus that 5,000 students came out the next day in support of the SDS fighters."[5]

Cleveland, Detroit, Chicago, Brooklyn—all of them became home to Weatherman organizing endeavors. Weatherman/SDS began the summer of 1969 by moving into working class sections of cities across the country to expand their base and recruit street fighters for the upcoming National Action planned for October in Chicago. Sometimes the Weather collectives set up shop in white working class neighborhoods; other times, the Weatherpeople were the only white folks around. As part of preparing themselves for violence, something they felt working class kids were already accustomed to, Weather collectives tried to show their militancy through fighting local street toughs and through sheer spectacle. "Weatherman wants to get at high school and community college drop-outs—not middle-class university kids—and it believes that the way to do it is to convince them that they can fight the authorities who daily oppress them: cops, principals, bosses," Kopkind wrote in 1969 of the "exemplary action" strategy.[6] So Weatherman collectives began to fight: street gangs, cops, working class toughs—all as a way of organizing. The emphasis on shock value also led to such puerile actions as running up and down the aisle of an airplane taking food from startled passengers.[7]

As an organizing strategy, it was less than successful: white working class youths were more alienated than organized by Weather's spectacles, and even some of those interested in the group were turned off by its early hijinks.

The Weatherman collective in Detroit emerged out of an SDS organizing project initiated in April 1969 by Diana Oughton and Bill Ayers, both of whom played leading roles in getting early Weather established. Michigan native Lyndon Comstock joined the Detroit collective after his freshman year at the University of Michigan. Unlike many of the other Weatherpeople, who had been in SDS for years, Comstock had joined in 1968 after watching the protests (and beatings) at the Democratic National Convention on television. The idea in Detroit was to work in factories, organize GIs, and engage in intensive political study. Comstock remembers the Detroit Weatherman collective as a successful cadre-building experience for the fifty or so individuals involved, with him "trying to grow up as an activist in the space of weeks." But as an organizing endeavor, it was "a total flop." The Weather cadre went out daily to organize, but passing out leaflets supporting the National Liberation Front and fighting security guards did little to enlarge the movement.

Columbia graduate student Mark Naison was briefly associated with a New York Weatherman/SDS collective in 1969. Hyped up by a karate workout in Brooklyn's Prospect Park, the collective conducted an impromptu sit-in at a coffee shop that refused to serve hippies. When the police came to eject them, "within seconds we had the restaurant workers on the floor and had taken away the cops' nightsticks," Naison recalls in his memoir. More officers arrived, and the arrests and beatings began. The experience of needlessly picking a fight, combined with the rigorous criticism session—a defining trait of Weatherman at this time—that followed the action, inspired Naison to withdraw from the group and focus on his studies.[8]

In his book on SDS, Kirkpatrick Sale tells how a group of about twenty Boston Weatherpeople "invaded the Harvard Center for International Affairs, whose work included counterinsurgency research for various branches of the government, and ran screaming through the building, smashing windows, shoving secretaries, kicking and hitting professors, dumping over typewriters and files, pulling out telephones, and then running away before police could make arrests." Five were ultimately arrested; one ended up with a two-year jail sentence for assault and battery.[9]

Former *New Left Notes* editor Cathy Wilkerson was among the crowd in Chicago that summer who ran through public beaches waving the NLF flag and chanting "Ho, Ho, Ho Chi Minh, the NLF is gonna win!" In reflecting on the summer and fall of 1969, Wilkerson says it was "confrontational politics run amok.... The beach strategy appealed to [people's] most reactionary macho instincts.... [It was] the macho toughness of it, not the NLF flag. To get to people through their reactionary characteristics...has never been a winning strategy in my opinion."[10]

And then there were the "jailbreaks"—and not the kind the Weather Underground would later do for imprisoned LSD enthusiast Timothy Leary. These jailbreaks were for high school kids and students at community colleges. The initial "Weatherman" statement defined school as one of four areas where youth are particularly oppressed by the system (the other three being jobs, the military, and the judicial system). "In jail-like schools, kids are fed a mish-mash of racist, male chauvinist, anti-working class, anti-communist lies while being channelled [*sic*] into job and career paths set up according to the priorities of monopoly capital," the statement asserted.[11] And even metaphorical prisoners should be freed.

Over the summer and fall of 1969, Weatherman/SDS tried to "liberate" students from their school oppression. The result was a dramatic increase, not in recruits—but in arrests and alienated former allies. Bob Feldman, whose close friends and former Columbia roommates David Gilbert and Ted Gold had already joined Weatherman, remembers a 1969 meeting where high school organizers were gathered to discuss how to support the Panther 21, then on trial. Weather's representative at the meeting "urged the students to run through the high school shouting 'jailbreak,' no matter how few they were in numbers, instead of just handing out leaflets," Feldman writes in an unpublished memoir. To her critics, the Weatherwoman had an immediate reply: "If you're too chickenshit to do anything more than leaflet at your high school, then you're part of the problem."[12]

As can be imagined, "jailbreaks" accomplished little in the way of organizing. A jailbreak in Boston, Dave Dellinger writes in *More Power Than We Know*, led to an anti-SDS march the following day.[13] In Detroit, a squad of Weatherwomen invaded a classroom at McComb Community College, lectured the students on war and racism, and—using karate moves—blocked those who tried to escape. The "Motor City Nine" were arrested and charged with disorderly conduct and assault and battery.[14] Weather championed the women's physical acumen, but, Kopkind says, much of the radical Left in Detroit "tried to form coalitions specifically aimed at destroying Weatherman."[15] In Pittsburgh, another "jailbreak," complete with NLF flag, ended in arrest for two dozen Weatherwomen—and the fictitious report that still lingers to this day that they ran through the school topless.[16] (Naomi Jaffe was one of those arrested during the Pittsburgh jailbreak. The only clothing missing that day was not her shirt but her shoes, given to her by Vietnamese fighters, which she lost in the melee when police arrived.) But militant women were scary, and a spectacle-based organizing strategy has a way of engendering apocryphal stories.

Judy Siff, who came to Weather out of Seattle's militant antiwar movement, remembers the jailbreaks as guerrilla theatre, designed to shake people out of their complacency. "We felt like we could do anything—and we did," she says of Weather's early months. From July 1969 until March 1970, Weatherman/SDS "elevated tactics over politics, over a broader strategic view," Bernardine Dohrn recalls. It was all legitimized by Debray's *foco* theory, which measured a group's importance by its audacity. *Foco* held that, in Jeff Jones' words, "a small group of very politically advanced, ideologically committed militant people can carry out revolutionary actions that will serve as an inspiration for other people."[17] Almost anything was acceptable, as long as it was *action*.

In ways good and bad, politics and action became melded in the group's early months. "You couldn't really separate the politics from the action orientation…. The action was very political," Siff says. "The politics around national liberation and militance about the war—nobody else articulated it in that way. And it resonated; it made total sense in such a profound way." Thinking about it more than thirty years later, Robert Roth sums up Weather's early politics by saying that the group "represented an insistence on up-front support for Black liberation as a centerpiece for any political movement among white people. It represented total commitment to a high level of militancy in relation to Vietnam. And it represented a fundamental drive toward action—that you had to act, that you had to act immediately, and that you had to act strongly."

Such politics, Roth says, "created waves within the white Left." Indeed, Weatherman almost got swamped. Kopkind wrote that much of the white Left was "almost viciously anti-Weatherman," representing "total rejection of Weatherman's revolutionary form."[18] Gilbert recalls feeling "under attack," noting, however, that the group's response to its sense of embattlement was less than ideal. "We mystified violence. We psyched ourselves up. We had great contempt for people who weren't willing to do the same things that we were willing to do."[19] Michael Novick, a Brooklyn College SDS supporter of the "Weatherman" analysis who became a member of an early Weatherman collective in California, remembers this as Weather's "fairly clear strategy of 'rule or ruin'; that if the (white) Left didn't get with the program, it was an obstacle to revolution and needed to be dismantled."

An example: While many in and around Columbia SDS—including David Gilbert, Ted Gold, Robert Roth, and Mark Rudd—had enthusiastically joined Weatherman/SDS, others had followed a different path. Herb Dreyer, a Columbia SDS veteran, worked at a GI coffeehouse at Fort Dix, New Jersey.[20] Similar coffeehouses had sprung up across the country, as antiwar activists sought to create spaces where they could reach out to GIs who were opposed to the war. It was productive and meaningful antiwar work, building bridges between soldiers and the antiwar movement. Activists involved with the Fort Dix coffeehouse were planning a demonstration in solidarity with twenty-eight soldiers being punished for refusing to fight in Vietnam. Dreyer welcomed his old Columbia comrades from Weatherman/SDS—until they began arguing enthusiastically for a violent confrontation with the military. Recognizing the sheer idiocy of staging a violent demonstration on a military base, Dreyer and the other Fort Dix organizers scheduled their demonstration on the same weekend as Weatherman's big National Action in Chicago. They didn't want Weather around—they wanted to build solidarity with the soldiers, not stage a bloodbath.

The frenetic period of the group's early months wasn't just alienating would-be supporters but even recruits and developing cadre. Michael Novick, a working-class former Yeshiva student from an immigrant Brooklyn family who had joined SDS at Brooklyn College, was recruited to join a Weatherman collective in the San Francisco Bay Area in 1969. After an outdoor collective strategy session, he contracted poison oak. "I ended up with my eyes swollen shut, my ears oozing, lying in the corner of a room of a house where the toilet flushed into a hole in the floor into the basement and everybody got crabs," he remembers. A Weatherman leader passing through town had Novick taken to a free clinic and joked that if Novick hadn't yet left the group, he deserved a leadership post for his endurance. Instead, as Weather transitioned underground in early 1970, Novick was among several people in the area "cut loose" from the group.

INTO THE WEATHER MACHINE

THE PERIOD FROM the June SDS convention through the end of 1969 was an intense one for Weatherman/SDS—a time of building collectives, developing cadre, preparing for armed struggle, facing police repression on a level members had never experienced, and becoming isolated from large sectors of activists, especially the burgeoning women's liberation movement. Confrontational street demonstrations mixed with intensive collective discipline. The period was so dramatic and unconventional that, although it lasted only a few months, many who lived through it remember it as lasting for more than a year.

It was also a time of growing internationalism, as several Weatherpeople went to Cuba in July to meet with representatives from the North Vietnamese government, the National Liberation Front of Vietnam, and Cuba's revolutionary government. The Cuban Revolution, a decade old by 1969, had long been an inspiration to the militant sectors of SDS. Mark Rudd was radicalized by a trip to Cuba during the Tet Offensive in 1968, and Donna Willmott remembers the inspiration she felt from seeing a society that had been able to carry out a successful armed struggle and build a socialist state without, it seemed, sacrificing its humanist grounding.[21] The experience of seeing a revolutionary country that not only was trying to build socialism economically and culturally, but also modeled internationalist solidarity with its unflinching material and political support for Vietnam, served as an important influence on and inspiration to Weather.

The Vietnamese and the Cubans both told the Americans that the best thing they could do for Vietnam and the rest of the Third World was to make a revolution in the United States—and soon, because Third World people were being killed at an astronomical rate. The Vietnamese spoke of organizing, the Cubans of militancy. Weatherman hoped it could bridge the two.[22] (The FBI later claimed, with its trademark cryptic vagueness, that "Cuban espionage agents...supplied limited aid to the Weather Underground.")[23]

While some Weatherpeople went to Cuba, the rest were building America's Red Army. "The view was that the revolutionary struggle against imperialism had gotten underway all over the world, what were we waiting for here?" Lyndon Comstock remembers. "Let's get moving." People rarely slept, as they worked daily at promoting the big action Weatherman/SDS had called for October in Chicago. Comstock was sent from Detroit to Lansing, Michigan, with three others to organize. After stealing a mimeo machine from the SDS office at Michigan State University, they printed leaflets at dawn and passed them out to high school and community college students. "We put our phone number on the leaflets for a while, but we got so many death threats that we eventually had to unplug the phone," he says. (As in Detroit, the Lansing collective lived in a Black community, which Comstock speculates may have kept hostile police or white vigilantes away.) At night, the collective would spray-paint antiwar graffiti on local schools or campuses.

In Lansing, New York, Detroit, and elsewhere, Weather collectives engaged in militant protests that regularly turned into small-scale riots, and cadre were arrested for vandalism and other minor crimes. Sent from New York to work with a small Weather collective in Denver, David Gilbert was arrested twice: once while passing out leaflets outside a mall (while his comrades were setting off a smoke bomb inside) and once for "assault with a deadly weapon" after police found a rock in his pocket.[24] Cadre were regularly arrested during these confrontational protests, and whatever money the group had went into bail or lawyer fees.[25]

Collective discipline and training were highly valued. Taking its cue from the Chinese Communist Party, Weatherman/SDS instituted the practice of "criticism/self-criticism," which was ostensibly to help people become better activists and human beings. In practice, however, it became a weapon of manipulation, of rigid discipline in the interest of smashing individualism. Although some in SDS had begun the criticism/self-criticism process earlier, it was taken to extreme conclusions in Weatherman. It got more intense as repression heightened, although its severity receded once the group went underground.

A criticism/self-criticism session could begin at any time. They were rarely scheduled; sometimes they included an entire collective, and at other times they included whoever was there. "It got really hard to differentiate between good criticism and bad criticism, and after awhile it just sort of rotted your brain," Scott Braley remembers. "You'd be there for two, three, four, or six hours with people telling you how awfully you've done." Sometimes everyone would get criticized; at other times one person received the full weight. Male supremacy was a frequent criticism—which isn't to say that men learned from or listened to the criticism, or even that all the criticisms were useful. In the East Bay area, Michael Novick remembers criticism/self-criticism focusing on "the smashing monogamy line and on cutting all your ties to your old comfortable way of life." Looking for support to come out of the closet or at least experiment sexually with other men, Novick was instead criticized by men for supposedly denying his desire to have sex with a lot of women, and criticized by women for being a "cry-baby." Braley remembers similar criticisms, where people challenged each other for being too macho and, simultaneously, for not being tough or hard-line enough. It was not uncommon for someone to get up silently in the middle of a session, leave the house, and never return.

Also at this time, the "Weather Bureau," as the group's leadership body was calling itself at the time, moved cadre around—both to encourage individual political development and also to separate people from the comforts of their previous "bourgeois" life. People often left friends, family, and romantic partners to commit themselves to the organization and to the revolution. It was a jarring move for most who went through it, although at the time it all seemed part of the process. People cut themselves off from those they knew and moved across the state or across the country, wherever they were sent.

As with everything Weatherman did, the summer organizing was an amalgamation of politics and culture. They weren't just becoming revolutionaries—they were becoming outlaws, both in terms of how they thought of themselves and in their daily practice. "Smash monogamy" was a guiding principle, as promiscuity and even the occasional orgy were encouraged—which isn't to say that collectives engaged in discussions about consent and healthy sexuality.[26] Shoplifting and smoking pot were political acts, separating cadre from bourgeois American life. Yet it could be easily overblown. "The idea of it [becoming outlaws] had significant romantic appeal from a distance," Comstock remembers. "But the reality of doing things every single day, often multiple times per day, that could get one busted, does get wearying."

All this activity brought down intense, systematic repression on the young activists. The "Weatherman" statement predicted—and even welcomed—an increase in repression as movements grew and as whites began to ally with the struggles of Third World people and take some of the state's pressure off of them.[27] Repression was particularly intense in Chicago, where the SDS National Office and a very active chapter of the Black Panthers were located—and where Weatherman/SDS had scheduled a militant demonstration for October. The Weather Bureau sent Robert Roth to the Chicago collective in September 1969, and he noticed the police presence immediately. It would have been hard not to. The Chicago police's "gang intelligence unit" camped out on the lawns of activists' houses, followed them constantly, and threatened individuals by name. "I don't think any of us had experienced that before, either [that level of] surveillance or personal connection to the police force," Roth says.

As the Chicago collective was meeting one night, police officers climbed up the rickety back stairs and came into the third floor apartment through an open window with guns drawn. One cop forced two female members of the group into the bedroom with him. Another grabbed Roth and hung him by his ankles outside of the window, threatening to drop him. "I could smell the liquor on his breath," Roth remembers. "Then they pulled me in, and it was a big joke." No one was arrested in the incident.

The SDS National Office was also under attack. Scott Braley doesn't remember a time that he went to the National Office when he was *not* stopped by the police, even before Weatherman took it over. "If it was at night, we would have to get out of the car, and they would search us, search the car, then tell us what terrible people we were and the awful things they were going to do to us," he says. Despite their rhetoric around self-defense, Weatherpeople did not engage in armed confrontations with the police. Although the SDS National Office eventually pledged that it would meet gunfire with gunfire should police attack, it avoided such a move when police inevitably raided the office in late 1969. Although police blew the heavy steel door off its hinges with shotguns, they did not come in shooting against SDS as they had against the Panthers.

BRINGING THE WAR HOME, TO CHICAGO

A LIENATING THE MOVEMENT became increasingly common. Activists in Madison, Wisconsin, turned their backs on Weatherman militants when they tried to take over an SDS event as part of the lead-up to the Chicago demonstration, billed as the "SDS National Action."[28] Chicago newspapers dubbed the mayhem "Days of Rage," and the name has stuck ever since.[29]

The National Action, scheduled for October 8–11, reflected the most elitist aspects of Weather's Fight the People attitude. It was to be, in the parlance of the times, the action that would "bring the war home!" The demonstration was called to coincide with the opening of the Chicago 8 conspiracy trial as well as with the second anniversary of the murder of Che Guevara. SDS was intentionally returning to the city where police had brutally beaten demonstrators the previous summer, in order to show that the movement was on the offensive. A Weatherman poster reflected this aggressive stance: "During the 1960s, the American government was on trial for crimes against the people of the world. We now find the government guilty and sentence it to death in the streets."[30] The National Action was advertised not just through leaflets but through actions themselves; an October 4 protest against Nelson Rockefeller in New York was as much about building for Chicago as it was about confronting a member of the hated ruling class family.[31]

The focus on getting people to Chicago in that four-day period in October wasn't just coming from Weatherman. A coalition of the Black Panther Party, RYM II, and the Young Lords (a Puerto Rican organization) planned a series of marches and rallies for the same time.[32] Weatherman argued for the centrality of race, RYM II for class—this even though RYM II had put together an impressive multiracial coalition whereas Weatherman was awaiting thousands of working-class white youths to descend on Chicago for a violent anti-imperialist street fight.

Three days prior to the so-called Days of Rage, Weatherman/SDS blew up a statue commemorating the policemen killed in the "Haymarket Riots" in May 1886 during the labor union struggle for the eight-hour day. (Eight anarchist labor leaders were framed for the murder, and four of them executed, although there was little evidence against them).[33] To kick off its big protest, Weatherman destroyed the only police statue in the country. "It was a declaration of war," Weatherman Scott Braley says of the action, "which is how the police understood it." The gauntlet had been thrown down.

Meanwhile, the movement was battling it out behind the scenes. Chicago Black Panther leader Fred Hampton, who had endorsed the RYM II march, was critical of Weatherman's planned battle with police, thinking it foolish and dangerous. From midnight to 3 a.m. on October 8, Hampton met with the Weather Bureau in a last minute conversation mediated by pacifist activist Dave Dellinger and radical attorney William Kunstler—two movement elders respected by both sides. By the end of the meeting, Dellinger later wrote, the Weather Bureau agreed to tone down the demonstration; in exchange Hampton agreed not to publicly criticize the action.[34] Neither side lived up to the bargain. Weather went on its planned rampage, and Hampton denounced the group as "anarchistic, opportunistic, individualist, chauvinistic, and Custeristic," referencing the ill-fated nineteenth century U.S. army general who died in battle with indigenous people, not police; but the point was that Weatherman was masochistic and suicidal.[35]

How could a group that so extolled the Black Panther Party ignore the sharp criticism of one of its most respected leaders? Surely, there was a contradiction in organizing for a violent mass action in a city where the head of the local Black Panthers opposed it. But the Black Panther Party was not a monolithic organization, and by 1969 fissures within the group were becoming more apparent. Some of these differences mirrored the debates in SDS over the strategic role of militancy, although the Panthers were under much more severe pressure from the state. Indeed, because the Panthers were under such heavy attack, many in the group (including Hampton) wanted to build a broad united front for their own self-preservation. Weatherman's street antics were thus seen as alienating potential allies and bringing down serious repression. However, the New York Black Panthers largely cheered Weather's militancy. And Hampton, despite his vehement disagreement with the Days of Rage, maintained a friendly relationship with Weatherman/SDS. Indeed, he had served as mentor to some in the group and overall seemed to respect its intentions, if he questioned some of its practice.[36]

★ ★ ★

The movement voted on the SDS National Action with its feet—by not showing up. Though Weatherman had predicted that thousands of eager militants would descend upon the Windy City, October 8 found only a couple of hundred gathered to do battle with the police and the property of Chicago's ritzy Gold Coast neighborhood. The masses of angry anti-racist whites that Weather had been expecting never materialized. The weeks of organizing in cities across the country had resulted in a flop. Police ridiculed the small numbers attending the demonstration. Historian Jeremy Varon reports that when the New York collective was leaving for Chicago, the police (who had of course been surveilling their organizing efforts) "taunted the departing Weathermen about their meager numbers."[37] But there was no turning back, especially after the organization's bombast in promoting the event as *the* mass revolutionary action. "We had drawn a line in the sand that said we were going to fight, so we had to [fight]," Braley recalls. As a result, several Weather activists ended up with serious charges, which then increased the pressure to build the underground.

The action represented a conscious departure from previous mass demonstrations where people fought police only in self-defense, if at all. At the Days of Rage, many in the ranks wore helmets and steel-toed boots. They carried makeshift weapons—rocks, lead pipes, baseball bats—for use against property (car, store, and bank windows) and police. While the vast majority were between their late teens and mid-twenties, the demonstrators ranged in age from pre-teens to at least two people in their fifties.[38]

The first protest began after darkness had settled in. October 8, 1969: the second anniversary of the CIA-orchestrated murder of Che Guevara; across town the Chicago 8 conspiracy trial was in full swing. A few hundred people gathered in Lincoln Park—where police had attacked demonstrators during the 1968 Democratic Convention—and built a bonfire out of park benches. They talked quietly, masking their anxiety. A bloc of about 150 marched in, and it soon became clear that this small crowd would be the only street fighters this evening.[39] Speakers railed against imperialism; three of the Chicago 8 made a brief appearance, including Tom Hayden, who told the assembled crowd that he and his codefendants were pleased to see activists return to Lincoln Park and "glad to see the militancy of Chicago increased."[40]

It was time to go on the offensive and "bring the war home." America could not export violence to the Third World, attack people of color domestically, and expect to sleep easy at night. Not anymore.

After 10 p.m., Jeff Jones took the bullhorn and, introducing himself as Marion Delgado (a five year old who had derailed a passenger train in California by placing a concrete slab on the tracks for kicks; an unlikely yet strangely fitting icon for Weather at this point), told the crowd that they were going to attack the Drake Hotel, where Chicago conspiracy trial Judge Julius Hoffman lived.[41] Several affinity groups had been sent to smash the big plate glass windows at the bank across the street. People were told to move out of the park and head toward the Gold Coast neighborhood as soon as they heard the windows break.[42] It's theater: "Delgado" tells the crowd it's time to go after Judge Hoffman; the sound of shattering glass fills the air, and people are off and running.

The police, for their part, were stunned. Although hundreds of them had been watching the park intensely for hours, they were caught off guard by such a bold move. It took them a few moments to recover and go after the Weatherpeople. Chants of "Ho, Ho, Ho Chi Minh, The NLF is Gonna Win!" mingled with the loud whir of police sirens, the repeated crash of breaking glass, and the fast-paced footsteps of a few hundred white youths trying to create "chaos in the mother country." Approaching a heavy police barricade, the protesters do the only thing they can: they charge into it with all their fury. Some make it through while others get stuck in hand-to-hand (and bat-to-baton) combat.

Breaking through police lines, Gilbert remembers, was a "rush," a heady pleasure. After so many demonstrations where police had contained and corralled protesters, telling them where and how long they could march, a long-suppressed fury was being released on the streets of Chicago.[43] Having gotten through the police lines, the remaining protesters came face-to-face with Chicago's Tactical Police Force. The police began shooting; some from their vehicles, some on foot, but they were shooting all the same.

"They're just shooting in the air," Lyndon Comstock remembers yelling, after seeing police with their guns pointed up toward the pitch-black sky. "Don't run; those are just blanks. They're firing to scare you away," an insurgent Vietnam vet shouted at the same corner. Hedging his bets, Gilbert stopped, threw another rock at the police (he missed)—and then ran.[44]

As it turns out, several Weatherpeople were shot at this intersection, including three who needed serious medical attention. One was shot in the neck and shoulder and left for dead by the police in the street. (He was eventually taken to the hospital and suffered permanent paralysis in his left arm.) With the upper hand for the first time that evening, police began grabbing anyone they could, beating and arresting as many as possible. Some of those beaten got away; others were only beaten after they were apprehended. Comstock, who was caught at the intersection shortly after shooting erupted, remembers lying face down on the ground, his hands cuffed, while a policeman kicked him in the face and broke his cheekbone.

The surviving protesters retreated to nurse their wounds and conduct a casualty count. At a regrouping area later in the evening, Gilbert remembers seeing a female comrade who had been clubbed directly in the mouth. "She'd lost some teeth, had stitches and had a bloody lip which was swollen beyond all belief. I'd never seen anything like that," he says. "She was in a lot of pain, but her morale was strong."

Morale was in short supply after that first night. The next morning, about seventy women wearing helmets and carrying NLF flags marched to shut down the Chicago Armed Forces Induction Center. Learning their lesson from the previous night, police set up a barricade just outside of Grant Park. A dozen women were arrested after rushing the police line (Bernardine Dohrn was charged with battery, mob action, and resisting arrest) and the march ended not long afterward.[45] The scheduled "jailbreaks" and an evening rally, billed as a "wargasm," were both cancelled.

Subsequent Weather Chicago actions didn't match the intensity or ferocity of that first night, though street battles and property destruction continued throughout the week. Later on in the Days of Rage, Gilbert was part of a four-person affinity group. A plainclothes cop surprised him while he was breaking the window of a big store, but when he attempted a karate kick against Gilbert, the other Weatherpeople knocked the officer down, and the four activists quickly fled in different directions. With some pulled muscles but otherwise OK, Gilbert called the SDS office and asked what to do next. "They told me to collect people and charge into some place or other," he remembers. He couldn't find anyone, however, and decided against a one-man charge.[46]

In total, almost 300 people were arrested, dozens of them with serious felony charges; many protesters (and some police officers) were injured in street fights; and police shot eight of the demonstrators.[47] The National

Guard was deployed after the first night. Assistant Corporation Counsel Richard Elrod—mastermind of the Chicago 8 indictments and a close friend of Mayor Daley—took to the streets as a semi-vigilante against Weatherman; he missed a flying tackle, hit a concrete wall, and was paralyzed.[48] One Weatherperson estimated that the group spent $150,000 on bail; combined, the 287 people arrested at the Days of Rage were held for more than $2 million total bail money.[49] While the demonstration was directed at the wealthy, the windows of numerous independent stores and of working class people's cars were also smashed.[50] By the time it was over, Varon recounts, more than "800 automobile and 600 residential or store windows had been smashed."[51]

In court, captured Weather activists continued the heroic antics of the street as best they could: everyone demanded immediate jury trials, forcing the prosecutors to ask for delays. (As with most everything in Weatherman, this strategy was decided by the leadership and passed on to the rank-and-file via a secret leaflet.)[52] Asking for an immediate trial was a way, perhaps the only way, "to go onto the offensive in a situation which was inherently very defensive," Comstock remembers. "We just didn't have any back-down in us as a group."

Reviews of the Days of Rage were mixed. Several Weatherpeople recall meeting Black Chicagoans—on the streets, in prison, in the hospital—who were impressed that white youth had done battle with the notorious and hated Chicago police, who had long been oppressing Black communities.[53] In the white Left, however, the tone was more guarded. *The Second Battle of Chicago*, a one-time, independently produced newspaper covering both the Weatherman protest and the Black Panthers–Young Lords–RYM II march, found something to praise in both. "On the one hand," *Second Battle* reported, "Chicago witnessed the first major white radical action in which the protesters moved on the offensive.... Secondly, actions by another faction of SDS marked the first major event in which [mostly white, middle class] student radicals worked in a functioning alliance with black, brown, and working class peoples."[54]

The Berkeley *Tribe* joined with the Chicago *Seed*, New York's *RAT*, and the Newsreel video collective for a roundtable on the Days of Rage. Though questioning the efficacy of running wild in the streets, several participants praised Weatherman/SDS for making discussions of armed struggle less abstract. Many radicals had been favorably discussing armed struggle since at least 1967, and support for armed movements outside this country was on the rise.[55] Now, it seemed, armed struggle was being brought home to U.S. soil, and people had to decide where they stood.

Meanwhile, Weatherman/SDS, still caught in a web of self-aggrandizement, was critical of those who did not support the action. In a pamphlet published shortly after the demonstration, they boasted: "We left Chicago with a clear sense that the level of struggle had been raised and we had won a victory." Calling itself "the only revolutionary organization for white people," Weather dismissed its movement critics: "They know we're right and yet they hope we fail so they won't have to give up their pleasant but miserable lives." People without the same revolutionary analysis as Weatherman were "fools, unless they work for the government and are [therefore] liars." These "fools" included everyone from antiwar liberals (too bourgeois to take on the system in its entirety) to feminists (racists who focused narrowly on the self-interest of white women) to deluded radicals (not ready or willing to begin armed struggle).

As with the rest of early Weather politics, the broad critiques had kernels of truth to them. Elements of the women's movement (like everything in the United States) were tainted by racism, and liberals often did not have a systemic critique of the war or a sweeping vision of social change. And there were real, legitimate political differences between Weatherman and the liberal Mobilization to End the War in Vietnam (the Mobe), just as there were political differences between Weatherman and RYM II. The Mobe did not support Vietnam's National Liberation Front, whereas Weatherman (and other antiwar radicals) insisted on solidarity with the NLF as a fundamental principle of opposing the war. But Weatherman/SDS often took political criticism to absurd lengths, posturing and presenting itself as the only solution. "Weatherman understands that we aren't the vanguard just because we would like to be.... Weatherman becomes the leadership by taking exemplary action," a pamphlet circularly explained.[56]

This was not a strategy for winning allies or building a movement. "So we turned against our closest friends," Bernardine Dohrn says today. "If you weren't willing to be with us, you were counter-revolutionary. We did damage with that, both with the arrogance and with the certainty." Many people interested in Weatherman dropped out after the Chicago protest, or as a result of the manipulative, often ruthless, criticism/self-criticism sessions.[57] People with a remarkably similar world outlook to Weather's were denounced as wimps or pseudo-radicals. "A lot of genuine, even militant, anti-imperialists were turned off," says Robert Roth, "including many within the women's movement—for correct reasons."

"One of the great mistakes of 1969 is that we thought we [alone] had it right," Bill Ayers says. "The main failures we had were those of smugness and certainty and arrogance." Others struggling with questions of empire and white supremacy were treated as antagonists rather than as allies in the struggle. By viewing themselves as the only true white revolutionary group, Gilbert now says, "we really turned off and alienated a lot of people who were decent people and potential allies. Not only is that a wrong way to deal with people, it really weakened achieving our own goals, which were to build as strong a movement as we could against the war and against racism."[58]

Scott Braley puts it more succinctly: "A little humility would have gone a long way."

THE DAYS OF RAGE AND ANTI-IMPERIALIST VIOLENCE IN THE UNITED STATES

SECTARIANISM NOTWITHSTANDING, the Days of Rage demonstration was important for several reasons. Other demonstrations in the later part of the 1960s left open the *possibility* for violence, and even encouraged it with such slogans as "Confront the war makers," "Shut down the war machine," or "Kick [military or CIA] recruiters off campus." But Days of Rage was a *planned* street fight. Indeed, the opening march began under the cover of darkness, thus forfeiting media attention that might have served to restrain police violence or spread an organizing message. Weatherman carried no leaflets or placards on the streets of Chicago, only weapons and National Liberation Front flags. And although Weatherman told people not to bring guns or knives, it was clear that the National Action was organized as a street fight. In a memo sent to SDS members in August 1969 in preparation for the event, SDS National Secretary Mark Rudd said that Chicago was chosen "precisely because it has come to symbolize what a government held together by force is all about."[59] It was hoped that the protest would help contribute to unraveling the government, spurring people to action through "exemplary action" and direct confrontation.

While a planned street fight with a notoriously brutal police force may seem like pure insanity, Days of Rage cannot be separated from the context of the times, including the Chicago 8 trial, the saturation bombing of Hanoi, and the Panther 21 conspiracy case. Cathy Wilkerson says that if Days of Rage is examined "from the standpoint of rational politics and organization, we were out of our minds. On the other hand, as a response to what was going on in Vietnam, it was the very sane response of total outrage. It was a gesture of total frustration to just go bananas, and as such was a very sane response."[60] Sane or not, the prospect of taking on Chicago's infamous cops was appealing to only the most hardcore SDS activists. "Even if we'd had a few more than the four hundred that did show up, so what?" Lyndon Comstock asks. "Take on the entire Chicago police department toe-to-toe in street fighting—who wants to join up for that? It was sheer bravado on our part, but with a political message: the war has come to the heartland of the Mother Country."

Days of Rage was a warning to the country and a challenge to the movement. Michael Novick remembers thinking that "only actually 'raising the level of struggle' would create the political dynamic that could force more of the Left to shit or get off the pot." Indeed, Days of Rage was not organized with the goal of enlarging the antiwar movement. Instead, says Comstock, it was a roll call. The plan was for a massive, disciplined, and organized riot. "We wanted to sharpen the level of contradictions, to push the country out of business-as-usual and into confrontation.... We were doing the best we could to take the movement to a higher level of struggle."

While trying to push the movement's tactical limits, Days of Rage also attempted to call into question what constituted the greatest violence. "Doing nothing in a period of repressive violence is itself a form of violence," Naomi Jaffe says in the documentary *The Weather Underground*. Remaining passive in opposition while the government was murdering people all over the world was an act of violence.[61] Though he now thinks the Days of Rage was a "suicidal, no-win situation," former Young Lords activist Panama Alba remembers being inspired at the time by the gutsy action. The Young Lords had their own Days of Rage, complete with football helmets, in the summer of 1971, battling the New York City police during the annual Puerto Rican Day Parade. The Puerto Rican version fared little better.

Whatever the problems with the Days of Rage, however, militancy was not an anomaly. Scholar-activist George Katsiaficas writes that the Days of Rage made "window breaking and street fighting ... commonplace."[62]

Actually, however, such acts of property destruction were already common-place by October 1969. Revolutionary violence—which in the United States consisted mostly of property destruction ("trashing") and symbolic bomb-ings—became an important component of movement tactics in the late 1960s and 1970s, existing both before and after the Weather Underground. In the fall of 1968, there were forty-one bombings on college campuses, almost double what the Weather Underground did in total throughout its seven-year existence. In the spring of 1969, before the "Weatherman" state-ment even appeared, there were eighty-four bombings on school campuses and ten off-campus by movement radicals. In the 1969–1970 school year, extremely conservative estimates say that there were at least 174—and as many as 5,000—bombings and attempted bombings on campuses nation-wide and at least another seventy off-campus. From September 1969 to May 1970, there was *at least one* bombing or attempted bombing somewhere in the United States *every day* by the progressive and radical movements.[63] A map of the United States printed in a (temporarily censored) 1971 special issue of the radical *Scanlan's Monthly* magazine on guerrilla war listed thou-sands of acts of political violence from 1965 to 1970; there were more than 500 acts of sabotage by the Left in 1969 alone.[64] The U.S. government, meanwhile, "dropped over 7.5 million tons (that's fifteen billion pounds) of bombs on Vietnam…equivalent to 700 bombs the size of the one dropped on Hiroshima or three times the tonnage dropped during the entire Second World War."[65]

And this was just the bombings. The movement had become increasingly radicalized to the point where political graffiti, fighting back against police at demonstrations, and breaking windows at corporate or government institutions were increasingly common. There was a shift away from nonviolence as a strat-egy and way of life, to nonviolence as a tactic, to be used when expedient—if at all. The political motion of the period was moving increasingly toward armed struggle. "1969 was an incredible time to be alive and political," Siff recalls. "It was a [time] in which it was very hard to be single-issue oriented because you were surrounded by activist Blacks, Chicanos, Native Americans, and women and gay people of all ethnicities who were looking at the world in a very dy-namic way, which is why the development of anti-imperialist politics seemed totally natural." This widespread militancy is the environment that birthed Weatherman. "It was a broad understanding that there was both a cultural and a political fight going on," says Scott Braley. "We said, 'this is what's important and we're going to organize publicly for it.'"

Just over a month after the Days of Rage, more than a half-million people descended on Washington, D.C., in the largest antiwar demonstration to date. The Vietnam Moratorium Committee and the New Mobilization Committee were the official sponsors for the November 15, 1969, demonstration, though people of all political persuasions flooded the streets to protest Nixon's continued aggression in Vietnam. Three days before the protest, a group of white anti-imperialists unconnected with Weatherman blew up the New York offices of Chase Manhattan, Standard Oil, and General Motors—and a day later, the Criminal Courts Building. The same group had been responsible for causing hundreds of thousands of dollars in damage in earlier bombings against the Whitehall Street Military Induction Center, the New York Federal Building, and a Marine Midland Bank.[66]

During the November march in D.C., a contingent of nearly 10,000, led in part—but only in part—by Weatherman/SDS, broke away from the main march to surround the Justice Department, trashing it and the South Vietnamese embassy. From different perspectives, with different connotations, both Weather leader Bill Ayers and Attorney General John Mitchell observed that the scene looked like the Russian Revolution.[67] This level of militancy would return in February 1970, when riots erupted in The Day After (TDA) demonstrations following the conviction of the Chicago 7 (Seale's case having been separated from the others). Michael Novick, for instance, was part of a Weatherman affinity group interested in "upping the ante" during the TDA in Berkeley. During the demonstration, his affinity group was "breaking windows, helping people get away from cops, [and] throwing back tear gas canisters," he says. And in May of that year, after Weather was already underground, campuses exploded, literally and figuratively, in response to the invasion of Cambodia and to the Kent State shootings.[68]

Weatherman's militancy, which seemed so maniacally expressed in the Days of Rage, was reflective of much of the movement's own politics in 1969. In spite of its sectarianism, the group had a finger on the pulse of much of the antiwar movement. Indeed, Comstock says, the difference between Weatherman and others from SDS was often just a couple of months—what Weather was doing at one point was accepted by broader swaths of people shortly thereafter. "Weather attracted the people who were most ready to do that, but most of the SDS membership wasn't that far behind," he says. In this context, Comstock identified the major difference as emotional rather than political. "That is, the real issue wasn't the tormented ideological maneuvering…but where you were at emotionally. Were you ready to go for it, to shut the motherfucker down?"

Thus, its arrogance notwithstanding, it was not surprising or irrational that Weather continued its demonstrations, even as charges continued to mount against both leaders and rank-and-file members. Now, however, Weather was beginning to realize that it couldn't make a revolution by itself. "That whole forced march leading up to Days of Rage and Days of Rage itself was too much, too fast, too profligate," says Comstock. "The hothouse effect from spending too much time listening only to each other…let us convince ourselves that Days of Rage was the right way to go, even though it meant going it alone." For Weather, the Days of Rage were significant because the mass arrests and heavy charges against many of its leading members meant that the organization was functionally finished as an aboveground entity, at least in Chicago, unless it wanted to concentrate its time and resources on lengthy legal battles. With its flashy actions and confrontational protest, the group had made going underground almost a self-fulfilling prophecy.

"The period after Days of Rage got very grim," Comstock remembers. The criticism/self-criticism sessions increased in both frequency and intensity, court cases were piling up for almost every member, and money was running out. The Weather Bureau again moved people across the country to work in collectives with people (and in cities) they barely knew, if at all. Freaked out or turned off, militants began to abandon Weatherman. "The horizon looked very dark," Comstock says; "we were either going underground or going to jail; either way, life was going to be very tough."

BORN IN BLOOD:
POLICE MURDER OF FRED HAMPTON AND MARK CLARK AS CATALYST FOR THE WEATHER UNDERGROUND

> *To us it was clear. The government was at war to smash the Black movement, and most of the white movement was not willing to fight [back].*
> —*David Gilbert*[69]

TWO MONTHS AFTER the Days of Rage, Chicago police, with the help of an FBI informant, murdered Panthers Fred Hampton and Mark Clark in their sleep. As Ward Churchill and Jim Vander Wall report in their exhaustive study on state repression of the 1960s and 1970s:

> On the evening of December 3, 1969, shortly before the planned raid, [FBI] infiltrator [William] O'Neal seems to have slipped Hampton a substantial dose of secobarbital in a glass of kool-aid. The BPP leader was thus comatose in his bed when the fourteen-man police team—armed with a submachinegun [sic] and other special hardware—slammed into his home at about 4 a.m. on the morning of December 4. He was nonetheless shot three times, once more-or-less slightly in the chest, and then twice more in the head at point-blank range.[70]

To counter the lies put forth in the mainstream media by Illinois State Attorney Edward Hanrahan, who said the Panthers had started a fierce gun battle with police, Chicago Panthers opened the bullet-riddled apartment up for tours.[71] People from across the country saw the blood-soaked mattress where Hampton was sleeping when he was murdered. Visitors to the apartment saw the holes from the ninety-eight shots fired by police, more than forty of them into Hampton's bedroom alone, including some at point-blank range. Only one shot came from the Panthers. Doing security by the front door, Mark Clark fired once, likely a reflexive action in his death convulsions.[72]

The twenty-one-year-old Hampton had been engaged in powerful organizing work: uniting street gangs and political groups in a progressive Rainbow Coalition (the radical precursor to the Jesse Jackson electoral campaign of the same name). Hampton had also coordinated free-breakfast-for-kids and free community healthcare programs in the city. He was an emerging national leader within the Panthers.[73] All of which had made him a target. Robert Roth recalls being in an elevator in a Chicago police station with other Weathermen, all of whom had been arrested during a militant protest in late September in support of the Chicago 8. Police had badly beaten one of the cadre about the face—and then boasted "wait until you see what we do to Hampton." None of the police who carried out Hampton's murder or the government officials who authorized it were ever charged with a crime.[74]

Members of Weatherman/SDS had all seen and experienced police brutality, in Chicago and elsewhere, but this assassination was something different. "It was so brutal," Cathy Wilkerson says. "We felt like we were in way over our heads, and that we didn't have time to figure [it] out.... The time was now. People were getting killed, and we had to go underground."[75] David Gilbert agrees: "It was the murder of Fred Hampton more than any other factor that compelled us to feel [that] we had to take up armed struggle."[76] With the saturation bombing of Vietnam and the police murder or harassment of Black leaders, something more needed to be done.[77]

The Hampton-Clark murders signaled to the nascent Weatherman that, as Gilbert tells it, it was "time to move to other forms of struggle." Hand-wringing and apologies were not going to stop the repression. "We wanted to create some pressure, to overextend the police so they couldn't concentrate all their forces on the Panthers. We wanted to create a political cost for what they were doing. And we also felt that to build a movement among whites that was a revolutionary movement, a radical movement...it had to respond when our government in our name was destroying the most promising, exciting, and charismatic leadership to come out of the Black movement in a long time."[78]

Michael Novick was one of a group who "concluded that war was upon us and that Weatherman was the only formation that white people who were serious about it could join. In that regard, the murder of Fred Hampton, who was younger than I was at the time when he was killed, was a huge factor for me. I basically felt that I was living on borrowed or stolen time and had to step up to the demands of the hour." Lyndon Comstock remembers the Hampton-Clark murders as proof that Weather's doomsday predictions were accurate. "It was fucked, but that was where we thought the whole situation was heading. We expected that it would happen even to white people before too much longer."

The belief in the need for militancy would be bolstered by events just four days after the Hampton-Clark murders, when the Los Angeles Black Panther headquarters survived an unprovoked pre-dawn attack from police that lasted five hours. Learning from Chicago, the Los Angeles Panthers had established tight security, and were able to hold police off until the media and the community arrived, assuring that they could surrender to arrest, however unwarranted, without being murdered in the streets.[79]

But LA was the exception, not the rule. COINTELPRO was in full swing, and twenty-seven Panthers were murdered and 749 arrested in 1969 alone.[80] An anti-racist movement needed to do more than wave signs in response to such blatant attacks; militant solidarity was an urgent priority. Indeed, many in and around Weatherman criticized the lack of response by the white Left—with the exception of militant pacifist Dave Dellinger, who did respond—when Bobby Seale was bound and gagged during the Chicago 8 trial. As Weather saw it, such passivity signaled to the government that it would face little resistance to anti-Black repression, thus opening the door for it to murder Hampton.[81] As a result, there was an urgent need for whites to put their bodies on the line in solidarity with the Black movement—to put themselves, in Bernardine Dohrn's words, "between Black freedom fighters and the police." The sides seemed clearly drawn.

More than any other single incident, the Hampton-Clark assassination pushed Weatherman to respond directly, even violently, to the state. "When Fred Hampton was killed, it was clear that there was no room for a genuine democratic Black movement in terms of what the United States would allow," says Laura Whitehorn, who had participated in study groups with the slain Panther leader. "I was not just full of rage; I was also full of sorrow at the thought of what it was going to take to change anything in this country."[82] The Hampton-Clark murders, together with other repression against the Black movement, showed Scott Braley that "the stakes really were what we thought they were." In spite of her mixed feelings about the group, Donna Willmott, a longtime pacifist from Ohio who had seen Hampton speak while a student in Chicago, was moved to join Weatherman after the murder. "Fred and Mark's assassination really brought home to me the nature of the state and the fact that this was a war that was happening—one being waged against Black revolutionaries and the Black community," she says. "Seeing what the state was prepared to do to stop revolution made me feel like I had to rethink my feelings about violence and nonviolence."

The rage at Hampton's assassination melded with fury at the continuing aggression in Vietnam in the December 9 demonstration against Nixon at New York's Waldorf Astoria hotel, where the president was receiving an award. (That week, Nixon had also announced the draft lottery.)[83] After arguing with his Weatherman friends for months against armed struggle, Jonah Raskin was now convinced that they were right. All the letters, pickets, guerrilla theater, sit-ins, hunger strikes, and teach-ins—and yet the police could openly murder a Black revolutionary. "There was a war going on," Raskin writes in his memoir. "We had to take the side of the blacks. We had to force the pigs to overextend themselves, to expose them, and to go on the offensive."[84] After performing street theater at the Waldorf Astoria protest, Raskin was among those who smashed windows and did their best to make midtown New York at least temporarily ungovernable. Unsurprisingly, he was beaten repeatedly and systematically after being arrested.[85]

Meanwhile, in response to the murders of Fred Hampton and Mark Clark, Weatherman anonymously firebombed several empty police cars in Chicago.[86]

"PSYCHING OURSELVES UP"
THE FLINT WAR COUNCIL AND GOING UNDERGROUND

WITH THE HAMPTON-CLARK murders fresh in everyone's mind, Weatherman/SDS held its last public gathering in late December. Billed as the "SDS National War Council," the meeting took place in Flint, Michigan, and was the culmination of the past few frenzied months. It was here that the decision to go underground was officially announced, although preparations had been ongoing since the aftermath of the Days of Rage and especially since the Chicago Panther murders.

Attended by approximately 300 people, the Flint meeting was a bizarre celebration of violence as the organization sought to prepare for the big shift underground.[87] Looking back, Judy Siff calls the "War Council" an exciting, frightening, and ultimately cartoonish event. "It was as if everything was in bold and italics. Sometimes you have to really psych yourself up to take on what you believe in…. It was like doing a hundred pushups—you just got energized by it, even if there were things that you really couldn't relate to." Despite its elements of self-parody, Flint was a rite of passage, a testament to the seriousness of the choice that many of those assembled had made. "We had committed ourselves," Braley says. "Part of the terror of that commitment was not seeing a lot of other things we should have seen. It was somewhat blinding."

A flyer for the meeting showed a sinister Santa (after all, it was Christmas) wearing a bandolier and holding a gift bag overflowing with weapons. It read: "Over the holidays we plotted war on Amerika" and "Ho Ho Ho Chi Minh!—National War Council, Weatherman."[88] The walls of the meeting hall were adorned with such artistry as a large cardboard machine gun with the words "PIECE NOW" above it; posters of revolutionary icons such as Fidel, Che, and Ho Chi Minh; and mug shots of enemies of the people, including Vice President Spiro Agnew.[89] The Hampton assassination was front and center—an entire wall featured pictures of the murdered Panther leader, the crime scene, and his bullet-ridden body. There was morbid humor, too: a songbook, filled with Christmas carols and pop songs rewritten to express the joys of communism, street fighting, and revolutionary violence. Even the Supremes were drafted into the revolution. "Stop in the Name of Love" became "Stop this Imperialist Plunder." (Rhythm, it would seem, was a bourgeois trait.)

It got worse as things got underway. Raising three fingers to signify the fork used as a murder weapon by the Manson "family," speaker Dohrn praised the recent murders in Los Angeles. (She would later say that her remarks were meant to be satirical, "mocking America's unabashed love affair with violence.") Weather leaders proudly proclaimed themselves "the new barbarians" and pondered aloud whether it would be acceptable to kill white children to prevent the further spread of white supremacy. They worked themselves up into a laughing frenzy, chanting "Explode!"

But Flint had serious political underpinnings, even if they came dressed in misanthropy. To many of those present, the spectacle was an expression of outrage, but one whose hyperbole was self-evident. "Every radio disc jockey talked about 'dynamite' records, and almost everyone in the movement at the end of 1969 talked about bombings and kidnappings," Jonah Raskin writes of the event. "The talk [at Flint] indicated our real anger, but there was an air of unreality about our talk. We daydreamed about guns and bombs." For Raskin, Flint represented the logical and the illogical extremes of Weather's politics. "On one hand there was a coherent political analysis, a disciplined organization, an ideology, and leadership. There was an understanding of imperialism, especially the war in Vietnam, and black oppression and rebellion in the United States. There was also a firm grasp of the strengths and weaknesses of youth culture and an insistence on the importance of women's liberation. On the other hand, there was a chaotic and frenetic life-style and an intense, irrational moral fervor."[90]

Today Dohrn, like everyone else, is critical of Flint, even as she acknowledges the context. "I don't know how you get yourself to take risks and do things you weren't brought up to do without trying to change yourself," she says. For most in the group, going underground was a conscious decision, one made politically and deliberately, for all the bluster that accompanied it. But Flint frightened away many would-be supporters, who agreed with the group's politics but were disgusted with the violent rhetoric.

"That meant that the number of people left was very small, and the support was less than it should have been," Braley recalls (adding that Flint's theatrics also "declared publicly to the state a lot earlier than anybody should" what the group was intending to do). Following Flint, Weatherman stepped up its preparations to go underground. In the rush, some of the cadre were separated from the organization. "Developing cadre was very nearly the only thing that Weather had been good at," says Comstock, who was "cut loose" because he was in jail during the major thrust of the move underground. "And whoever heard of a revolutionary organization that was so focused on shrinking, rather than growing?"

In January 1970, Weatherman officially closed the SDS National Office in Chicago; its plans of turning SDS into a revolutionary mass organization were abandoned in lieu of building its own, independent revolutionary organization.[91] Many of the SDS files were donated to the University of Wisconsin library, although some, such as the member list, were destroyed.[92]

Flint was a point of no return for Weatherman. From here on, everything was full speed ahead in building a white anti-racist fighting force inside the United States of America.

The remnants of the Greenwich Village townhouse on West 11th Street after an accidental explosion on March 6, 1970. The blast killed Weather activists Ted Gold, Diana Oughton, and Terry Robbins.

> *Under the pressure of those times and still expressing
> our very competitive culture, we made many
> serious and interrelated errors: romanticization
> of violence, sectarianism, dismissing the potential
> to have both an underground and a militant
> mass movement, substituting status ratings on
> who is most "revolutionary" for honest political
> debate, perpetuating macho values and failing
> to work with and foster potential allies for Black
> liberation. These errors, this wrong politics, were
> not only extremely costly in our loss of three bright,
> lovely, idealistic young lives, but also a setback in
> the broader struggle against imperialism.*
>
> —David Gilbert[1]

FOR ALL HE KNEW, DUSTIN HOFFMAN LIVED ON A QUIET block on West 11th Street in Greenwich Village, not far from Washington Square Park, in an area known for its unique architecture. So when the townhouse adjoining his was reduced to rubble in a powerful blast around noon on March 6, 1970, Hoffman believed the fire marshals who said that a gas pipe had exploded in the basement of 18 W. 11th Street. The famed actor made a few trips into his own house, which was damaged in the explosion, to save paintings and a Tiffany lampshade, until police prevented him from entering the building, which was still in flames.[2]

In the early evening, when the fires were finally quelled, firemen searching through the wreckage found the body of one man crushed under a fallen beam on the second floor, and it was unclear whether other bodies would be found amidst the debris.[3] It soon became clear that the four-story townhouse had not exploded because of a gas leak. Police and fire marshals found "reams of pamphlets" for SDS and Weatherman in the townhouse

127

owned by James Wilkerson, a radio executive, who was vacationing in the Caribbean at the time.[4] The dead man was soon identified as Ted Gold, a twenty-three-year-old Brooklyn native, honor student, teacher, and leader of Columbia SDS (who also was the primary author of the Weatherman songbook). Meanwhile, police couldn't locate the two women who had emerged, dazed but not seriously hurt, from the wreckage: Kathy Boudin, twenty-six, and Cathy Wilkerson, twenty-five, whose father owned the house. The two were longtime SDS organizers associated with Weatherman. Boudin was a Bryn Mawr graduate from an Old Left family; Wilkerson, the former editor of *New Left Notes*, was a Swarthmore alumnus with Quaker roots. After they escaped the burning townhouse, the two were briefly taken into a neighbor's house (by Susan Wagner, Henry Fonda's ex-wife), where they showered, dressed their wounds, and disappeared for the next ten years.

Four days after the blast, police and firefighters discovered in the basement the "headless body of a young woman, missing both hands and a foot and riddled with roofing nails." Also in the basement were "57 sticks of dynamite, 30 blasting caps, lengths of doorbell wire, several clockwork timing mechanisms, and four crude but deadly fragmentation bombs." The basement, it was estimated, contained "enough explosives to level half the block."[5] The woman was later identified as Diana Oughton, a twenty-eight-year-old Bryn Mawr grad, Peace Corps veteran and teacher from Dwight, Illinois. Like Gold, she had gone on the trip to Cuba the previous summer with other Weatherpeople to meet Vietnamese and Cuban revolutionaries. She had been a leader of early Weatherman in the Midwest.

Another torso was found in the basement of the townhouse on March 14. It was so thoroughly dismembered that it wasn't until the Weather Underground released a communiqué ten weeks later that twenty-one-year-old Terry Robbins was identified. One of the signers of the founding "Weatherman" statement, Robbins had been a leader in the Midwest, especially in Ohio where he had organized a large and militant SDS chapter at Kent State University.

While Weatherman had been building its underground capacity for several months in preparation for the shift to clandestinity, this accidental explosion led to the organization's immediate submersion. Aided by friends and comrades, many people instantly disappeared within America, especially those who had been moving in that direction for the past several months. Some of those without serious charges were told by the leadership to remain aboveground and help build the support apparatus—either as "public" activists who were secretly members of the Weather Underground, or separate from the organization, as unaffiliated anti-imperialists. Some were simply abandoned in the frenzied process, while others freaked out at the deaths and left the organization, even the country, altogether.[6] David Gilbert remembers the moment as one of the two loneliest times in his life, when he felt "overwhelmed by the heaviness of it all. That was really a loss."[7] It was Ted Gold who had recruited him into Weatherman.

Even those who remained committed to the organization were devastated and confused after the explosion. Scott Braley remembers being wracked with indecision. "I found it very difficult to decide anything," he remembers. "One morning I would think, 'we just have to keep going and do what we're doing. That's the right thing to do.' The next morning I'd say, 'that's wrong, we have to go a different direction.' That evening, I'd say, 'this is crazy, we're all going to be killed, I want to leave.'" It was, he says, a "shattering" period for everyone.

As tragedies often do, the townhouse explosion forced a reconfiguring process and a change. All Weather actions were called to a halt—including one plan involving bombs that, like the ones at West 11th Street, were to be used against human targets. (An action attempted outside a Detroit police station used a shoddily constructed bomb that would have surely caused significant injury or loss of life, but failed to detonate; it was built in part by an FBI infiltrator.)[8] In a self-criticism session done after the explosion, it was revealed that the bombs being built at the townhouse were to be used against people, not just property. The specific target was a non-commissioned officers' dance at an Army base.[9] Operating under the logic that "the bigger the bang the better," the action was to be a pre-emptive strike against those who would soon drop bombs over Vietnam, thus "bringing the war home" with all the intensity that the slogan implied.[10]

Weatherman, soon to become the Weatherman Underground, now had to deal directly and immediately with the meaning of armed struggle; it was no longer an abstract concept. "Bringing the war home" had real consequences—in flesh and blood and friends and family. "The dead end of militancy and violence for their own sake was obvious" after the townhouse explosion, says Laura Whitehorn. Which way forward for a group that had spent the past nine months preparing for and boasting about revolutionary armed struggle?

To decide this question, Weather held a strategic retreat in northern California in late April. There, the group intensified its organizational consolidation. The leadership body was shrunk in size and soon changed from the Weather Bureau to the Central Committee. More importantly, the group defined the greatest error to be its own political thinking and attitude, rather than just the bomb's inadvertent detonation or the group's technical inexperience. It was decided that armed propaganda—targeting only property—was a more appropriate level of struggle at the time. The decision to engage in armed propaganda was political as well as moral. It was understood that there was less support for armed struggle in the white Left than in Black and Puerto Rican communities, due in part to the higher level of repression against Third World communities.[11]

As a result of the shift to armed propaganda, the Weather leadership expelled John Jacobs from the group. An ex-Progressive Labor member known as JJ, Jacobs was the principle author of the original "Weatherman" statement and was a leading figure in pushing militancy in SDS and early Weather. Even after the townhouse blast, JJ argued for "armed squads" that would pursue a similar strategy, only with better technical training. The group, however, took a firm position against injuring anyone, and JJ was out. He remained underground, living under assumed names until his death in Canada in 1997.[12]

After the California meeting, Weather collectives lost some of their bleak tone and ascetic rigidity. The group stopped denouncing others in the movement, and criticism/self-criticism sessions ceased to be marathon sessions of manipulation. Collectives became more mutually supportive, acknowledging that, as Braley puts it, "we're in this together, this is really intense, we better figure out how to make this work."

THE TOWNHOUSE EXPLOSION IN CONTEXT

THE TOWNHOUSE EXPLOSION was the tragic and dramatic culmination of the grim political direction in which Weatherman had been headed. "We were out of touch with what was going on," says Laura Whitehorn, "and we lost sight of the fact that if you're a revolutionary, the first thing you have to try to do is preserve human life."[13] For that reason, Braley calls the townhouse explosion "a foregone conclusion.... It was bound to happen. There were just too many people running around doing too many things with too little political and technical preparation." Indeed, Cathy Wilkerson says the townhouse explosion followed from the political direction presented at the Flint War Council, just three months prior. "The townhouse is just an enactment of those politics" from Flint, Wilkerson says. Although the group had been headed toward catastrophe in one form or another, Weatherman's actions prior to the townhouse blast had not injured anyone, despite the group's apocalyptic rhetoric.

However painful the deaths of Gold, Oughton, and Robbins were, the broader context quickly underscored for Weatherman that a complete reversal of its path was not the right decision. Three days after the Greenwich Village townhouse was reduced to rubble, a car bomb in Bel Air, Maryland, killed SNCC activists Ralph Featherstone and William "Che" Payne. The pair was in town for the trial of SNCC leader H. Rap Brown (now Jamil Al-Amin) on incitement charges for his fiery speeches in nearby Cambridge; the trial was slated to start the next day. FBI and police alleged that the two men had intended to use the bomb in the courthouse. SNCC activists contended that the bomb was planted in the car, possibly under the notion that Brown would be in it as well. SNCC called for "massive retribution and revenge," and a fearful Brown went underground.[14]

There were other bombings at this time whose targets were clear. On March 12, a group calling itself "Revolutionary Force 9" placed bombs at the New York City headquarters for IBM, Mobile, and General Telephone and Electronics, accusing them of profiting "not only from death in Vietnam but also from Amerikan imperialism in all of the Third World."[15] At the same time, Cambodia was becoming increasingly embroiled in a bitter civil war, unleashed by General Lon Nol with the help of U.S. military advisors.[16]

The townhouse blast was a grievous error, but Weather's broader analysis of the political context still held true. For Gilbert, an underground strategy still made sense as a way "to stop the much greater violence that was going on." And that greater social violence continued, despite the three deaths on West 11th Street. "The fact that we had three people killed was *horrible* but it actually hadn't changed the world. It had only changed our world," Braley says, explaining his decision to stay with the group because, after all, "imperialism was still imperialism."

AMERICA'S MOST WANTED

THE STATE SEIZED on the negative publicity created by the lev-
eled townhouse on West 11th Street to launch an attack on the dazed
Weatherman organization, now hastening to go underground. "On April
2," wrote historian Jeremy Varon, "Attorney General John Mitchell personally announced a fifteen-count federal indictment of twelve Weather
leaders and named twenty-eight unindicted co-conspirators for the Days
of Rage, making many of the elusive Weathermen fugitives from U.S. law."
These indictments followed the Cook County grand jury indictments of
sixty-four people on thirty-seven counts in December 1969, following the
Days of Rage.[17] Having gone underground after the townhouse explosion,
those indicted became federal fugitives. In desperate need of an arrest to
match the bold language of the indictment, the FBI blew the cover of its
only undercover operative in the group, Larry Grathwohl, and arrested
Weatherwomen Dianne Donghi and Linda Evans on April 15—one of
the few times any clandestine member of the Weather Underground was
arrested following the townhouse explosion.[18]

A month before the townhouse explosion, J. Edgar Hoover had publicly called Weatherman/SDS the "most violent, persistent and pernicious
of revolutionary groups." And now the chase was on. In May 1970, the FBI
announced "one of the most intensive manhunts in history" for nine suspected Weather leaders.[19] Bernardine Dohrn was now on the FBI's "Most
Wanted List," as were lesbian feminists Susan Saxe and Kathy Power, wanted in connection with the murder of a police officer killed during a Boston
bank robbery that was to fund radical activities.[20] In November, the FBI
expanded the Top Ten list to include sixteen people, nine of them wanted
for radical activities.[21] Even the Weatherpeople who hadn't made the FBI's
Top Ten still found their faces plastered on Most Wanted posters in post
offices across the country. The group was, as it had pledged, starting to take
some of the repressive attention away from the Panthers and other Third
World groups in the United States—even if Weather never received the full
brunt of repression that its nonwhite comrades faced.

Meanwhile, the war in Vietnam was expanding. The United States invaded
Cambodia on April 30, 1970, in stark contradiction to Nixon's pre-election

promise to end the war. Militant protests erupted nationwide, resulting in the destruction of numerous ROTC buildings and other institutions related to the war. "Students at sixty institutions declared themselves on strike, with demonstrations, sometimes violent, on more than three dozen campuses," Kirkpatrick Sale writes in his history of SDS. At Kent State University in Ohio, the National Guard was called in after an ROTC building was torched. On May 4, twenty-eight guardsmen fired sixty-one shots in thirteen seconds into a crowd of about 200 unarmed student protestors, killing four and wounding nine. The response was immediate. According to Sale:

> There were major campus demonstrations at the rate of more than a hundred a day, students at a total of at least 350 institutions went out on strike and 536 schools were shut down completely for some period of time, 51 of them for the entire year. More than half the colleges and universities in the country (1350) were ultimately touched by protest demonstrations, involving nearly 60 percent of the student population—some 4,350,000 people—in every kind of institution in every state of the union. Violent demonstrations occurred on at least 73 campuses (that was only 4 percent of all institutions but included roughly a third of the country's largest and most prestigious schools), and at 26 schools the demonstrations were serious, prolonged, and marked by brutal clashes between students and police, with tear gas, broken windows, fires, clubbings, injuries, and multiple arrests; altogether, more than 1800 people were arrested between May 1 and May 15.... The National Guard was activated twenty-four times at 21 universities in sixteen states.... Capping all this, there were this month no fewer than 169 incidents of bombings and arson, 95 of them associated with college campuses and another 36 at government and corporate buildings, the most for any single month in all the time government records have been kept; in the first week of May, 30 ROTC buildings on college campuses were burned or bombed, at the rate of more than four every single day.[22]

Within ten days of the Kent State murders, six Black people were killed in demonstrations in Augusta, Georgia, and two at Jackson State University in Mississippi; in both instances, students and community residents were not just protesting the war but voicing opposition to police violence and other forms of U.S. racial oppression. Weatherman bombed the National Guard headquarters in Washington, D.C., on May 10. (The group didn't claim responsibility for this action until four years later. When it took credit, Weather said the bombing was in response to the murders in Ohio and Mississippi, although the bombing occurred before the Jackson murders, and it was local and state police rather than the guard that opened fire in Jackson and Augusta.)[23] The lack of significant outrage among whites following the Augusta and Jackson murders, as well as following the murders that summer of three Chicanos during the Chicano Moratorium antiwar protest in Los Angeles, proved Weather's point about racism, repression, and the dangers of white passivity.

MILITANT ANTI-RACISM:
THE POLITICS OF WEATHERMAN UNDERGROUND

GIVEN THE RHETORICAL and tactical excesses characterizing Weatherman/SDS from its founding in June 1969 until March 1970, it can be easy to forget the political, and quite rational, substance of its program: the need for white opposition to war and racism in solidarity with people of color. Those who joined the group, in Gilbert's view, "supported the perspective that the struggle against racism was a life-and-death struggle that mandated militancy." Weather activists thought it hypocritical to support the risks Third World people were taking without taking their own risks in the struggle. This decision was a conscious political choice, not the psychological malfunction of "white guilt" that some have proposed.[24] "Calling Weather's politics 'guilt' comes from an upper class world view," Gilbert says. "There is nothing guilt-ridden about identifying with oppressed people—especially when they have been blazing the trail toward humane social change."[25] Indeed, some ex-Weatherpeople argue that the "guilt" accusation says more about the accuser than the accused. "To say anti-racism is pathological does say something about this country," Laura Whitehorn observes.

The leading example of armed liberation movements in the Third World and in the United States had a ripple effect throughout the white Left, breeding in many a sense of urgency. Even longtime pacifist Dave Dellinger gave "critical support" to certain groups that used violence, although he himself never departed from nonviolence.[26] (Unlike many white activists who more openly supported armed struggle, Dellinger also remained in dialogue with the Weather Underground.) Even the Old Left was moved. Independent journalist and pacifist I.F. Stone (whose niece, Kathy Boudin, was a Weather fugitive) said, "Weathermen are the most sensitive of a generation that feels in its bones what we older people only grasp as an unreal abstraction: that the world is headed for nuclear annihilation and something must be done to stop it." [27]

The basis for the Weather Underground, Braley says, was the notion that "it *is* right to fight back, particularly when the rest of the world is dying by the millions because of your own country. It is right to fight back and you have to stand in solidarity with people who are [fighting back] and people who are being repressed." It was, in many ways, a frightening revelation, if only for the implications; Braley remembers being "often scared and sometimes terrified" in his years underground. "You knew that if something went wrong on an action, you would likely be dead or in prison forever. It was often incredibly scary," he says. "Because of that, you had to decide whether what you were doing was really a good thing or not. You had to make a decision based on politics and not on fear."

The politics, not just of the group but of the period, pointed toward the underground. Weather's turn to clandestinity was not simply a flight from repression. Although the Days of Rage indictments and the townhouse explosion expedited the process, most people in the group *chose* to go underground rather than being forced per se. It was a strategic move. There were plenty of role models, both historical and contemporary: the Cuban revolution, the National Liberation Front, the Tupamaros of Uruguay, the African National Congress in South Africa, an assortment of Palestinian guerrilla organizations, the Black Liberation Army (formed in 1971), the Puerto Rican Nationalists of the 1950s (a new generation of which cropped up in the 1970s and 1980s), and others. And it wasn't just the Third World; people of comparable age and social background were forming similar armed clandestine groups in Europe, most famously the Red Army Faction in Germany and the Red Brigades in Italy.[28]

The rise of armed revolutionary groups elsewhere provided the context for Weatherman's militancy; national liberation struggles were the context for Weather's all-white composition. Lyndon Comstock remembers it being "a process of political education for most of us to start seeing past the propaganda that we've been raised with and [to start] identifying the U.S. as an empire." But the strength and presence of the liberation movements had already defined the issues. "All those movements for self-determination pushed us to think about what it means to support someone as an ally instead of as a missionary," Donna Willmott says. "On the other hand, the war that the state waged against them also pushed us to figure out what our stand was and what it meant [to act in solidarity]." And it had to be figured out quickly.

DECLARATION OF WAR

THE TIME PERIOD following the townhouse blast had been a hectic one for Weatherman, complete with internal restructuring, federal indictments, and adapting to life underground. Now it was time to get back to business. After its hasty and difficult self-examination and self-criticism, Weatherman released its first "communiqué" from underground. It was titled "A Declaration of a State of War."

As far as war declarations go, this one was short, although at fourteen (small) paragraphs, it is among the longer statements to emerge during that first year underground. Dated May 21, 1970, and signed by Bernardine Dohrn, the communiqué stated that "revolutionary violence is the only way" to overcome "the frustration and impotence that comes from trying to reform this system."[29] In its championing of violence as a strategy (rather than a tactic) and its uncritical celebration of drug culture ("guns and grass are united in the youth underground"), the statement showed that the organization was still somewhat enamored of a militarist vision of being outlaws. Still, the overall message was a sharply political one.

After making the first public acknowledgement that Terry Robbins was the third person to die in the townhouse blast, the statement ended by commemorating the three dead comrades and by reaffirming the Weatherman Underground (as the first communiqué called the group) as a white revolutionary organization fighting in solidarity with the Black liberation struggle:

> For Diana Oughton, Ted Gold and Terry Robbins, and for all the revolutionaries who are still on the move here, there has been no question for a long time now—we will never go back.
>
> Within the next fourteen days we will attack a symbol or institution of Amerikan injustice. This is the way we celebrate the example of Eldridge Cleaver, H. Rap Brown

and all black revolutionaries who first inspired us by their fight behind enemy lines for the liberation of their people.
Never again will they fight alone.

On June 10, 1970, at 7 p.m., the Weatherman Underground bombed New York City police headquarters. A little more than 14 days, but close.[30] With widespread resentment and anger at police violence—from communities of color as well as white youth—the police station was a logical choice as the most visible manifestation of a racist state.[31] Seven police officers were cut from shattered glass in the explosion, but there were no serious injuries.[32] Due to Weather's commitment to engaging in armed propaganda only, no one else was injured by a Weather Underground bombing in the ensuing seven years.

Just as not causing injury was part of Weather's calling card, so too was releasing a communiqué with each action, and sometimes even without an action. So when part of the New York City police headquarters blew up, a communiqué immediately followed. In a mark of professionalism, the second sentence points out that the group called in a warning before the bomb detonated. But there was still some counterculture posturing. "Every time the pigs think they've stopped us, we come back a little stronger and a lot smarter. They guard their buildings and we walk right past their guards. They look for us—we get to them first.... They outlaw grass, we build a culture of life and music." More impressively, the communiqué tied police violence against white antiwar activists, Black and Chicano/a militants, and counter-culturalists to a system that thrives on repression. It was a unifying message of all-out resistance against the state.[33]

A month after the police headquarters attack, a Weatherman letter (not tied to any action) published in the underground press stressed the need for a global activist approach. "Our task now is to join the people of the world in destroying U.S. imperialism and building a socialist society.... Our struggle must be waged on every level, on every front," the letter said, going on to express solidarity with urban guerrilla movements in Southeast Asia, Latin America, and the Middle East.[34] Already the group was starting to shed its narrow commitment to violence alone, celebrating the guerrilla and the outlaw while also supporting other forms of activism.

A federal grand jury in Detroit indicted thirteen Weather activists on July 23, 1970, for conspiracy charges emanating from the Flint War Council, where, the indictment alleged, the group had conspired to commit bombings and murders and had illegally carried weapons.[35] Weatherman's defiant response came just two days later, in a communiqué entitled "Honk Amerika." The new Central Committee addressed Attorney General Mitchell directly: "Don't look for us, Dog; we'll find you first." Dated July 25, 1970, the communiqué originated in Detroit.

The next day, in celebration of the eleventh anniversary of the Cuban revolution, the Weather Underground blew up a Military Police Station at the Presidio Army Base in San Francisco and a Bank of America branch in New York City. Damage in both cases was minor.[36]

TUNE IN, TURN ON—AND BREAK OUT

AFTER A BRIEF lull in August, two actions in the fall of 1970 illustrated the strengths and weaknesses of Weather's connection to youth culture. Indeed, the group in this period was being pulled (or, more precisely, was pulling itself) in two directions: between being the white anti-racist fighting force the "Weatherman" statement had pledged to build, and being the "outlaw" underground of the white youth culture. These different directions coexisted in a sometimes unhappy, if unnamed, tension. While the group had formed to act in solidarity with national liberation movements, Weather was also shaped by the political elements of the counterculture, and it was from these sectors of the white Left (especially the Yippies) that early support for the group came.[37] Recognizing the problems of its isolation from the Days of Rage through the beginning of 1970, Weather thought that increased celebration of youth culture would speak to, even broaden, its base of support among white youth. Although Weather hoped to bridge the thoroughly political with the thoroughly cultural, the two were often at odds in practice.

On September 15, 1970, the Weatherman Underground "sprung" LSD guru Timothy Leary from a minimum security prison in San Luis Obispo, California, and helped him escape to Algeria to join with Eldridge Cleaver and the international chapter of the Black Panther Party.[38] (Weather's main role in the escape was getting Leary from the prison to Algeria; Leary got over the fence on his own.)[39] A drug-based underground group calling itself the Brotherhood of Eternal Love had approached the Weather Underground about the escape—and even covered expenses.[40] "They regarded him as one of their heroes, their radical prophet and high priest," Jonah Raskin writes of Weather and the Leary escape, "but they also sprung him from jail to build support for themselves in the hippie world."[41]

Two communiqués accompanied the escape—one by Weather, the other by Leary himself, both praising LSD's supposedly revolutionary qualities. The ex-Harvard professor's statement was far more rambling and hard to follow than Weather's communiqué. In explaining the action, Weather said, "Dr. Leary was being held against his will and against the will of millions of kids in this country. He was a political prisoner, captured for the work he did in helping all of us begin the task of creating a new culture on the barren wasteland that has been imposed on this country by Democrats, Republicans, Capitalists and creeps." The communiqué goes on to mention some of the many radicals then imprisoned (and more accurately defined as political prisoners), such as SNCC leader H. Rap Brown and Black communist Angela Davis, and closes: "Our organization commits itself to the task of freeing these prisoners of war. We are outlaws, we are free!"

But Leary is the only person the Weather Underground ever helped escape, which proved to be a sore point: an organization formed in solidarity with Third World revolutionaries, instead freeing a white counterculture drug enthusiast lacking much political commitment.[42] On a tactical level, of course, the minimum-security Leary was much easier to help escape than the Black or Puerto Rican revolutionaries, who were held under heavy guard. But the disparity is something some former members regret. "We should have never done the Timothy Leary escape," says Naomi Jaffe, "since we could not do others. It made no sense politically." Fellow Weatherwoman Donna Willmott agrees, adding that the escape was "not one of the high points" in the group's history. While the escape bolstered the group's outlaw status, it was an action with more cultural power than political. Years later, Leary testified against the Weather Underground—although his stories were too inconsistent and incomprehensible to be of much value to law enforcement. Some speculate that this was intentional on Leary's part, while others insist that he was indeed cooperating with the police but that his brain was addled from too much drug use. Either way, his escape in September 1970 was a short-term, if contradictory, victory for the Weather Underground.[43]

On the flip side was an action three weeks later in Chicago. One year after the police memorial in Haymarket Square was destroyed in the build-up to the Days of Rage, the Weatherman Underground blew up the (since-rebuilt) statue again. The communiqué, signed by Dohrn, Bill Ayers, and Jeff Jones, the only publicly identified leaders of the group, read: "A year ago we blew away the Haymarket pig statue at the start of a youth riot in Chicago. The head of the Police Sergeants' Association called emotionally for all-out war between the pigs and us. We accepted. Last night we destroyed the pig again."[44] Weather's communiqué proved that a humorous tone could appeal to the frivolity of youth culture while still keeping politics at the forefront. People could immediately connect the statue with police violence, even without knowing that the memorial commemorated police repression against the nineteenth-century workers' movement. It was armed propaganda at work, raising consciousness through armed action.

In a more serious tone, the communiqué accompanying the second destruction of the statue announced a "fall offensive" against imperialism. "It is our job to blast away the myths of total superiority of the man," Weather said. "We did not choose to live in a time of war. We choose only to become guerillas and to urge our people to prepare for war rather than become accomplices in the genocide of our sisters and brothers." The communiqué then called for more active public support, for "the underground and the mass movement responding together.... Surround every armed attack with rallies, phone calls, posters, and celebrations. We are not just 'attacking targets'—we are bringing a pitiful helpless giant to its knees."[45] Abandoning its earlier go-it-alone mentality, Weather was now looking to engender mutually supportive aboveground-underground relationships, intent on building a revolutionary movement.

As this communiqué reached the newspapers, the Fall Offensive had already begun—not just in Chicago but in California and New York, where the Weatherman Underground was settling old debts and showing its ability to respond in solidarity to attacks on the Black movement.

PRISONS AND WAR:
ATTACKING THE HEART OF IMPERIALISM

THE FALL OFFENSIVE targeted imperialism in its most repressive entities: the prison system and the war machine. Weather described prisons as "instruments of genocide against the entire black and Latin community," and called for solidarity with prisoners in building a movement against "the final solution of the Amerikan state." Such solidarity was necessary, both because the group saw prisons being used as a bludgeon against

Third World communities, and because numerous revolutionary leaders had passed through or emerged from the ranks of prison.

George Jackson was one such leader. Sentenced in 1960 at the age of eighteen to one-year-to-life for a $71 robbery—effectively placing his life permanently in the hands of the state—Jackson had become a revolutionary thinker and writer in California's prison system. Along with prisoners John Clutchette and Fleeta Drumgo, Jackson was charged in 1970 with the murder of a prison guard after three Black activists were murdered in the prison. Jackson and company became known as the "Soledad Brothers," and supporters launched an international campaign for their release. His book of prison letters, *Soledad Brother*, was a best-selling revolutionary classic, making him an instant icon of the burgeoning prison movement. Jackson became Field Marshal of the Black Panther Party and an inspiration to many activists.[46]

His younger brother, Jonathan, was one of those he inspired to take action. On August 7, 1970, seventeen-year-old Jonathan marched into the Marin County courthouse in California. He sat for awhile, watching the trial in progress of James McClain, a San Quentin prisoner. "Then he stood up, a carbine in his hand, and directed everyone in the courtroom to freeze," writes Angela Davis, a Black activist professor who at the time was a Communist Party leader and close friend of George Jackson. Jonathan provided weapons to all the prisoners in court that day—McClain, William Christmas, and Ruchell Magee. Shouting for the freedom of the Soledad Brothers and all political prisoners, the four men took the judge, the district attorney, and several jurors hostage. They tried to escape in a van, but "a barrage of shots tore into the van and when the smoke had cleared, all except one inside had either been killed or wounded." The survivors included a woman juror, the district attorney, and Magee—who remains in prison.[47]

Two months later, on October 8, the Weatherman Underground bombed the Marin County Hall of Justice (the courthouse), claiming solidarity with all prisoners, who have "turned every prison in Amerika into an advance guerrilla post of the war against pig Amerika."[48] Weather's action was specifically dedicated to Jonathan Jackson and to Angela Davis, who was then being sought in conjunction with Jackson's raid. (Jonathan had been her bodyguard, and one of the guns used in the raid was licensed to Davis. Although she had no prior knowledge of the raid and was not present at the scene, she was charged with conspiracy, kidnapping, and homicide. She was underground for two months, and placed on the FBI's Most Wanted list, before being arrested in mid-October 1970; she was acquitted of all charges in 1972.)[49] The *New York Times* reported that the Marin courthouse blast caused an estimated $100,000 in damage.[50]

Four days after the Haymarket action and one day after the Marin County bombing, the Weatherman Underground attacked a New York City courthouse in Queens in solidarity with a five-day revolt in the Tombs, the city's infamous detention center. The insurgent prisoners' concerns would become familiar over the next few years: brutal and racist treatment by guards, bad food, overcrowding. Weather's six-paragraph communiqué described U.S. prisons as "machines for breaking men and women with filth, rats, isolation, brutality and torture," and called for radicals outside of prison to take action: "With thousands of pigs mobilized to guard the jails, those of us on the outside should move to aid the prisoners. Put out wanted posters for [Judge John] Murtagh and [Corrections Commissioner George] McGrath. Wherever they go treat them with the respect due enemies of the people. Keep them scared. The people will free the Soledad Brothers and the Panther 21." The communiqué concluded on a high note: "With rallies and riots, with marches and Molotovs, kids in New York City and around the country will continue the battle."[51] The bombing rendered the Queens courthouse temporarily unusable.[52]

The Marin and New York bombings, occurring within a day of each other and less than a week after the Haymarket police statue bombing in Chicago, demonstrated that the Weatherman Underground was coast-to-coast ("part of an international conspiracy," bragged one communiqué, in an apparent parody of the FBI's Cold War mentality) and could mobilize resources and carry out actions with relative speed.[53] It was, depending on your perspective, an ominous or inspiring message. Either way, it was a new front in a movement on the upswing.

Weather's last bombing in 1970 also happened to be the first by the organization's women's brigade, initially called (in a casual rip-off of Native cultures) the Proud Eagle Tribe. Their October 15 bombing targeted the Center for International Affairs at Harvard. Before going underground, Weather members had raided the center, destroying property and attacking employees. Now they returned, under the cloak of darkness, to attack the home of the "strategic hamlet program" and the former employer of Nixon's imperial crusader, Henry Kissinger. The hamlet program was, historian Stanley Karnow writes, a plan developed in 1962 to "corral peasants into armed stockades," thereby preventing the Vietnamese population from joining or supporting the guerrillas.[54] The Weatherwomen chose an institution tied to the war in Vietnam as their target in order to counter the notion current among some feminists that Vietnam was not a women's issue.

In the communiqué, the Weatherwomen pledged to "build a militant women's movement that commits itself to the destruction of Amerikan imperialism" and exploit "the Man's chauvinism" as a "strategic weakness."[55] The communiqué ended with a handwritten postscript expressing solidarity with Angela Davis, recently captured after months underground.

WEATHER'S IMPACT ON THE ABOVEGROUND

MILITANCY WAS SPREADING, beneath the surface and above. By 1970, Yippie founder Abbie Hoffman recalled in his memoir, "there was just the frustration that arises from seeing no choices but electoral politics or armed struggle, which in this period meant bombings. The underground was cheered. On most campuses you could see T-shirts with the rainbow-lighting insignia of the Weatherpeople and posters announcing 'Bernardine Welcome Here.'"[56] A year later, scholar-activist Roxanne Dunbar-Ortiz determined that radical movements had three choices: "sell out, drop out, or go underground." Highly critical of the Weather Underground, she chose to go underground with her own group.[57]

Full-fledged armed struggle was seen as an imminent reality, including many aboveground activists. Lyndon Comstock was one of those "cut loose" from Weather as the group went underground. In jail for a Weatherman action until late February 1970, he had not been privy to most of the plans for submersion. A week before the townhouse explosion, he met with some of the mid-level leaders in the group, who told him that Weather was no longer an aboveground organization. Comstock estimates there were another thirty people from the New York City Weather collectives who were similarly informed about the group's change in status. They committed themselves to aboveground work; collectives of former Weatherpeople and other anti-imperialists sprung up across the country. "We were actively preparing for the armed struggle phase that seemed inevitable," he remembers.

The ex-Weather members brought what Comstock calls their "intense training in both ideology and in doing actions" to the mass movement, helping give it political and tactical direction. Anti-imperialist collectives were inspired and propelled by Weather's bombings. Suzanne Ross, an activist and psychology professor at Lehman College in the Bronx, says that "in the early years, every action the Weather Underground did made me more militant in the work I was doing." Whatever problems there were with the initial "Weatherman" statement, Ross says she "fundamentally agreed with the Weatherman focus on the centrality of national liberation struggles both in Vietnam and elsewhere around the globe, as well as within the borders of the United States at that moment in history." In that context, she says, Weather was on target. "Vietnamese people were being massacred on a very broad scale in campaigns such as Operation Phoenix, which was meant to wipe out the NLF leadership and cadre in the South, let alone the massive bombings throughout Vietnam," Ross says. "And Black revolutionaries were being picked off one after another for targeted assassination at home to avoid the rising up of the 'Black Messiah' of FBI Director Hoover's nightmare." The choice, for Ross, was clear. "We had to up the level of struggle in this country. An underground structure seemed essential both to carry out a more militant level of resistance and impose visible material damage on the enemy, as well as to develop organizational structures less penetrable by the state's intrusions."

For Comstock, 1970 began with the belief that full-scale revolutionary war was around the corner. Hippies, Yippies, and others had obtained guns; bombs were thought to be sexy; and repression seemed to be reaching a crescendo. "As the leading elements of the black movement had already done, we were acquiring guns and would, sometime soon, start shooting back when the cops opened up on us again," he says. Whether they agreed with its direction or not, many people were looking to see what the Weatherman Underground, as the "heaviest organization in the white Left," would do next. It had declared war in May, targeted property throughout the summer and fall. Did the organization still believe that People's War was imminent in the United States and that, as the first communiqué asserted, "revolutionary violence is the only way"?[58] As 1970 came to a close, the answers were literally blowing in the wind.

A COMMUNIQUÉ OF REFLECTION

DECEMBER 1970 WAS a time for the Weather Underground to pause and reflect. The loss of three comrades in the townhouse explosion, a slew of indictments, at least seven well-publicized bombings in eight months, and the Leary escape had all made 1970 a dramatic year for a group still in its infancy.[59] Yet the seven Weather actions in 1970 were only a tiny percentage of the 330 incidents of sabotage *Scanlan's* magazine reported against police, military, or government buildings and corporations profiting from the war.[60]

To close out and sum up the year, the group released a lengthy communiqué. "New Morning, Changing Weather" was not directly tied to an action and was signed by Bernardine Dohrn, on behalf of the Weather Underground (rather than Weatherman or Weatherman Underground). The name was used for the first time in this statement, reflecting not only the group's clandestine status but a new gender-neutral name that would stay through until the end. Beyond the name change, "New Morning" marked a new communiqué format; from now on, public statements would be longer, trading slang and swagger for detail and documentation. (Although the connection with youth culture remained; indeed, the "New Morning, Changing Weather" communiqué took its title from the new Bob Dylan album. No one knows what Bob thought of all this.)

The "New Morning, Changing Weather" communiqué was mailed to the Liberation News Service and delivered to the *Liberated Guardian* (a spin-off of the leftist weekly *Guardian).* Pictures of Black Panthers, Vietnamese fighters, Native American warriors, and mass demonstrations surround the text. "New Morning" was an attempt at building relationships with the mass movement Weather had previously scorned. "We were trying to be accountable to a base from the position of underground, trying to figure out what the range of communiqués could be," says Dohrn today. "New Morning" was Weather's attempt to separate rhetoric from reality. "We really thought that our own language from '69 required us to take account of the fact that 'by any means necessary' didn't quite catch the nuance necessary...." The communiqué identified Weather's "core mission to organize, educate, agitate, oppose and not elevate tactics to a certain level."

The communiqué opened by repudiating several written statements that were alleged to have come from the underground but did not, thus expressing the group's desire to "be clear about who we are and what we are doing." "New Morning" was a "communication for our friends," an attempt to share the lessons Weather had learned from the townhouse explosion and its time underground to date. Again without irony at how it was co-opting indigenous social structures, the group said it wished to "express ourselves to the mass movement not as military leaders, but as tribes at council." Announcing that "the townhouse forever destroyed our belief that armed struggle is the only real revolutionary struggle," the Weather Underground acknowledged its "military error," "wrong direction," and "technical inexperience."[61]

If the townhouse was the culmination of the politics put forth at the Flint War Council, "New Morning" was proof of the group's internal restructuring and turn from undefined "armed struggle" to armed propaganda. By criticizing the military error, "New Morning" put renewed emphasis on building mass movements rather than isolated actions. It was, however limited, a critique of the *foco* theory that had shaped early Weatherman. "Twos and threes is not a good form for anything—it won't put out a newspaper, organize a conference on the war, or do an armed action without getting caught," the communiqué said.[62] "New Morning" paid tribute to women's leadership and traded in the bravado of "bringing the war home" for "a seriousness about how hard it will be to fight in Amerika and how long it will take us to win."

NEW MORNING—STORMY WEATHER?

"NEW MORNING" ENDS with a celebration of youth culture, even calling it a "New Nation that will grow out of the struggles of the next year." Along with championing the "Youth Nation," the communiqué also celebrated the alleged revolutionary potential of drug use. According to Robert Roth, this statement was the organization's attempt to correct the narrow sectarianism and dogmatism of Weather's early months. But, he adds, the group went too far, failing to address racism in white subcultures and the negative impact of drugs on oppressed communities. Judy Siff says "New Morning" exposed the tension within the organization between organizing hippies versus exacting a cost for Black oppression. David Gilbert agrees, calling Weather's uncritical embrace of youth culture in "New Morning" a repeat of the "classic error of the predominantly white

Left: seeking a base among white people (working class, women, or youth) at the price of compromising anti-racism."[63] Cathy Wilkerson also criticizes the statement for not suggesting a way forward for the group. "The political shift embodied in 'New Morning' is real, but it wasn't 'to' anything, just 'away' from something," she says.

Of course, these criticisms are offered largely in retrospect. At the time, it was members of the New York chapter of the Black Panther Party, then in jail on specious conspiracy charges, who raised the sharpest criticism of "New Morning." In an "open letter," the imprisoned Panthers particularly criticized the group for not recognizing that drugs, both in terms of addiction as well as arrests, were a form of chemical warfare against Black and Latino people. The Panthers also chastised the Weather Underground for what seemed like a retreat from armed struggle; the open letter reminded Weather that the Panthers had also "lost dearly loved comrades" but retained a stiff and militant opposition to the state.[64] Like the Black Power theorists in SNCC, the Panther 21 emphasized the responsibility of white radicals to fight racism, noting in particular how the antiwar movement and white youth culture (Weather's support bases) were tainted with racism. The New York Panthers didn't mince words; they criticized the Weather Underground because they saw it as the most promising development among whites. "We wish you revolutionary victory in all that you do. But remember—the degree of racial co-existence greatly depends on your successes."

The open letter was printed in radical papers when it was issued in January 1971 and even reprinted later in the decade.[65] In the course of supporting Weather, the Panther 21 also challenged the Black Panther Party leadership for ignoring their needs while in jail. Even more critical of Weather and upset at the insubordination, Huey Newton and the West Coast Panther leadership viewed the letter as a sellout and expelled its authors from the party.[66]

Despite its media savvy and its political focus on solidarity, the Weather Underground chose *not* to answer this criticism. By failing to respond to constructive criticism offered by the main U.S. Third World group they were supposedly fighting in solidarity with, Weather missed a crucial opportunity to be accountable anti-racist allies, to forge a public sense of accountability and a level of movement-wide, aboveground/underground discourse.[67] In its book, *Prairie Fire*, the Weather Underground acknowledged the error in not responding to the Panthers. But that was more than three years later, and damage to the group's credibility had been done. Now, former members regret the mistake. Robert Roth says "blowing off" the Panther 21 showed arrogance and a "staggering" lack of accountability to Black revolutionaries. Naomi Jaffe calls the organization's silence regarding the Panther critique "outrageous."

This silence was made more egregious by the fact that the organization had already responded to a constructive criticism raised months earlier by white pacifist and radical priest Daniel Berrigan. A Jesuit priest and committed antiwar militant, Berrigan went underground to evade capture for his role with eight other radical Catholics (including his brother) in the burning of more than 300 draft records with napalm in Catonsville, Maryland. The group was collectively known as the Catonsville 9.[68] In an open letter written August 8, 1970, three days before his capture, Berrigan cautioned the young activists against embracing violence. Along with announcing its Fall Offensive, the Weather Underground issued a brief statement of solidarity with Berrigan, praising him for having "refused the corruption of your generation." Even if Weather's letter did not grapple with the issues Berrigan raised, it was nevertheless an acknowledgement of Berrigan's efforts at dialogue and an expression of solidarity, showing a willingness to communicate with comrades. And yet, the organization failed to do exactly that with the main group inspiring its move underground.[69]

ARMED PROPAGANDA:
THE WEATHER UNDERGROUND MODEL

"NEW MORNING" EMERGED from Weather's clandestine political work, which included not only the high-profile bombings but also building an underground network and engaging in intensive study of revolutionary history and theory. (Joining Weather in the mid-1970s, Suzanne Ross said she never read as much as in the five years when she was underground.)[70] The group was now clear in the propagandistic quality of its actions. Its actions were explicitly aimed at supporting the aboveground organizing, showing the Left that it was possible to build an underground and successfully elude the state, and expanding the range of what constituted dissent.

The organization succeeded with armed propaganda because, as Naomi Jaffe puts it, "we always were focused on targets that were participants in repression." The organization concentrated all its efforts against a great bully that had once seemed untouchable. For that reason, Scott Braley says the Weather Underground served mainly as a "retaliatory capacity." In going underground, the group opened up a new site from which to respond to the crimes of the state. By attacking the halls of power, the group was attempting to retaliate while also pushing people to connect the particular issue to the broader system of imperialism. It wanted to bring under public scrutiny those institutions that were so often able to function in relative obscurity.

In an article critically reflecting on the Weather Underground, Gilbert identified five key aspects of the organization's program:

1. Draw off some of the repressive heat concentrated on Black, Native and Latino movements,
2. Create a leading political example of white solidarity with national liberation,
3. Educate about key political issues,
4. Identify the institutions most responsible for oppression, and
5. Encourage others to intensify activism despite state repression.[71]

In short, the organization engaged in bombings and other acts of armed propaganda to, as Weather supporter-turned-member Suzanne Ross puts it, "highlight who the enemy is and the nature of the enemy."[72] The actions weren't important as a military challenge to imperialism—the Weather Underground had no illusion that it was going toe-to-toe with the U.S. government—but rather as part of building what Robert Roth calls a "culture of resistance." Building an underground and engaging in armed propaganda were broadening the contours of struggle, one of many ways in which white radicals had, in Roth's words, "moved into a militant confrontational stance with the government." This culture of resistance was important, Gilbert says, to counter the demoralization that state repression could engender. "It was very important to show that there were many ways to continue and advance the struggle."[73] Writing shortly after the Days of Rage, Andrew Kopkind defined Weather's politics by saying, "It isn't enough to march or leaflet in support of the Vietnamese or the Black Panthers; there has to be an active effort to pull the machinery of empire off their backs."[74] Weather recognized solidarity with Third World movements as the only way to build a liberating movement among whites. And now, here was the first anti-racist movement to voluntarily build a clandestine component since the Underground Railroad.[75]

And there was something else. Even before Weather's submersion, the group presciently observed that racism and white privilege were hallmarks of American life; to fight white supremacy necessitated a break from Americanism. And because America was steeped in—maybe even inseparable from—white supremacy, it was especially necessary for white people to break from it, because it was an ideology and an ethos designed precisely for them. At a press conference after the Hampton-Clark murders, the not-yet-underground Weather leader Bernardine Dohrn said: "the notion that we're outlaws has got to be put together with the fact that America created us."[76] In other words, unlike the Black militants, the Puerto Rican radicals, and other Third World insurgents who rebelled because the United States was trying to destroy them as a people, Weather was America's favorite child gone astray and turned rebel, the embodiment of everything good whites fear. It was Made in the USA and yet attempted to break from all the privileges and domination that label carried with it. The group's existence was a warning: white skin and U.S. citizenship could no longer buy complicity with white supremacy. Not one for subtlety, Weather displayed its anti-imperialism as a badge, telling the ruling class to "guard your children," lest they be corrupted by the Weather bogeyman.[77] Speaking more broadly than just about Weatherman, Daniel Berrigan likened the white anti-racist underground to being "kicked out of America," offering the opportunity to "join...those who have never been inside at all, the Blacks and the Puerto Ricans and the Chicanos."[78]

If people of color were the despised targets of a racist America, the Weather Underground was made up of its darling children. Its members were largely college graduates, some with advanced degrees, from elite institutions like Brandeis, Columbia, and Swarthmore, and often on their way toward careers as doctors, lawyers, academics, and other professionals. But they seemingly rejected all the comforts being white and middle class afforded them to help build an anti-racist movement, to work fulltime for the revolution. As the first communiqué explained, "The parents of 'privileged' kids have been saying for years that the revolution was a game for us. But the war and racism of this society show that it is too fucked up. We will never live peaceably under this system."[79] Even in its less eloquent moments—such as when early Weatherman ideologue John Jacobs said in Flint that the group was "the incubation of your mother's nightmare"—Weather dedicated itself to shattering white American allegiance with anti-Black and Third World oppression.[80] All bets were off. "We have learned that to be honest we must live outside the law, to be free we must fight," a later communiqué proclaimed.[81] In his letter to the group, Berrigan also underscored this point, noting that "your lives could have been posh and secure; but you said no. And you said it by attacking the very properties you were supposed to have inherited and expanded—an amazing kind of turnabout."[82]

It was political theater, performed amidst a real battle for hearts and minds of American youth. And it worked, at least on a certain level. "It freaked out the ruling class that so many white kids were alienated by what empire had to offer," Donna Willmott says. "I think it was a real threat to them, both by the mass-based antiwar movement but also the number of people who did not identify with what this government was about.... I do think we were somewhat of a threat politically—and could have been more of one."

This *political* threat to white supremacy—not physical damage to government or corporate buildings—is the central tenet of what the Weather Underground means. White activists, mainly from the middle class, rejected what most people of color were never offered, at least not in as meaningful a way. The refusal of white people to embrace the system was significant because it tied their hopes and aspirations to the oppressed world majority rather than to the oppressor minority. The organization grounded its strategic decisions in the issues facing most people of the world, rather than white North American people alone—a pivotal difference from most white-led social movements in this country.

If causing only relatively minor material damage, Weather's actions were of tremendous importance on a symbolic level. Indeed, the symbolic resonance of Weather's actions led Jeff Jones to call the bombings themselves a form of media—not done *for* media attention, but actions that themselves communicated a message. No matter how fiery the rhetoric, the group's actions largely fell in the realm of militant political theater, dramatizing its attempted break from the spoils of white supremacy and empire. "The world knows that even the white youth of Babylon will resort to force to bring down imperialism," the group announced in "New Morning."[83]

Bombings also pierced the myth of government invincibility—one of Weather's most important accomplishments, some former members argue.[84] In disrupting the smooth functioning of U.S. imperialism, in exposing the malfeasance of power, the Weather Underground's actions showed that the government could be opposed at many different levels. Bombings were about dramatizing and humanizing revolutionary politics, about exacting a political cost for state or corporate terror, about challenging the institutions responsible for oppression. With bombs and with words the Weather Underground was taking on the most powerful country the world has ever seen.

It was, former members still argue, the least they could do.

A police station after unknown radicals
attacked it in the early 1970s.

When you're underground, you can't go around saying, "I'm your local representative from the Weather Underground. Let's discuss politics." And you can't be in Left centers where certain issues are being discussed. So that was a limitation.

But on the other hand, we went more into communities that weren't Left communities, whether it was youth communities or working class communities or whatever. And we got to get more of the pulse of what a range of people were thinking. So it had that benefit.

—David Gilbert[1]

WEATHERMAN WAS NOW THE WEATHER UNDERground: less sexist, more serious. Having defined itself—its goals and its limits—in relation to violence, through armed propaganda, the group went forward in the task of building a nationwide clandestine movement. "We spent a lot of time and energy trying to invent a way to live, a way to have jobs and yet be flexible, live in communes, stay politically connected," Dohrn says of the years following the townhouse blast. Thus the group spent considerable time and effort building the organization's infrastructure—from IDs to safe houses to money and other vital issues. The organization also cultivated more of a base of support, in both youth culture communities and the Left.

But first there were fences to mend. "We started to go around and make amends to a lot of people with whom we had split in utterly sectarian and unnecessary ways," Dohrn says. "A lot of that middle period included going back to people and talking over and listening to what had happened by cutting people out, by accusations, by charges against people, and taking seriously the need to repair the harm for which we were responsible.

Sometimes those flowered into ongoing relationships of support and political unity. And sometimes they were just attending to accountability.... It wasn't just a few us doing it. All of us did it in our lives with former friends and comrades."

As a result of this making of amends, the group was able to build an underground that guarded clandestine members without severing the organization completely from the mass movement. Although the Weather Underground was never more than a few dozen active members, there was a large ocean of supporters and colleagues in which the guerrillas swam. Living mostly in collectives dispersed on either coast, Weather Underground members built enough of a buffer between them and the police to allow them to do their work and live their lives without being in constant peril.[2] There were no guarantees, of course, but the group was careful and cautious enough to ensure its safety as well as that of others.

It is, of course, a lot easier to hurt people with a bomb than it is to avoid injury. But after the townhouse blast, the Weather Underground was intractable on this point. How did the group ensure people's safety? It first chose a target on political grounds, a symbol or institution representing state violence domestically or an increase in U.S. aggression overseas. From there, it was a question of accessibility: which buildings could be gotten to? When? How? This part of the process included "casing" a building at the time the bomb would go off (usually around 2 or 3 a.m.) to make sure that there were no overnight workers. (The importance of such reconnaissance was brought home in August 1970, when an underground group called the New Year's Gang inadvertently killed a graduate student when it bombed an Army research institute at the University of Wisconsin.)[3] Of course, the early morning is an odd time for people in their late 20s to be sitting outside police stations, corporate headquarters, and government buildings, so extra care was needed. People also needed to go inside the building during business hours to get a lay of the structure and find an accessible spot to place the bomb.

Once a location was chosen, a bomb with a safety device and timer would be placed inside the building, usually in a duct in a bathroom. Then, calls went out to police and media; the latter being called not just to get coverage but as an extra precaution to ensure that the building would be evacuated.[4] Whoever was making the phone call had only a short time to do all this, given the state's ability to trace phone calls. Sometimes the group was able to set its own timeline for this process; other times, however,

Weather was responding to a particularly egregious act and needed to move quickly. Regardless of the timeframe, such safety precautions were a constant feature.

Learning how to do all of this, how to live underground and engage in illegal actions, took serious work. While some people may have had personal experience with some aspects of clandestinity—procuring false IDs, for instance—the main lessons came from research. Robert Roth remembers a whole "cottage industry" of materials on the ins and outs of fugitive life. Abbie Hoffman's *Steal This Book* was a guide to guerrilla living, including directions on everything from stealing food to bomb making. Régis Debray's *Revolution in the Revolution?* presented strategies for armed struggle, as did the writings of Che Guevara, Brazil's Carlos Marighella, and other proponents of clandestinity. Even the U.S. government provided instruction; one clandestine militant told of gleaning useful information from the "several manuals published by the U.S. Army on sabotage, [and] on construction of bombs."[5] And, of course, angry veterans were returning to this country, and some helped militarily train activists or went underground themselves.[6]

Class background and access to resources also affected the ability to carry out actions. Although some would deride the Weather Underground as a bunch of spoiled rich kids, their class background was solidly middle class, with a few members from working class backgrounds and a few from wealthy families. Dismissing the entire organization as wealthy both inflates the class status of many in the group and renders invisible the working class members of the group. It further presents a false dichotomy between the Weather Underground and other white Leftists of the period, who generally came from similar backgrounds. The organization presented no deviation from the average class background of most other post-SDS formations in the white Left.[7]

Whatever their individual background, Weatherpeople once underground were, as Jeremy Varon notes in his book on the group, "nearly broke and lived in Spartan dwellings on a diet of noodles and other simple foods." To get by, they "begged or borrowed money from friends and family (though some held jobs, turning their income over to the group)."[8] On special occasions—to celebrate a successful action, for instance—members would go out to a decent restaurant.[9] Otherwise, they lived as cheaply as possible. Collectives often lived together in the same house, cutting down on expenses and making it easier to coordinate the group's political work (such as study groups, writing, and building the underground).

But in the panoply of clandestine groups, the Weather Underground was still among the more privileged. In fact, privilege was its *raison d'etre*—the group set out to use its privilege in service of revolutionary change. Not surprisingly, such privilege also affected how the group operated. It didn't have to turn to bank robberies ("expropriations") for money as some others did. Early on, in the transition underground, the group carried out a few armed robberies but quickly abandoned the idea as dangerous and, given its access to other resources, unnecessary.[10] In addition to material support from aboveground allies, some Weatherpeople used money they had from their families. David Gilbert, for instance, cashed in his Israel bonds before going underground—fitting, since the organization claimed solidarity with the Palestinian struggle. Half of the cash he received went to Weather, the other half to the Black Panther bail fund.[11]

On a day-to-day level, the group received money from the Left. The ties the group maintained (or re-established, following the townhouse explosion) with the Left proved valuable in funding the Weather Underground with both small and large donations. Collectives nurtured their own connections for money, and the central organization chipped in when necessary to ensure that collectives could pay the bills and get by. Although some members of the organization worked or even went to school while living underground, this was usually dependent on people's own desire. Living cheaply and with a broad base of support, the Weather Underground carried out its political work while eluding capture. And the government was none too happy.

UNDERGROUND, UNDER INVESTIGATION, UNDER ATTACK:
GOVERNMENT ATTEMPTS TO BREAK THE WEATHER UNDERGROUND

BEGINNING IN 1969, the state showered Weatherman/SDS with indictments for inciting to riot, conspiracy, and mob action against the state. When Weather went underground, such criminal charges were useless unless the fugitives could be found. The placing of Bernardine Dohrn and others on the FBI's Ten Most Wanted list only enhanced the group's "outlaw" glamour. Police were unable to find America's white urban guerrillas, and hippies and activists alike demurred at police questioning.

Then in December 1970, a member of the group was recognized in New York City and arrested on charges stemming from the Days of Rage.

Still learning the art of forging IDs, the group had neglected to observe certain safeguards; Weather's ID system was compromised because there was enough of a paper trail between the identification the captured Weatherwoman had on her at the time and other IDs the group was using. It wasn't a direct connection, but it provided the state with an entry point into the clandestine network.

Soon there were indicators, some more direct than others, that the FBI was starting to close in. David Gilbert's first inkling that something might be wrong came when two men in suits, claiming to be real estate agents, approached him and a fellow Weather member as they were fixing one of the group's cars in the spring of 1971. The "suits" asked a few questions and left suspiciously enough, convincing Gilbert and his friend that they were definitely agents, but not the kind that sells real estate. In retrospect, it seems that Gilbert and his comrade were spared arrest because the FBI was still trying to draw a net around the group (specifically its leadership body), and busting these two would have blown the FBI's cover before it could make a substantial dent in the organization, as had happened with the Donghi-Evans busts in April 1970. Whatever the FBI's intentions, Gilbert was convinced that there was cause for alarm.

After several meetings, Gilbert's collective decided not to abandon its San Francisco apartment, even though it could possibly be traced through the ID link. Resources were scarce, and it wasn't yet certain that the location was "blown." Abandoning the home base would be costly, and other members weren't yet persuaded that police were on their tail. They were learning how to live in clandestinity, and perhaps their fears were an over-reaction. Gilbert remembers being unconvinced. The COINTELPRO-initiated split between Black Panther leaders Eldridge Cleaver and Huey Newton was underway (and being publicly broadcast) at the time, and he remembers thinking how damaging it would be for movement morale if the Panthers split and the Weather Underground was busted at the same time.[12]

A few days later, the other shoe dropped. Weather leaders Bernardine Dohrn and Jeff Jones went to a Western Union office to pick up money from supporters in the East. Three suspicious people, two whites and one Asian, lurked inside the office. Unlike everyone else in the office, these three weren't standing in line, which made them seem suspicious. Dohrn spotted another checking out the license plate of the car she was driving. Trying not to appear suspicious or give in to what could be spurious paranoia, Jones picked up the money as casually as possible. But his experience combined with Dohrn's perceptions convinced the pair to not wait around and see if their fears were justified. They peeled out from in front of the Western Union office, noticing that a black car across the street did an immediate U-turn to get behind them. After a short car chase through the streets of San Francisco, Dohrn and Jones lost their tail.

Still thinking that they were perhaps being needlessly paranoid, they loaned the car that night to some aboveground friends—who were soon surrounded by a phalanx of police and G-men who interrogated them, bugged the car, and let them go.[13] At 2 a.m., one of them called the Pine Street apartment where Gilbert and others were staying. (The collective had recently decided to get a phone.)[14] Everyone in the apartment, including Gilbert, immediately fled—"with just the clothes on our back," he remembers. The group sent an aboveground friend to check out the apartment at 6 a.m. that morning. The person found the place swarming with police and FBI agents. Weather "ended up having to leave that city completely at that period of time," Gilbert says.[15] Given how close the FBI had come, the Weather Underground would later call the affair "the encirclement."

The Bay Area was no longer safe, at least for the time being; the FBI had broken their ID system, rendering the entire clandestine infrastructure in that area vulnerable to attack. They had lost a car, an apartment—and who knew how many IDs were compromised? The Weather collective immediately left San Francisco, heading north, frustrated but trying to keep things in perspective. Gilbert remembers the group "holed up in a motel near Portland on a rainy night with our whole infrastructure gone, and as we're watching TV, Bernardine exclaims, 'After the revolution there won't be any commercials.'" It would take more than a year to rebuild the West coast infrastructure of the Weather Underground, and years before there was another Weather bombing on the West coast.

The narrow escape was due less to underground skills or harrowing Hollywood tricks than to the political context and the support the Weather Underground had. "While quick wits and fast maneuvers provide the most dramatic story," Gilbert says, "the basic reason for our escape was the anti-state political consciousness that prevailed in youth culture, which meant that information did not flow to the state but flowed to us." he says. Even people who weren't directly aware of or in contact with the Weather Underground tended to resist police questioning and spread the word when the FBI was around. That support, Gilbert says, is what thwarted the encirclement.[16]

The encirclement happened because the FBI had been working diligently and methodically on tracking the group since its members disappeared in 1970. Efforts to find the Weather Underground led to a host of dirty tricks against those in and around the militant white Left, including family and friends of Weather Underground members. While the Black, Latino/a, and indigenous liberation movements received the bulk of state repression, the Weather Underground and its "periphery" were particularly of interest to the bureau. "Obviously they didn't murder people to get us, and that's everything about white privilege," Dohrn says. "But they did have a white version of their strategies to harass, [use] dirty tricks, plant false information to link us to international terrorists."

How much the government had invested into destroying the Left became known in March 1971. A clandestine group calling itself "The Citizen's Commission to Investigate the FBI" broke into the Media, Pennsylvania, office of the FBI in March 1971, and exposed the existence of COINTELPRO through the release of secret files, first to the radical press, ultimately picked up by the mainstream media. Public scrutiny focused on the FBI as a result, just as the leak of the Pentagon Papers that June by Daniel Ellsberg fixed attention on the government's longstanding duplicity in the Vietnam War.[17]

But in his paranoid zeal to crush his opponents, Richard Nixon didn't know when to quit; instead, he stretched himself too thin. The "Plumbers," Nixon's cabal of thugs famous for the Watergate break-in, also carried out many of the acts against associates and relatives of the Weather Underground.[18] COINTELPRO was said to have stopped after the 1971 break-in at the Pennsylvania office, but experience showed otherwise. In 2005, ninety-one-year-old Mark Felt revealed that he was "Deep Throat," the famed insider who provided *Washington Post* reporter Bob Woodward with the dirt on Nixon's domestic crimes. In 1972, however, Felt was the deputy associate director of the FBI, the number-two man at the agency. In addition to harassing groups such as the Arab Information Center, Felt personally oversaw and ordered surveillance, break-ins ("black bag jobs," in FBI parlance), and other forms of harassment against the friends and families of Weather fugitives.[19]

The state's tactics against the Weather Underground included unauthorized wiretaps of more than 12,000 separate conversations by 1973

---

alone; grand juries convened in eight cities "to gather evidence and launder illegally obtained evidence"; physically assaulting "relatives, friends, and acquaintances of Weathermen to gain information against us through intimidation"; home and office burglaries of those associated with the group (including attorneys); burglaries of institutions (e.g., universities) where Weather members had once been; and intercepting and opening mail to and from friends and family.[20] In 1972, for instance, an ex-member had her apartment broken into three times, her phone tapped, her activities monitored, and her mail opened and read.[21] Other attempts to catch the group included monetary rewards—as high as $100,000—for anyone who turned them in, and the attempted infiltration of the underground.[22] The FBI even concocted a plan (never carried out) to kidnap Bernardine Dohrn's infant nephew as a way of getting her to surrender.[23]

None of these tactics proved particularly effective—the underground thrived and few people cooperated with the police. To mask the full extent of the dirty tricks—and because the FBI likely worked in concert with agencies barred from domestic spying (such as the CIA)—the state decided it was easier to drop the charges against many of the Weather Underground fugitives.[24] The Detroit indictments against Weather activists were dropped in October 1973, and the Chicago indictments were dropped three months later.[25] Bernardine Dohrn was removed from the Most Wanted List—and yet, people stayed underground.

Grand juries were a particularly important tactic against the Left. Convened by Guy Goodwin, Nixon's man in the Justice Department, more than 100 grand juries returned more than 400 indictments against a spate of movement groups in the early to mid-1970s.[26] Associates of the Weather Underground were targeted by grand juries in California, New York, Ohio, Vermont, and Washington.[27] "They themselves decided...that the strategy of trying to find people [by] knocking on doors was a total failure because of massive opposition to the Nixon administration and due to a campaign to not cooperate with police or FBI," Dohrn says of the state's attempts to find fugitives. But the grand juries would also fail, due to popular resistance against them.

Held in closed, secret sessions to determine if there is enough information for an indictment, grand juries are "fishing expeditions" whereby friends, family, and associates are subpoenaed and compelled to answer any question asked of them. Prosecutors are free to ask about friends, family, acquaintances, habits, whereabouts, or beliefs—and those who refuse to cooperate can be jailed for contempt of court for up to eighteen months. There are no rules of evidence; those subpoenaed are not allowed an attorney at their table, nor does a judge preside over the hearing. Spectators are traditionally barred from the proceedings.[28]

Having come so close to catching members of the Weather Underground in San Francisco in 1971, the FBI and the Justice Department weren't ready to give up on the Bay Area. Starting in 1972, a grand jury was impaneled in San Francisco that would subpoena more than a dozen activists from the area—including one ex-member, Lyndon Comstock, whose 1969 draft card the FBI claimed to have found in Weather's Pine Street safe house. Comstock hadn't been associated with the group or any of its members since early 1970, and he had never been to the Pine Street house. Perhaps Weather's "pack-rat mentality" of holding onto IDs was to blame, or perhaps the FBI concocted the story. Either way, Comstock now found himself subpoenaed.

Of the seventeen subpoenaed, only Comstock and Clayton Van Lydegraf, a former member of the Communist Party, had ever been associated with the Weather Underground. Although Comstock had briefly met Van Lydegraf before, none of those subpoenaed knew each other. Still, Comstock remembers, "all of us were quite clear that this grand jury was about applying political pressure." They also bristled at the anti-democratic nature of the proceedings, which compelled people to testify: anyone taking the Fifth Amendment before a grand jury can be given immunity from prosecution; once granted immunity, people *must* testify or risk going to jail for contempt of court. When the grand jury was announced, all seventeen defiantly refused to cooperate.

The National Lawyers Guild, an activist association of legal professionals and students (which also happened to have a Grand Jury Defense Committee) put together a legal team of a dozen people to defend the activists and try to get the subpoenas quashed. They fought the grand jury in the courtroom and in the court of public opinion, using the media, demonstrations, and literature to build public sympathy while the lawyers worked the legal angle. If nothing else, Comstock says, these efforts slowed the grand jury process down, which worked to their advantage as 1972 became 1973 and the rank corruption of the Nixon administration became known, threatening to unravel his presidency.

When the lawyers were unable to get the subpoenas thrown out, individuals were called one by one to testify. At that point, Comstock says, those subpoenaed "made a very strong effort…to appeal, over the head of the prosecutor, directly to the grand jury members to take control of the process during the time that we were in the room with them." When Comstock was called, he told the jurors (not the prosecutor) why he was refusing to cooperate, telling them that the jurors were supposed to head the proceedings and not just bend to the will of the prosecutor. Still on probation from the Days of Rage, Comstock joined with the others in risking time in jail rather than cooperate with the FBI investigation. If held in contempt, any one of them could have been incarcerated for as long as the grand jury was in session—up to eighteen months.

"That was a heavy price to pay for simply taking a principled stand on non-cooperation, since I wasn't going to be providing any information anyway," he says. Ultimately, though, the principle won out; it was more important to stand firm in refusing to cooperate, even if they had no information to give. "Civil liberties are a hard-won and important defense against domineering and repressive governments, and we shouldn't give them up lightly," Comstock says. Eventually, a couple of people with no information to give did end up testifying, but only one of the resisters ended up with contempt charges, serving one month in jail. No indictments were issued by this grand jury as the Watergate scandal took the Justice Department, at least temporarily, away from its attempts to find the Weather Underground. Repressive grand juries would make a strong comeback in the 1980s, as the government attempted to track down a new crop of clandestine movements, and they are still in use today against some 1960s-era movement veterans and against sectors of the radical animal rights and environmental movements.[29]

EMERGING UNDERGROUND IN THE BLACK MOVEMENT

THE EXACT ORIGINS of the Black Liberation Army (BLA) are purposefully shadowy, but the group was shaped predominantly by members of the Panther 21 conspiracy case, even though work on developing a Black underground predates their acquittal; indeed, some would argue that the BLA was a parallel development to the Black Panthers and not just an outgrowth of it.[30] Found innocent of all charges in the spring of 1971, several members of the Panther 21 went underground, convinced by experience that the government intended to crush radical aboveground organizing in Black communities. (Some of their comrades were already underground, having escaped arrest in 1969.) The move underground was also a response to the bitter split in the Black Panther Party. Huey Newton, cofounder and ostensible head of the Party, based in Oakland, expelled many of the more militant East Coast Panthers who were suspected of being supporters of Eldridge Cleaver, then in exile in Algeria. These members would form the heart and soul of the Black Liberation Army, while the Oakland Panther office pursued an electoral strategy.[31]

The BLA's program included three components: retaliation against police violence in Black communities; elimination of drugs and drug dealers from Black communities; and helping captured BLA members escape from prison. Coming mostly from poor and working class backgrounds, the BLA resorted to bank expropriations (robberies for political ends) to fund its armed work.[32] The BLA was an attempt to carry on the Panthers' legacy underground—building an armed component as part of the war for Black self-determination and national liberation. As a mid-1970s statement put it, the BLA was a necessary supplement to aboveground organizing. In "creating the apparatus of revolutionary violence...to weaken the enemy capitalist state," the BLA described its goal as working toward "a national Black Liberation Front composed of many progressive, revolutionary, and nationalist groupings."[33]

Like other clandestine groups of this period, the BLA was not contending for state power. The three components of its program came from a desire to promote revolutionary Black Nationalism and exact a material cost from the state for its continued repression of Black people—as one former member put it, "to prove that we could fight back."[34] Given the heightened levels of repression against the Black movement, combined with the history and daily experience of white supremacy, the BLA's strategy differed from that of the Weather Underground. The BLA had no compunctions against injuring the armed enforcers of the state (such as police), because of the murderous repression that had forced them under in the first place. Still, the group's mission was thoroughly political, and it avoided harming civilians. For BLA soldier Ashanti Alston, "our history in this country—Black people, indigenous folks in this country, the history of what this country has done to Puerto Ricans, Hawaiians, Mexicans and others—shows that our fight back is always going to take different forms."

Despite the tactical differences between the Black Liberation Army and the Weather Underground, the two groups supported each other's existence. Alston remembers the Weather Underground as one of the few groups in the white Left that supported the BLA's right to tactical self-definition and political self-determination. In a communiqué, Weather urged people to support the BLA as one of many righteous expressions of Black anger at racism.[35] And the Weather Underground crafted its own response to racism.

RESPONDING TO STATE VIOLENCE

WITH THE INVASION of Cambodia in the spring of 1970, Nixon had betrayed his promise to end the war in Vietnam. But he thought he had at least figured out a way to placate the American public through "Vietnamization," whereby the major onus for the war would be shifted to the South Vietnamese Army (ARVN). The United States would still supply the ARVN with weapons, training, and funding—but the South Vietnamese would fight America's war, thus limiting troop count overseas and reducing the number of dead Americans.[36] Vietnamization also let Nixon make an end run around the 1970 congressional amendment banning U.S. troops from entering Cambodia or Laos. Without wasting any time, Nixon put Vietnamization to work and invaded Laos on February 8, 1971, ostensibly to destroy the National Liberation Front's rear base.[37]

And without wasting any time, the Weather Underground bombed the U.S. Capitol on February 28.

Weather's bombing was a particularly audacious expression of the widespread protests against the Laos invasion (which was a resounding failure, complete with heavy casualties and a hasty retreat).[38] According to Ron Jacobs, Weather's first action since its Fall Offensive "confronted the lie put forth by Nixon and many Congress members that the Vietnamization of the war meant peace."[39] The Weather Underground declared that it "attacked the Capitol because it is, along with the White House and the Pentagon, the worldwide symbol of the government which is now attacking Indochina. To millions of people here and in Latin America, Africa and Asia, it is a monument to U.S. domination over the planet."[40] The communiqué went on to detail the ferocity and frequency of the U.S. bombings in Laos, and presciently denounced the use of defoliants (Agent Orange) as a "war against the future."

A subsequent communiqué identified three reasons for the Capitol bombing: "to express our love and solidarity with the nonwhite people of the world who always happen to be the victims of 200 years of U.S. technological warfare"; "to freak out the warmongers and remind them that they have created guerrillas here"; and "to bring a smile and a wink to the kids and people here who hate this government."[41] During the Mayday antiwar protests in D.C., at which more than 12,000 people were arrested, some of the protestors said of the Capitol bombing: "We didn't do it, but we dug it."[42] One Yippie demonstrator said that the Weather Underground bombed the Capitol "to bring joy into the world."[43] The group also received what it took to be a compliment, when President Nixon himself went on national television and denounced the bombing as "the most dastardly act in American history."[44]

The Capitol bombing communiqué modeled the best of the Weather Underground: staunchly supporting people's struggles, promoting unity among their allies, focusing attention on those responsible for devastation, and exhibiting the hope central to any revolutionary movement. "Together there comes great power," the communiqué stated. "The combined strength of armed underground attacks, propaganda, demonstrations in the cities and campuses, actions by local collectives, all forms of organizing and political warfare can wreck the Amerikan warmachine. Everything we do makes a difference.... People all over the world are encouraged by what we do here in the heart of Empire." The group was exposing "the arrogance of the white man" and having a good time at it. Countering the administration's claims that the antiwar movement was in decline, the communiqué closed with a warning: "Nixon will see that what he took for acquiescence was really the calm before the storm."[45]

The storm arguably materialized in May 1972. In response to an offensive by the National Liberation Front, Nixon initiated massive bombings in both North and South Vietnam. He also ordered the mining of North Vietnamese harbors, and the bombing of ports and dikes. In response, the Weather Underground bombed the Pentagon on May 19. The bombing temporarily knocked out Pentagon computers and caused "tens of thousands of dollars in damage."[46] More than the economic damage, however, the bombing showed that even the Pentagon could be attacked. It was, one aboveground supporter said, "a great accomplishment."[47]

On August 21, 1971—almost exactly a year after his brother's daring action ended in bloody mayhem—George Jackson was murdered by guards at San Quentin during an alleged escape attempt. Many believed that the murder was the culmination of state efforts to silence the Black leader. "George was a symbol of the will of all of us behind bars, and of that strength which oppressed people always seem to be able to pull together," Angela Davis wrote of her friend and comrade.[48] Nine days after the murder—and hours before Jackson's funeral—the Weather Underground simultaneously bombed the California State Department of Corrections offices in San Francisco and in Sacramento.[49] (A third bombing that night targeted a prison office in San Mateo, California, also in response to Jackson's murder, though it was not carried out by the Weather Underground.)[50]

Interspersed with quotes from Jackson's writings, the Weather communiqué articulated the need for a white anti-racist movement to take pressure off Third World movements—and the terrible cost of not doing so. "Mass actions outside the Tombs [detention center in New York] last year might have prevented the murder of two Puerto Rican prisoners a week after the rebellions. If [Illinois state attorney] Edward Hanrahan had been dealt with for the murder of Fred Hampton, [associate warden] James Parks might have thought twice before participating in the murder of George Jackson.... White people on the outside have a deep responsibility to enter the battle at every level. Each of us can turn our grief into the righteous anger and our anger into action."[51]

The killing of Jackson also sparked a silent protest at a medieval prison far across the country, in rural western New York. More than 800 prisoners at Attica Correctional Facility held a silent protest wearing makeshift black armbands and refusing to eat breakfast the day after Jackson's murder. The protest was organized in part by Sam Melville, a white political prisoner incarcerated for a string of Weather-type political bombings against government and corporate property.[52] The Attica protest frightened the prison authorities, who feared any kind of organizing behind the walls. Their fears multiplied when prisoners began to seek redress for grievances, including racist and religious persecution by the white, rural, Christian guards of the largely urban Black and Latino prisoners, including several who had converted to Islam. Prison authorities responded to the organizing with cell searches and increased harassment.

On September 9, prisoners seized the prison's D yard following a scuffle with guards.[53] Prisoner leaders quickly moved to turn an inchoate uprising into a strategic and very political rebellion. To forestall the immediate retaliation and retaking of the prison by the police, the prisoners seized guards as hostages.

The Attica rebellion lasted for four days, involving 1,300 prisoners and modeling an interracial solidarity rare in the racially polarized world of prison. The prisoners' collective statement was a passionate declaration of self-determination and resistance:

> WE are MEN! We are not beasts and do not intend to be beaten or driven as such. The entire prison populace has set forth to change forever the ruthless brutalization and disregard for the lives of the prisoners here and throughout the United States. What has happened here is but the sound before the fury of those who are oppressed.
>
> We will not compromise on any terms except those that are agreeable to us. We call upon all the conscientious citizens of America to assist us in putting an end to this situation that threatens the lives of not only us [prisoners], but each and everyone of us [in society] as well.
>
> We have set forth demands that will bring closer to reality the demise of these prisons institutions that serve no useful purpose to the People of America, but to those who would enslave and exploit the people of America.[54]

The prisoners developed a list of fifteen "practical proposals" for prison reform. The demands included minimum wage for labor, the freedom to practice and congregate based on political or religious beliefs, better food and medical care, a grievance process, improved training for the guards, better visiting rules, and education and rehabilitation programs.[55] In addition to these calls for basic human rights, five additional demands were later added: amnesty from reprisals for participating in the uprising, transport to a friendly country (such as Cuba or Algeria), intervention by the federal government, prisoner participation in restructuring the prison, and a team of negotiators/observers. Of the additional demands, the government agreed to the negotiating team. This team included representatives of the Black Panthers, the Young Lords, government representatives, *New York Times* columnist Tom Wicker, and activist attorney William Kunstler.[56]

But the state was never serious about negotiating. After a four-day standoff, New York Governor Nelson Rockefeller—who from the beginning had refused to go to Attica—gave the nod. While a helicopter dropped tear gas over the D yard, more than 500 New York State Troopers opened fire from the walls with a nine-minute torrent from countless shotguns, sniper rifles, and automatic weapons. When the smoke cleared, they had killed thirty-nine men—twenty-nine prisoners and ten hostage guards. Some prisoners, such as Melville, were shot at close range and left to bleed to death.[57] Then it was time for revenge. Police made each prisoner strip, crawl through mud, and run naked through a gauntlet of clubs, gun butts, fists, and racial epithets. The leaders were singled out for special treatment. One of them, Wicker reports, "was made to lie [naked] on his back across a recreational table, and a football was placed under his chin. He was told that if the football fell he would be killed."[58] He was left in that position for more than three hours. He was also beaten, threatened with castration, and burned with cigarettes.

Scott Braley was driving on the highway when he heard on the radio that the state police had moved to retake the prison. "You could hear it in the background—this fusillade. It sounded like someone kicking off a dozen machine guns all at the same time," he remembers. "You just knew that people were dropping like flies. I pulled over to the side of the highway and burst into tears. It was so wrenching…. I just sat there and cried for a half an hour because it was so awful." The tragedy of Attica wasn't just the thirty-nine people who died when police retook the prison, in addition to the four people who died after the start of the rebellion and before the police assault. The tragedy was what the police action, carried out on order from Governor Rockefeller (soon to be named Vice President), represented about the United States. "All of us keep believing that maybe things aren't really as bad as we say they are," Braley says. "Maybe there will be a reformer [who will] come along. Maybe it isn't really *truly* innate, maybe it isn't systemic and unsalvageable. Then you find out that it isn't salvageable, that it's as brutal and horrible as you ever thought it was. That's hard to live with on a day-to-day basis and still have a life."

On September 17, the Weather Underground placed a bomb in the New York State Corrections Office in Albany, New York. The bomb went off after 7:30 p.m. on Friday evening, near the office of Russell Oswald, the Commissioner of Corrections who had long rebuffed the prisoners' human rights demands. The communiqué accompanying the action called the prison system "how a society run by white racists maintains its control," with white supremacy being the "main question white people have to face."[59]

The group's anger at racist police violence continued. When a police officer in Queens murdered a 10-year-old Black youth in the spring of 1973, the Weather Underground responded by bombing the 103rd Precinct of the New York Police Department. The communiqué noted that New York police "have already killed ten Third World people this year." The action was dedicated to "the families and communities of the dead and in solidarity with the living—those in prison, those who continue the struggle."[60]

This period also saw the Weather Underground responding to events abroad, and not just in Vietnam. On September 4, 1970, the people of Chile made what apparently proved to be a huge mistake: democratically electing a leftist president, Salvador Allende, without clearing it with the U.S. State Department. Three months earlier, Secretary of State Henry Kissinger had said, "I don't see why we need to stand by and watch a country go communist because of the irresponsibility of its own people."[61] No armchair counterrevolutionary, Kissinger helped correct the situation, first by embargo (starting after the election in 1970), then by isolation (including a propaganda assault), and finally by funding, arming, and training anti-Allende forces. The Chilean Right was also helped by U.S. corporations: copper companies Anaconda and Kennecott as well as International Telephone and Telegraph (ITT), which had invested $200 million in the country. Allende's plans for nationalizing key industries didn't bode well for these multinational corporations, which continued trying to destabilize or oust the Marxist president in favor of one willing to play ball. Allende was murdered on September 11, 1973, in a military coup that installed General Augusto Pinochet in power and launched a long reign of repression and state murder—ultimately leaving 300,000 dead.[62]

On September 28, 1973, the Weather Underground bombed ITT headquarters in New York City, "in support of the people of Chile." The communiqué indicted ITT and the U.S. government for subverting Allende's Chile and supporting and supplying weapons to the Chilean police and military. The ITT bombing was Weather's first major attack on a corporate rather than a government target. Given that ITT had long been funding and pushing for a coup—telling Kissinger's deputy in 1971 that "everything should be done quietly but effectively to see that Allende does not get through the crucial next six months"—the target was a logical one.[63] It also marked Weather's departure from an exclusive focus on targeting the state.

WOMEN IN THE LEAD

ALSO SIGNIFICANT FOR the Weather Underground in this period was a new emphasis on women. Kicking off this process was a document circulated in January 1973 suggesting ways to strengthen the organization. It was simply titled "on structure," and one of its major proposals was a women's caucus.[64] This idea was taken up shortly thereafter in a separate article, "Mountain Moving Day," which called for Weatherwomen to "autonomously take on the responsibility of developing a feminist politics and program." The article was the first of several attempts by women to push the organization in a more feminist direction.[65] Similar position papers circulated underground, as women began meeting together to chart a feminist course for the Weather Underground.

"Mountain Moving Day" is a fascinating and timely document that attempts to untangle the organization's inconsistent politics regarding women's liberation and to determine a new direction in light of the January 1973 cease-fire between the United States and Vietnam. With the war less pressing, Weatherwomen "should seize this chance and delve deeper into feminism, in study, organizing, writings, and actions," the paper asserted, noting that women's liberation should be at the heart of whatever the group decided to focus on next. The paper argued for the centrality of women's liberation both because of Weather's public weakness on feminism to date, and because "the liberation struggle of women is and will be one of the important, decisive ones" globally. In acknowledging that "anti-imperialism, anti-racism, [and] anti-sexism all intermingle but are not all the same," the paper argued for Weather's immersion in the women's movement, to push for internationalism and anti-racism in that sector while also learning and benefiting from what the women's liberation movement had to offer. Noting that feminism "has played a crucial role internally" for women, the paper pushed the organization to take a more public pro-feminist stance. It was an uphill battle, the statement acknowledged, because much of the women's movement felt at odds with the Weather Underground.

"Mountain Moving Day" resulted in a feminist initiative within the organization, which revolved around three goals: "1. to encourage solidarity among women, to make work among women a priority (geographically, structurally, programmatically) 2. to develop a women's program, for and about women; to actively participate in building the women's movement 3. to recognize the need for solidarity among men."[66] Criticisms women raised while the organization was falling apart and afterward suggest that these policies were never consistently applied. And the principles say nothing directly about the biggest obstacle to women's liberation: male supremacy, and how the organization as a whole could fight it.[67]

Still, the impact of the article was significant, if only for women in the group. Six months after this historic document, women in the organization initiated a summer project—a six-week study group by women underground, with some key aboveground supporters, focusing on women's oppression and its relationship to anti-imperialist politics. A particular focus of this group was the Department of Health, Education, and Welfare, or HEW—which women in the group called "the major government vehicle of social control of women," comparing it to the Bureau of Indian Affairs. Meeting twice a week, this summer study session continued the efforts begun in "Mountain Moving Day" to grapple with the correlations between race, class, and gender in U.S. politics—and suggest better ways for the Weather Underground to respond to what sociologists and feminists have since called the "intersections of oppression."[68]

The women who convened the study distributed a packet entitled "Six Sisters," explaining their motivations, their wide-ranging reading list, meeting notes, and plans for action. In it, the authors tell how the lack of attention the group paid to women up to that point made them feel anxious going into the summer. But once the study group began, women wrote later, "the synthesis of sexism with our previous understandings of imperialism and racism was natural and easy."[69] Weatherwomen started to bond over common experiences and shared commitments in a way that had largely eluded them to date. Solidarity was engendered, and some began living in all-women collectives.

"Mountain Moving Day" and "Six Sisters" were efforts to solidify an emerging revolutionary perspective. The "youth nation" politics of the "New Morning" statement were being replaced with a more conscious and thorough Marxist-Leninist outlook, to which it was hoped a lasting commitment to women's liberation would be added. Throughout these documents and others, women in the organization rejected separatism, even as they pushed for greater autonomy within the organization. Separatism, they said, divided women from the world situation, whereas autonomy afforded women the space to organize with and foster solidarity among other women while still locating feminism "in a world wide context."

The public was first made aware of these scholarly efforts in the first week of March 1974, when the Women's Brigade of the Weather Underground bombed the San Francisco HEW office in honor of International Women's Day (March 8) and in remembrance of Diana Oughton, Ted Gold, and Terry Robbins. This action was the third (and final) bombing carried out by the all-women unit, which had abandoned the "Proud Eagle" name. Their accompanying communiqué argued that women's liberation required decent schools, healthcare, adequate food, and childcare—and that such demands could not be fulfilled without a socialist revolution. Poor women of color were particularly hard-hit by government policy regarding women, the communiqué said, noting that reactionary policy makers such as Richard Nixon, Ronald Reagan, and Casper Weinberger held the reins over poor women's lives.[70] After the HEW action, women in the Weather Underground continued to meet periodically. In reflecting on women's organizational status more than thirty years later, however, ex-Weatherwomen note that there was some solidarity among women but little else in the way of feminist politics. Men tended to be more shielded from criticism and often didn't embrace women's liberation as integral to revolutionary politics, and the organization never adopted a feminist program.[71]

Although the women's brigade hadn't done an action between 1971 and 1974, women of the Weather Underground had been vocal eight months prior to the HEW bombing. This time, they were publicly responding to the "fighting words" of a fellow fugitive.

Jane Alpert had been part of an earlier (non-Weather) armed undergound collective led by her partner, Sam Melville. The group carried out a string of bombings against military and corporate targets, most famously the 1969 bombing and temporary disabling of the Whitehall Induction Center in New York City. The group was infiltrated by an FBI agent, and Melville, Alpert, and one other were arrested on November 12.[72] Another alleged conspirator eluded capture altogether, and Alpert jumped bail and went underground shortly before being sentenced. When Melville was murdered in the state's retaking of the Attica prison in 1971, Alpert wrote (from underground) the forward to his posthumous book, *Letters From Attica*, eloquently describing Melville's manipulative and sexist behavior alongside his anti-racist commitment; it was a nuanced character portrait of a complex person, detailing what she saw as Sam's strengths and his weaknesses.[73]

By 1973, however, Alpert had grown tired of the underground and felt drawn more to a separatist, biologically deterministic section of the women's movement hostile to the Left and anything mixed-gendered. She wrote an open letter called "Mother Right" and addressed to the women of the Weather Underground, which was published in the feminist journal *off our backs* in May of that year and shortly thereafter published in *Ms.* magazine. In it, Alpert denounced the Left, her own political history, and the Weather Underground. Individual men were responsible for women's oppression, Alpert wrote; the state and capitalism were irrelevant, and women in mixed-gender groups were misguided at best, cooperating in their own demise at worst. In discussing Weather, Alpert particularly called out Mark Rudd, a founding Weatherman who was no longer a part of the group. She and Rudd had met underground in New Mexico, and Alpert vilified him as the embodiment of patriarchy not only in the Weather Underground but in the mixed-gender Left as a whole. But Alpert reserved special vitriol for her one-time partner, Melville. "I will mourn the loss of 42 [*sic*] male supremacists no longer," she wrote of the dead at Attica. (The total death toll from the rebellion was forty-three).[74]

"Mother Right" was the retrograde version of feminism that Weather had tarred the entire women's liberation movement with in its early months. It focused narrowly on white self-interest, calling feminism a "religious transformation," and urging Weatherwomen to "leave the dying left."[75] Yet the response to Alpert proved difficult for the Weather Underground. Although Weatherwomen had attempted to structure feminism into the organization, the women weren't all of the same opinion, nor had the group established a collective position. For Naomi Jaffe, the fact that Alpert addressed the letter *to women* in the Weather Underground necessitated a strong response *as women* anti-imperialists. She was to be disappointed.

The group's response to Alpert was delayed, and the final product, after much internal back-and-forth, failed to make an anti-imperialist *and thoroughly feminist* answer to her biologically deterministic and separatist arguments. The July letter vacillated, both criticizing Alpert for revealing information about fugitives, and praising her (falsely, it would seem), for spurring the organization to confront its own stance on women's liberation. Addressed to the women's movement, the lengthy Weather communiqué offered self-criticism of Weather's early practice regarding the women's movement and gave tribute to the Black movement in defining the enemy. But it was defensive and didn't offer a way forward or commit the organization to specific change.[76] The group's lack of cohesion on the place of feminism within an anti-imperialist political framework led to what was, in Jaffe's view, a watered-down response. A chance to put forward the Weather underground as firmly part of and accountable to the women's movement had been lost. An internal paper written afterward about the exchange called the response a "compromise document, reflecting the achievement of certain unities among us, and many disunities."[77] It was proof of the indecision gripping the Weather Underground when it came to "the women's question."

In November 1974, Alpert turned herself in—and began cooperating with the FBI. Several Weatherwomen wanted to write another open letter denouncing Alpert's cooperation and her reactionary feminism in no uncertain terms. The information she shared with the police was especially dangerous, given that the organization had temporarily provided her with shelter in her time underground. Her description of Rudd and his partner (never a Weatherwoman or a fugitive) in Santa Fe led FBI agents to converge on the town, although the couple had long since left. The result of Alpert's cooperation was predictable: harassment, arrests, and beatings of movement people and counterculture youth Rudd had known.[78] Rudd was furious. In his unpublished memoir, he writes of pressuring the organization to denounce Alpert for cooperating with the hated FBI. "I was quite open about my motive—revenge. Why not hit her back if we could?"[79] But neither vengeance nor denunciation was forthcoming from the underground, despite the drafts some Weatherwomen circulated.

While the organization publicly remained silent on Alpert's surrender and collaboration, the earlier response to her in the summer of 1973 had a surprise twist. In addition to the Weatherwomen's open letter to the women's movement came a personal letter to Alpert herself. The letter was from Mary Moylan, a Catholic antiwar activist and one of the Catonsville 9, who destroyed draft records. Like the Berrigan brothers, Moylan had jumped bail and gone underground; unlike the Berrigans, who were both captured within a few months, she remained outside the state's grasp. And now here she was with the Weather Underground, expressing her anger at Alpert's "odd twist to sisterhood" in bringing down the state on other women just to criticize Rudd. Of course, Moylan's letter also expressed something beyond what she wrote to Alpert; among the ranks of the Weather Underground could now be found a former member of the Catholic Left.[80]

COMMUNICATING REVOLUTION:
THE COMMUNIQUÉS OF THE WEATHER UNDERGROUND

IN THE 1975 film *Underground*, Weather members spoke of being "professional revolutionaries." Arrogant, perhaps, but still true. The Weather Underground Organization (as it ultimately became known) of the 1970s was professional in its operations. In addition to the high level of technical skill that went into making bombs and conducting actions without injuring anyone while still attacking major institutions, this professionalism carried over into the organization's public relations. Most of the group's communiqués after 1970 were press packets, often seven or eight pages long and as slick as the press releases of the corporate or government agencies being attacked. Communiqués were arguably the most important way the group defined itself and its actions, built accountability with the movement, and countered the lies, omissions, and half-truths of the government and the media.

Claiming and explaining actions became particularly important when frustrated law enforcement agencies began falsely accusing the aboveground movement, such as when police arrested an antiwar activist for the Weather Underground's 1971 Capitol bombing. In an open letter addressed to the mother of the arrested woman, published in the radical newspapers, Weather affirmed that the accused had nothing to do with the action and placed the blame squarely with the war makers and the forces of repression. "The issue is the war in Indochina, the murderous policy of a lying government bent on dominating the Third World," the letter said. "As long as there is an Amerikan soldier, gun, bomb, or plane attacking the people of Southeast Asia, we must continue our fight. We hope our own mothers also understand how passionately we feel this."[81]

Using the underground press was a creative and important way of communicating and fostering accountability among revolutionaries at different levels of legality—the aboveground, the underground, and those in between. And it worked. The success of the communiqués was due in part to the expansive network of alternative newspapers. In *Revolution in the Air*, Max Elbaum writes that by 1970, "the Underground Press Syndicate included 200 papers with six million readers, not counting another 500 underground papers in high schools." Papers such as the *Berkeley Tribe*, the *Liberated Guardian* (for the short time it existed), the *Quicksilver Times*, *RAT*, the *San Francisco Express*, and *Takeover* regularly published communiqués. Radio stations such as KPFA in the San Francisco Bay Area also aired communiqués—either by reading them or playing pre-recorded versions the station received. "The Weather Underground was really good about communicating actions," recalls former KPFA reporter Claude Marks. "We were inventing a way of debating politics and talking from a clandestine situation," says Bernardine Dohrn. "That was pretty interesting, to have these forces at work, all trying to sort it all out."

Communiqués were political education. The 1973 WUO statement on the cease-fire in Vietnam, not tied to a bombing, shows the group's efforts to celebrate movement victories and draw out the lessons of the recent past. In an introductory letter and in the communiqué itself, Weather acknowledged the significance of the cease-fire for the radical anti-imperialist movements in the United States and throughout the world:

> Dear Friends,
> The enclosed statement expresses our thoughts on the cease-fire in Vietnam. The signing of the cease-fire agreement marks a great victory, not only for the Vietnamese people, but for everyone who has protested the war and fought for an end to U.S. aggression. It is a time to share in the celebrations of the Vietnamese, to reflect on our movement's history, and renew our resistance.
> Nixon and his supporters will spread the lie that U.S. terror-bombing "won the war" and "forced" the Vietnamese to sign the agreement. This lie cannot affect the continuing progress of the Vietnamese revolution. It is aimed at deceiving the American people and silencing millions in this country who have opposed the war. Many clear voices need to be heard right now—to tell the real history of the war, to draw the lessons from U.S. defeat.
> We hope that you will read this statement, print it if possible and circulate it among your friends.
> —Weather Underground[82]

Weather summed up the significance of the cease-fire by saying: "A small poor country can defeat the largest, richest power in the world, provided its people are united and its cause is just. What an ominous message for the American empire. What inspiration and comfort for all people." After further elaboration on the importance of the Vietnamese victory, the communiqué chronicled the history of the antiwar movement in true term-paper style, by analyzing six popular movement chants: "Hell No, We Won't Go!"; "Stop the Draft!"; "Dump Johnson!"; "Bring the Troops Home!"; "Stop the Bombing!" and "The NLF Will Win!" Each one, the communiqué said, signified a different stage of the antiwar movement, "from the first acts of conscience to the flowering of mass action."

Throughout its analysis, the communiqué put forward the importance of the Black freedom struggle and of Third World liberation movements in providing leadership and inspiration to the white antiwar movement. The Weather Underground did not separate the antiwar movement from the ghetto rebellions or the GI resistance movement, nor did it give the impression that the cease-fire signaled the end of struggle. And in keeping with Weather's insistence that "the cultural is political," the communiqué closed with a poem by Ho Chi Minh.

In its early years, Weather's communiqués consistently raised the issue of racism, seeking not only to affirm the group's solidarity with the Black movement domestically but to encourage antiwar activists to do the same, and to understand the war in Vietnam itself as a racist act. The group used communiqués to combat elitism, urging people to read and look to political leaders and cultural figures from the Third World. Ho Chi Minh, Pablo Neruda, and George Jackson weren't just activists but intellectuals who offered a gateway into understanding how and why colonized people resist. The communiqué accompanying the ITT bombing, for instance, said Weather wanted to let the "Chilean people themselves speak through our media."

As the 1970s wore on, the group released more communiqués not tied to actions. The Weather Underground was repositioning itself—not just as movement fighters but as thinkers and strategists. Communiqués underscored Weather's creativity, prompting Abbie Hoffman to call the leaders in the Weather Underground some of the most creative people he knew.[83] Communiqués were released to analyze world developments, rather than to just announce a bombing. Whether attached to bombings or not, communiqués began to offer specific strategies, plans of action, and even slogans for possible use by the aboveground. Bombings and statements were viewed in tandem with the mass movement—they fed and inspired each other. Together, it was hoped, the mass movement and the underground would expose and attack the enemy. "They were more thoroughly researched, and cogently argued," Raskin writes of the post-1970 statements. "They evidenced a dialectical understanding of history."[84] In 1972, the Weather Underground even stopped spelling America with a 'k.'

This analytical trend accelerated in 1973, with the release of the "Common Victories" communiqué analyzing the cease-fire in Vietnam. It continued with the letter to the women's movement that summer and through the next three years. There was even a public statement written by an individual in the group. Weatherman Howie Machtinger was arrested in New York City in April 1973, after three years underground. Freed on bail, he decided to rejoin his comrades underground, releasing a statement explaining his decision to flee rather than stand trial. Expressing his commitment to the potential and possibilities of the underground, Machtinger said he looked forward to figuring out a post-Vietnam War strategy. "I believe in the continuation and growth of what so many people fought so hard to build over the last years," he wrote. "There need to be bases beyond the reach of the state power—so that people have alternatives to going to jail, so that we can as much as possible meet, think, plot, study, work things out without the interference of our enemies (without being harassed, infiltrated or bugged)."[85]

Of particular interest in the turn to analytical communiqués was Weather's open dialogue with the Symbionese Liberation Army. The SLA was a predominantly white underground group based in the San Francisco Bay Area, led by a Black former prisoner who had taken the name Cinque, after a famous insurgent slave. The SLA first gained notoriety in November 1973 by assassinating Marcus Foster, a Black school superintendent in Oakland who was proposing a controversial student ID system. The Weather Underground, more sympathetic to the SLA than many other Left groups, criticized the SLA for the Foster killing, saying it couldn't "comprehend" why the SLA would do such an action.

In February 1974, the SLA kidnapped newspaper heiress Patty Hearst from her apartment in Berkeley, and demanded food for Oakland's poor as partial ransom. Of the spate of clandestine groups to emerge in the United States in the 1970s, the SLA was the first to turn to kidnappings, a tactic more common among Latin American guerrillas. Weather was cautiously supportive in a February 20 open letter:

> Committed political workers will be criticizing and discussing the Hearst kidnapping for a long time, but we must acknowledge that this audacious intervention has carried forward the basic public questions and starkly dramatized what many have come to understand through their own experience: It will be necessary to organize and to destroy this racist and cruel system.[86]

Weather had no sympathy for the captive's family, particularly Patty's grandfather, newspaper baron William Randolph Hearst. "For two generations, the Hearst newspapers themselves have wielded their power and profits by exploiting the most lurid aspects of war, irrational violence, and racist and sexist ideas. They have a lot of reckoning to account for." And now, "the guerrillas have kidnapped the daughter of a rich and powerful man in order to provide food to the poor."[87] The action, Weather said, offered the possibility to expose the great social violence of hunger, and to show the extent to which "American society is maintained by force and violence."[88]

The plot thickened when Patty Hearst apparently joined the SLA and even participated in a couple of bank robberies with and for the group. (She would later claim "Stockholm Syndrome" and testify against her former captors/comrades). With the SLA dominating the headlines, the Weather Underground suddenly found itself described in the mainstream media as the "moderate" revolutionary alternative.

That hurt. As the communiqué said, "It is a new experience for us to be described as a moderate alternative in the Hearst press. This has never happened before. New Left 'moderation' is invented now as another racist weapon against Black revolution." In response, Weather urged activists not "to do the enemy's work" by "asserting their own moderation and legitimacy" in contrast to the SLA.[89] Instead, Weather wished for the safety of both Patty Hearst and the SLA. Its wish was not fulfilled. On May 17, 1974—three months after the Hearst kidnapping—police surrounded an SLA safe house in Los Angeles, laid siege to it with tear gas and incendiary bombs, and burned six of them alive. "An FBI officer threatened to arrest a fire chief who wanted to go in and put out the flames," Roxanne Dunbar-Ortiz writes in her memoir.[90] The massacre was broadcast live on television. Patty Hearst and two other SLA members were not in the house and survived, although they would be arrested in September 1975. In response to the murder of the six SLA members, the Weather Underground bombed the Los Angeles office of the California attorney general on May 31.[91]

The communiqué following the June 13, 1974, bombing of the Gulf Oil Corporation headquarters in Pittsburgh highlights the group's style in the mid-1970s.[92] A small box in the upper left has "Weather Underground Bombs Gulf Oil" in all caps with the date; the Weather insignia of a rainbow with a lightening bolt is in the upper right. Beneath the insignia is a quote from Amilcar Cabral, the assassinated revolutionary leader of Guinea-Bissau, on "fighting against our common enemy…the best form of solidarity." From there, the communiqué begins:

> We have attacked the Gulf Oil Corporation at its executive headquarters in Pittsburgh, Pa., for enormous crimes:
>
> - Gulf finances the Portuguese colonial war against the people of Angola in Africa
>
> - Gulf steals bonanza profits from poor and working people in the U.S.
>
> - Gulf exploits the people and resources of 70 countries in the world.

Each of these allegations is then explained more thoroughly in the following pages. The bombing, which caused more than $350,000 in damage, was to express solidarity with the national liberation struggles in Angola, Mozambique, and Guinea-Bissau—all places where Portugal maintained a colonial presence with the help of the U.S. government and corporations such as Gulf.[93] Indeed, Angola and Mozambique were cutting-edge battlegrounds for post-Vietnam U.S. foreign policy. In both countries, the United States and South Africa armed and funded reactionary movements (UNITA in Angola, Renamo in Mozambique) as proxy armies against the national liberation movements (MPLA and FRELIMO, respectively).[94]

The first four pages of the Weather communiqué explained the struggle and guerrilla movements in those countries; the connection between Gulf Oil, the United States government, and African colonization; and other examples of Gulf's perfidy. The communiqué included a map of Africa with key regions highlighted, and the Gulf Oil logo, changed to read "Gulf Kills." The communiqué put forth a broad analysis of Western imperialism in Africa. Noting how Gulf bolstered Portuguese colonialism in Angola, Guinea-Bissau, and Mozambique through investments and support, the communiqué also examined Gulf's impact internationally and in the United States, particularly with the then-acute energy crisis. Although the bombing targeted Gulf, the communiqué also blasted the U.S. government's role in dominating Africa. This communiqué devoted three pages to the specific history and struggles of Guinea-Bissau, featuring a close-up map of the area. In these ways, the action represented a fairly successful model of armed propaganda—an action targeting a somewhat hidden but nonetheless major player in colonial oppression overseas, and a reasoned communiqué supporting African liberation struggles and urging others to do the same.

And something more. On the top of page five, there was an announcement: "This is the section on Guinea-Bissau from our political statement PRAIRIE FIRE, which will be released soon." A similar announcement had accompanied a lengthy analytical communiqué in April about Vietnam. It was the movement's first intimation that the Weather Underground had written a book.

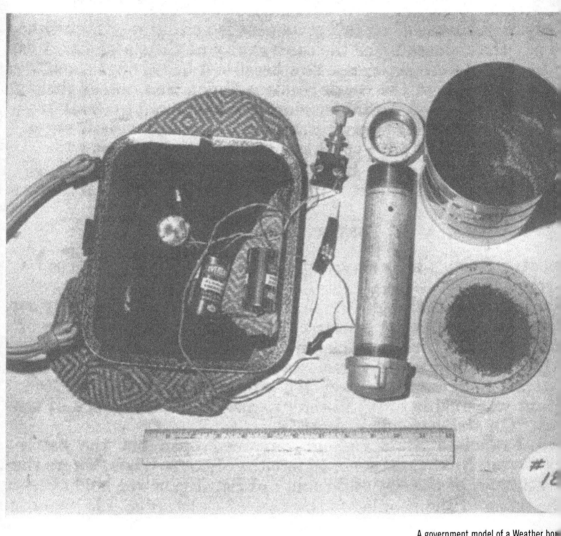

A government model of a Weather bom
Photo courtesy of Sam Gr

> *It was felt that by putting out a major statement about revolutionary anti-imperialism, what those politics meant and how it applied to our particular conditions in this country, that we'd be speaking to a larger movement. So it was partly to remobilize our own organization. But it was partly to overcome the error of what happened in 1970, when there was a real split…between us and the mass movement, and to try to put out a politics that are larger and that people aboveground could identify with and rally around.*
>
> —*David Gilbert* [1]

JULY 1974 WAS THE FIFTEENTH ANNIVERSARY OF THE Cuban revolution. Communists and anti-communists alike held marches and talks to either honor or pillory Fidel Castro. And the Weather Underground picked this time (July 24) for its most interesting clandestine action to date: distributing its book, *Prairie Fire: The Politics of Revolutionary Anti-Imperialism*.

The group had already released sections of the book through two communiqués in the spring of 1974. Now, the book was being distributed under the cover of darkness, in an action as carefully planned and executed as any the group had done. Copies were surreptitiously "dropped off" at hundreds of bookstores across the nation on a single night, along with boxes of books delivered to women's centers, movement groups, and other friendly associates in cities and towns nationwide.[2] Eventually more than 40,000 copies were distributed, making *Prairie Fire*, in fact, a trade paperback bestseller, even if the movement was the primary distributor.[3]

The book's title came from a quote from Chairman Mao Zedong, leader of revolutionary China: "A single spark can start a prairie fire."[4] It was hoped that the book might provide that spark.

PRAIRIE FIRE:
THE POLITICS OF REVOLUTIONARY ANTI-IMPERIALISM

SOMETIMES, YOU ACTUALLY can tell a book by its cover. *Prairie Fire*'s was bright red. The main edition was red with black flames and type, though the group also produced versions with blank red covers "for those who wanted to remain inconspicuous."[5] In just over 150 well-illustrated pages, *Prairie Fire* presented a concise yet surprisingly detailed analysis of the United States, the 1960s movements and the turn to armed struggle, the Vietnam War, the Third World and anti-imperialism. Throughout, it offered lessons to be applied by the movement. "Between the communiqués and *Prairie Fire*, we were trying to re-imagine ways to be in dialogue with lots of other forces—people who were doing grass-roots community organizing, people who were doing feminist organizing, [and] anti-imperialist forces" says Bernardine Dohrn.

Central Committee member Bill Ayers wrote a rough draft of the still-untitled book in 1972, sparking the project, which then became a group effort. This collective process, begun in earnest in the winter of 1973, yielded a rare moment of increased democracy within the organization, as drafts were traded back and forth, with the rank-and-file (as well as some key aboveground supporters) given more room than usual to help shape Weather's political line.[6] Indeed, the group even had its first of two Cadre Schools in 1974 as part of collectively working on the political line in the book. The week-long political education retreat brought many of the clandestine members of the organization, along with some aboveground friends, to a house in Maine.[7] The purpose was to discuss the book—but also to train one another in the politics of Marxist-Leninism. Some people in the group taught on particular subjects, and a few aboveground comrades were also brought in as instructors. The schools were a "cross between mobilizing people and browbeating people," says Gilbert, who was heavily involved in the first school.

In his memoir, Ayers says the book took two years to write and involved the entire organization, "pulling in the whole network of friends and supporters including the most far-flung contacts." *Prairie Fire* "was an attempt to sum up our thinking since the 'Weatherman' paper and especially since the townhouse. Through it we hoped to consolidate our political organization and to forge unity with progressive activists."[8] For much of 1973 until it was distributed, the book dominated Weather's political work. "We were taken with words…and practically taken over by words on occasion," Ayers writes.[9]

Gilbert was part of a small group that took a more hands-on role in editing and rewriting the book based on Ayers' initial draft. Of particular interest to this group was strengthening the book's class analysis without undercutting its emphasis on the leading role of national liberation struggles. Representatives of each region where Weather was based met to discuss the book's politics; from there, the representatives went back to the collectives to discuss the project more thoroughly.

Producing the book was also a collective, and clandestine, effort. The Weather Underground established a print shop, run by a small unit that was eventually formalized as the Red Dragon Print Collective.[10] The print shop was an important feature of the Weather Underground's last three years, and the group managed to keep it running even after having to move it twice for security reasons. The organization rented an apartment for a "social research and consulting company," made it soundproof, built a reception desk to give it an air of legitimacy, and bought (and fixed) a printing press. While radical media in the 1960s were popularly referred to as the "underground press," the Weather Underground's media unit was more literally an underground press.

"Nothing was particularly traceable," says Scott Braley, who helped run the print shop from its inception. "We could have gotten caught a couple of times, but it wasn't like, at that time, the state was running around looking for people who were buying illegal printing presses." Largely self-taught, Weather's production collective found itself running a full-fledged printing operation; it was responsible for design, camera work, and the actual printing, binding, and collating of materials. "Anybody who touched anything that was ever going to go out the door wore gloves," Braley says. "We ran the printing press with gloves, we did all the binding with gloves."

When it came time to distribute the book, the entire organization was involved, not just the production collective. In addition to those dropped at bookstores, a few thousand copies were hand-delivered or shipped (using false return-address labels) on July 24 to various collectives who then handled their own distribution. While Weather collectives handled the bulk of the distribution on that first night, the group also enlisted the support of aboveground helpers to ensure an even bigger release. "A huge number of people [were] involved in distributing it, which in itself was probably the largest number of people involved in a clandestine action since the underground railroad," Braley estimates.

Prairie Fire is less strident than Weather's early communiqués and writings. It is detailed, accessibly written, and well-designed, with little of the bravado and macho swagger that turned off many in the Left in 1969. And while the book generally calls for militancy, it doesn't demand it in the same way the "Weatherman" statement did.

The book opens with pictures of Diana Oughton, Teddy Gold, and Terry Robbins, paying tribute to three "comrades who gave their lives in the struggle." The next page, filled with names of current political prisoners, dedicates the book to Harriet Tubman, John Brown, "all who continue to fight [and] to all political prisoners in the U.S."[11] A later page features a picture of Sam Melville, the white anti-imperialist murdered by police at Attica, with a caption reading (in Spanish) "We won't forget." Although the group was tepid in the face of Jane Alpert's denunciation and publicly silent when she cooperated with the FBI, openly commemorating Melville was both honoring a fallen comrade and, in a subtle way, also thumbing a collective nose at Alpert.

An introductory letter signed by Central Committee members Bernardine Dohrn, Billy Ayers, Jeff Jones, and Celia Sojourn (a pseudonym), expresses the desire for communication and unity between the "mass and clandestine movements" and promises to respond to comments and criticisms "as best we can."[12] (Although the book was widely discussed and debated, Weather never did engage in any public dialogue about the book from underground.) The letter defines the book as written for "communist-minded people, independent organizers and anti-imperialists; those who carry the traditions and lessons of the struggles of the last decade, those who join in the struggles of today. PRAIRIE FIRE is written to all sisters and brothers who are engaged in armed struggle against the enemy. It is written to prisoners, women's groups, collectives, study groups, workers' organizing committees, communes, GI organizers, consciousness-raising groups, veterans, community groups, and revolutionaries of all kinds; to all who will read, criticize and bring its content to life in practice."

The book was trying to speak to broader segments of the movement—to "hold a debate about political theory," in Braley's words. The introductory letter explains the book's roots in the need to develop a cohesive movement strategy and ideology to build a "successful revolutionary movement and party."[13] Even though the Weather Underground and the party-building

Left had significant political differences, Weather was increasingly drawn to the idea of creating a communist party. While support for national liberation remained a running theme throughout Weather's existence, the allure of "youth nation" politics common in 1970 had by 1974 been replaced by a pull toward "party-building" politics.

The first chapter identifies the Weather Underground as a "guerrilla organization" intending to "disrupt the empire," "engage the enemy," "encourage the people," and "forge an underground." This chapter explains Weather's formation as inspired by the Vietnamese struggle and the Black Liberation Movement; declares the need for revolution, including armed struggle; and argues for a symbiotic relationship between above and underground movements. The book was a step toward institutionalizing such mutually supportive relationships.

This chapter also contains a list of Weather bombings up until that point, divided into three categories. There were bombings to "retaliate for the most savage criminal attacks against Black and Third World people, especially by the police apparatus"; those done "to disrupt and agitate against U.S. aggression and terror against Vietnam and the Third World"; and bombings "to expose and focus attention against the power and institutions which most cruelly oppress, exploit and delude the people."[14]

Category one included the bombing of Chicago police cars after the assassination of Black Panthers Hampton and Clark (1969), the bombing of Department of Corrections offices in San Francisco and in Sacramento after the murder of Black radical George Jackson (1971), and the bombing of the 103rd precinct of the New York City Police Department after the murder of a 10-year-old Black boy (1973). Bombings against U.S. aggression included the Harvard Center for International Affairs (1970), William Bundy's office at MIT (1971), and ITT's Latin America Headquarters after the U.S.-supported 1973 coup in Chile. To expose illegitimate state power, the Weather Underground bombed National Guard headquarters after the murders at Kent State University (1970); the Presidio Army Base and MP Station (1970); and the Health, Education, and Welfare federal office (1974). The women's brigade of the Weather Underground carried out the Harvard, MIT, and HEW actions.

Prairie Fire acknowledges five key achievements of the 1960s: proving the vulnerability of the U.S. empire; contributing to victory in Vietnam; anti-racism; building alternative institutions and cultures; and recognizing "the need to fight and the terrible cost of not doing all we can." As many historic works have done since, the book labels 1968 a "high point and a turning point" in revolutionary anti-imperialist struggle.[15] The year was important for several reasons: the Tet Offensive in Vietnam, the Chinese Cultural Revolution, the near shutdown of Paris by strikes, rebellions at Columbia University, the rise in women's liberation, and an increased Black militancy (especially after Martin Luther King's assassination). *Prairie Fire* also notes that 1968 marked the official beginning of COINTELPRO efforts against the predominantly white New Left, particularly SDS. Repression and hope, death and resistance—these were the forces that gave rise to the Weather Underground and the movement at large.

After pointing out the strengths and weaknesses of 1960s movements in general, *Prairie Fire* applies a critical lens to Weather itself. While defending the decision to "prepare and build the armed struggle," the book criticizes the organization's failure to prioritize and lead mass movements.[16] By focusing only on "white people's complicity with empire," Weather lost its "identification with the people—the promise, the yearnings, the defeats." This led to a "mistaking [of] friends for enemies" that alienated would-be (and one-time) comrades. The book also criticizes the failure to respond and learn from constructive criticisms, acknowledging publicly for the first time the error of not responding to the Panther 21 critique.

Moving on from the 1960s, *Prairie Fire* identifies the obstacles to 1970s movements, which include "anti-organization tendencies, cynicism, sexism, and racism." These obstacles are compounded by the "anti-revolutionary errors in the movement" of "American exceptionalism" and "reformism." Reformism was obviously anathema to a revolutionary group because it sapped the strength and vision of long-term, structural change. But, given the organizing focus of the book, *Prairie Fire* differentiates between fighting for reforms as a way of pushing the struggle forward and an ethos of reformism, which sees Band-Aid solutions to institutional problems as the end goal.

The critique of American exceptionalism was an especially important one. Exceptionalism, *Prairie Fire* states, is "the assumption that…our revolutionary struggle is not subject to the same general conditions and the general necessities as others." In practice, the book argues, U.S. exceptionalism is manifested in two ways: first, in the belief that the U.S. Left is politically above and strategically beyond Left movements in other countries; and second, in the rejection of forms of struggle for the United States "which are obviously necessary in other parts of the world."[17] This criticism refers to those radicals, pacifist and otherwise, who may have supported self-defense and armed struggle in Third World countries but demanded only nonviolence within the United States.

Indeed, this critique of exceptionalism was the key to the Weather Underground's very existence. "It seemed racist to say 'it's OK for Black people or for Vietnamese people to fight for their liberation, but it's OK if white people only struggle politely,'" says Judy Siff, reflecting on what drew her to the group. "And I think that was a big deal for us, to not see ourselves as exceptions to the revolutionary processes that were really going on in the world."

Other members agree, even as they wonder whether the organization took this argument too far. "We rejected American exceptionalism, and yet we weren't South Africa," Bernardine Dohrn points out. "There still were methods of struggle here that were public and open, even with COINTELPRO, even with the kind of repression that was going on, even with the white supremacist way in which one group of activists was murdered and another had dirty tricks unleashed on them. Even with all that, there was room here that wasn't there in apartheid South Africa, let alone the Belgian Congo."

Subsequent chapters of *Prairie Fire* mix history, current affairs, and revolutionary theory. The second chapter—which had been released as a communiqué that April—analyzes the Vietnam War and the strengths of the antiwar movement. Of particular interest and prescience here is the book's emphasis on "the war to explain the war"—the propaganda offensive to present the Vietnam War as a noble cause, the antiwar movement as puerile and meaningless, and the outcome as other than the defeat for the United States that it was. This war of words has, it can be argued, become a real war in the thirty years since, with easily winnable U.S.-led wars in small Third World countries such as Grenada, Panama, Kosovo, Iraq (the first time), and elsewhere to beat the "Vietnam syndrome" and restore domestic confidence in U.S. military supremacy.[18] (George Bush I seemed to confirm this hypothesis after the first Gulf War, when he declared "By God, we've kicked the Vietnam syndrome once and for all.")[19] That the Weather Underground was able to recognize this process while the ink had not yet dried on the Paris peace treaty—and as the U.S. involvement in Southeast Asia continued—was an accomplishment, to be sure.

Prairie Fire also presents an anti-imperialist history of the United States, from the first days of Native American genocide through post-Civil War reconstruction and up to the Great Depression, paying particular attention to resistance struggles waged by oppressed and marginalized people. This section was proof of how voraciously the group read, how intensively it studied, in its time underground. *Prairie Fire* examines the history not just of the "internal colonies" but of the Industrial Workers of the World, the Communist Party, and the early women's movement. In looking at such a wide swath of U.S. history, the group tried to grapple with the complexity of oppression and privilege, noting how white-led social movements of oppressed workers or women historically abandoned anti-racism and eventually allied with white supremacy at the expense of people of color. Even when these movements started off in opposition to racism, the book said, white-led movements have undercut the autonomy of Third World struggles.

This anti-racist guide to U.S. history rooted the book in real-life struggles, Gilbert says, at a time when "so many debates…in the movement were competing quotes between Marx and Lenin."[20] *Prairie Fire* also avoided lining up behind either China or the Soviet Union in the running Sino-Soviet split that was then wracking the party-building sector of the Left.[21] Instead, the book defines national liberation as the cutting-edge issue and urges revolutionaries to support mass-based movements for self-determination, regardless of whether they are supported by the Soviet Union, China, or neither. *Prairie Fire* was a unifying message at a time when much of the Left was fractured and at one another's throats.

Building off its discussion of U.S. history, *Prairie Fire* then examines "Imperialism in Crisis" in two chapters: one dealing with the international situation, the other with the United States. These chapters are on-the-ground analyses of the struggles then being waged against colonialism and neo-colonialism (formal independence but economic and cultural domination). Internationally, *Prairie Fire* describes how racism, sexism, and underdevelopment are guiding features of U.S. imperialism, by both the government and corporations. Neocolonialism—"Vietnamization on a world-wide scale"—features prominently in this process, the book argues, as imperialism seeks continued domination over the Third World and violently suppresses progressive and socialist movements without directly colonizing a country. *Prairie Fire* then points to three movements Weather saw as leading national liberation struggles on a world stage: Puerto Rican independence, Guinea-Bissau's anti-colonialism, and the Palestinian movement.[22]

Domestically, *Prairie Fire* sees "Imperialism in Crisis." The United States was in the grips of an economic recession—particularly affecting women, children, and the elderly—while multinational corporations grew wealthier and fled overseas. "Violent counterrevolution" was accomplished through the prison system, and racism and sexism were used to maintain control. Domestic national liberation movements, along with women's and youth rebellion, were at the forefront of creating positive change.[23]

The last chapter, "Against the Common Enemy," presents Weather's strategies for building a revitalized mass radical movement. Its program includes everything from opposing war and the "cultural and economic penetration" by U.S. government and corporate entities, to active engagement in struggle around the prison system, to reading Black and Third World publications.[24] *Prairie Fire* ends with a call for organization—especially among poor and working people, among youth, and among women—to unify and mobilize people to fight for revolution, "the midwife bringing the new society into being from the old."[25]

PRAIRIE FIRE:
ONE STEP FORWARD, ONE STEP BACKWARD?

PRAIRIE FIRE EMERGED out of a growing internal political crisis. The Weather Underground didn't want to be known simply as a group that only did a bombing every few months. Especially with the cease-fire in Vietnam, Weather was figuring out what it should do next, and the book was a part of that process. "We needed something to remobilize us, we needed to have an organization to fight imperialism," Gilbert says. "We had sort of floundered."[26] And it wasn't just the Weather Underground experiencing this crisis. Donna Willmott says the book was an attempt to deal with the disorientation many committed anti-imperialists felt at the time. "We had to figure out our purpose and what we were doing," she says. "I think so many things changed in the whole movement, not just for us…. The book seemed like a good opportunity to try and articulate what our definition of anti-imperialism was, to try and be organizers with those politics, and to be accountable to the movement for what we thought."

With the mass movement on the decline following the cease-fire, the book was a step toward solidifying Weather as an integral and even leading part of the Left. Beginning in 1972, bombings were less frequent as the group experimented with what it meant to be clandestine. The early burst of actions in 1970–1971 flaunted Weather's militancy and defined the organization as an anti-racist fighting force, but that level of activity was not sustainable in terms of the people and resources required. The encirclement showed the need for support and security. The group spent the next three years consolidating its politics, building support, and doing the occasional action while settling into life underground—turning the Weather Underground into an established and well-protected entity. Communiqués had shown the group to be an analytical force, and now *Prairie Fire* presented Weather as historians and strategists—an anti-imperialist political organization and not just hippie bombers. The book publicly displayed and explained Weather's political program and perspective.

Speaking broadly about Weather's propaganda, historian Jeremy Varon says that the organization used its media "to consciously cultivate a kind of mythology of the underground as a free space of outlaw-rebels, the New Left's righteous avengers. And [its] media provides a fascinating window into a small, intense, radical subculture which, for all its bluster, still captures and denounces some basic, awful truths about the corruption of the American empire."[27]

Black Liberation Army soldier Ashanti Alston was in prison when he got a copy of *Prairie Fire*. He remembers being "really amazed" at the "imaginative" book. He also remembers the dedication, which showed an appreciation and recognition of the sacrifice political prisoners were making. "I liked the spirit of the book and using it as a way to continue to mobilize people into the movement," he says. To Mark Rudd, no longer in the organization but still living underground, the book "was an attempt to influence the movement that we had abandoned back in 1969. It tried to reach out to the many thousands of New leftists and former New leftists by saying, in effect, 'Don't despair, we're all part of the same thing,'" despite political differences within the Left. Rudd remembers talking to people who felt the book was "welcome news to many leftists that the underground was still alive."[28]

The book's success was not just measured in moral support. At the time *Prairie Fire* was released, "more than two hundred people had affiliated themselves with the WUO," and thousands more were aligned with anti-imperialist politics.[29] The organization experienced an influx of members, popularity, and donations.[30] Supporters distributed the book and organized study groups around it. Seeking to use the book's success to build a strong national organization, the Weather Underground supported and encouraged the establishing of the aboveground Prairie Fire Distribution Committee (PFDC) to ensure widespread circulation. PFDC not only distributed the book but was one of the aboveground organizations that reprinted it and even organized a book tour. Five aboveground members of the Weather Underground, including Laura Whitehorn, were sent on a nationwide PFDC tour of college towns, women's groups, community and antiwar groups to talk about the book, especially its views on anti-racism and armed struggle.

The creation of PFDC—soon to take off as its own organization, the Prairie Fire Organizing Committee (PFOC)—showed that Weather was reorienting itself toward the mass movement, trying to do in 1974 what it had been unable (or unwilling) to do in 1969. To show the clandestine possibilities for fighting back, the Weather Underground also experimented with other types of actions, transcending both incendiary devices and fiery communiqués. In March 1974, four months before *Prairie Fire* hit the streets, the group stink-bombed the Hilton Hotel where Nelson Rockefeller was to receive a "humanitarian" award. The communiqué afterward was especially critical of Rockefeller's recently enacted drug laws, draconian measures that dramatically extended prison sentences (along with life-time parole) for those arrested on drug charges.[31] This action, along with the print shop and the increased emphasis on attacking both corporations and the state, showed the expressive range of clandestinity. For the Weather Underground during this time, Raskin notes, the "underground is not simply or primarily an escape route, a place of refuge or retreat, but one of many roads to the frontier of revolutionary thought and action."[32]

Not surprisingly, the expansion of the underground had aboveground reverberations. Susan Rosenberg worked at an anti-racist women's center in Brooklyn that distributed the book. The center was one of many Left groups that participated in a *Prairie Fire* study group held at the Washington Square Church. The women's center joined with other local groups to form a New York chapter of PFOC, hoping that their individual projects would cohere into a mass and national anti-imperialist organization. It was an aboveground version of Weather's politics. And for a time, it seemed as if the Weather Underground would get its wish for *Prairie Fire*.

In the best tradition of radical media, *Prairie Fire* was an attempt to be accountable to the broader movement by putting forth a political statement and platform. Judged by the standards of the time, the Weather Underground's opus was an accomplishment. Bernardine Dohrn calls the book a "period piece" but one that still "gets the main threads right" in its analytic approach. For Cathy Wilkerson, the analysis presented in *Prairie Fire* is, by and large, one that still holds up today.

It was, however, *Prairie Fire*'s inconsistencies that were to prove most prophetic. They arose, in part, because of the collective authorship, and in part because of real, if unacknowledged, political differences within the organization. The group's relation to and analysis of class was the central terrain on which these battles were fought. Whereas most of the book highlighted the leading role of national liberation movements (including those within this country), other parts suggested instead that the ultimate strength rests with the "industrial proletariat," without a clear explanation of the differences or how the group intended to reconcile these two notions of the *leading* agent for social change. The book, Braley says, alternately argued that national liberation was critical and had to be staunchly supported by whites, and that the primary task was to build a communist party to lead the working class. These inconsistencies led former Weatherwoman Judy Siff to call the book a "collection of essays" rather than a coherent text. "Even though as an organization, we were a 'we,' we weren't a unified political 'we,'" Siff says. "We were many people with different political influences trying to come together with a coherent ideology."

In general, Weather was undergoing an increasing turn to Marxism and class; a communiqué released shortly before *Prairie Fire* described "fundamental reality" as the "war between the rich and poor."[33] The turn to a more thorough class analysis wasn't inherently problematic. Indeed, growing attention to class could have sharpened Weather's analytical framework, enabling it to better navigate the troubled waters of race, class, gender, and national oppression on a global scale. But as the group knew from its own methodical study of U.S. history, a Marxist class analysis needed to be joined with ongoing commitment to fighting white supremacy rather than juxtaposed against it. But with the Left wrapped up in the Maoist hunt for the "primary contradiction," it often became a question of race versus class. At the first Cadre School, Siff remembers one of the most respected instructors telling the group that it was time for a revolutionary analysis—and staunch support for national liberation wasn't it. For Siff, it was a sign of things to come.

And it wasn't just class at stake. As Naomi Jaffe pointed out in an unpublished criticism of *Prairie Fire*, written as the group disbanded, the book contained little self-criticism of Weather's sexist behavior or its dismissal of the women's movement as racist and bourgeois in its totality.[34] For that reason, Jaffe wrote, the book's "main purpose was the self-justification of a hegemonic, white organization that thought it was going to be the vanguard of the revolutionary movement. This white, male [dominated] organization was not going to be the vanguard of the revolution, in this country or anywhere."

The publication of *Prairie Fire* brought the best of the organization to the surface while also foreshadowing the group's demise. Many of the issues that would play out over the next two years, as Weather fell apart, were present in *Prairie Fire*, from women's liberation to the relevance of class politics and armed struggle. The success of *Prairie Fire* was aided by the group's reputation of staunch support for national liberation politics in opposition to a classical white Marxism that downplayed race. As such, the book effectively provided the Weather Underground with, in Siff's words, an "anti-imperialist calling card." That is, *Prairie Fire* solidified the organization as a white anti-imperialist group, broadened its politics to include more about class and women's liberation—and became a "blank check" for the group to move in a more traditional Marxist perspective, with the politics of the book as a shield from both external and internal criticism.

The book also begged the question of Weather's continued clandestinity—an issue that would come to the surface much more dramatically over the next two years. After the book, the group produced and distributed a regular newsmagazine, was featured in a documentary, and released a pamphlet of women's poetry (among other statements). All were remarkable accomplishments for a clandestine grouping—but none of them required being underground.[35] Much of the organization's money beyond living expenses was now going into running the Red Dragon Print Shop and mailing out the group's political statements. If the Weather Underground was turning increasingly from armed propaganda to printed propaganda, did people need to remain underground?

The group struggled, if unevenly, with where to go next, with how much publishing should play a role in that process, and with who was leading the revolution. "Even the way *Prairie Fire* (which does have good politics) developed" was problematic, David Gilbert says. "I remember being shocked when a Central Committee member argued for doing it to establish 'our leadership over the Left.'"[36]

The book met with success, but the Weather Underground was headed toward implosion.

WANTED BY FBI

The persons shown here are active members of the militant Weatherman faction of the Students for a Democratic Society - SDS.

Federal warrants have been issued at Chicago, Illinois, concerning these individuals, charging them with a variety of Federal violations including interstate flight to avoid prosecution, mob action, Antiriot Laws and conspiracy. Some of these individuals were also charged in an indictment returned 7/23/70, at Detroit, Michigan, with conspiracy to violate Federal Bombing and Gun Control Laws.

These individuals should be considered dangerous because of their known advocacy and use of explosives, reported acquisition of firearms and incendiary devices, and known propensity for violence.

If you have information concerning these persons please contact your local FBI Office.

William Charles Ayers
W/M, 25, 5-10, 170
brn hair, brn eyes

Kathie Boudin
W/F, 26, 5-4, 128
brn hair, blue eyes

Judith Alice Clark
W/F, 20, 5-3, 125
brn hair, brn eyes

Bernardine Rae Dohrn
W/F, 28, 5-5, 125
drk brn hair, brn eyes

Ronald D. Fliegelman
W/M, 26, 5-9, 175
black hair, blue eyes

John Allen Fuerst
W/M, 26, 5-10, 145
brn hair, brn eyes

Leonard Handelsman
W/M, 24, 6-5, 210
brn hair, blue eyes

John Gregory Jacobs
W/M, 23, 5-9, 150
lt brn hair, gray eyes

Federal wanted poster for Weather fugitives, 1970.
Courtesy of Roz Payne (www.newsreel.us)

> *The radical impulse in our own movement had dissipated a lot with the ending of the draft and then the peace treaty in Vietnam. And we were somewhat floundering. And I think part of our solution was to retreat into the sort of traditional [Marxist politics] which we had critiqued so many times.*
>
> *—David Gilbert[1]*

THE PUBLICATION OF PRAIRIE FIRE MARKED A TURNING point for the Weather Underground. With the book came a flurry of support for Weather, even as it was trying to decide on its next steps. Meanwhile, the group continued to carry out armed propaganda actions against imperialism—now against the economic interests driving the system (corporations) and not just against the political/repressive apparatus (the state).

On September 11, 1974, the one-year anniversary of the U.S.-supported coup in Chile, the group bombed the Oakland offices of Anaconda Copper, a main supporter of the Pinochet regime. The front page of the communiqué featured a box with the action and date at the top, followed by the Weather insignia.[2] This communiqué was the first from the Weather Underground *Organization* (WUO). Proclaiming "Free Chile!" it detailed why the group had bombed the copper company:

> We attack Anaconda Corporation in international solidarity with the Chilean people and their revolutionary struggle.
>
> • Anaconda is controlled by the Rockefeller family, part of Rocky's vast empire of power in Latin America and at home. Anaconda is but one substantial piece of the Rockefeller fortune, which is worth about as much as the combined wealth of all the Black, Chicano, Indian, Puerto Rican and 40 million poor white people in the US put together.

> • Anaconda, along with ITT and Kennecott, played a decisive role
> in the US-sponsored fascist coup in Chile. They were the force
> behind suspension of aid and credits, the continuing military aid
> to the generals, and the policies of economic aggression....
>
> Anaconda is one with the US/Kissinger policy toward Chile, a
> policy of BRIBES AND BLOOD.

The focus on corporate power was something new. Until now, Weather had concentrated almost exclusively on the state: the Pentagon, the U.S. Capitol, police stations, and courthouses. The first corporate attack had come a year earlier, when the group bombed ITT, also in solidarity with the Chilean people. In the mid-1970s, the WUO was shifting emphasis to corporate involvement in supporting repressive regimes in Latin America and Africa. Without ignoring the state, attacking corporate power was seen as a way to help rekindle mass action during economic recession. The shift was, in part, a prescient move, given the heightened role of transnational corporate power that accelerated in the 1980s and remains central today.[3]

Publicly, the WUO was expanding its realm of targets. Privately, the group was also undergoing a political shift. The Weather Underground was now an *organization*. The change in thinking included an increasing and systematic study of Marxist-Leninist theory (begun in 1973), a heightened focus on the U.S. working class, and a growing belief in the need for a communist party. Although the group never declared itself a party (as numerous post-SDS formations had done), the language around party-building suggested a change in political orientation. After all, the party is supposed to represent the workers in assuming the mantle of state power and overseeing the "dictatorship of the proletariat." It is primarily a leadership entity. But if the WUO now supported party-building, what did that mean for its support of national liberation movements, especially those within this country? The WUO had long proclaimed that those movements, spearheaded by the Black liberation struggle, would be leading the revolution in the United States. Elsewhere in the world, of course, many of the national liberation movements *were* communist parties, built over decades of struggle. But the United States was a different situation. Who would be at the helm—a communist party or the national liberation movements? Different answers required different organizational priorities.

TURNING TO THE MASS MOVEMENT:
THE PRAIRIE FIRE ORGANIZING COMMITTEE

WITH THE SUCCESS and popularity of *Prairie Fire*, organizers aboveground and under hoped to put the book's politics into practice with a national mass organization. The Prairie Fire Distributing Committee became the Prairie Fire Organizing Committee (PFOC) and quickly grew into an organization in its own right, with a viable presence in cities and struggles across the country.[4] Indeed, longtime anti-racist organizer Sharon Martinas called PFOC the best thing to come out of the WUO, because of the role it played in pushing militant anti-racism on the mass level, especially after the WUO's demise.[5] And PFOC was valuable while Weather still existed. Although Weather's actions served as inspiration to some activists—and did take some heat off Third World groups in the United States—there was only so much organizing it could do from underground. PFOC, then, was formed to help build the legal, mass wing of a militant anti-imperialist movement among whites. It was, in many ways, what the organization tried to but couldn't do in 1969 and 1970: have both aboveground and clandestine anti-imperialist fronts, with each side following Che Guevara's strategy of creating "two, three, many Vietnams."

From its founding at a 1975 conference in Boston, PFOC expressed similar politics to *Prairie Fire*: staunch support for Black liberation, the National Liberation Front of Vietnam, and Puerto Rican independence as primary political tasks. PFOC also defined itself by upfront and militant support for women's liberation, improving on Weather's politics. Judith Mirkinson, a native of New York City, joined the Bay Area PFOC after working for one and a half years in a GI organizing project in Okinawa. Previously, she had worked in the Black Panther Defense Committee in New Haven. Like many other anti-imperialist women, Mirkinson saw a connection between this work and the struggle for women's liberation. She considered herself part of the women's movement and had helped to organize a march in Washington, D.C., of 10,000 women against the war in April 1971. "The issue of women's liberation was central to our politics," she says.

Bernardine Dohrn's younger sister, Jennifer, played a leadership role in PFOC, as did Annie Stein, the mother of WUO fugitive Eleanor Stein.[6] Some former Weatherman members joined PFOC. And surreptitiously there were also aboveground current members of the WUO who joined and took on leading roles in PFOC.[7] For the WUO, the Prairie Fire

---

groups were an attempt to institutionalize mass support for armed struggle and the underground, as in Ireland (Sinn Fein/Irish Republican Army) or South Africa (African National Congress/Umkhonto we Sizwe), where such aboveground-underground formations had proved powerful. For those aboveground, says New York City PFOC organizer Susan Rosenberg, PFOC was a chance to build a national organization, united by "an overall strategy, an anti-imperialist set of politics, and a program."

Building off the prestige of the WUO, PFOC chapters built relationships with many revolutionary Third World groups, especially in Black and Puerto Rican communities, while trying to organize other whites against racism and in support of national liberation. Indeed, Puerto Rican radical Esperanza Martell remembers PFOC members in New York City (as in Boston, Chicago, San Francisco, and elsewhere) being involved in all the crucial issues facing poor people of color, including education, healthcare, and prisons. Ashanti Alston notes that PFOC members were some of the few white people who attended the trials of captured BLA members. "I always appreciated that they were there," he says today.

CONTEXT RAISES NEW QUESTIONS

WITH THE SIGNING of the Paris Peace Accords on January 27, 1973, the Weather Underground, like other Left organizations shaped by the war in Vietnam, began to struggle for direction. Granted, the war didn't really end for another two years, during which time the United States continued to supply weapons, funding, public support, and military aid to the reactionary and unpopular Thieu regime of South Vietnam and Lon Nol in Cambodia. The WUO didn't lose sight of that fact, carrying out a bombing of the Vietnam section of the U.S. Agency for International Development in the State Department building in Washington, D.C., on January 28, 1975. (Weather also attempted to hit the Defense Department Supply Agency in Oakland that same night, but the bomb failed to detonate.)[8]

Still, given that opposition to the conflagration in Vietnam was a major source of unity for the WUO, it had to decide which way to move after the Vietnamese victory, the end of the draft, and Nixon's fall from power. "We saw it as a turning point in U.S. imperial power," Bernardine Dohrn says of the U.S. defeat in Vietnam. "We saw it as a real beginning of the decline of the American empire." At the same time, however, the winding down of the war meant a waning mass movement in the United States. Dohrn remembers the WUO "groping for relevance, groping for an analysis of how to be effective and where to be effective." Donna Willmott says the WUO at this time was "not sure of the role of a clandestine organization and armed actions in a period of time that was clearly moving away from a high tide of militancy."

But the Weather Underground Organization wasn't just an antiwar group; it was unified around revolutionary politics and resistance to the system. The group had defined itself as anti-imperialist; now it had a book and a publicly allied mass organization to back up its politics. And organizations of anti-imperialist whites were clearly needed. The Black movement that had so inspired the WUO's formation was no longer experiencing a high tide. Indeed, the Black Liberation Army had been experiencing debilitating setbacks. Between 1971 and 1975, police killed at least eight suspected BLA members and captured more than twenty; this in a time that saw nearly 1,000 Black "civilians" killed by police.[9] The Native American movement was also under attack. The Pine Ridge reservation in South Dakota was an especially contested space; AIM occupied Wounded Knee, site of an 1890 massacre of indigenous people, in 1973 and found itself facing harassment, beatings, arrests, and murder. In 1975, two FBI agents and one Native American were killed in a shootout on the reservation, leading to the arrest of four AIM activists, most notably Leonard Peltier, the only one of the group who still remains in prison.[10]

Despite the repression, the 1970s were still alive with action. Throughout the decade, the Puerto Rican movement was on the upsurge; new organizations hit the streets advocating for Puerto Rican independence and the freeing of five Puerto Rican Nationalist prisoners held since the 1950s. Armed actions by *independentistas* on U.S. soil, with the same demands for independence and amnesty, were also on the rise, starting in 1974.[11] The mid-1970s also saw the emergence of multiracial and explicitly women-of-color feminist organizing. Groups such as the National Black Feminist Organization (NBFO), the Mexican American Women's National Association (MANA), and Women of All Red Nations (WARN, sister organization to AIM) began targeting the intersections of race, class, and gender oppression. In particular, these organizations and others all opposed the sterilization abuses targeting women of color.[12] And it wasn't just feminist organizing; the National Bisexual Liberation Movement was formed in 1973, with the National Gay Task Force emerging the following year.

Weather's post-*Prairie Fire*, and post-Vietnam War, political shift included a renewed interest in mass work and a new incorporation of class into its political platform. The group had always been focused on the mass movement, viewing its actions as along a spectrum of movement resistance. Most people in the WUO had been successful organizers with SDS, and their skills and growing aboveground-underground relationships were now put to use in helping a mass movement struggling to find its footing. The question then became, what kind of mass work should be done? What were the effective strategies for the time? The need for a resurgent mass movement was unquestioned. But how to get there was an open debate.

As the political limits of the white youth counterculture became more evident, as it became clear that revolution was not imminent, the WUO attempted to develop a more long-term strategy. It increasingly found itself pulled toward the traditional communist political ideas and organizational forms it had denounced. Armed actions came into question and the "multinational working class" began to be considered a leading force.

It was a shift for the WUO to not only consider abandoning armed work but to speak of a multinational working class at all. After all, this was a group that had always said that "the working class" was too amorphous a group to organize around a common platform, that whiteness often proved a stronger bond of solidarity than class exploitation. More than that, Weather had always identified itself with a political analysis that defined white supremacy as the main enemy, with the leading forces to be found among national liberation movements. To talk of organizing the *multinational* working class within the United States raised a host of new political questions—including the central strategic divide between a class-based movement and a national liberation one. A communist party, in theory anyway, could lead the multinational working class—but that meant viewing national liberation as one progressive force among many, rather than the leading one. Having expelled PL from SDS for emphasizing class over race, and having split from RYM II in part over differences with a class-based, party-building philosophy, many WUO activists objected to this political shift—even though many of them went along with it at the time.

Until the end, the WUO talked about racism, but its shift of emphasis to the "multinational working class" led by a revolutionary communist party was a deep change in its view of what the struggle was about and who would lead it. The WUO's core political analysis was being called into question. Was national liberation the leading force (with its own timetable and direction), or was the leading force instead the multinational working class (under the direction of a communist party)? Was anti-racism the linchpin to a revolutionary strategy in the United States, or was racism simply a barrier to working class organizing? Fundamentally, who were the leading agents of social change?

"I'm not sure now what we should have done at that point," Scott Braley says. "I certainly didn't know then." But there was undeniably a different public presentation of the WUO, along with a different internal culture. Many in the group identify it as a time when it was losing its commitment to national liberation and armed struggle. Looking back, several former members lament this political shift. Robert Roth, who advocated the "multinational working class" direction at the time, now regrets it. "I think that we backed off from some of the foundations of our politics and purpose, especially at a time when the Black movement was under extreme attack and the Puerto Rican movement was on the upsurge." Referencing the long history of white-led social movements abandoning the principle of anti-racism and ceasing (or refusing) to follow Third World leadership, Donna Willmott says simply and with regret that, "We did what those before us had done."

The group lost some of its political edge, and it is for this reason that many members reflect with dismay on the last two years of the Weather Underground. These political shifts were reflected in two of the major endeavors the group carried out after *Prairie Fire*, both of them involving media: the WUO produced a regular magazine and was featured in a film.

OSAWATOMIE: NOT IN KANSAS ANYMORE

OSAWATOMIE IS THE name of a town in Kansas where white abolitionist John Brown and a small band of anti-slavery guerrillas held off a much larger pro-slavery force in 1856. This battle was a boon to the abolitionist movement, decisive in securing Kansas as a "free state"—and proof that a small group can accomplish a great deal in the struggle against white supremacy. In honor of Brown, the WUO named its magazine *Osawatomie*. It was to be one of the last projects of the Weather Underground Organization.

As a white man who was willing to pick up arms against slavery, John Brown was in many ways a perfect icon for the WUO (minus his patriarchal mindset and fervent Christianity). The symbol of Brown was fitting for the WUO because the organization tried to carry on his tradition of militant white anti-racism. Indeed, Black Liberation Army soldier Ashanti Alston called the WUO "John Brown's children." In 1969, Mark Rudd said Weatherman was an attempt to create "two, three, many John Browns."[13] A century after Brown was killed, Malcolm X posited Brown as the litmus test for white anti-racists: "If a white person wants to help our cause, ask him what he thinks of John Brown. Do you know what Brown did? He went to war."[14]

And that's what the Weather Underground did as well, although more symbolically than Brown. After years of anti-racist struggle across the country, Brown was hanged after he led a multiracial abolitionist army in a failed 1859 raid on a federal arms arsenal in Harper's Ferry, Virginia (now West Virginia). The raid was an attempt to secure arms for abolitionist forces and mobilize the slaves in the South. A devout Christian and militant anti-racist at a time when Christianity was used as a justification for slavery and many white abolitionists were still openly anti-Black, Brown has been deemed crazy by some historians. But Brown's actions helped initiate the Civil War. He showed the United States—North and South alike—that there were some white people willing to fight and, if need be, die in the struggle against white supremacy.[15]

Besides providing a historical backing for the WUO's militant anti-racism, Brown's image was also perfect for the WUO as a counter to the pathologizing process that deems white anti-racism "crazy" and "guilt-ridden." Coming of age amidst Black ghetto rebellions and open repression of the Black freedom movement (whether nonviolent civil rights marches or Black Power militants), the Weather Underground identified with Brown's staunch anti-racism. The risk of being branded crazy by the war-makers, the racists—even by liberals—was worth it if it meant the WUO was standing up for humanity and on the right side of history. Perhaps one of Brown's contemporaries put it best, saying that all people "who are ready to die for their principles have been charged in their day and age as impractical and unbalanced. It is the explanation mediocrity offers for greatness."[16]

The WUO itself, in a brief mention of Brown in *Prairie Fire*, called him an "example to us of dedication, belief in people's power to affect history and the willingness to risk everything in the cause of liberation."[17] And yet, there was a tragic irony in calling the newsmagazine *Osawatomie*. It became the mouthpiece for the new WUO line of "organizing the multinational working class," which in practice moved the organization away from the staunch support for Third World leadership that had been its hallmark.

The premier issue of *Osawatomie* came out in March 1975 and was available for 40 cents, including postage, with bulk orders of six or more costing only 25 cents each. (The price eventually went up to 50 cents for individual copies.) The Weather Underground printed and distributed each issue of the magazine clandestinely; once it was distributed, PFOC and associated groups would reprint the magazine for a wider circulation. (The same was true not only of *Prairie Fire* but also of *Sing a Battle Song*, a collection of poetry by Weatherwomen released on International Women's Day in 1975 but reprinted by aboveground groups.) Issues were almost always twenty-eight or thirty-two pages long. Each issue featured a "Who We Are" box, usually on page 2, which explained the WUO's history, gave examples of its actions, and stated its official program. The WUO produced six issues of *Osawatomie* before the organization imploded, taking the magazine with it. Publishing required the "total mobilization of our forces," Jeff Jones says in the film *Underground.* Also in the film, Cathy Wilkerson says that a lot of time was now spent writing and licking stamps.[18]

In "Who We Are," the WUO claimed to have caused approximately $10 million worth of damage in its attacks (although no source for this calculation was given). While calling its bombings a "significant blow to [imperialism's] arrogance," the WUO acknowledged that its actions were but a "bee sting against such a powerful enemy."[19] In describing its mission as such, the Weather Underground highlighted its political nature; this was not a group defined by its military deeds. Bee stings were part of a movement that attacked an imperialist system through a variety of means.

The group's program, listed in the first issue, consisted of five key areas:

- U.S. imperialism out of the Third World.
- Peace. Oppose imperialist war and U.S. intervention.
- Fight racism. Build an anti-racist base among white people.
- Support self-determination for oppressed peoples.
- Struggle against sexism and for the freedom of women.
- Wage the class struggle. Fight for socialism. Power to the people.

> In one single phrase, the program means this: Mobilize the people
> to fight U.S. imperialism, the common enemy.[20]

There was still no mention of lesbian or gay liberation struggles (bisexual and transgender liberation being issues that were marginalized even within the gay liberation movement at the time) and there was little understanding of the interconnected structure of oppression—reflecting a crisis for the Left at large, not simply for the WUO. In that sense, given where the U.S. Left was at, the WUO's stated program was an impressive and rather wide-ranging platform. *Osawatomie* was taking the broad political view of *Prairie Fire* and trying to develop it into an organizing program.

Donna Willmott, who worked on *Osawatomie* as a member of the publishing collective, describes the magazine as a way of "letting the movement know what we were thinking," even as that thinking shifted. But the group's identity crisis was growing. Though the magazine was said to be the WUO's voice, it spoke more for a certain element of the group rather than the organization as a whole. Behind the scenes, the Weather Underground was falling apart. "As words came off the press, the organization was unraveling," Cathy Wilkerson says of the "chaotic" magazine.

"We were telling ourselves that this [media production] was a way to be more than an organization that did periodic bombings," Willmott recalls. "[Media] was a way to try and diversify different kinds of actions. But what was the point of it all coming from clandestinity? It doesn't make a whole lot of sense in retrospect." The running of an underground press shop was surely impressive, proving that it was possible to outwit the FBI with words as well as with bombs—"an act of defiance and a clandestine action in itself," Willmott says. But the Red Dragon Print Collective raised the question for many WUO members of why the group was still underground if it wasn't going to continue more direct, and illegal, actions. Exploring the range of clandestine possibilities was a positive development, but the group now found itself doing entirely legal things with the rigmarole of clandestinity, which made them all the more expensive and time consuming. It was, Willmott says, "undercutting a lot of what we used to do." Something had to give.

The WUO concentrated on media production for political, not purely logistical, reasons. Media was a way to maintain a clandestine identity without engaging in bombings or other armed actions. As the Central Committee began to wonder about the efficacy of remaining underground, making media was a way to build support for the WUO as a respectable radical organization. *Osawatomie* was a way for the WUO to gain political credibility in the movement separate from armed actions. It wasn't an overnight decision or even one that was expressed in a direct or coherent way. But media became a way of negotiating the WUO's shifting role and self-conception. Though most members of the organization remained underground until at least 1977, the WUO's clandestine life in the mid-to-late 1970s consisted largely of media production, study, and in Boston, surveillance of a white supremacist anti-busing group—none of which required clandestinity to accomplish. The WUO's main work, Mark Rudd writes, "had become communication with the aboveground—trying to spread the politics of antiimperialism through words instead of by deeds."[21]

Today, former leaders of the WUO tend to have a more positive view of the magazine than many former members do. Bernardine Dohrn calls *Osawatomie* "an effort to try and link our politics to community organizing, to worker organizing, to women's organizing." For her, the magazine was a political reformulation, a resuscitation for the WUO and for the movement at large, which had waned once the immediate threat of the draft had disappeared. The magazine recognized that "the main task at hand was an organizing task" and required building bridges among different groups and movements. It was *Prairie Fire…* applied more analytically to current events." Importantly, Dohrn insists that *Osawatomie* was "not an abandonment of our politics."

Other members differ, viewing the magazine instead as an expression of communist populism that ignored the leading role of Third World movements, and thus compromised the WUO's anti-racism. "In the name of broadening, we abandoned some key strengths of the politics," says Robert Roth, who was a leader of the editorial collective. The problem some former members have with the publication is not with the idea of broadening support, but with the political shift accompanying it. "We wanted to have a bigger influence on people, and in order for that to happen, we thought we had to do things, and especially write things, that were more understandable—which was another word for 'acceptable'—to greater numbers of people," Judy Siff recalls.

In practice, she says, it meant a significantly reduced focus on oppression, especially regarding white or male privilege. So the BLA largely disappeared from consideration, and there was scant attention to the blossoming feminist and lesbian and gay movements, despite the solid anti-imperialism of many people active in those struggles. "The difficulty in maintaining an anti-racist, pro-Black liberation political line was phenomenal," Siff says. "Every time we tried to 'broaden,' we stepped back from that anti-white supremacist perspective. I guess the most amazing thing to me is that we developed it in the first place.... It's not what America wants you to think."

Siff's take on *Osawatomie* helps get at the complexities of the magazine, which succeeded in writing accessibly about various resistance struggles at the time, from those of California's farmworkers to Angolan liberation fighters. But absent from the magazine is what was once the cornerstone of Weather Underground politics: militant struggle against privilege—the flipside to oppression—and the recognition and insistence that systematic oppression rests on the unearned social, political, and economic capital afforded whites, men, and others in a society defined by institutional subjugation. By its very nature, the structural marginalization of one group requires the privileging of another. Much to its credit, "Weatherman" raised the struggle against white privilege to a central political principle in 1969. Indeed, the fight against white privilege took precedence for the Weather Underground over other considerations, including any notion of "organizing the working class." Absent a militant commitment to toppling white supremacy, especially working as white people against white privilege, a political program among whites would ultimately yield to white supremacy, Weather argued in its auspicious beginning.

Now, however, it was 1975—the war was over, the country was gripped by recession, and combating privilege was no longer the centerpiece of the WUO's strategy. The leadership was no longer convinced that an underground strategy was viable or appropriate, and it was rethinking its program. Without the same emphasis on fighting privilege and on continuing underground actions in some form, the magazine disappointed many members of the organization, who defined their politics as fighting privilege and armed struggle as a way to express solidarity with Third World struggles—especially the Black Liberation Movement.

The Central Committee's shifting politics were revealed in the pages of *Osawatomie*. By the time of *Osawatomie*'s demise, the five-point program aimed to "Build an anti-racist base within the working class" rather than among white people specifically—a noticeable shift from race- and nation-based politics to a class-based analysis.[22] "Independence for Puerto Rico" had been added to the first point.[23] The fifth point was changed to "Organize the working class," instead of "Wage the class struggle." And the single phrase consolidation of the program now read: "Mobilize the exploited and oppressed people to wage the class struggle against U.S. imperialism, the common enemy." The program was thus an illustration of the internal political change, where "the class struggle" was now paramount.

Articulating its program as "building an anti-racist base in the working class" moved the WUO away from organizing other whites and toward organizing a multinational/multiracial working class. In focusing on an ostensibly broader class struggle, discussion or program about challenging white privilege was dropped. The WUO had said from the beginning that there *was* a white working class, but that it was an inherently contradictory sector that could not be organized until whites confronted white supremacy as a whole. The new political line assumed a broad, working-class political unity—which the WUO had once argued was illusory—to be harnessed and led by a communist party. It was unclear whether the WUO saw itself as still having a special responsibility to work with whites under the directives of a Black Power-inspired program. If organizing the entire working class was now the goal, organizing whites against racism was a "narrower" program.

This was not a semantic squabble, but one that struck at the heart of what the group was and what it was trying to. Theoretically and practically, mobilizing the working class was different from supporting national liberation. The WUO had never been the only white anti-racist force on the Left. Its strength, however, rested on its emphatic support for national liberation movements—its insistence that these movements were *the* leading forces and that white revolutionaries must ally with them. White supremacy, in this analysis, was an entrenched and embedded system defining the United States, and fighting it was the primary duty of any white revolutionary. If the WUO's primary purpose was now to be organizing the U.S. working class, rather than organizing whites against racism, the group was subordinating Third World movements in the United States to the struggles of the multinational working class—which is exactly what Weather had expelled PL from SDS for doing. Such a political position also rendered an underground organization increasingly irrelevant. Most U.S. workers were not under direct attack by the state in the way national liberation movements were, and the struggle of workers in this country had—with some important exceptions—not advanced to open, long-term levels of confrontation.[24] Equally important, the U.S. working class was not, in any organized capacity, supportive of armed struggle or the national liberation movements that had been Weather's guiding inspiration.

The first issue revealed surprisingly little about the publishing of *Osawatomie*—the risks taken to produce it, the goals the organization hoped to achieve by publishing a newsmagazine, or what its publication would mean for the organization.[25] The final two paragraphs of a three-page editorial briefly mentioned the magazine's goals for the organization: "OSAWATOMIE is written to demystify the workings of the system, to expose and clarify the political meaning of things. Our purpose is to contribute to the unity of progressive forces around a revolutionary line." The editorial, signed by the Central Committee, urged activists to share, discuss, and reprint the magazine to help it expand.

Issues two through six described *Osawatomie* as "the revolutionary voice of the WUO," which was "guided by a commitment to struggle, a determination to fight the enemy, the certainty that we will see revolution in our lifetime, and a spirit of love for the exploited people of the world. In order to build a successful struggle, the people need strong organization and a revolutionary party."[26] In explaining the role of the magazine in Leninist terms—as a voice for the party—the WUO was positioning itself similarly to the aboveground Left publications in the New Communist Movement and taking another step in a party-building direction.[27]

Osawatomie's regular features included an editorial, usually signed by the Central Committee; news and book reviews; the "toolbox" section, which attempted to explain, in understandable language, certain communist ideas the WUO found important; and the "fireworks" section, which, depending on the issue, was an interesting amalgamation of history and current possibilities for incendiary movements. Most issues featured information on prison issues along with stories specifically related to the economy or working people (including a lengthy examination of women workers in *Osawatomie*'s second issue).[28] There were also stories about struggles by farmworkers in the United States and movements in parts of the Third World. Like good journalists, the WUO tried to explain issues with a focus on how different communities were impacted. For instance, the first issue featured articles on what the economic crisis meant for women and for the elderly.[29] An article in the third issue highlighted the effect of the booming prison industry on different populations.[30] There was also usually an artistic centerfold design of some kind, like the bilingual report on the Puerto Rican Nationalist political prisoners in issue one; or the final issue's drawing of Frederick Douglass that accompanied a reprint of his speech "What does the Fourth of July mean to the slave?"[31] It was an innovative production, if ultimately a confusing one.

Despite the WUO's political shift, *Osawatomie* attempted to articulate aspects of its theoretical understanding in a fairly accessible way, at least given the limitations of the stilted Marxist-Leninist diction seemingly required by many groups on the Left at this time. Puerto Rican independence was a recurring theme in *Osawatomie*, as it was in PFOC's aboveground work—not surprising, given the growth of the independence movement, encouraged by a 1973 UN resolution calling for the end of U.S. colonialism over the island.[32] Now with the grandiose title of "First Secretary" of the WUO, Bernardine Dohrn wrote "An Open Letter to U.S. Workers" in the penultimate issue of *Osawatomie*, to encourage support for the Puerto Rican workers' movement.[33] While it was a positive step to connect U.S.-based class struggle with that in Puerto Rico, the letter also makes the grievous mistake of appointing the Puerto Rican Socialist Party (PSP) as the "leading" force of the Puerto Rican struggle (a designation the WUO lavished on the PSP more than once). The PSP was certainly an audacious and impressive group in 1976, but it was not the place of a white group to proclaim the vanguard of a Third World struggle.[34] More than that, by throwing its support primarily behind the PSP, the WUO inserted itself in the Puerto Rican struggle at a time when other forces were also emerging, both aboveground and underground.

Like all of Weather's political work, *Osawatomie* was a well-done clandestine action. Even as she grew horrified by the politics, Laura Whitehorn remembers thinking that each issue was "always beautiful, and I was impressed that something like that could come out." Naomi Jaffe was part of the publishing collective, which was responsible for magazine design and layout. "We were very proud of it and justly so," she says today. The magazine was aesthetically pleasing, with lots of pictures and artwork, and well written—both of which, she says, reflected a care and respect for the politics and how they were presented. But because it reflected a new political direction, the clandestine print shop "exemplified the best and the worst" of the organization. Fellow publishing collective member Donna Willmott felt good to be producing something but was unclear how the magazine fit with the group's program. "It was a tangible reflection of our continued existence," she says today of *Osawatomie*. "[But] sometimes I think it masked the level of lack of strategy and direction that we were feeling."

Although one of its purposes was to build support for the WUO as an organization, *Osawatomie* was no mere cheerleader for WUO actions; even when reporting on a particular bombing, the magazine focused very little on the action itself, choosing instead to focus on broader political objectives and attempts to unify with other movements.

 Osawatomie reported on the three WUO bombings that occurred while the publication was in print, but the bombings received even less coverage than in the mainstream media. They were not front-page news for the magazine the way prison struggles, Vietnam, and the economic crisis were. An *Osawatomie* article in support of striking cement workers in Puerto Rico mentions the WUO bombing done in solidarity only once, even though the bombing took place shortly before press time (June 16, 1975, before the summer issue).[35] The braggadocio of 1969 was replaced with a quiet modesty about bombing the halls of power.

 Osawatomie did not shy away from controversial issues, including those topics that the Left was divided over. The WUO continued to critically engage with the Symbionese Liberation Army through the pages of the magazine, writing a second open letter about the SLA in the fourth issue of *Osawatomie* (published in winter 1975–1976).[36] This open letter, appearing after SLA members were captured, was critical of the SLA's belief that "the leadership of the movement is established through armed actions alone," but supportive of them as comrades-in-arms. The WUO was particularly critical of the SLA for repeating an error Weatherman originally made: using the *foco* theory in the misguided belief that "guerrilla struggle itself politicizes and activates the people." The open letter to the SLA in *Osawatomie* displayed the organization's thinking about the purpose of clandestine work. It argued for building mass organizations led by a revolutionary party that supports armed struggle, but which would also be in a position to lead "the powerful discontent of the oppressed and exploited." The message seemed to foreshadow the WUO's demise as an underground force.

The WUO emphasized mass movement work in other public statements, not just through *Osawatomie*. In spring 1975, the Red Dragon Print Collective released an editorial by Celia Sojourn (a pseudonym) and Billy Ayers entitled "Politics in Command." It defended the use of armed struggle, even as it argued that armed struggle "is the work of the masses of oppressed and exploited people." While that statement, and others like it in the essay, may seem intuitive, they express the WUO's changing attitudes about armed work. The Weather Underground and other clandestine armed struggle groups were definitely *not* the work of the masses; even those groups with the broadest support in Third World communities, such as the BLA or the FALN, did not command majority sentiment. And if "the test of action is primarily the ability to win the people," as the 1975 statement argued, how important or effective was an armed component in this period? Could it still contribute to building a mass movement? Armed propaganda, once conceived of as way to bring resistance to a new level, was no longer deemed a viable strategy for the WUO of the mid-1970s, even if this was never explicitly stated.[37] By defining armed struggle as only the expression of the masses, the WUO was arguing against itself. Without much input from rank-and-file members, the leadership of the organization began to move the group away from armed acts. "The dynamics of the period were pulling Weatherman away from armed struggle and pulling it toward public organizing," Robert Roth says. "The Weather Underground didn't grapple with this openly or clearly enough—either publicly or internally."

With armed acts no longer a high priority, and with the public organizing (PFOC) going strong, the WUO now began to question the utility of staying underground at all. Some former WUO members claim that the leadership of the organization began pursuing a strategy called "inversion," planning for the group to surface and assume a leading role in what would be the multinational working class revolution, led by a communist party. "The way things worked in the WUO was, the Central Committee made a decision and then won over the cadres," Gilbert says, "and it sure felt like that was what was going on with inversion."[38] Even asking these questions was a big shift, given that the WUO's *raison d'être* was to be a white fighting force in solidarity with national liberation. To suggest that the group not only leave the underground but try to play a leading role in multiracial, class-based formations was a shock to many. There was also a sense that it would be wrong to disband underground work after all that people had been through. "I felt like I had gone through so much stuff, I was so emotionally invested in building clandestine organization, that the idea of anything else was too shocking," Scott Braley recalls, remembering being "aghast" when someone suggested bluntly that the group should disband and people should surface.[39]

The inversion strategy, to the extent it held sway, can be seen as part of larger attempts in the post-SDS Left at party-building, despite the acrimony between WUO and PFOC, on the one hand, and those building communist parties on the other.[40] It is not clear, however, that inversion was a planned, coherent strategy. Former Central Committee member Bill Ayers acknowledges that the leadership was asking whether it was appropriate to remain underground, given the end of the Vietnam War and the related decline in both movement work among whites and support for militancy. But both Ayers and Dohrn say now that there was no organizational *plan* to carry out inversion. Instead, they say the group was doing what it should have done: looking for ways to be relevant to the political climate of the time—and it wasn't a time for bombs.

Jeff Jones, the Central Committee member who first proposed inversion (or at least raised it as a question), says today that inversion, while not *a plan*, was nevertheless *in motion* as a possible course, even though the organization at large opposed such a move. "I certainly knew as a leader that [inversion] was controversial, and if put to the membership as a whole, it stood a good chance of being rejected for the same reason it was subsequently rejected," Jones says. It wasn't just the leaders who thought of it. Mark Rudd remembers suggesting to the Central Committee that those remaining underground (himself included) begin to surface, seeing a clandestine capacity as futile at that point.[41] A longtime radical with roots in the Communist Party, PFOC leader Annie Stein similarly argued that clandestinity was unnecessary.[42]

Remaining underground was "an increasingly high-cost fantasy," Ayers says. "What was it accomplishing?" Indeed, some members of the WUO even left the organization after the end of the war, he says. Jeff Jones says he also felt that "the underground had run its course by 1975." Dohrn seconds this view, saying that for the organization to continue "to do what we had been doing, in the sense of doing a couple actions a year and releasing communiqués, seemed inappropriate [in 1975]. And I think it *was* inappropriate. It didn't have the kind of shock value and interpretive value that it had during the war."

Jones, however, is quick to distinguish between withdrawing from armed actions and abandoning a clandestine capacity. The goal of inversion, he claims, called for maintaining the underground networks to protect those in need and provide space for thinking and strategizing away from the eyes and ears of the state. In Jones' view, inversion would apply only to those without charges who wanted to surface. This move, it was hoped, would contribute to the mass movement, such as it was then, without sacrificing the underground as a clandestine support network. But the time for armed acts was over, he felt.

THE BATTLE OF BOSTON

IN ADDITION TO the process of dialoguing with other sectors of the Left, the Weather Underground used *Osawatomie* to experiment with investigative journalism by covering the busing struggle in the Boston area. A court order had demanded that Boston desegregate its schools through busing, and a white backlash ensued. Many elements were at play in the anti-busing movement, but at the frontlines were predominantly working-class white mothers and youth who physically attacked Black families, including the bused children—and even the police who tried to safeguard children on their way to school. The complexities and tensions of race, class, and geography were being played out for the country to see.[43]

The Boston busing crisis—which the WUO referred to as "the Battle of Boston"—was a mainstay in *Osawatomie*, featured as the cover story in the first issue. In its exposé of the racist anti-busing movement, the WUO revealed that the leaders of one of the main groups spearheading the campaign, Restore Our Alienated Rights (ROAR), included representatives of the openly racist John Birch Society, Boston city council members, and supporters of segregationist and former presidential candidate George Wallace. The seven-page article on Boston in the first issue included smaller accompanying stories on key ROAR leaders and on the demographics of South Boston, a predominantly Irish neighborhood where much of the opposition to busing was based. The article also described what the WUO had done to date. "From underground, we have put up antiracist stickers and talked with people in white working-class communities, stink-bombed the offices of the School Committee and marched in the National March Against Racism on December 14. We've also secretly attended weekly meetings of ROAR.... Our purpose has been to gain knowledge of the enemy's strategy and goals, to expose ROAR's purposes, and to discover its vulnerable points."[44] Much of the main article consisted of reports from ROAR meetings and an analysis of ROAR's actions.

In response to the Boston crisis, the WUO engaged in only minor confrontational tactics. To have done a bombing would likely have been ill-advised and only added to the problems of Black families, who were under physical assault by racists. While the organization never did an armed action relating to the Boston crisis, it did support the work of its aboveground cadre, who were defending Black families. For two years, Laura Whitehorn was among a small group of PFOC activists in the Boston area who sat with baseball bats in people's homes (every night in the summer, on weekends during the winter) protecting families from local white supremacists who tried to attack with bats, Molotov cocktails, and spray-paint.[45]

Weather's stance in Boston stood in stark contrast to that of the Revolutionary Union (RU), a post-SDS communist group that opposed busing and functionally aligned themselves with racists in the supposed interest of preserving "working class unity." Much of the Left opposed RU and the racist attacks on Black Boston, but "was divided over the basic issue of whether the Boston battle was mainly a fight against racism or a confrontation with a ruling class plot to use busing to divide workers," Max Elbaum writes in his history of the New Communist Movement. "And even those organizations with a sound basic stance were unable to unite on a common program of action."[46] That the WUO recognized "The Battle of Boston" as fundamentally an anti-racist struggle was an advance from the sectarian rigidity gripping much of the Left. Still, even the WUO was not fully unified on what the correct response to the crisis should have been; a faction that emerged within the group as it split criticized the organization for pulling back from militant action in Boston.[47]

STRUGGLING FOR DIRECTION:
CLASS, GENDER, AND THE WEATHER UNDERGROUND

THE WUO LEADERSHIP viewed *Osawatomie* as a way to popularize its program, which was growing increasingly unpopular inside the organization. Everything from women's liberation to the energy crisis was explained in *Osawatomie* in terms of class, specifically vis-à-vis the "multinational working class" the WUO was now committed to organizing. Discussion of the BLA was limited, and AIM was almost nonexistent in the pages of *Osawatomie*.

The women's movement was also slighted. In an editorial signed by Celia Sojourn, the leadership argued that "The Women's Question is a Class Question," asserting that only socialism and the destruction of capitalism could free women, with "the working class" as the "motor force in making this revolution."[48] Women's liberation was thus seen as dependent on working class struggle rather than on any feminist movement. The editorial neglected to mention anything about patriarchy as a system or that women's oppression was deeper than just the class system. Male supremacy and sexism were presented as bad ideas implanted by capitalism without any material basis in their own right. PFOC activist Judith Mirkinson refused to distribute that issue of the magazine because of the article. The editorial also created ripples within the WUO, reigniting meetings by Weatherwomen, who demanded that the organization issue a self-criticism renouncing the article's politics.[49] It never happened.

The "Women's Question" editorial emerged at a time of tremendous feminist organizing, including impressive political work by women of color, which the editorial either ignored or inadvertently maligned by deriding the women's movement for not focusing on class. Indeed, the editorial made no mention of the array of organizing projects at the time, which included highly publicized defense work for two women on trial for the self-defense murders of men who had raped them. Joan (pronounced Jo-Anne) Little was an African American woman imprisoned in North Carolina who had killed a jail guard attempting to force her into performing oral sex. Inez Garcia, a Chicana in California, had shot and killed one of two men who raped her. The two women's trials took place in 1975 and 1976, creating a public stir over racialized sexual violence and women's self-defense. (Both were acquitted on grounds of self-defense.)[50]

Also in 1975, lesbian feminist Susan Saxe was arrested after five years underground for clandestine activities. An antiwar militant from the Boston area, Saxe publicly said her "armed struggle against the Amerikan state was a valid and necessary escalation of the politics of the '60s." She denounced Jane Alpert's collaboration as anti-feminist, pledged solidarity with the "sisters and brothers who are our natural allies in revolution," and connected her anti-imperialism to her lesbianism and her feminism. The government had been hunting Saxe since she participated in a 1970 bank robbery gone awry, leaving a police officer dead. Women's and lesbian activist communities in New Haven, Connecticut, and Lexington, Kentucky, were targeted by grand juries hunting for Saxe. As with the grand juries impaneled for the WUO, women refused to cooperate, and about a dozen people went to jail.[51]

So it's not just that "The Women's Question" offered a rather static political framework for women's liberation, but that it missed the beat of a militant women's movement on the rise. Problems had emerged prior to the offending editorial. As part of the organization's attempt to consolidate its new politics around class, the WUO held its second Cadre School in September 1975. Out of it emerged an *Osawatomie* editorial (reprinted as a speech by Bernardine Dohrn) outlining the WUO's "Class Stand." More than the first one, this Cadre School was indoctrinating WUO rank-and-file with a class line; the leadership was excited about the potential for the schools to teach members economics from a Marxist-Leninist perspective and possibly create new momentum within the group. And the subsequent editorial in the autumn 1975 issue of *Osawatomie* reflected the change in organizational focus not only since 1969, but even since the publication of Prairie Fire a year previously.

"We are building a communist organization to be part of the forces which build a revolutionary communist party to lead the working class to seize power and build socialism," the editorial announced. Although the organization had been engaged in a serious study of Marxism-Leninism for more than two years, the editorial dubbed the "struggle for Marxism-Leninism" to be the "most significant development in [the WUO's] recent history." The statement offered a self-criticism of the WUO for dismissing the progressive potential of the (white) working class. The group had now gone to the opposite side of the spectrum, saying that although racism was a problem among the working class, the main struggle was between the multinational working class and the ruling class.[52]

Absent a broader discussion, and with the emphasis in *Osawatomie* on a "revolutionary party" of the "multinational working class," many members felt that the organization was moving backward, not forward. "We settled for the simple and familiar," Willmott says, calling the organization's later "Marxoid" politics a "throwback" rather than an advance. As the organization went from viewing race to class as "the primary contradiction," facile answers often usurped careful debate and even became institutionalized within the WUO. "I remember having an informal conversation with a leading member of the organization about anti-Semitism at this time," says Suzanne Ross, a Jewish member of the group born in Nazi Europe. "And this woman said, 'It's simple. It's a class question.' Suddenly, everything became a 'class question.' Not only was that kind of thinking simplistic and one-sided, but because members did not feel free to seriously question and challenge it, weak and incorrect positions were accepted and imposed on Weather collectives and supporters. Worse, sloppy thinking became the norm."

FROM UNDERGROUND TO *UNDERGROUND*:
THE WUO ON THE BIG SCREEN

FOLLOWING THE PRECEDENT of combining underground actions with underground media that began by writing a book and continued by producing a newsmagazine, the Weather Underground next turned to visual media. The idea for the project came from radical filmmaker Emile de Antonio, who was inspired by reading *Prairie Fire*. *Underground* is the only film or TV appearance the WUO ever did while underground, although it is revealed in the film that there were "other offers." De Antonio's history of radical filmmaking and sympathetic approach made him the obvious choice.[53] De Antonio teamed up with Mary Lampson and Haskell Wexler in May 1975 to make the documentary. The film featured Central Committee members Bill Ayers, Bernardine Dohrn, and Jeff Jones along with townhouse survivors Kathy Boudin and Cathy Wilkerson—the five best-known members of the group. The film, a fascinating 88-minute glimpse at the underground and a further attempt to communicate from clandestinity, seems also to reflect the leadership's move away from armed struggle.

The film consists mostly of interviews with the five Weatherpeople done in a two-day period in a Los Angeles safe house, with an additional day of filming with Boudin and Jones talking to random people at a Los Angeles employment office about the economy (then in recession) and revolution (also in recession at the time). Spliced with footage taken from the safe house interviews are various images of 1960s and '70s struggles, from Malcolm X to the U.S. army fleeing Saigon to the Boston busing crisis. From a security perspective, the film is almost comical. Throughout it, the famous fugitives appear either behind a cheesecloth scrim, or with only their backs visible as cameraman Haskell Wexler filmed a mirror placed behind them. The cheesecloth was abandoned after the first day of shooting to provide a more intimate setting, although there is no clear break in the film from day one to day two; footage is spliced together throughout. The film also shows old pictures and footage of all five from before they went underground, providing viewers and law enforcement alike with before and (fuzzy) after images of the radicals.[54]

Immediately after the filming was complete, the FBI subjected the filmmakers to surveillance and harassment. This harassment ranged from getting de Antonio's financial records from banks and credit card companies, to phone taps, to a plot (never carried out) to steal a copy of the film from his studio. Cameraman Haskell Wexler was followed by a helicopter; his house was burglarized and his Oscar for a previous film was stolen.[55] The harassment culminated in a subpoena of the filmmakers to testify before a grand jury and turn over the film and negatives. The subpoena drew the ire of actors, civil libertarians, and movement activists, who feared a return to Senator Joe McCarthy's red-baiting and blacklisting of Hollywood radicals and rallied to the defense of de Antonio, Lampson, and Wexler.[56] A petition on their behalf featured such celebrities as Warren Beatty, Mel Brooks, Sally Field, and Jack Nicholson, as well as Daniel Ellsberg, the ex-government employee who leaked the documents that became known as the Pentagon Papers. The filmmakers were defended by three prominent radical lawyers (including Leonard Boudin, Kathy's father) and staunchly refused to cooperate. De Antonio argued that asking for a filmmaker's unedited film was like asking for a journalist's notebook.[57] The ACLU said the grand jury was being used as a "blunderbuss" by the government because it was unable to capture the WUO. De Antonio went a step further, saying that the grand jury was the government's attempt to stop a film "that would embarrass a government whose vast resources had failed to locate a network of fugitives that a middle-aged film director had found with little difficulty."[58]

Amidst public support for the filmmakers, the FBI dropped the subpoena. *Underground* was released and billed as "the film the FBI didn't want you to see." Although the film received surprisingly good reviews from many mainstream publications, its box office success was limited.[59] The WUO advertised the film through a centerfold spread in the third issue of *Osawatomie*, complete with snippets from de Antonio's original letter proposing the film to the WUO and a letter from Jeff Jones congratulating the filmmakers on their "principled stand of non-collaboration" with the grand jury.[60] The filmmakers' resistance to the grand jury built on the successful resistance of the Left throughout the 1970s. It was also proof that, though the mass movement was in abeyance, a healthy distrust of the state's repressive apparatus continued and even extended to include parts of Hollywood.

Opinions on the film among activists differed. Some were pleased with it, viewing its release as proof that the system could be outwitted. Just by its existence, the film was a taunt and a challenge to the state. It even played in Europe.[61] But some radicals were angered at the way the WUO used the film as a means to build support for its own well-being. A letter signed by twelve political prisoners (who had no way of seeing the film but had plenty of secondhand reports) and published in a letters section in the fifth issue of *Osawatomie* criticized the WUO for using the film "*almost* exclusively [for] comrades who have the most support nationally."[62] The WUO should set up showings of the film to build support for other political prisoners and political people awaiting trial, the letter said.

In reflecting on the film in his memoir, Bill Ayers writes that, while the politics espoused in the film "held up remarkably well," he was not all pleased to see the film more recently. "I was embarrassed by the arrogance, the solipsism, the absolute certainty that we and we alone knew the way. The rigidity and the narcissism.... We can, as well, be carried along toward an easy belief, toward the decisiveness of our dogma."[63] Other members of the group didn't share Ayers' sanguine view of the politics expressed in the film. Later, as the organization was falling apart, one faction was particularly vocal in criticizing the film for being used opportunistically as a way to improve the standing of the organization and its leaders, to reacquaint the mass movement with the group, and to establish a leadership position for the WUO in the event that members should surface.[64]

Donna Willmott remembers being excited that the film could be made but frustrated by its politics. "*Osawatomie* I wasn't critical of until years later. But when I saw the film, I really didn't like it," she says. "I was embarrassed by the self-centeredness of it. It didn't feel right." Jeff Jones, who pioneered the idea for the film within the organization, agrees that criticisms of the film were mostly on target. "We got carried away with ourselves as individuals," he says. Cathy Wilkerson says the film was well done but politically absurd. Dohrn says the film was another effort at communicating from underground, but that it didn't serve a strategic purpose. Other members call it "a snore," "boring," and a "self-promotion" tool, among other things.[65] Mark Rudd writes that people in and around the organization dubbed the film, with its endless talking, "Jaws."[66] Of its various media projects, then, it seems that the group's book (*Prairie Fire*) was much better than its movie (*Underground*).

In 1976 Mark Felt, second in command at the FBI and later revealed as Deep Throat, holds a copy of a magazine produced by the Weather Underground to defend the warrantless break-ins against radical groups.

> *By the time of its demise in 1976, the WUO had evolved basically to the position of traditional white left groups: denying the leading, or even independent, role of national liberation; seeing itself as the leadership of the entire "US revolution"; and pulling out of armed struggle. Ironically, Weather's claim to leadership was based solely on the prestige of the armed struggle and the support for national liberation that it was now abandoning.* —David Gilbert[1]

WITHIN A YEAR AND A HALF OF UNDERGROUND'S release, the Weather Underground was no more. The group did two actions in the four months following the May 1975 filming of *Underground*: one against the Banco de Ponce offices in New York's Rockefeller Center (June 16, 1975) in solidarity with a strike in Puerto Rico, and the other against the Kennecott Corporation in Salt Lake City (September 5, 1975).[2] Kennecott, a copper company, was the final entity in the corporate triumvirate that the WUO had identified as dominant U.S. players in the coup that had ousted Allende and installed the Pinochet regime. The Kennecott bombing was the third against U.S. support for the coup in Chile—and the last WUO bombing prior to the group's factional split.[3]

While a bomb exploded in a bathroom at the multinational copper company, the Prairie Fire Organizing Committee was planning for the Hard Times Conference, with WUO support and (surreptitious) leadership. To the Central Committee, who came up with the idea (and went ahead with it over the objections of some aboveground organizers), the conference was a way of building a national multiracial coalition—with the WUO in a leading role. The plan was doomed to fail, partly because of Weather's confusion over its connection to the aboveground. "I don't feel like we really ever came to an appropriate definition or view of the relationship between clandestine forces and aboveground organizing," says Donna Willmott. Others, such as Bernardine Dohrn, see the conference as a deviation from Weather's traditional practice, whereby the group was "very careful…to not interfere with aboveground activity" because it "didn't have a good enough grasp" on aboveground needs. But excited by the aboveground-underground relationships fostered through the writing and publishing of *Prairie Fire*, she says, the group thought it could pull off a conference to serve as a catalyst for aboveground organizing.

The slogan for the conference was "Hard Times are Fighting Times." Although the idea and the political direction originated with the WUO, PFOC was the public convener and organizer of the Hard Times Conference. It had been planning for the conference since its official inception in 1975. PFOC established conference organizing committees in a dozen cities nationwide.[4] They worked with the Puerto Rican Socialist Party (PSP), United Black Workers, the Republic of New Afrika (RNA), Youth Against War and Fascism, the Workers World Party (WWP), the American Indian Movement (AIM), a Mexicano-Chicano workers' organization called CASA, several unions, and others to bring together a multiracial crowd of more than 2,000 people to the University of Illinois Circle Campus in Chicago from January 30 to February 1, 1976. The conference was endorsed by a spate of movement groups and well-known activists such as Black feminist author Toni Cade Bambara and radical historian Howard Zinn.[5] Even famed SNCC leader Ella Baker and radical lawyer William Kunstler were at the conference, which was "broadcast live on Pacifica radio."[6] The widespread participation in and support for the conference testified to the respect both the WUO, and by extension the PFOC, commanded among progressives and radicals—and also to the fact that people were hungry for a revived mass movement.

The goal of the conference was to forge a national organization with a unified program to fight those issues impacting "working and oppressed people in the US [who] are under assault."[7] PFOC leader Jennifer Dohrn (Bernardine's little sister) told the crowd that they were there to "develop a program of demands for the working class as a whole in this period to fight the depression."[8] While the overwhelming tone of the conference was in response to the economic recession, there was also some discussion of struggles in Vietnam, Angola, Zimbabwe, South Africa, and elsewhere. With thousands gathered in Chicago, it looked like the conference would be a success. The attendance far surpassed what the WUO and PFOC had anticipated. "Action proposals" were discussed, with the conference delegates voting to support the PSP's planned demonstration against colonialism to be held that summer in Philadelphia during the bicentennial celebrations. Demonstrations to be held in solidarity with Vietnam, Chile, women's struggles, and labor fights were also discussed.[9]

But the unity quickly unraveled, and the conference became a political disaster. A Black caucus—led by the RNA, which had asked to make a formal presentation but was denied by the conference organizers—and a women's caucus both formed during the conference. Each caucus was upset with the reformist Hard Times agenda. Both were furious that the WUO and PFOC had backed away from support of self-determination for women and Third World people in the United States—positions on which the convening organizations had staked their political credentials. Instead, the conference spoke of creating an organization of the "multinational working class" to lead the entire political struggle in America. The Black caucus critiqued the conference program and platform, Susan Rosenberg remembers, and the women's caucus "critiqued it as being male-defined and not pro-lesbian." Both caucuses denounced the event for abandoning self-determination in favor of party-building.[10] As with *Osawatomie*, the worthwhile goal of broad Left unity was undercut at Hard Times by a platform attempting a lowest-common-denominator politics.

PFOC activists were devastated—but not necessarily surprised. Judith Mirkinson, a Bay Area PFOC member, says the severely critical response by Third World people to the conference was to be expected, given that the conference put forward "this classic [white] Marxist perspective." She remembers "sitting there, listening to the speeches and hating it." Michael Novick, who had been in Weatherman when it first began, went to the Hard Times Conference with a contingent from the June 28 Union, an anti-imperialist and pro-feminist gay men's collective. Already upset with the "right turn" presented in *Osawatomie*, Novick and his group were supportive when the caucuses criticized the "obsolete, economist definition of the struggle and the organization needed to wage it." It was antithetical to the politics that had defined the WUO and PFOC—and people were angry at the reversal. "Struggle seemed to emerge at every workshop and plenary," Novick remembers.

Even though unity was a worthy, indeed necessary, goal, the question was what kind of unity. Susan Rosenberg remembers feeling that the event marked "a sell out of anti-imperialist politics in general" by both the WUO and PFOC. She was somewhat prepared for the criticisms that emerged; in organizing for the conference, Rosenberg and other New York City PFOC activists had traveled south and met with people from the RNA. Like the Panther 21, the RNA activists regarded the WUO and its sector of the movement as the best of the white Left. They were upset that the WUO and PFOC had seemingly backed off from addressing white privilege and supporting self-determination and were positioning themselves more as leaders of an overall U.S. struggle. "It was a shift in organizational focus, and it was taking away concrete support and solidarity from the Black Power Movement," Rosenberg says. "I thought that that [criticism] made sense."

STRUGGLING FOR DIRECTION: HARD TIMES AND THE WUO

LIKE OSAWATOMIE, THE Hard Times Conference was an attempt to find relevance in the postwar-but-still-imperialist United States. As longtime activists, members of the WUO realized that bombings themselves weren't a strategy, that the time period raised new questions for a group formed amidst a strong mass movement, and that class was central to revolutionary process. And yet what these generalities meant specifically and in practice were open questions. By and large, the WUO leadership and the membership had different answers to the question: What is to be done?

"I think that we were influenced by a sense that we hadn't paid appropriate attention to a class analysis," Bernardine Dohrn says today, although she takes issue with the notion that the group's politics at the time were retrograde. "You could call that traditional Marxist, but I think that what wasn't traditional Marxist about it was that we were trying to recognize that it necessarily involved Black and Latino and white forces." The broad-based approach that Hard Times put forth was a positive aspiration and a "good-faith" effort, she says.

Other Weather veterans disagree. To many of them, the Hard Times Conference was a betrayal. Naomi Jaffe calls the conference "the most visible manifestation of the WUO's lack of accountability to people of color leadership." Rather than looking to the leadership of Black, Puerto Rican, Native, and other Third World movements, the WUO was now positioning itself as a "pre-party formation" to lead the "multinational working class." As always, it wasn't just race and class at stake but gender. As Weatherwomen would later write, the Central Committee opposed instituting an autonomous women's caucus on the grounds that "it would become a bastion of 'bourgeois feminism.'"[11] (Of course, upset at the absence of a women's caucus, women conference participants formed their own caucus, which then denounced the sexism of Hard Times.)

In an organization where, as Judy Siff notes, "you'd rather die than be characterized as racist and sexist," the criticisms of Hard Times had a shattering effect. If the internal problems following *Prairie Fire* were the "warning signs" of trouble for Siff, the conference was the "loud noise" that dramatized the depth of the problems. Donna Willmott remembers feeling "a tremendous loss and defeat" after Hard Times when she realized "how far [the WUO] had sunk." Similarly, Suzanne Ross regrets not listening to earlier "disturbing observations" about the group's political direction. When everything blew up around the Hard Times Conference, Ross says she was upset at "having participated in a development that had become so corrupt."

As fugitives, underground members of the WUO couldn't attend the conference that they had been mobilizing for since the Central Committee came up with the idea. But that doesn't mean that the WUO missed the conference altogether; there were always people living and acting aboveground who were unidentified members of the WUO and involved in mass movement work. These people not only attended the conference but had a major role in organizing for it. Laura Whitehorn was one such member. "I hated it more than anything else I've ever done," she says today. Whitehorn was so nauseated by the politics of the conference that she became physically ill in the middle of it—right after the RNA delegation was denied its request to make a presentation. Afterward, she began to pull away from the WUO.[12]

But it wasn't that simple. Like other aboveground WUO members surreptitiously in PFOC, Whitehorn was kicked out of PFOC when her clandestine affiliation was discovered. PFOC members were furious when they found out that leading members of their organization were "double agents" secretly in the WUO. It was an unprincipled and unaccountable position. Despite similar politics, PFOC was not merely a WUO support group; it had its own identity and wanted to maintain its autonomy. The close political (and in some cases, personal) ties between the WUO and

PFOC meant both organizations were discredited, at least temporarily, as a result of the conference fallout.

Hard Times begat hard times, for the WUO as well as PFOC. The conference set in motion parallel crises for both organizations. Within a year, one organization would be destroyed, the other dramatically reshaped.

Publicly, the WUO left the Hard Times Conference showing no signs of defeat—even as it was internally coming apart at the seams. The WUO still managed to release two more issues of *Osawatomie* before the group was hopelessly fragmented. In fact, the magazine increased the frequency of publication following Hard Times, likely as a last-ditch effort to rescue the organization. Neither the April–May issue nor the June–July issue—which proved to be the final one—mentions the Hard Times Conference or the fallout from it. But this silence is not quite the paradox it seems; issues of the magazine prior to the conference didn't advertise for it, since the WUO's role in it was supposed to be secret. The closest thing to a public acknowledgement of the WUO's role in the conference was a self-criticism by the Central Committee printed in the June–July issue that acknowledged many of the criticisms raised at Hard Times.

In *Osawatomie*, the WUO put forth a façade of remobilization. An introductory letter in the April–May issue, signed by Central Committee members and *Osawatomie* editors Bill Ayers and Joe Reed (a pseudonym), announced that *Osawatomie* would now appear bimonthly instead of quarterly.[13] The change, according to the letter, reflected the WUO's growth and "the importance we attach to the continued development of OSAWATOMIE as the revolutionary voice of the WUO." Rather than backing down from what led to the problems at Hard Times, this issue expressed an entrenchment of those politics. The editors described the development of the publication as a way to "mobilize and organize the working class" and to "organize and build a revolutionary Marxist-Leninist party of the working class."

Two months later, the sixth and what turned out to be the final issue of *Osawatomie* appeared. The June–July cover photo, from the Boston busing struggle, showed a white man attempting to spear a Black man with a flag pole flying the American flag. Beneath the picture, in promotion of the upcoming PSP-initiated bicentennial protest in Philadelphia, was a headline proclaiming "200 Years is Enough!" Inside was a sometimes odd, sometimes engaging collection of news stories, radical theory, book reviews, and literary fiction. (It was the most frazzled issue to date.) There was nothing to mark it as the last issue, except perhaps for a self-critical editorial on "anti-imperialism vs. opportunism" which discussed many of the errors exposed at the Hard Times Conference. Without mentioning the conference, the editorial identified the errors as:

> 1. abandoning revolutionary anti-imperialism
> 2. submerging the national question into the class question, especially in relation to the Black liberation struggle
> 3. downplaying the struggle against the special oppression of women/sexism and male supremacy
> 4. downplaying the essential role of revolutionary theory and communist organization.[14]

This self-criticism by the Central Committee did nothing to avert, and little to slow, the collapse of the organization. Realistically, no self-criticism, no matter how public or sincere, could have prevented the split that occurred, given how deeply divided the organization was. This internal dissension, built up over years, reflected a general confusion and disagreement over strategy. The group's head had tried to move in a different direction than most of the body wanted to go. But given the top-down structure characterizing the WUO, the rank-and-file members had followed. And now they were furious. Indeed, the lack of internal democracy was a powerful force precipitating not just the breakup of the WUO but the bitterness and quick dispersal that followed the group's collapse.

The self-criticism itself embodied these tensions, on the one hand saying that the organization didn't identify strongly enough with the working class, and on the other acknowledging that the working class is not a monolithic entity but is racialized, gendered, and more complex, even contradictory, a grouping than can be led under one communist party. The editorial was a fairly thorough criticism of (and by) the WUO leadership and the direction it had put forth. But the criticism offered no sense of how or if the organization intended on correcting these errors and moving forward. The damage had already been done.

FALLING APART...

AFTER HARD TIMES, the Weather Underground Organization began to disintegrate with surprising speed. For those who had spent six or more years building this unprecedented anti-imperialist group, the implosion was tragic. "It dissolved like sand through our fingers," recalls Donna Willmott.

Prairie Fire, too, was shaken in the conference fallout. Shortly after the conference, the Bay Area PFOC released an essay called "Class and Revolutionary Politics" that criticized the conference and the political direction the WUO had argued for. "We were emphatically reminded that for revolutionaries of an imperialist country the distinction between oppressor and oppressed nations is the main thing," the article declared. "This means that to be a communist it is not enough to be for class struggle, for socialism, the dictatorship of the proletariat. A white communist must especially fight for the national liberation of oppressed peoples, for self-determination and against special privilege, white supremacy, chauvinism."[15] In thoroughly trouncing the WUO and the Hard Times Conference, PFOC hoped to reverse its errors and find solid grounding on which to move forward.

This article was part of "rectification," an intense period (with an appropriately tough-sounding name) during which PFOC and Weather members were trying to identify and correct the mistakes of both organizations that had been exposed during the Hard Times Conference. Rectification happened at both the aboveground and clandestine levels, each one feeding the other. Central to this process were the countless criticisms of the Central Committee circulating in the underground, some of which made their way to key aboveground supporters. WUO members, PFOC activists, and others close to the underground all put forth written criticisms.

Other groups also weighed in on rectification. The George Jackson Brigade, a multiracial Seattle-based clandestine organization, released a public criticism of the John Brown Book Club (a project of PFOC). Expressing hope that the process of rectification within PFOC would lead to better political practice, the brigade pointed out numerous instances when WUO/PFOC supporters had withheld support from clandestine groups such as themselves. Through the open letter, the brigade said it hoped to help move the Seattle-area Weather supporters "forward [with] your rectification. We are encouraged because your statement is one step in material proof of real change. We are encouraged to see you begin this hard struggle. We are eager to hear more. We are also anxious to see a closer link between your words and your actions."[16] Some unidentified Native American activists similarly criticized the WUO in an open letter.[17]

Among WUO members underground, position papers proliferated. Some focused on the group's racism, others on its sexism, still others on the lack of democracy. New factions began to coalesce around shared criticisms of the WUO's direction, but few lasted in the frenzied atmosphere of denunciations and counter-denunciations.[18] It was, Suzanne Ross says, a "chaotic and totally dangerous situation." Those underground were also, as Cathy Wilkerson recalls, "scurrying for how you're going to survive tomorrow"—for housing, money, and other needs that the organizational apparatus had coordinated. Lots of criticisms called for disbanding the organization entirely. Gripped with paranoia and anger, many in the underground felt it was too risky to travel. This made group discussion or meetings difficult, adding to the sectarian and divided atmosphere.

Rectification for the WUO became a collective fury unleashed at the Central Committee. For the first time, rank-and-file members sat down with leadership and demanded to know the details of what had until then been the province of leaders: how did the group relate to revolutionary nationalist groups? What was the rationale driving decisions the WUO made after (and even before) the publishing of *Prairie Fire*? At the same time, Weatherpeople read and reread criticisms of the group—from the Panther 21 criticism in 1971 to post-Hard Times critiques. Criticism mounted, and it wasn't pretty or neat or nice. Weather's process of rectification would soon rectify the organization out of existence.

By and large, the organization's leadership responded to the inquiries from cadre, in some cases revealing information about the group's practice over the years that rank-and-file members did not know. In other instances, Judy Siff recalls, self-criticism by the leaders vindicated criticisms some Third World revolutionaries had raised of the group. The Central Committee was more open in acknowledging the political direction it had taken the organization—although the intensity of the way in which things fell apart may have made the leaders feel pressured to denounce their own errors more strongly than they would have otherwise done.

Indeed, some rank-and-file members interrogated the leadership with an intensity that placed little value on treating comrades with respect and even surpassed the group's early criticism/self-criticism sessions. At the time, it was felt that a thorough criticism/self-criticism of those who had seemingly led the group astray might save it. Led by rank-and-file members, the criticism/self-criticism sessions started with the national leadership but also criticized local leaders. As a result of these criticisms, Bernardine Dohrn even wrote a self-flagellating letter denouncing herself and the rest of the leadership, a move she now calls her "most embarrassing moment in my whole political life." Dohrn's letter appeared among the handful of statements printed in the *The Split of the Weather Underground Organization: Struggling Against White and Male Supremacy*, a shrill 1977 pamphlet compiled and edited by the John Brown Book Club.[19] Amidst valid criticisms are some ludicrous assertions: that Weather's recent support for union struggles resulted in de facto support for prosecuting undocumented workers, that the group had worked to "destroy" the prison solidarity movement, and that Weather completely abandoned anti-racist work during the Boston busing crisis.[20]

As critiques deepened in the rectification process, paranoia swirled and people were isolated from all but their closest friends.[21] "You didn't know who you could trust, what was going to happen next…. It got really crazy," Ross recalls, noting that "accusatory and guilt-ridden rhetoric was rampant" in the split period. Chaos defined the group's demise. "When Weatherman fell apart, there wasn't a coherent debate," Cathy Wilkerson says. Many of the Weatherwomen in heterosexual relationships (temporarily) broke up with their male partners as a result of the sexism in the organization—although some mainstream media accounts erroneously claim that the men walked out on the women.[22] David Gilbert remembers this period and the period following the townhouse explosion as being the two loneliest times in his life. Committed revolutionaries found themselves adrift when the clandestine organization they had dedicated years to—not to mention risked their lives for—fell apart. "I felt like I had lost my political bearings," says Robert Roth, echoing sentiments many have expressed about the bitter last days of the Weather Underground.[23]

…AND TRYING TO MOVE FORWARD AMIDST THE WRECKAGE

A S THE WUO began to unravel following the Hard Times criticisms, a grouping of Weather cadre on the West coast emerged, calling itself the Revolutionary Committee of the Weather Underground Organization. The Revolutionary Committee (RC) pledged to return to the best of WUO politics, including armed struggle. "When criticism started to happen from outside the organization, we became empowered to add our voices to it," Judy Siff says of the committee's audacious beginnings. The Revolutionary Committee held up the political line of *Prairie Fire* as the model to be returned to—and expelled the Central Committee from the organization, although the WUO had all but disintegrated by that point. Demoralized, defeated, and in certain agreement with many of the criticisms, the Central Committee had already disbanded.

The Revolutionary Committee "wasn't a very pleasant place to be at the time of the split," Siff says. "We knew what the problems were, but we had no idea how to lead out of them. There was no end to seeing the problems rather than the strengths." Feeling like "the movement we had built had been betrayed," that core principles to which people had committed themselves had been abandoned, the Revolutionary Committee was one expression of the deep anger many in and close to the WUO felt. Though various ad-hoc groupings were circulating criticisms and self-criticisms, the Revolutionary Committee was the only formation to publish these criticisms—in *The Split* pamphlet, which was distributed by PFOC. Although it had sharply criticized the Central Committee for abandoning armed support for national liberation and women's liberation, the Revolutionary Committee's only proposal for correcting that error was that those underground should surface in order to spread the criticisms while their small group would continue clandestine work.

A very strong influence on the Revolutionary Committee was Clayton Van Lydegraf, a sixty-two-year-old militant and ex–Communist Party cadre who was known to his comrades as "Van." A leader of PFOC, Van Lydegraf was a powerful force; he had influenced the organization's politics throughout its existence and had the respect of the Central Committee. As a PFOC leader and longtime radical, Van Lydegraf was a particular target for police surveillance. He had already stood down the House Un-American Activities Committee in the 1950s and resisted a grand jury investigating the WUO in 1972. And one of his longtime roommates—"Phil Gamachi," an activist recruit claiming to be a Vietnam vet—was in reality an undercover FBI agent. In 1977, based on the trust built after eight years of living together, Van Lydegraf recruited "Phil" to join the Revolutionary Committee, and "Phil" subsequently introduced "Dick Regan" (another agent) to the group as well. The Revolutionary Committee was thus successfully infiltrated within a few months of its beginnings.[24]

In its zeal to capture the WUO or any segment of it, the FBI had put 150 agents to work on arresting the Revolutionary Committee, Freedom of Information Act documents later revealed. To give credibility to "Dick's" story—that he was on the run from the Canadian government for radical activities there—the FBI (through its Radical Activities Informant Program, which was used to target the WUO) staged a well-publicized "search" of San Francisco for the "fugitive," going door-to-door with his picture. As a result, the movement perceived "Dick" as a bona fide fugitive, and he was welcomed into the Revolutionary Committee.[25] The two FBI agents immediately began pressuring the group to take action and plan for a bombing. The office of California state senator (and gubernatorial candidate) John Briggs was selected. Briggs was notorious in the Bay Area for trying to make it illegal for lesbians and gays to teach in public schools. This issue is what attracted the Revolutionary Committee's attention, although Briggs was also the author of a ballot initiative aiming to reinstate the death penalty in California.[26]

In November 1977, the FBI arrested Van Lydegraf and four members of the Revolutionary Committee. Two were arrested in California and three in Texas, where they were conducting surveillance at a convention of the Klan and affiliated white supremacists. For all the agents involved and the number of years it spent on infiltration, the FBI still could not claim full success. The bureau thought it was tracking the WUO's Central Committee, and was furious when it discovered that Bernardine Dohrn was not a part of the Revolutionary Committee.

The "L.A. 5," as the captured RC activists came to be called, did not conduct a political trial. "For us at the time," Siff explains, "a political trial meant seeking support for the political thinking behind the action in spite of the fact that the action never took place—and we did not think we could do this." The five were self-critical that they had focused on Briggs' homophobic initiative without paying attention to his racist death penalty proposal. "We did not believe that trial was the place to be self-critical in terms of our political thinking," she says. "As a result, we did not feel we could ask support for the case." In the end, the group accepted a plea bargain. Four served sentences of two years, and Siff served four years. (Her longer sentence was due to an outstanding political charge from before she went underground.) The arrest and imprisonment of the Revolutionary Committee marked the end of anti-imperialism under the name of the Weather Underground Organization.

SECTARIANISM IN THE FALL OF THE WEATHER UNDERGROUND

A S IN THE 1968–1970 period when SDS split apart, the issues facing the Weather Underground in 1976–1977 were complex. But this time, there were no ready answers. "Nobody had a corner on *the* right way to move," says Bill Ayers today. "Debates were more fraught, more sharp, but no one had anything to point to other than their own ideas." Despite "clubbing each other with a lot of rhetoric," Ayers says, no one "knew what was to be done."

Political questions were made more challenging by the fact that the Left was then gripped by the Maoist paradigm of seeking "the primary contradiction." The problem with that, Dohrn recalls, was that "nobody ever got to the second contradiction and the primary became everything." Complexity and nuance were ignored when revolutionaries had such a narrow theoretical vision of the problems facing the world. Real questions over effective strategy instead became an issue of ranking political problems, with built-in conflict based on how someone measured the "primary contradiction."

The dangers of this thinking were especially apparent in the split, when criticisms of the WUO mounted from within and without the organization. *The Split of the WUO* pamphlet collected some of the critiques of the Revolutionary Committee and Van Lydegraf, who was then a public PFOC leader covertly trying to re-initiate armed struggle. (An ironic position, given that the WUO was under fire for having some of its members secretly play leading roles in PFOC.) By the time *The Split* appeared in the spring of 1977, the apparatus of the WUO had essentially fallen apart. Although these were the only such communiqués to be published, *The Split* documents are but a reflection of the statements then circulating the underground.

Reflecting the intensity of the break-up and the atmosphere of the Left in general at the time, *The Split* named and called out members of the Central Committee individually and listed their alleged "crimes" against the people.[27] Historian Jeremy Varon calls *The Split* "creepily hermetic, dogmatic, sloganistic, and censorious—almost unreadably dated and Byzantine."[28] Even where the critiques had validity, David Gilbert says, the tone oversimplified complex issues and demeaned old comrades.[29] But the harsh criticisms of *The Split* cannot be separated from the overall intensity of the WUO's dissolution. To some outside observers, such as Panama Alba, it seemed that the organization had lost its humanist grounding.

People not involved in the WUO's infighting called attention to the rancorous tone characterizing *The Split*, including the claim that members of the Central Committee were "an obstacle to revolution."[30] In criticizing the pamphlet's tone, *The YIPster Times* noted, "apparently, if you're a member of a Weather Underground faction you never just call someone a jerk." The article, entitled "W.U.O. Blows Self Up!" criticizes the invective accompanying the WUO's implosion, noting that *The Split* document denounces as "crimes" what "common folk might refer to as fuck-ups and the WUO used to call 'errors.'"[31]

"There were political differences and criticisms to be made," says Suzanne Ross. "But political criticisms can be made in a rational and even a loving tone. As far as I know, none of us succeeded in doing that." The acrimony of the split contributed to a general diminution of support for armed struggle. This made it easier for the government and police to isolate post-WUO armed struggle efforts among the white Left, she says. "This wing of the movement consequently paid the very heavy price of having so many of its cadre imprisoned without getting the kind of support they should have [had] from the rest of us."

ABOVEGROUND REVERBERATIONS

THE PRAIRIE FIRE Organizing Committee went through its own process of rectification following the Hard Times Conference. PFOC chapters in the Bay Area, Chicago, New York, and Seattle led the process, which ultimately consisted of severing ties with the underground and changing the political line back to what it had been when the organization first started, making support for national liberation and feminist work primary. Untangling the PFOC from the WUO was a difficult but rewarding process. "For Prairie Fire, in a sense, it was liberating…because then we were charting our own course," Mirkinson says. Still, PFOC was weakened by the implosion of the WUO. "A lot of people got disillusioned with the split of the Weather Underground," she says, noting that PFOC lost members as a result. And in keeping with the intensity of the times, PFOC's rectification also required people associated with the WUO to write public letters repudiating their former politics and the organization as a whole. Even those who weren't actual members of the WUO but just aboveground supporters had to do this in order to join PFOC.[32]

After the Hard Times Conference, PFOC tried to rebuild itself. But finding its footing proved slow and difficult. Differences began to emerge within PFOC over how to relate to Black forces and how much (and how best) to support revolutionary armed struggle in the United States. In hindsight, PFOC activists were more united than not on these issues, but at the time, minor differences were treated as major points of division. Competition for leadership also played a defining role in the growing tensions within PFOC. What people now recognize as sectarianism run amuck seemed at the time vital to saving the revolutionary movement.

Tension within PFOC finally erupted at an organizational conference in San Francisco in the summer of 1976. The organization split along coastal lines, with the West Coast branch retaining the name, and the East Coast ultimately reconstituting itself as the May 19th Communist Organization. (The Chicago branch initially went with May 19th, though it soon separated and went its own way.) As with the WUO implosion, PFOC's split was a bitter and ugly one among friends and comrades. May 19th cofounder Susan Rosenberg remembers the split as a "very shell-shocked period…of great, intense emotion and activity." The political differences between the West Coast PFOC and the East Coast May 19th became more defined *after* the split, former members of both groups say. Activists on the East Coast wanted to build an organization of whites "under the direct leadership of the Black liberation struggle" and to fully support armed work. West Coast PFOC was more reticent, wanting to keep the organization independent.[33]

Named in honor of the birthday of Ho Chi Minh and Malcolm X, May 19th set out to build political relationships, including providing material aid, with revolutionary nationalist African and African American liberation movements, in the militant tradition of the WUO but with much more of a feminist bent.[34] Composed primarily of women, it was a small, severe group, never numbering more than 100 people. According to its points of unity, the group's primary task was "supporting, both politically and with material aid, the wars of national liberation, outside and within the borders of the US."[35]

And May 19th lived up to it, in its way. Before the 1981 Brink's robbery debacle and the resulting legal woes that effectively destroyed the organization, May 19th members were involved in public support for clandestine Black and Puerto Rican actions, mobilizations against the KKK, political prisoner defense, and fundraising for and militant demonstrations in solidarity with the anti-apartheid movement in South Africa. The group had a graphics collective that produced political posters and also participated in a lawsuit against the FBI for COINTELPRO abuses. Ex-Panther Afeni Shakur and RNA activist Mutulu Shakur formed the National Task Force for COINTELPRO Litigation and Research in the late 1970s to expose the FBI's war against dissent. While its focus was on lawsuits to help Black dissidents, the task force also encouraged May 19th activists and other white anti-imperialists to sue the FBI for its legal violations in pursuing the WUO. The multimillion-dollar lawsuit ultimately resulted in the 1980 convictions of top FBI officials Mark Felt and Edward Miller, though both were pardoned by Ronald Reagan as his first act in office.[36]

PFOC, meanwhile, continued in the Bay Area. As May 19th became closer to Black liberation forces in the East Coast, PFOC built political relationships with Puerto Rican independence organizations. But about a year and a half after the internal split, PFOC was rocked by the arrest of Van Lydegraf and four members of the Revolutionary Committee in November 1977. Van Lydegraf's arrest proved embarrassing to an organization trying to establish itself as more than a front group for the underground. People in PFOC were also freaked out that Van Lydegraf and the RC were arrested due to FBI infiltration.

Still, PFOC was able to recover. It changed its leadership structure, and once and for all severed all organizational ties to the underground. After that, the organization was on the ascendant. It lasted until the mid-1990s, organizing around Central America solidarity, Puerto Rican independence, and in support of U.S. political prisoners. It strongly supported feminism and gay liberation. Throughout its existence, PFOC regularly published a journal of world news and analysis called *Breakthrough*, which covered a wide range of political issues. It also had a graphics collective that produced more than 100 posters.[37] PFOC sought to continue the anti-imperialist politics that had shaped it, building relationships with liberation movements inside and outside the United States. Prior to its dissolution, May 19th worked with PFOC on specific projects, and both groups built chapters of the John Brown Anti-Klan Committee to engage in mass movement work against neo-Nazis and others in the fascist Right, as well as against police brutality.

RE-EVALUATING, RE-EMERGING, REBUILDING:
LIFE AFTER THE WEATHER UNDERGROUND

THE BREAKUP OF the WUO was a reality check for all involved. Many former WUO members agreed with the substance of the Revolutionary Committee's criticisms of the organization's political direction, if not the tone.[38] "I think a lot of people in the organization probably agreed that the organization had strayed from its original mission," Suzanne Ross says. "An awful lot of people seemed to agree that the commitment to national liberation struggles and the struggle against white supremacy had been too much abandoned or weakened."

When the WUO collapsed, so did the support apparatus for those underground. For many, there was no choice but to surface. Scott Braley, for one, didn't really want to come aboveground. He felt it would be a repudiation of the politics the WUO had so long defended and by which it defined itself. But after the dissolution of the group, he decided to surface, convinced by the intensity of the split that "nobody in our crew could honestly say, 'we know what to do'.... It seemed like the only way I was going to know [what to do] was to go back as a public person and see what the hell was happening. That was a really tormenting decision, but that's what I felt." Braley and his then-partner, also in the group, moved to California upon surfacing. "You had to choose—you either went West, you went East, or you disappeared into something else."

People started surfacing to begin life anew as legal members of society—to, as Naomi Jaffe remembers, put their lives back together politically as well as personally. Robert Roth and Phoebe Hirsch, who turned themselves in together, were among the first in 1977. The first famous member to surface was Columbia strike leader Mark Rudd, who turned himself in to New York City authorities in September 1977—even though, unbeknownst to the public and the phalanx of reporters surrounding him as he arrived to surrender to authorities, Rudd had left the Weather Underground in 1970.[39]

As the disco decade drew to a close, others began to surface. "I decided I could no longer be useful underground," says Suzanne Ross. "In the aftermath of the dissolution of the WUO, I did not trust enough people underground to take the risks necessary to be effective on that level. I felt that once I surfaced, I would be able to draw on the support of old friends and comrades and would be better able to make a contribution." For Ross, it was back to the unfinished tasks of Vietnam solidarity work in the wake of Pol Pot, the Chinese invasion of Vietnam, the U.S. manipulation of the Vietnamese refugee issue, and the continued Vietnamese request for support. For others, the return to aboveground activism entailed work against police violence in communities of color, for Puerto Rican independence, in solidarity with Central American and African liberation movements, for women's liberation, or anti-nuclear activism—in addition to the personal work of finishing college or graduate degrees and reuniting with friends and family.[40]

In prison as a result of BLA activities when all this was happening, former Panther Ashanti Alston says it was depressing to hear about, noting that however complex and legitimate the reasons WUO members had for surfacing, it was a privilege BLA members were denied. Young Lord Panama Alba agrees with this assessment, but he still thought it pointless for whites to remain underground just to prove their rejection of white privilege. He didn't think staying underground was worth it unless they were both willing and had the capacity to continue at that level, he says. "The reality is that people in the Weather Underground got away with a lot because they're white…. [But] we took a position that it served no purpose to have people remain clandestine just because Blacks and Latinos [living] clandestinely couldn't resurface."

People surfaced throughout the last years of the 1970s and early 1980. The other high-profile surrenders came in 1980 as first Cathy Wilkerson, and then Bill Ayers and Bernardine Dohrn, gave themselves over to authorities in Chicago to answer to charges stemming from the Days of Rage and the September 1969 demonstrations at the start of the Chicago 8 conspiracy trial.[41] Most WUO members who surfaced did little jail time. In its zeal to catch them, the FBI had cut too many corners and broken too many laws. Many charges had to be reduced or dropped altogether, including the two major federal conspiracy indictments, which were dropped due to government misconduct. Most of the Weather Underground members who surfaced between 1976 and 1980 received fines and probation. Others, including Bill Ayers, had all charges against them dropped. In fact, of the four best-known members to surface (Ayers, Dohrn, Rudd, and Wilkerson), only Cathy Wilkerson did any time for WUO activities.[42]

When he turned himself in to authorities in Chicago in 1977, Robert Roth didn't know how much time he was facing, although he was sure that it would be substantial. After eight days in Cook County Jail uncertain of what charges would be filed against him, Roth and his then-partner, also a member of the group, pleaded guilty to charges that predated their participation in the underground. They received a fine and two years' probation. The state "just wanted it to end," Roth says. Reflecting on the fact that most Weatherpeople got away with probation and fines, Donna Willmott says: "The message of the state was that 'you can always come home again…. Look, it wasn't worth it, come home, there's a place for you.' That was never extended to Black revolutionaries, it was never extended to Native American people—there was no 'home' to come back to. That was always part of the reality for us, even though we were being looked for."

In his unpublished memoir, Mark Rudd recalls the process of turning himself in. Waiting for arraignment, he was the only white person in the jail cells. The district attorney was willing to let Rudd go on his own recognizance (i.e., without bail), but the judge was reluctant, given Rudd's seven years as a fugitive, and wanted to keep Rudd behind bars. "Remembering the holding cells filled with black and Latino men who could not make bail, I agreed with the judge," Rudd writes. But the district attorney prevailed, and Rudd was released without having to pay a cent or say a word.[43] These American outlaws were allowed to come back into the fold.

David Gilbert surfaced briefly from 1977 until around 1979 in Denver, Colorado, the city where he had helped organize a Weather collective in October 1969. He was able to get his existing (minor) charges dropped before he surfaced and suffered no legal penalties.[44] "It was a difficult time for me," he says about surfacing, "and I was trying to understand the political errors I made, why Weather disintegrated, what it had to do with my life, and my commitment to revolution."[45] Like most former Weathermembers, he became politically involved fairly quickly, joining a local Men Against Sexism group and trying to plug into organizing support for national liberation movements in the Denver area.

Still, Gilbert opposed abandoning the underground and did not think his surfacing would be the best help to the movement. The Black movement had been his inspiration since he became an activist in high school. The WUO's inglorious ending, he felt, was at least partly due to its abandoning clandestine armed actions in support of the Black liberation struggle. And overseas, the late 1970s saw militant struggles in Iran, Nicaragua, Puerto Rico, South Africa, and Zimbabwe (some of them successful in seizing state power)—showing, it would seem, that national liberation remained a major world player. As a result, the Columbia and New School graduate with a penchant for political theory slipped back into what revolutionaries called "the forest."

The Weather Underground Organization was no more, but the underground continued.

David Gilbert's mug shot after being arrested October 20, 1981, following the failed Brink's robbery.

> *We are neither terrorists nor criminals. It is*
> *precisely because of our love of life, because we*
> *revel in the human spirit, that we became freedom*
> *fighters against this racist and deadly imperialist*
> *system.* —David Gilbert[1]

THE WEATHER UNDERGROUND WAS NO MORE, BUT the underground persisted; indeed, it seemed to be experiencing a resurgence. In the late 1970s and early 1980s, the most prominent clandestine groups in the United States were the Black Liberation Army and the Puerto Rican *Fuerzas Armadas de Liberación Nacional* (Armed Forces for National Liberation; FALN). Between 1974 and 1981, the FALN claimed responsibility for 120 bombings or incendiary attacks, mostly in New York and Chicago, directed against U.S. government, military, and corporate targets.[2] The BLA, meanwhile, appeared to be at a standstill in the mid-1970s, after several members had been arrested or killed by police.[3] Some incarcerated members formed a "Coordinating Committee" of the BLA in late 1975, releasing "an ideological document depicting the theoretical foundations of the Black Liberation Army's political determination." This statement was followed by a small-circulation BLA newsletter and by ongoing campaigns to support incarcerated BLA members.[4] But BLA actions were, it seemed, largely a thing of the past.

And then it happened: on November 2, 1979, celebrated BLA leader Assata Shakur escaped from a prison in Clinton, New Jersey, about 15 miles east of the Pennsylvania border. According to the *New York Times*, the ex-Panther escaped with the help of three armed visitors, who "seized two guards as hostages and commandeered a prison van in the escape."[5] The guards were released unharmed and the van abandoned after everyone fled the scene. The operation was so quick, quiet, and painless that

245

other guards in the prison weren't aware that anything was happening until the alarm was sounded.[6] In the 1980s, Shakur revealed that she was living in Cuba, where she had been granted political asylum.[7]

Shakur had been held in captivity since a 1973 New Jersey Turnpike encounter in which a New Jersey state trooper, Werner Foerster, and a BLA member, Zayd Shakur, were killed. Assata was wounded, shot with both her hands in the air. Despite ballistics evidence showing that she did not shoot a gun, Shakur and a BLA comrade, Sundiata Acoli, were both charged with Foerster's death. Characterized by police as "the soul" and "mother hen" of the BLA, Shakur was also charged with a string of bank robberies and attacks on police officers.[8] Scholar-activist Akinyele Umoja notes that "any suspected BLA action involving a woman" was pinned on Shakur, eventually totaling six cases.[9] In a series of highly publicized trials, she beat all of the charges against her but one: she was convicted and sentenced to life in prison for Foerster's death.[10]

Denied medical care for her wounds and convicted by an all-white jury after months of prejudicial news stories, Assata Shakur (known in the press by her "slave name," Joanne Chesimard) became a symbol for the Black Liberation Movement. (Shakur is also a symbol for the state of New Jersey, which has diligently tried to extradite her back to the United States from Cuba through both traditional channels and otherwise. In 2005, New Jersey offered a $1 million bounty for her capture, raising it from the $100,000 it had offered in 1998. Also in 1998, the state appealed to the U.S. attorney general and secretary of state, suggesting that the United States drop the embargo against Cuba in exchange for the country turning over Shakur and other U.S. fugitives. Shakur remains in Cuba.)[11] Prior to her incarceration in Clinton, Shakur was held under draconian conditions in a men's prison, denied visits and reading materials, housed with open white supremacists, and placed under constant surveillance with lights on in her cell twenty-four hours a day.

Still, she managed to escape, with the help of her comrades.

Assata's liberation from prison was a bold move that countered FBI and police claims to have "broken the back of the BLA." The BLA's audacious action also had a good measure of community support. Posters in support of Shakur could be found throughout New York and across the nation. An article (December 1979) and an advertisement (January 1980) were placed in the Black-owned *Amsterdam News*, encouraging Shakur to "stay strong and free" and expressing appreciation to the BLA for its action.[12]

Three days after Shakur escaped, 3,000 people marched from Harlem to the United Nations in honor of Black Solidarity Day.[13] Amidst signs demanding self-determination and human rights, hundreds carried signs proclaiming "Assata Shakur Is Welcome Here." Near the UN building, a BLA communiqué about the escape was read: "In freeing Comrade-Sister Assata we have made it clear that such treatment and the criminal 'guilt' or innocence of a Black freedom fighter is irrelevant when measured by our people's history of struggle against racist domination."[14]

While Assata's escape and the attempts to capture her received considerable media attention, it was in October 1981 that the Black Liberation Army would find a more lasting place in the public consciousness. Even the Weather Underground, then dead for four years, would capture the headlines in ways it hadn't since its auspicious beginnings. It was another audacious action, but unlike the Shakur escape, this one went terribly wrong: three cops were dead, four revolutionaries were captured at the scene, and that was just the beginning.

The place was Nyack, New York, a sleepy town about twenty-five miles north of New York City. A Brink's truck was making a cash delivery at the Nanuet Mall around 3:45 p.m. on October 20, when a group of men in ski masks, with guns drawn, yelled "Freeze!"[15] Police maintain that the radicals opened fire without cause, but the BLA's track record suggests otherwise; it had never before come out shooting during a robbery attempt. Gunfire attracts attention, and the goal of expropriations is to get funds and get away, not cause injury.[16] In his closing statement at the Brink's trial, Kuwasi Balagoon said that it was only when Brink's guard Peter Paige reached for his gun that the BLA began firing.[17] Firing broke out, regardless, and Paige was killed. Francis Joseph Trombino, his partner, was shot in the arm. Six bags containing $1.6 million were quickly removed from the truck, and the masked men fled.[18]

With the money in hand, the revolutionary bandits sped a few miles east and switched vehicles, getting into the back of a waiting U-Haul truck. A woman watching out the window of her house called the police as the U-Haul sped off.[19] Nyack police pulled over a U-Haul a few miles away. They were on the lookout for Black men, but the driver of this particular U-Haul, David Gilbert, was white. Still, police ordered him and his female passenger, also white, out of the vehicle.[20] Then, the back of the U-Haul opened from the inside, several men jumped out, and a shootout erupted. Nyack officers Waverly Brown and Edward O'Grady were killed.

Pandemonium ensued, as more police arrived and people tried to flee, on foot or by car (including, in at least one instance, a car commandeered from the early rush hour traffic).[21] Some managed to escape—briefly. Others weren't so lucky. Sam Brown, Judy Clark, and David Gilbert were in a tan Honda that crashed trying to make a sharp turn. They were captured at the scene of the crash. Kathy Boudin, the female passenger in the U-Haul, was arrested by an off-duty prison guard as she scampered from the gunfire. Boudin and Gilbert were, of course, former members of the Weather Underground. Clark, briefly associated with the group in 1969–1970, was an aboveground organizer and leader of the May 19th Communist Organization. Brown, a Black man, was the least political of the crew; after a series of arrests for non-political offenses, he had recently hooked up with some former Black Panthers.[22]

The investigation began immediately, as authorities traced everyone associated with the captured individuals. As a result of this investigation, police cornered BLA militants Sekou Odinga and Mtayari Shabaka Sundiata in New York City three days later. What started as a twenty-minute car chase through Queens turned into a running gunfight between Odinga and Sundiata and the police. Sundiata, former head of the Brooklyn chapter of the Republic of New Afrika, was shot and killed as he tried to scale a fence. After his gun jammed, Odinga threw it down and surrendered.[23]

Police soon found out that they were not dealing with common criminals, but with conscious revolutionaries who saw themselves as engaging in an "expropriation," or robbery for political purposes. Such "unauthorized withdrawals" were part of a long tradition, extending from Josef Stalin to Nelson Mandela and beyond, of using capitalist banks to finance revolutionary programs—because, as Gilbert dryly notes, revolutionaries are "just not going to get donations from the Ford or Rockefeller foundations."[24] This expropriation was, in Gilbert's words, "under the leadership of the Black Liberation Army with white revolutionaries participating in alliance with them."[25]

Police were quick to abuse their detainees. Gilbert was beaten for several hours, leaving visible black eyes and bruises. At one point, police jammed a shotgun against his neck, telling him to talk. (He demurred.)[26] But the treatment accorded Sam Brown and Sekou Odinga, the two Black men arrested, was much worse—and more methodical in its application. Police broke Sam Brown's neck in two places and denied him medical care for eleven weeks—until he agreed to cooperate with the police against his comrades.[27] During the beatings, police at Rockland Jail called Brown a "nigger" as they threatened to kill him.[28] Gilbert estimates that police beat him and Brown for several hours—roughly from the time of arrest in the early evening until police began to prepare the men for their midnight arraignment.[29] Sekou Odinga, one of the original Panther 21 who had served in the Panthers' international chapter in Algeria, was more stalwart. Even after police burned him with cigarettes, almost drowned him in a urine-filled toilet, ripped out his nails, and beat him so badly that his pancreas had to be removed, he had nothing to say to the police.[30] He had to be fed intravenously for three months afterward.[31] Despite medical records (and visual evidence) proving the contrary, the Rockland County district attorney said no beatings of any kind took place.[32]

In the days, weeks, and months following the Brink's debacle, police arrested dozens more radicals, mostly in the New York metropolitan area, as well as on a farm in Mississippi associated with the Republic of New Afrika. Some, such as ex-Panther Kuwasi Balagoon, were involved in the events of October 20. Others simply had personal or political ties to radical movements or the people involved; still others had no connection at all and were just victims of the broad police sweep that brought more than 1,000 FBI agents into New York City, working in concert with the local police through the so-called "Joint Terrorism Task Force." Freaked out by what appeared to be a Black-white alliance, police especially targeted interracial couples, arresting at least one that had no connection to either Brink's or the movement.[33]

Ex-Weatherpeople Jeff Jones and Eleanor Stein, still underground after the dissolution of the WUO, were arrested by a dozen-member SWAT team on October 23 while watching the World Series in their Bronx apartment. They knew nothing about the Brink's robbery, and had, in fact, been negotiating for their surrender at the time of their arrest—but were initially lumped in with those captured at Nyack. (That they were not involved was quickly established.)[34] Suspected BLA members Bashir Hameed and Abdul Majid were also arrested at this time and initially thought to be co-conspirators in the Nyack fiasco. They, too, soon had their cases severed when it was shown they were not involved.

★ ★ ★

To say that it is difficult to write about "Brinks" is like calling the Grand Canyon a pothole; it's an understatement of several orders of magnitude. People died that day, and three days later, and others received long prison sentences. Personally, politically, it was a disaster. The Brink's affair is nonetheless an important event to explore in understanding the lessons and legacies of Sixties-era movements, particularly the Weather Underground and the Black Liberation Army.

The Brink's fallout was part of a steep downward turn for the Left underground in the United States. Eleven Puerto Rican *independentistas* suspected of underground activities with the FALN had been captured outside Chicago in April 1980, tried on charges of sedition, and given lengthy prison sentences (one was sentenced to more than 100 years, even though none of them were charged with any actual bombings or use of force).[35] This arrest was followed by the Brink's arrests in October 1981 and the related federal conspiracy trials and grand juries that led to more than a dozen incarcerations throughout the next two years. There were more arrests in 1984 and 1985: six white anti-racists (mostly former WUO and May 19th members) allegedly associated with armed clandestine groups calling themselves the Armed Resistance Unit and Red Guerrilla Resistance; eight Black radicals in a military raid for charges (which proved spurious) of planning to free two BLA prisoners; seven activists accused of being in the United Freedom Front, a Boston-based white anti-imperialist underground group; and eleven more Puerto Ricans for suspected participation in the armed clandestine group known as *Los Macheteros*.[36] Prior to these arrests, the early 1980s saw WUO-style bombings of the Capitol, various U.S. companies involved in support for the apartheid regime and death squads in Central America (such as IBM, Union Carbide, and Motorola), and the South African Airways office in New York, among other targets.[37] In Puerto Rico, *independentistas* attacked U.S. military establishments, and the *Macheteros* were also wanted for a $7 million expropriation from a Wells Fargo branch in Connecticut.[38] But by the end of the decade, leftist armed struggle in the United States seemed to be thoroughly smashed, with dozens of radicals behind bars on various charges for their alleged involvement in clandestine actions.

It was not just the clandestine Left facing these setbacks; 1985 also saw the Philadelphia police drop a bomb on a house, killing eleven members of the radical MOVE organization (six adults and five children) and letting much of the block go up in flames (a crime for which no one was ever charged, except for Ramona Africa, the only surviving adult MOVE member).[39] Amidst all of this, of course, was the ascendancy of the Reagan administration and all the related issues: the Iran-Contra scandal; the attacks on the unions, affirmative action, sexual health and freedom, welfare, and social services more generally; and U.S. involvement in "low intensity" conflicts in the Caribbean (Grenada) and Latin America (El Salvador and Nicaragua).[40]

The 1980s, then, can be seen as a time of tremendous setbacks for the Left, resulting in the almost total obliteration of the revolutionary underground movements that were born in the late 1960s and lasted for approximately fifteen years. It was a destruction resulting from both internal and external factors: a waning mass movement that resulted in minimal support for clandestine actions; increased vigilance by an ever-more reactionary state; and failed actions that ended in arrest, sometimes stemming from strategic as well as tactical failures.

"The people arrested in the eighties were real serious, committed revolutionaries," says social worker Esperanza Martell, who has been an ardent defender of U.S. political prisoners for the past forty years. But their commitment did not make support work easier; Martell says that the string of arrests and repressive legal climate of the 1980s put the Left on the defensive because people "had to pull at a lot of resources [for legal defense] when the legal movement had also been killed. Organizing around political prisoners in the eighties was a real challenge."[41] This was especially true for the Brink's expropriation, an illegal, high-risk fundraiser to support future clandestine actions. It lacked political or popular appeal to begin with. Now that it had gone so terribly wrong, the small sector of the Left that normally championed political prisoners found itself in a difficult spot. This difficulty was particularly palpable with those arrested in Nyack, as public animosity reached a fever pitch. The town of 6,500 had never had a police officer killed before, and they were out for blood. From the beginning, Nyack residents publicly and virulently cried out for the death penalty.[42]

LEGAL BATTLES: ROUND ONE

THERE WERE TWO levels of legal proceedings to emerge out of the attempted expropriation in Nyack: state trials for those captured or placed at the scene, and federal conspiracy trials for those the government accused of plotting robberies and conspiring to free Assata Shakur.[43] The government also subpoenaed more than a dozen people to grand juries; most refused to cooperate and spent time in jail as a result. In all levels of the legal struggle, politics took center stage, with many of those captured demanding that they be treated as political prisoners or as prisoners of war. The government, meanwhile, used the defendants' politics to justify extraordinary (and prejudicial) security procedures.[44] This battle was especially apparent in the first state trial, which one attorney said resembled hearings in a "police state."[45]

At the state level, Kuwasi Balagoon, Judy Clark, and David Gilbert stood trial together. (Kathy Boudin and Sam Brown were each tried individually, also at the state level.) Security at the trial was particularly intense.[46] Defendants were driven in unmarked police vans and brought into court cuffed, shackled, and wearing bulletproof vests. Jurors were taken to and from court in buses with blackened windows.[47] Guards packed the courtroom, and snipers and police photographers sat atop buildings surrounding the courthouse. Police on horseback also monitored the area. People entering the courthouse had to go through two metal detector searches (normal now, but unusual then) and had to give their names to deputy sheriffs.[48] The prosecutor maintained that the security was necessary because of the fifty or so demonstrators rallying outside the courthouse in solidarity with the defendants—a group of mainly May 19th and Republic of New Afrika activists calling itself the Coalition to Defend the October 20 Freedom Fighters.[49]

Calling themselves "captured freedom fighters," Balagoon, Clark, and Gilbert sat out much of their own trial. They argued that to participate would be to recognize the legitimacy of the court to criminalize *political* acts. When they did appear, it was to make statements condemning white supremacy and U.S. imperialism. They called only one witness: Sekou Odinga, who had been separated from the state trial to face federal conspiracy charges. Odinga's testimony was a defense of the right of revolutionary movements to expropriate from the ruling class.[50] With Balagoon arguing that he was a *prisoner of war* and Clark and Gilbert maintaining their position as anti-imperialists acting in solidarity with the Black Liberation

Movement (thus making them *political prisoners*), the three asserted that the United States government lacked the legal basis to try them, both because of the political character of their actions, and because of the government's own illegitimacy. They demanded to be tried as political combatants in an international court under UN jurisdiction, noting that international law is supposed to supersede national legal proceedings.[51]

It was never about innocence. And as a legal strategy, it was less than successful. But for those on trial, it was important to resist the state's attempts to criminalize and deny the political motivations of their actions.

"I never had any criminal history," Gilbert says. "I never even shoplifted a candy bar; the only conflict I ever came into with the government or with the law had to do with responding to their much greater criminal behavior.... There's not one minute of my life where I was ever involved in criminal activity, ever thought about it, or ever did anything for personal or economic gain. Since I was 15, I've been completely conscious and aware of the injustices, the inhumanity of the system." With all that in mind, he couldn't bring himself to participate in a criminal trial for an action undertaken for political reasons—no matter how badly it had turned out.[52]

By proclaiming themselves political internees, the three radicals argued for the Black struggle as a national liberation movement. But the three defendants did not make the same claim: the two white people called themselves political prisoners, and the one Black person called himself a prisoner of war. As a result, Balagoon's courtroom statements highlighted the colonial condition of Black people in the United States, with Clark and Gilbert following suit as allies in the struggle.[53] It was an argument appealing to international law, where the United Nations had laid out firm guidelines for the protection of "persons detained or imprisoned as a result of their struggle against apartheid, racism and racial discrimination, colonialism, aggression and foreign occupation and for self-determination, independence and social progress for their people."[54]

The United Nations Geneva Convention protocols of 1949 define prisoners of war not just as captured soldiers from a standing army, but also as members of "organized resistance movements." If detained or arrested, these combatants are to be treated as prisoners of war under the conditions set forth in the Geneva Convention.[55] Additions to the protocols in 1977—which the United States did not sign, though most other countries did—make provisions for national liberation fighters to engage in guerrilla war and other forms of unconventional warfare and still be considered prisoners of war once captured.[56] Thus, as Puerto Rican activist Julio Rosado notes, under the UN rules it is *not* required that combatants belong to a "standing, recognizable army, or a fighter clothed in the usual garb of war" to be considered prisoners of war. Instead, "all that is required for such individuals to have a legitimate status as prisoners of war is that they advance a claim to that status and be identified with a recognized national liberation movement."[57]

International law on political prisoners and prisoners of war operates on the assumption that those on trial have engaged in some sort of illegal act, and yet merit protection above and beyond what is called for in criminal cases. After all, what government would legalize revolution against itself? As radical journalist I.F. Stone said of the Weather Underground in 1970, "A guerrilla movement is a political, not a criminal, phenomenon, however many crimes it may commit."[58] It must, therefore, be dealt with politically. Whether someone "did it" or not is not the issue. Nelson Mandela "did it" in the sense that he was a leader of the armed wing of the African National Congress, a group that was illegal under the brutal apartheid system of South Africa. Yet Mandela was arguably the most famous and celebrated of the world's political prisoners before his release in 1990 and the collapse of apartheid.[59]

Four years before the Brink's robbery, the United Nations General Assembly passed a resolution for the "Protection of Persons Detained or Imprisoned As a Result of Their Struggle Against Apartheid, Racism and Racial Discrimination, Colonialism, Aggression and Foreign Occupation and for Self-Determination, Independence and Social Progress for Their People."[60] The resolution "expresses its solidarity with the fighters for national independence...against racism" and "demands the release of all individuals detained or imprisoned as a result of their struggle against...racism and racial discrimination...and for self-determination."[61] This resolution and others like it constitute the foundation of international law regarding the treatment of political prisoners and prisoners of war (since undermined by the U.S. government with the Guantánamo gulag). These resolutions demand that member nation-states treat captured combatants in accordance with the Geneva Convention's rules on the treatment of political prisoners. In many cases, these resolutions support the unconditional release of political prisoners, including those who used armed struggle to secure liberation from racist or colonial oppression. (Hence James Forman, former executive secretary of the Student Nonviolent Coordinating Committee, writes bluntly in his memoir that, "all political prisoners are innocent and the U.S. government is always wrong. That is the political truth, regardless of so-called 'legal' technicalities.")[62]

The Black freedom movement was, of course, structured around opposition to racism and white supremacy. And the movement's revolutionary nationalist tenets (from which the BLA emerged) helped popularize the notion that the struggle was not just against racism but against colonialism. Thus, for instance, the final demand of the Black Panther Party's ten-point program in 1966 called for a "United Nations-supervised plebiscite to be held throughout the black colony...for the purpose of determining the will of black people as to their national destiny."[63] Two years later, the Republic of New Afrika "declared [its] independence from the U.S. government and called for a Black nation-state" to be established in the five "Black belt" states of the South (Alabama, Georgia, Louisiana, Mississippi, and South Carolina).[64] The RNA set up a provisional government and even presented the State Department "with a petition for land for the New Afrikan nation."[65]

In his trial statements, Balagoon described the Black struggle for national liberation and self-determination, political positions Sekou Odinga and Dr. Mutulu Shakur (who co-founded the RNA) articulated in later trials. Indeed, Balagoon said in his opening statement that he had hoped to be tried together with Odinga, so that the two former Panthers could articulate their position as captured freedom fighters.[66] A criminal trial negated the political foundations of the war for Black liberation. "I am a prisoner of war and I reject the crap about me being a defendant, and I do not recognize the legitimacy of this court," Balagoon proclaimed in his opening statement. "The term defendant applies to someone involved in a criminal matter, in an internal search for guilt or innocence. It is clear that I've been a part of the Black Liberation Movement all of my adult life and have been involved in a war against the American Imperialist, in order to free New Afrikan people from its yoke."[67] (The press, meanwhile, held up the fact that Balagoon and Odinga were both indicted as part of the Panther 21 case to show their criminality—never mentioning that the case was a COINTELPRO frame-up.)[68]

As a white person, David Gilbert was not about to call himself a prisoner of war. He saw himself as a captured ally of the Black Liberation Movement, not a direct combatant from a colonized nation. The result, however, was the same: he didn't accept the authority of the courts to try him, and like Balagoon and Clark, was ejected from the courtroom when he tried to talk about politics, including his political motivations for being under-ground in the United States in the 1980s.[69]

The defendants had legal standing to call themselves political prisoners and prisoners of war, according to attorney Michael Tarif Warren, even if it was ignored by the courts. "Their legal standing was totally disregarded," Warren says, adding that one reason the courts ignored it was because "the courts didn't really understand it themselves." Attempts to be treated as prisoners of war and political prisoners proved futile.

When the first state trial ended on September 15, 1983, Kuwasi Bala-goon, Judy Clark, and David Gilbert were each convicted and given the maxi-mum sentence: seventy-five years to life on charges of triple murder. The district attorney who prosecuted the case said he was upset that there was no death penalty, even though the sentence is, in effect, a death sentence.[70] In New York state, there is no shortcut around the minimum; the earliest Gilbert could see the parole board is in the year 2056, at the age of 112. He was never charged with shooting anyone or even possessing a gun; he was not at the scene where Brink's guard Peter Paige was killed and was at no time armed.[71] Further, *none* of the prosecution's eighty-one witnesses identified Balagoon, Clark, or Gilbert as the people who killed Paige, Brown, or O'Grady.[72] Balagoon died of AIDS in prison in 1986. Clark remains incarcerated at the Bedford Hills Correctional Facility, and Gilbert has been subjected to a Department of Corrections' version of musical chairs, being moved among the three toughest prisons in the state (Attica, Clinton, and Comstock), despite a pristine disciplinary record.

Kathy Boudin and Sam Brown, each tried individually, put up tradition-al legal defenses, though both were still given hefty sentences. After a plea bar-gain, Boudin received twenty years to life; she was paroled in August 2003 after twenty-two years in prison. Brown's cooperation with the federal investigation didn't win him any leniency. District Attorney Kenneth Gribetz tried to pin all three killings of October 20 on Brown because witnesses described seeing only Black people with guns, and Brown was the only Black person captured at the scene.[73] He, too, got the max: seventy-five years to life.

LEGAL BATTLES: ROUND TWO

SEKOU ODINGA WAS tried with five others on federal conspiracy charges stemming from robberies attributed to the BLA and the es-cape of Assata Shakur. They were tried under the Racketeer Influenced and Corrupt Organizations Act, otherwise known as RICO, which was originally designed for use against the Mafia. Those on trial at the state level rejected criminal charges for what they deemed political acts, but the federal RICO charges were even worse. Using RICO statutes as the basis for trial compared the defendants to the mob and described their actions as being done solely for personal gain. And the charges didn't just cover the Brink's expropriation; the court alleged that from "December 1976 to October 1981," the defendants "committed a succession of robberies and attempted robberies of armored trucks in the Northeast."[74] Some of the people in the federal case—including Odinga—were known to have not participated in the Brink's robbery.[75] Unable to connect them to a specific act, the government instead retreated to the vague territory of conspiracy charges. Of the six people tried in this case, Odinga and former SDS and May 19th leader Sylvia Baraldini, the two most politically outspoken and involved of those on trial, received the longest sentence: forty years each.[76] Two people received sentences of twelve and a half years for being accessories after the fact, and two others were acquitted.[77]

Initially indicted with Odinga et al., Dr. Mutulu Shakur and Marilyn Buck were still underground at the time of the first federal trial. Buck was arrested in Dobbs Ferry, New York, in 1985, Shakur in Los Angeles in 1986, and the two stood trial together on the same RICO charges.[78] Like Odinga and Balagoon, Shakur presented himself as a captured prisoner of war, with Buck (who prosecutors described as "the only white member of the BLA") arguing she was a political prisoner fighting in solidarity with the Black Liberation Movement. And as in the first federal trial and the state trial before that, this political strategy did not pan out as a legal endeavor, even though Shakur and Buck argued their political position in court with more traditional means than their comrades in earlier trials had used.[79] They were convicted in 1988; Dr. Shakur was sentenced to 60 years and Buck to 50 years, although with other charges against her, Buck ended up with an 80-year sentence.[80]

Both federal prosecutions benefited considerably from four people associated with the defendants to varying degrees who decided to cooperate: Sam Brown, Kamau Bayete, Tyrone Rison, and Yvonne Thomas. Only Rison, however, was of much use. Beaten and broken down, Brown was of little help to authorities, given that, as the court said, he was "at times disjointed, dishonest, and agitated" as a result of his torture.[81] Bayete had worked at the Black Acupuncture Advisory Association of North America

(BAAANA), a Harlem-based clinic founded by Dr. Mutulu Shakur that used acupuncture to treat drug addiction.[82] The court acknowledged that he was less than credible as a witness: "Bayete is an admitted drug abuser whose primary motive in testifying appeared to be to avoid imprisonment for drug offenses. He also admitted to lying both to the grand jury and to the FBI on numerous occasions," wrote one judge.[83] Thomas, the girlfriend of the late Mtayari Shabaka Sundiata, had a history of mental illness.[84] The FBI found her in a psychiatric institution; besides providing details of BLA robberies (some of which she later recanted as lies), Thomas told authorities that "she had swum the Atlantic to Zimbabwe in twenty-four hours...had sex with 1,000,001 men at a party, headed the Ku Klux Klan and Mafia, and brought apes and cavemen back to life."[85]

Although the court still allowed the affidavits and testimony of Bayete, Brown, and Thomas, it was Tyrone Rison who became the star witness for the prosecution. Arrested in Georgia as a result of information Thomas gave to the FBI, Rison spent seven months in jail before he agreed to cooperate—after seeing that Thomas would be testifying against him at trial.[86] A former Republic of New Afrika activist who was mentored by Dr. Mutulu Shakur, Rison testified in both federal trials about Assata Shakur's escape and about armored car robberies in which he had participated from the late 1970s into 1981. His testimony linked several of the defendants to various illegal actions, which he admitted on cross-examination were undertaken to "free oppressed people in this country,"[87] with money going "to the political struggle."[88] Rison also took responsibility for killing a guard during a June 1981 robbery—the only time before the Brink's expropriation that anyone was hurt in a BLA-credited robbery.[89] But his cooperation paid off handsomely. Rison, the only one the state could directly link to violence, pleaded guilty to one racketeering charge and received a ten-year sentence.[90]

The final arena of legal contestation, the Brink's grand juries, was seen by many as a repressive measure against the Left, and more than a dozen people were jailed for periods of seven to eighteen months for refusing to cooperate.[91] Casting a wide net, the state targeted an array of Black liberationists, white anti-imperialists, and their friends. Attorney and longtime activist Susan Tipograph described the post-Brink's grand juries as an effort to "compel testimony which provides comprehensive general intelligence on personal and organization relationships within the left as a whole."[92] Through his work with the National Conference of Black Lawyers, Michael Tarif Warren served as legal counsel for some of the Black activists subpoenaed for the Brink's grand jury. He called the legal proceedings attempts "to create not only disarray...[but] to destroy families, to attempt to destroy allegiances between people."

Bernardine Dohrn was one of the white radicals who refused to testify. Dohrn had surfaced in December 1980. She was living and working in New York City, preparing to return to a career in the law, when the robbery occurred; she was not involved in May 19th, as many of the white people subpoenaed were. By the time the grand jury began, Dohrn and husband Bill Ayers had three children—now including Kathy Boudin and David Gilbert's son, Chesa Boudin, for whom they had assumed legal custody in November 1981 from Kathy Boudin's aging parents.

"For me, the grand jury was agonizing because I had three young kids," Dohrn says. "But it wasn't agonizing in terms of the choice. I feel like one of the great things we [the WUO] did in our time underground was build a real campaign, a widespread, popular campaign, against cooperation with the FBI and the repressive strategies." For Dohrn, the fact that the campaign against cooperating with the state's repressive apparatus had been so widespread and people were willing to go to jail for the Weather Underground "meant that there was no question" in the Brink's grand jury: "Even though I had no information to give.... I felt I had to resist." She spent seven months of 1982 in jail rather than testify, even though she disagreed with the Brink's action.

PRISONS AND POLITICAL PRISONERS IN THE UNITED STATES

IN *LOCKDOWN AMERICA: Police and Prisons in an Age of Crisis*, Christian Parenti traces the rise of the modern prison industrial complex in the United States. Parenti anchors the prison system's rising trajectory in the growth of militarized policing and increasingly repressive laws, partially as a response to the movements of the 1960s and 1970s and also as a way of controlling poor populations made poorer by the economic restructuring of the late twentieth century.[93] The "War on Drugs" is a prime example of the mass internment of poor people and people of color.[94] The incarceration and treatment of political prisoners further reveals the use of prisons as a means of control. Put simply, political prisoners do harder

---

time, even if arrested on the same charges as an apolitical person. This is a common practice of governments the world over, whether in Robben Island (South Africa), Long Kesh (Ireland), Stammheim (Germany), Marion (Illinois), Leavenworth (Kansas), or Attica (New York). "The state treats each political prisoner in a similar fashion, irrespective of geography," says Michael Tarif Warren, speaking from years of experience representing U.S. political prisoners. "That's the dilemma that we have been faced with and that we're still faced with in this country."

Political prisoners and prisoners of war are routinely given longer sentences and harsher prison conditions than even serious repeat offenders. As political prisoner Marilyn Buck notes, "those imprisoned for political actions and offenses are...subject to preventive detention or astronomically high bails; courtroom security is used to prejudice the jury; we receive disproportionate sentences; and we are subjected to isolation and efforts to break or destroy those who do not repent our political ideologies."[95] Political prisoners are often housed in the most repressive institutions—control units inside existing prisons, where prisoners are confined to their cells for 23 hours a day, or specially designed federal prisons such as Marion or the "maxi-max" prison in Florence, Colorado. In these "supermaxes," prisoners are constantly monitored on closed-circuit televisions and separated from human contact for most of the day. Political prisoners who have been held in super-maximum prisons and control units include Sundiata Acoli, Marilyn Buck, Yu Kikumura, Tom Manning, Leonard Peltier, and Russell Maroon Shoatz.[96]

One of the most notorious super-maximum prisons was the Lexington High Security Unit in the basement of a Kentucky federal prison. The whole unit was painted white, creating an environment of sensory deprivation for those incarcerated there—in addition to being denied human contact and living under constant surveillance. One of the prisoners called it a "white tomb," similar to the Stammheim prison in Germany, which housed many of that country's political prisoners.[97] Lexington's first guinea pigs were political prisoners Silvia Baraldini, Susan Rosenberg, and Alejandrina Torres: a May 19th leader convicted of conspiracy, a former May 19th leader arrested for suspected clandestine activity, and an alleged FALN member.[98] An ACLU report on Lexington by psychologist Richard Korn said that such extreme incarceration creates a host of psychological and physical conditions, including depression, claustrophobia, hallucinations, withdrawal, dizziness, heart disturbances, and visual problems.[99] The Lexington control unit was declared cruel and unusual punishment by Amnesty International and closed following a grassroots campaign.

The prisons reflect the bias exhibited by the courts against the Left. The International Tribunal on Political Prisoners and Prisoners of War in the United States, held in 1990, found that those captured from the Right—mainly abortion clinic bombers and violent white supremacists—received much lighter sentences than those of the Left. This was true even when the neo-Nazis and fundamentalists were arrested on similar or even more serious charges than the anti-racist revolutionaries. Michael Donald Bray served forty-six months for bombing ten *occupied* abortion clinics, and Dennis Malvesi, another clinic bomber, received seven years for possessing more than 100 pounds of explosives in a New York City apartment. (Susan Rosenberg served sixteen years of a fifty-eight-year sentence for keeping explosives in an empty storage unit in a sparsely populated neighborhood.)[100] Klansmen who murdered five anti-racist communists in North Carolina at an anti-Klan rally in 1979, and were later found to have been helped by the police, served no time.[101] Ex-Klansman Don Black, who violated the Neutrality Act with his attempted takeover of the Caribbean nation of Dominica, was back on the streets after two years of a ten-year sentence, despite being caught with a boatload of explosives and illegal weapons.[102]

Political prisoners have been released in Ireland, the Middle East, and even under the most brutal regimes, such as those of Augusto Pinochet in Chile and Robert D'Aubisson in El Salvador in the 1980s. Even among countries reluctant to acknowledge a legitimate internal opposition, there is a global history of political prisoners being released on a somewhat regular basis.[103] Not so here. "Only in the United States," Julio Rosado writes, "where deviation from political orthodoxy is typically presented as common criminal conduct, and where the act of resisting the objectives of the status quo is cast as something unnatural, akin to child molestation, selling drugs, or running a prostitution ring, do we find a refusal to recognize any category of political 'criminality.'"[104] This criminalization of political opposition allows the United States to find itself in the absurd position of having the highest incarceration rate in the world while simultaneously having no officially designated political prisoners. Absent a category for political offenses, the country justifies its continued imprisonment of its political internees as criminals. And a vengeance-based legal system results in lengthy sentences for political prisoners, with amnesty rarely granted.

Being a political prisoner does not mean never having to say you're sorry. Pure motives are not carte blanche for any behavior; in the Brink's case, there were several real mistakes leading up to the action, even before the deadly shootouts that occurred that day (as well as the one three days later that killed Mtayari Sundiata). A communiqué issued two and a half weeks afterward claimed that the action was done by "the Revolutionary Armed Task Force," a Black Liberation Army unit with allied white anti-imperialists working under their direction.[105] The communiqué said the RATF was formed to oppose the "Black Holocaust" and to support revolutionary nationalist programs for youth and the Black community at large. But this statement, the first in which the "RATF" acronym was ever used, assumed a level of cohesion and unity that was not actually there.

Almost immediately upon their arrest, Gilbert remembers engaging in political discussions with Balagoon and Odinga about the mistakes and failures. It was an eye-opening experience for him, in which he realized the problems of his own involvement. Feeling "shattered by the collapse of the WUO," he had entered into what he now calls an "apolitical relationship"—absent any discussion over politics and strategy—because he was looking for validation from "the heaviest Third World group going." Frustrated by the mistakes he felt the WUO had made, and "anxious to prove I could be of service," he had thrown all of his support behind one particular group that didn't have a clear mass base of support in Black communities, inadvertently meddling in the Black Liberation Movement in the process. He had neglected his responsibility to work with other whites against racism, a particularly urgent and difficult task at the start of the Reagan era. He went from a group that lacked direct mechanisms of accountability to Third World groups, to an equally untenable position of choosing "the most revolutionary" people of color to follow.

Problems emerged among the Black comrades as well. Based partly on Rison's testimony, the *New York Times* reported in March 1983 that some BLA members (including but not limited to Rison and Bayette) were using cocaine, and that one of those on trial in the federal conspiracy case ran a small prostitution ring.[106] Ashanti Alston, in prison for BLA activities when Brink's happened, recalls feeling extremely upset when he found out about the problems among his BLA comrades. Especially infuriating for Alston was hearing that some of his comrades had been involved in drugs and had been lax on security, thus enabling so many people to later cooperate with the state. It was a slap in the face that BLA members would be involved with drugs, given that the BLA was formed in part to rid Black communities of drugs. He was also upset with white comrades for entering into a relationship that excluded them from all decisions and plans.

The mistakes of the Brink's action have not been lost on those incarcerated. During his years in prison, Gilbert has tried to openly and honestly criticize his own errors without losing sight of the greater ills caused by social violence. In a 2004 public statement, Gilbert apologized for his role in "the grievous mistakes" made in Nyack twenty-three years earlier. Affirming his history of and commitment to "solidarity with the Black Liberation Movement," Gilbert wrote that "my actions on 10/20/81 were wrong, and I deeply apologize for their role in the tragic loss of lives."[107] Gilbert had taken up the issue of remorse before his 2004 statement, writing elsewhere: "Even in a battle for a just cause, we can't lose our feeling for the human element.... I feel sorry for the losses and pain of the families of those who were killed." Gilbert also expressed regret for the pain to his own family, "who never got to make choices about the risks I would take."[108]

THE WEATHER UNDERGROUND LEGACY AND THE BRINK'S AFFAIR

THE BRINK'S AFFAIR captured public attention as proof of the Left gone awry. The story dominated newspaper headlines throughout the 1980s, and two journalists published books about the case (with a third on the Boudin family devoting considerable space to the Brink's affair).[109] An easily discernible pattern runs through all these narratives. This "Brink's formula" should be familiar by now: privileged white radicals, feeling guilty about their race and class background, have allied with Black thugs with disastrous results. This dollar-store pop psychiatry, conducted by people with no apparent training in psychology, produces little in the way of meaningful explanation. The deeper implication of this pathologizing process is that whites who resist class and racial privilege, especially those who ally with militant Black people, have somehow "gone wrong." The Black people involved, dismissed as criminals, are of course of little interest.

In reducing the captured white anti-racists to a tortured psychological profile, the dominant narrative misses the fact that, in a certain sense, any former member of the WUO, among other militant anti-racist whites, could have been there with (or instead of) David Gilbert that day. Laura Whitehorn, who was in the May 19th Communist Organization at the time, says she can easily imagine herself there—not because she knew anything about its planning, but because she shared a politics of staunch, full-fledged support for the Black Liberation Movement. Just weeks before Brink's occurred, Judy Siff was released from prison for her role in the Revolutionary Committee of the WUO. As the political problems of Brink's became known, Siff says she "felt completely horrible because I knew that our mistakes were the background to what was now happening." And Naomi Jaffe, Gilbert's comrade and dear friend since graduate school, recalls a young, heartbroken Chesa Boudin asking why his biological parents were both in jail.

"Wait, while I sob my heart out, and I'll try to give you an answer," Jaffe later imagined as her response. "They did what we all did, only for a minute longer."[110]

PART THREE

...a single spark can

start a prairie fire...

Anti-imperialists at a demonstration countering the Republican National Convention in 2004.
Photo by Andrew Stern

THE POLITICS OF SOLIDARITY

LESSONS AND LEGACIES OF THE WEATHER UNDERGROUND

12

> *In learning from history, we need to break from the mainstream culture that defines people as either purely "good guys" or purely "bad guys," which can lead to the self-delusion that getting certain basics down guarantees that everything else we do is right. The WUO made giant errors along with trailblazing advances. Hopefully both are rich in lessons for a new generation of activists.*
> —*David Gilbert*[1]

THE REVOLUTIONARY GROUPS TO EMERGE OUT OF THE twenty-year period known as the Sixties didn't win. But they didn't lose, either. Real gains arose from the social movements of that period, many of which are still being contested today. For that reason, and because dozens of veterans of that era remain incarcerated for their political work, it is impossible to speak of the Sixties as "over and done."

That is not to suggest that we should live forever in nostalgia or that we must hearken back to a time when America was spelled with a "k" (or three). A mythology of the Sixties is unhelpful, even detrimental, to any attempts at understanding what happened, let alone to forging progressive movement strategy today. But the continuing arrests and convictions, as well as investigative grand juries, of veterans of the 1960s and 1970s movements—including members of the WUO, the Black Panthers and the Symbionese Liberation Army—show that the Sixties are still an ideological battleground, still a contested space.[2] The Sixties era still resonates today. And yet, our world in many ways is profoundly different. The goal, then, is to understand the politics and practices of the past without looking for mechanistic formulas or losing sight of today's realities.

In the thirty years since the dissolution of the Weather Underground, the world has undergone many changes. Globally, even though U.S.-led wars of conquest and occupation continue, national liberation movements are not major world players, even where they still exist (as in Venezuela and elsewhere in Latin America). Most of those that succeeded in obtaining state power in the 1960s and 1970s have been less than successful in building or maintaining revolutionary societies, because of U.S. malfeasances, the pressures of global capitalism, and weaknesses within those movements.[3] And the 1989 fall of the Eastern bloc proved the death knell for the bureaucratic and authoritarian state socialism of the Old Left variety. The international revolutionary elements so common and mass-based in the 1960s and 1970s no longer pose the credible alternative to Western hegemony that they once did. Instead of avowedly Left threats to state power, there are now a phalanx of groups, from globally dispersed reactionary political Islamists (some of whom were trained or funded by the United States during the Cold War) who view targeting civilians and non-combatants as a viable tactic, to those opposing U.S. military occupation in Afghanistan or Iraq from a variety of political perspectives, to a resurgent and virulently anti-government fascist movement within the United States (which, among other things, has violently targeted immigrants and abortion clinics).[4] Within the United States, Christian fundamentalism has found a comfortable home under George W. Bush.

Domestically, the past three decades have seen the growth of a wide range of social movements: welfare rights; HIV/AIDS care and prevention; international solidarity; global justice and global debt relief; prison reform and abolition; anti-nuclear, immigrant rights, anti-sweatshop and pro-living wage campaigns; reparations; education justice; environmentalism and animal rights; media democracy; lesbian, gay, bisexual and transgender rights; and gender and ethnicity based identity movements. With an estimated eleven million participants, the February 15, 2003, demonstration prior to the war in Iraq was the biggest global protest in the history of humankind, made even more noteworthy by the fact that it occurred before the invasion began. And a slew of academics who cut their teeth on the movements of the 1950s through the 1980s have entered academia, giving rise to a vast quantity of critical scholarship on race, ethnicity, class, gender, sexuality, culture, and U.S. foreign policy.[5] It is quite likely that there are more people active, in some way, today than in 1968.

At the same time, however, these diverse social movements have yet to cohere into a single mass movement with a shared set of principles, guided by a common strategy—as "two, three, many Vietnams" was for part of a previous generation of activists. Because of the right-wing backlash, many of the gains of the Sixties-era movements have been steadily contested or rolled back and eroded.[6] Since the Reagan years, the United States has been engaged in military conflicts in Afghanistan, Grenada, Haiti, Iraq (twice, with twelve years of bombings and sanctions killing an estimated 1.2 million people, 500,000 of them children, in between the two Bush-led wars),[7] Kosovo, Panama, Nicaragua, Serbia, Somalia—although, afraid of massive U.S. casualties and unable to mobilize significant world support, the country has been reluctant to engage in full-scale military force until recent years, opting instead for high-technology, "low-intensity" conflagrations.[8] At the same time, the nature of state power is itself changing through corporate-led globalization, so that significant power now rests with supranational entities devoted to the worldwide capitalist market and less beholden to the individual interests of any one nation-state (even if the United States, at least for the time being, is still the dominant world player).[9]

Given the conditions facing the world today, what does the legacy of the Weather Underground Organization have to offer? The lessons are not primarily to be found in the bombed buildings but in the politics and practice of the group. Weather must be examined both for what it stood for historically and for how such lessons translate to today's globalized, postmodern, permanent-war wonderland. A critical analysis reveals not only that the Weather Underground, and others from that sector of the Left, have had a role in shaping organizing action and academic discourse of the past thirty years, but also that their worldview, their victories and mistakes, still present a valuable guide to navigating the perilous path ahead.

PART I:

THE WEATHER UNDERGROUND IN HISTORY

L IKE ANY ORGANIZATION, the Weather Underground was complex—it had its high points and low, its positive attributes and its negative ones. Most importantly, it existed in a broad political context, in which it was one of many revolutionary groups grappling in both theory and practice with how to make fundamental change. The WUO pushed and was pushed by other groups and other sectors of the movement. It took its politics seriously, constantly seeking creative ways to response to oppression. Acknowledging that the WUO's advances came with a dose of sexism and bravado, among other things, diminishes neither the importance of the successes nor the weight of the errors. To that end, I will examine in this section five different but interrelated aspects of the legacy of the Weather Underground: race, class, militancy, democracy, and gender.

A WHITE FIGHTING FORCE
RACE, WHITE PRIVILEGE, AND WHITE SUPREMACY

THE MOVEMENTS OF the Sixties era put the issue of racism on the agenda not only for progressives and revolutionaries but for society as a whole. Today, white supremacy remains a constant source of social confusion and controversy. We are now said to be either in a "color blind" or a "multicultural" society (two popular but contradictory claims), and yet neither has solved the problem of the color line.[10] Tokenistic Bush appointees and a smattering of conservative people of color are held up as proof of progress or the dissolution of racism, although they support an agenda that is by design white supremacist. Race continues to be a battleground and a rallying point, despite the ample historical and sociological evidence proving it to be socially constructed rather than biologically determined.[11] And despite lots of talk to the contrary, racism remains a pivotal part of American society. Nonwhite, especially Black, people continue to face systemic oppression in the political, economic, and social realms—as the government's response to Hurricane Katrina so horrifically laid bare.[12]

And race and racism are at the heart of what the Weather Underground was all about. To me, these are the most important questions raised by the Weather Underground. What does it mean to be a white person opposing racism and imperialism? What does it mean to be born of privilege in a world defined by oppression? How can those with such unearned social benefits work in a way to undermine and ultimately dismantle systems of injustice? I pose the questions in political rather than tactical or military terms; the point is not that effective anti-racism necessarily leads to bombs. Politically, however, the Weather Underground offers valuable lessons for fighting institutional racism. The WUO experience revolved around fighting white supremacy in three concrete and challenging ways that still endure: it showed that racism is a defining feature of the United States, both domestically and in terms of foreign policy; it provided a lasting call for whites to support the progressive demands of people of color; and it mandated that white people challenge themselves and other whites, at personal and institutional levels, in the struggle for racial justice. Such a process entails taking risks, as white people, in solidarity with liberation movements in this country and across the planet.

"We saw U.S. imperialism for what it was," Scott Braley says. "We made a conscious decision to not acquiesce in that, that we were going to oppose that in all possible ways, that we were not going to allow ourselves any excuses for not doing everything we could to stop the war, to stop the attacks on Black people.... We saw ourselves as struggling over white supremacy as a principle. Doesn't mean we did it right all the time, doesn't mean we always do it correctly right now. But that was the commitment." In making the fight against white supremacy a guiding principle, the Weather Underground was trying to provide anti-racist leadership amongst white activists in a context established by the leadership of people of color. The group, in other words, was trying to both lead and get out of the way at the same time. At its best moments, Weather recognizing the need to provide leadership to whites without usurping the overarching leadership of Third World movements.[13] It was neither flawless nor hopeless in this regard, but it was rather unique in that era; it still provides a model for white people's participation in anti-racist movements. Such a complex legacy of resistance, Donna Willmott says, is "our gift to the next generation" of white activists.

This commitment to "see things as they were and to change them," as Braley puts it, is an important promise that many former members of Weather still try to live up to. "What was going on was so hideous that you had to give it your best shot," says Judy Siff, elucidating a point that almost every former member of the group expressed in interviews. It was "better to fail than sit home and wonder what the better way is." The centrality of anti-racism to the Weather Underground translates into the lives of former members today, whose commitment to racial justice is evident in their talk and work, although now without the bravado that characterized the earlier period. "I feel it is essential as a white person to define yourself in terms of race and militant opposition to white supremacy," Bernardine Dohrn says. "Whatever we do today requires you to change yourself, requires you to see the world constantly in a new way, requires you to not be un-self-conscious about white privilege."

Since the end of the WUO, white privilege and the very concept of whiteness have both become fields of academic study and even discussions of public policy. Scholars such as labor historian David Roediger and sociologist Becky Thompson have studied the relationships between race, class, and gender—insisting, as the WUO did, that any progressive movement must make the struggle against white supremacy and white privilege central to any political work.[14] Years before white privilege and the concept of whiteness became a mode of academic inquiry, the Weather Underground built an organization dedicated to fighting white privilege as a way of helping topple white supremacy. Those who joined the WUO, in Robert Roth's words, saw it as "our job to disrupt from within"—not only geographically but politically within institutions and communities once thought held together by white supremacy and thus by common opposition to the demands of people of color.[15]

"It was a time when movements for self-determination were saying that 'we need to decide on our own. You go home and organize other white people,'" recalls Donna Willmott. "You can look back on it now and wonder why we didn't follow a different model. But I think in the time period, it was really a challenging thing to grapple with the question, 'What does it mean to be in solidarity with people of color,' to be an ally when the push for national self-determination without interference was paramount?"

In attempting a break from whiteness, the Weather Underground flipped racial profiling on its head—promising outlaws in every dorm room and commune, proclaiming that white skin didn't buy complicity.[16] The message was that no white youth could necessarily be trusted; the nice college student or young factory worker could be a revolutionary whose allegiances lay with the oppressed people of the Third World, with Black and Native and Latino/a people in the United States. While widespread fear of white youth was not exactly the result, the FBI was especially obsessed with capturing the Weather Underground, with restoring the nation's surface unity.

Whiteness was also a protection for the WUO: members had a bigger population to blend into and could get into high-level government buildings without raising suspicion. Much as they loathed the reality, white privilege protected white radicals at all levels, including the clandestine Weatherman. It was a sobering reminder of the enduring presence of white supremacy. "We were being pursued and beaten, true," Bill Ayers writes in his memoir, "but our Black Panther comrades were being targeted and assassinated."[17] The same Chicago police who hung Weatherman Robert Roth outside a window by his ankles in 1969 murdered Black Panthers Fred Hampton and Mark Clark as they slept.

David Gilbert remembers being stopped twice by police while he was underground, and each time talking his way out of the situation without raising suspicion.[18] In contrast, police had shoot-to-kill orders for Assata Shakur and other members of the Black Liberation Army. Underground WUO members didn't have to fear "accidental" capture through racial profiling; simply being white in a society defined by racial oppression spared them the harassment of constant police stops. "It is a powerful lesson about racism that, even when taking on the high level of commitment of building an underground, there was such a big relative cushion of white privilege," Gilbert says in reflecting on the WUO.[19]

"I think there's some victory to be claimed in the fact that people were able to elude the FBI," says Willmott. "But there was just a lot of privilege in being white, which meant we could skip through a lot of situations because we were not viewed as a threat by the way people looked at us. People could get away with a lot more and not be viewed as suspect just because of the color of our skins and the way we carried ourselves and how we could talk our way out of situations. That's the privilege born to race and class."

White privilege was a reality beyond Weather's control. What the group *could* control was how it grappled with privilege and what relationships it sought to build with people of color within the United States. How accountable was the WUO to domestic Third World groups and movements? The issue is difficult to assess, given the secrecy still accompanying clandestinity. One criticism that has emerged is that the group failed to sufficiently aid liberation movements within the United States. This criticism was a running theme in *The Split of the Weather Underground* pamphlet and has been brought up by some former members and others in the years since the group's implosion.[20]

Decisions on whether to work with other groups were made by the leadership, most of whom say that the WUO did what it could to support the organizing of people of color. It is largely the rank-and-file members who raise criticisms about accountability. Haunting them all is the Leary escape: The WUO using its resources and expertise to help the LSD guru get "free and high," while Black, Puerto Rican, and Native American militants were being hunted down and thrown into maximum security prisons, where many remain to this day. In a recent interview, Gilbert acknowledged that Weather "should have had more of a focus and solidarity and support for Black, Puerto Rican, and Native American undergrounds because it was easier for us to have access to more resources; we had a bigger population to blend in to [and were] less likely to be harassed by the police."[21] There were also periods of organizational silence about the struggles of people of color in the United States, such as following AIM's 1973 standoff at Wounded Knee.

Reflecting on this history, Suzanne Ross says the WUO fell short of its goal of being an accountable anti-racist organization. "My criticism is that we did not engage adequately in discussion, struggle, and dialogue with revolutionary forces in the movements of color, and [we] relied on too small a group, our leadership, to pursue this process for us," she says. "Though the clandestine structure presented some obstacles to this kind of dialogue, it was certainly not the only obstacle and, I believe, could have been overcome." Ross is especially critical of the WUO for not engaging in dialogue with revolutionary women of color from the various Third World movements inside the United States. By "seeing itself as the vanguard and arbiter of revolutionary struggle—to the point of defining who the vanguard forces were of other movements—the WUO did not recognize the importance of listening to and learning from the truly leading forces," she says. "In short," she says, "there has to be an overall perspective on the leading role of national liberation struggles and of the negative role of white hegemony and privilege. It is not just a 'line.' It involves a fundamental way of approaching all aspects of the work. And it must address male supremacy as well, by relating in a significant way to revolutionary women of color."

There is no consensus among former Panthers and BLA members about the WUO's aid to the Black movement. Prior to Weather's submersion, the Black Panther Party had an uneven relationship with Weatherman, characterized by both support and hostility. Under tremendous pressure from the state and becoming increasingly divided internally, some Panthers objected to Weatherman's pervasive action focus. Panther leader Bobby Seale once described Weather as "jive bourgeois national socialists and national chauvinist" because the group refused to support a Panther demand for community control of police in white neighborhoods. While agreeing that community control of police was a righteous demand in Third World communities, Weather opposed it in white communities, saying it feared open white supremacy.[22] Controversy continues among ex-Panthers, but such disagreements must be located within the context of the political differences within the Black Panther Party.

Former Black Liberation Army member and current political prisoner Jalil Muntaqim says that the WUO neglected to aid captured BLA members when asked and failed to share resources or show public support when the BLA was under attack.[23] Others congratulate the group for its efforts. Ashanti Alston, also a former BLA soldier, credits the Weather Underground for supporting the BLA's right to tactical self-definition and political self-determination at a time when many in the Left did not. Some BLA cadres tell of instances when the Weather Underground helped Black Panther or BLA activists with money and personal contacts. The fact that the BLA was made up of groups working autonomously explains at least partially why BLA members could have had such different experiences with the WUO.

When former Young Lord Panama Alba was being hunted by the state in 1977 (after the WUO broke up), he went for help to ex-Weather activists who had not yet surfaced and still had access to a clandestine network. "I have a lot of respect and love for the individuals [in the WUO] and their commitment, professionalism, and willingness to sacrifice…. They made themselves available to us," Alba says, "and they had the operation in place to make that [escape] possible." (During Alba's brief stint underground, the case against him began to crumble and his attorney was able to negotiate a surrender absent the police violence that had forced him underground.) Without glossing over the WUO's mistakes, Alba views it as an organization that tried to use its advantages for the broader liberation struggle. "At the end of the day, we were glad that they used their white skin privilege to get into places…. You have to give people an A for effort and recognize the sacrifices."

To get beyond surface level dismissal requires critical engagement with the entire history of the Weather Underground Organization. "The Weather experience," says Robert Roth, "is too often exceptionalized. Actually, it needs to be seen within the framework of other activists grappling with the same issues and questions: how do you deal with fascism, how do you deal with a state that's killing Black revolutionaries, how do you deal with mounting resistance and knowing that you're going to be attacked, harassed, surveilled?"

The significance of the WUO is as an organization of whites willing to risk life and limb to take some of the pressure off Third World movements and open up a new front of struggle. There are, to be sure, ongoing political questions. Bernardine Dohrn, for instance, says "the dilemma has always been, how do you as white people support the Black freedom movement in the United States in a wholehearted way without choosing the vanguard, without appointing yourself the white equivalent of it? [How do you keep] your own balance, your own mind, your own sense of right and wrong?... The only thing one can conclude, if you think white supremacy is the crucial issue defining American life domestically, is that you have to throw yourself into the struggle for social justice."

Solidarity with Third World people and movements was the cornerstone of WUO politics and is what most former members are most proud of. "There are things I wish the WUO had done with more maturity or less sectarianism, but I have no regrets about the path we took," says Scott Braley. By virtue of its existence, the Weather Underground forced the government to allocate resources to catching white people that otherwise could have gone to repressing Black, Latino/a, and Native movements. The group, at its best, represented an important pole of the Left—one insisting that staunch and unyielding opposition to white supremacy was the necessary prerequisite for any social justice movement. In that, there is victory to be claimed for anti-racist solidarity.

RACE, CLASS, AND COLONIALISM:
WEATHER'S CLASS ANALYSIS

CLASS HAS BEEN a defining issue for both the liberal and radical Left. Central to Left criticisms of the Weather Underground is the assertion that the group had little class analysis; that it failed to recognize the centrality of the working class, or proved divisive by concentrating on race rather than class.[24] To be sure, the WUO presented (at least at times) a dramatic departure from the standard Left conception of class. But to say that the group had no class analysis overlooks how it tried to reshape a radical approach to class.

In what has since become a hallmark of critical labor studies, the Weather Underground recognized the inherent contradiction of the white working class, as both privileged and oppressed.[25] Weather's fervent, if not always articulate, insistence on this point was and remains a crucial challenge for the Left. Especially in its early period, the WUO recognized that white workers in the United States had historically sided with empire against Third World people—and even against their own long-term interests—for the short-term gains of white privilege. The founding "Weatherman" statement asserted that, even though the long-term interests of white workers lay with anti-capitalist revolution, they received short-term but nonetheless very real material (and psychological) benefits for siding with the ruling class against the Third World. This had disastrous consequences given that people of color, the world's majority, were leading revolutionary struggles, both here and across the world.[26] Such allegiances meant that many white workers not only thought themselves better than people of color but that they had real material privileges as a result. Whiteness trumped class solidarity, Weather said, in part because of the tangible gains white unity enabled. As the communiqué accompanying the Attica bombing said, the "main question white people have to face today is not the state of the economy (for many, the question of selling their second car) but whether they are going to continue to allow genocidal murder, in their name, of oppressed people in this country and around the world."[27]

At the same time, Weather also argued that (sectors of) white working class communities were a central organizing location, which it tried to reach through youth culture. From its inception the group committed itself, through its statements, to working in these communities to build support for national liberation movements—and, at its best, argued for connecting the demands of white working class youth to a broader and explicitly anti-racist systemic critique. And while sectarian arrogance prevented Weatherman from making much headway in these aboveground organizing attempts, the political message was that active solidarity with Third World struggles was the primary way by which whites could become revolutionary. The WUO didn't want to join in the established history of white-led social movements that treated anti-racist or anti-colonial movements as secondary, or that tried to position themselves as *the* leading force, domestically or internationally.

"At a time when people were talking about 'organizing the white working class,' Weather argued for a strategy to 'split the white working class,'" according to Robert Roth. "Weatherman said you couldn't just look at the white population as a whole and 'organize it,' especially in light of the white backlash and the rise of racist movements. The Weather strategy was to heighten divisions in the white population and attempt to build an anti-racist base, especially by targeting youth who were already in motion against racism and the war."

The WUO argued strategically for building an anti-imperialist base among as significant sectors of whites as possible, to counter the reactionary tendency among parts of the white working class. "The point of the Weather politics was not so much about being all-white as about respecting and recognizing national liberation leadership and the idea that the timetable of revolutionary struggle was set by the most oppressed and most advanced, which was not the white Left or the working class," says Michael Novick, who continued to struggle against white supremacy and "domestic colonialism" after leaving Weatherman.

Weather didn't ignore class, but flipped traditional white Left postulations of class on their head. In a society where white social movements have historically betrayed Third World movements, at a time when Black leaders were being openly assassinated and more bombs were being dropped on Vietnam than were used in all of World War II, the Weather Underground said it could not and would not wait for the white working class to be a unified and militant revolutionary class. The gravity of the situation was too great and merited a response from anti-racist whites. And, it was hoped, offering a militant response to repression and openly displaying solidarity with Third World movements would help push all whites in a more anti-racist direction.[28]

"Our wing of the movement was always considered anti-working class because we put an emphasis on the struggle against racism and white supremacy," says Judith Mirkinson of Bay Area PFOC. "I remember when I got interviewed before going to a GI [organizing] project in Okinawa, and I said, 'well, I think the rest of the world is the working class of America. We get certain rights and we have a certain life because we're oppressing everyone else.'" Perhaps this wasn't sophisticated enough, she says now, but it "hit upon a central truth which is still very much reflected in today's world."

A crucial lesson from the WUO, many former members say, is this identification with the rest of the world, the recognition that though they dominate (for now) in the United States, whites are but a minority in the world stage. "That sense that we were global citizens, that we needed to get off of the necks of people of the world, that we would actually be better people and happier people without trying to protect all of 'our stuff,' was a core thing we did right," says Bernardine Dohrn, noting that "American wealth and privilege and comfort and longevity and good teeth and cell phone technology is all at the expense of other people's poverty and commiseration." Similarly Mark Rudd, highly critical of his involvement with the group at many levels, still identifies the WUO's main strength as struggling over the role of the United States in the world.[29]

Such internationalism inspires hope. "One of the strengths of Weather was that people had a stake in the future, that people were willing to risk a lot to build a different kind of society," Donna Willmott recalls. "We felt connected to a worldwide struggle, and that was powerful. Everything we did was being shaped by what was happening in Vietnam or in the Black Power Movement—all these things were totally redefining the society that we lived in."

The WUO's political framework defined the enemy as an imperialist system, which was colonizing nonwhite nations in and outside the United States. Weather's focus on the primacy of colonialism in the world situation was itself an argument about class. After all, colonialism is a class relationship, even when played out in racial codes. The position that defeating colonialism was the leading strategy to global revolution asserted that those in the West, in the imperial centers, benefited from colonialism. And to benefit from colonialism is not just a racial privilege, but a class privilege as well—American wealth and well-being rested on the subjugation of the global working class, a proletariat that was largely not white.

This analysis was applied within the United States as well. Black, Latino/a, and Native people were seen not only as occupying the lowest rungs on the class ladder but also as citizens of nations subjugated by the United States. Just as external colonies could throw off oppressive foreign power, the internal colonies of New Afrika/the Black nation, Puerto Rico, occupied Mexico, and all the Native nations could play the decisive role in shutting down the system of U.S. imperialism. It seemed to the WUO (and others with this political perspective) that there was a much greater level of unity among the national liberation movements of the internal colonies than across the multiracial/multinational U.S. working class as a whole. Organizations such as the Black Panthers and the Black Liberation Army, the Provisional Government of the Republic of New Afrika, the Puerto Rican Socialist Party, the *Movimiento de Liberación Nacional*, the Young Lords, the American Indian Movement, and others were in regular communication; the organized sections of militant white workers appeared tiny and largely divided. All of these factors convinced the Weather Underground and others that people of the Third World—within and outside the United States—were the leading agents of change. Marx's classic working class, white industrial workers, formed a small and privileged sector of the proletariat, "racially and politically...members of the oppressor nation."[30] It seemed foolish to expect them to take the lead in defeating a system that gave them relative benefits.

It was a class analysis centered around white people's complicity with empire, and thus was not complex enough—but it was a reasoned, even detailed, class analysis of the world situation. The white working class wasn't dismissed, but it was approached and analyzed in terms of support for national liberation struggles. Weather understood and sought to organize around the global racialized class conflict that existed between imperial power and those colonized by it. The group, says Judy Siff, was trying to balance the tension between supporting national liberation politics on the one hand, while recognizing that no political framework is complete without a class component on the other.

Thus, it is not true to say that the group maligned, minimized, or missed the role of the white working class. Its emphasis on colonialism was a significant accomplishment in internationalizing class and anti-racist struggle. Operating with an anti-colonial paradigm both complicated and deepened discussions of class struggle (or Left populism) by insisting on the role white supremacy has played in sapping the progressive political strength of the white working class. There is surely a need to synthesize this history with the impact of class oppression among whites and the possibilities for the white working class to play important roles within radical movements. For Naomi Jaffe, the group's grappling with class expressed itself in one of two polar responses, depending on the time period. "It was reflected in the see-sawing from dismissing the white working class to glorifying the white working class. Obviously, both those positions are wrong," she says. "But they're both wrong because what's right is pretty difficult and complicated."

Looking back on the WUO's attempts to understand the role of the white working class in political struggle, Jaffe says it wasn't a surprise that the group failed to come up with a nuanced answer. "The fact that we didn't understand it [the complexity of the white working class] isn't stupid. The fact that we didn't know how complicated it was and what we were getting into was a little stupid." The group, she says, was grappling with difficult questions: "how do you build a movement in a society that's layered in so many different ways that cut against each other? What does that mean? Who leads it? What does it mean to have solidarity with the most oppressed—who's that?"[31]

MILITANCY, CONFRONTATION, AND THE UNDERGROUND

MILITANCY HAS COME to define who and what the WUO was—and, to be sure, there is justification for that. In practice, however, this has often meant combining the rhetorical flourishes of the group's early months with its bombings to suggest that militancy was naïvely misguided or pathologically foolish. Today, militancy easily gets one branded a terrorist, perhaps with an all-expenses-paid trip to the Guantánamo gulag. But what was militancy? What did it mean for the WUO? Is it necessarily violent? Is militancy the same as militarism? Is it the same as terrorism?

The Weather Underground still occupies a complex place historically. On the one hand, its emphasis on militancy argued that, in a time of mass murder and repression against people of color within the United States and in other parts of the world, white radicals had a special responsibility to join the fight. "We took a stand when it was necessary to stand," says Robert Roth. In Gilbert's view, "given the level of lethal attacks on Black, Latino, and Native revolutionaries, it was crucial for whites to raise the level of struggle to make more tangible the politics of solidarity—the totally necessary terms for building a revolution among whites." Such a politic, it was hoped, would counter the demoralizing effect of widespread repression and "show that there were many ways to continue and advance the struggle," that the state was vulnerable and could be defeated.[32]

But that same militancy, absent a deep political analysis or strategy, could easily be reactionary. At the 1972 Republican National Convention protests in Miami, for instance, Laura Whitehorn confronted other white activists who, after attacking the buses carrying Republican delegates, turned to the cars of Miami's Black citizens, determined to do *anything* to stop traffic. They told her she wasn't militant enough. "And at that moment I realized: no, I don't believe in militancy," she says. "I believe that we should allow for militancy when guided by a political framework…. But I don't believe in militancy [for itself]. I believe in national liberation, solidarity, democracy, socialism. But it was too late—that's what we had created."[33]

Thus, the climate of militancy—which both Weather emerged from and contributed to—was neither inherently revolutionary nor reactionary. Militancy, escalating confrontational tactics rooted within an understood strategic framework, had the *potential* to be a real, progressive threat to the established order. But it could also be militancy for militancy's sake. At its best—especially after the townhouse blast and until the publication of *Prairie Fire*—the militancy of the Weather Underground was not just a question of tactics but a political stance of resistance. Tactics, of course, matter when examining any movement organization. But tactics *alone* do not explain the significance of a political group, and militancy isn't inherently just a tactical question.

A militant tactic, whether it is a bomb in the Pentagon bathroom or a brick through a Starbucks window during a global justice protest, is flashy and grabs people's attention. But a militant strategy does not require the most extreme or the most violent response to every situation, nor does it necessarily close off possibilities for coalition with those less militant; this is what the Weather Underground began to understand as it started separating *militancy* from *militarism* in 1970. Militarism says "the bigger the bang, the better"; it is concerned with maximum damage. A militant position, on the other hand, can often be a restrained response, providing it is one that works to expand political consciousness and fight systemic oppression. Militancy expresses itself differently in different communities—those under more pressure from the state are often the most militant in opposition, even if they are not the ones seen today, by and large, breaking corporate windows or burning SUVs. The power of the Sixties era, though, was that the most oppressed were visibly rising up and using a wide range of militant tactics. From sit-ins to armed struggle, tactics adopted by the white movement were pioneered by people of color, especially Black activists.

At its best, the Weather Underground understood militancy to be more than a tactical expression, such as bombings or street fighting. Rather, the group took militancy to be, in the words of Bill Ayers, "a stance in the world, a stance of integrity." With that definition of militancy, Ayers says, a sit-in at a restaurant in the 1950s apartheid South was an expression of militancy, as was the 1981 starving death of Irish Republican Army political prisoner Bobby Sands (and others), who died in a hunger strike demanding political status for IRA prisoners.[34] Militancy, so defined, changes based on the circumstances, the situation, and the period (as well as on who is defining it). Militancy can be a butt on a stool, a fist in the air, or a helping hand to the underground. It emerges when legal and reform elements seem exhausted, when mass movements feel restless and discouraged by what the state has to offer.

Militancy as a stance can help determine or define tactics. This is because a *strategy of militancy* is concerned with challenging and overturning systems of power and recognizes that a healthy and persistent opposition to oppression is central to creating progressive change. Such a stance mandates that tactics flow from the exigencies of the movement and the moment; a militant stance neither requires violence nor precludes nonviolence.[35] It is not interchangeable with clandestinity and often express itself aboveground. The *tactic of militancy*, absent a political framework or clearly identifiable strategy, is just interested in flash and bravado. For Weather, it was the difference between turning every demonstration into a fight with police, and crafting a movement living in dynamic and intractable opposition to the root forces of domination.

By intentionally going underground to carry out a string of high-level bombings, the organization helped expand the range of protest. In Gilbert's words, it was successful in "piercing the myth of government invincibility."[36] (Ayers describes this as the WUO's intention "to show that the Man was penetrable.") Piercing that myth was important in securing a sense of the movement's own power, especially as the Nixon administration expanded the Vietnam War into Cambodia and Laos and increased its murderous attacks on the Black movement.[37] The Weather Underground showed that political struggle against war, racism, and repression would come in many forms—and from all sectors. Indeed, in their letter to the women's movement, Weatherwomen identified clandestinity as "a way of cutting through the myth of impenetrability of government. We believe that the continued existence of an underground shows that America is deeply divided within itself."[38] Longtime Puerto Rican activist Esperanza Martell calls the Weather Underground "courageous" in "relation to Vietnam" for taking on the state. While difficult to quantify, the militant antiwar resistance of the Sixties surely contributed to two decades of official reticence and public disfavor regarding open U.S. military operations overseas.

It is this political impact, rather than the armed acts themselves, that is the most palpable of the WUO's legacies. "What's the reason to even care about the Weather Underground now?" asks Robert Roth. " In a period of war and national liberation struggle and revolution worldwide, a significant number of white radicals moved into a militant confrontational stance with the government. Moved well outside of the boundaries of what we had been trained to believe was movement organizing and protest, into a stance that we were going to be part not just of protesting the war, but ending it; not just denouncing violence against the Black liberation movement but attempting to be in solidarity with the Black liberation movement." None would claim perfection in this regard—the WUO had failures, blind spots, and pitfalls. But for PFOC activist Mickey Ellinger, the WUO and its offshoots "were willing to make mistakes, big mistakes, rather than make the worst mistake of all, which was to do nothing."[39]

Indeed, the militancy of the WUO, as expressed through its bombings, draws a map of some of the defining issues of the 1970s: racism in America, bombings in Asia, colonialism in Africa, coups in Latin America. "Our actions and our communiqués did a pretty decent job of reflecting a vibrant politics that I still think is core in any radical analysis of American power," Bernardine Dohrn said in 2004.

Was the WUO a terrorist organization? Terrorism is a loaded word, especially since September 11, 2001. In the intervening years, the U.S. government has equated terrorism with any illegal or even oppositional act by any group or individual against the state. Fighting terrorism has been offered as rationale for indefinite detention, draconian laws, permanent war, and even torture. Although they succeed at keeping people generally fearful, color-coded terror alerts and random police searches don't offer a definition of what is said to be the defining issue of our time.

Conservative military historian Caleb Carr offers a definition of terrorism rooted in international law. He defines terrorism as "the contemporary name given to, and the modern permutation of, *warfare deliberately waged against civilians with the purpose of destroying their will* to support either leaders or policies that the agents of such violence find objectionable" (emphasis added).[40] Carr's definition is useful for two reasons: it makes intentional violence against civilians *the* defining issue, and it creates space to talk about both state and non-state terror. Terrorism, as the late Eqbal Ahmad argued, is a tactic at the disposal of both governments and private individuals; it knows no inherent political or organizational bounds.[41]

"Terrorists terrorize, they kill innocent civilians, while [the WUO] organized and agitated," Bill Ayers writes in his memoir. "Terrorists destroy randomly, while our actions bore, we hoped, the precise stamp of a cut diamond. Terrorists intimidate, while we aimed only to educate."[42] The WUO's actions were more than just educational—one could argue that there was a component of "intimidating" the government and police attached to the actions—but the group purposefully and successfully avoided injuring anyone, not just civilians but armed enforcers of the government. Its war against property by definition means that the WUO was not a terrorist organization—it was, indeed, one deeply opposed to the tactic of terrorism. A poem by a Weatherwoman illustrated the way in which the state hypocritically defined terrorism by saying, "They call it terror / if you are few / and have no B-52's."[43]

★　★　★

Terrorists? Apocalyptic nihilists? Hardly. The Weather Underground was, on the contrary, a militant continuation of the hopeful spirit characterizing the early to mid-1960s, inspired by the success of national liberation movements the world over. "What was driving everyone was the belief that you could make a difference," says Judy Siff. "Not just that you could wave your fist and express your opposition, but that your actions could actually make change happen." As a result, militancy both emanated from and was itself a source of hope. "What gives you courage to take risks is that you believe they're going to accomplish something," says Naomi Jaffe. "What gives you courage isn't rage but hope."[44]

Thus, the impact of Weather is not to be judged by its military or economic damage, which was admittedly tiny. Instead, its impact was in broadening the contours of struggle and adding to the range of responses to U.S. imperialism—a moral, pedagogical, and militant form of guerrilla theater with a bang. The fact that the WUO from underground (and PFOC and May 19th from aboveground) were willing to push the envelope was what appealed to many people. Suzanne Ross, for instance, abandoned her much publicized and widely supported fight for tenure at Lehman College, part of the City University of New York, to go underground with the WUO. "What attracted me to the politics were, one, the anti-racism, the position on national liberation struggles; and, two, the militance. I loved the militance," she says today.

Public support was both moral and material. On a moral level, David Gilbert remembers hitchhiking across the country in the 1970s and getting picked up by people who would speak favorably of the WUO and its actions. In his memoir, Bill Ayers recounts hearing the news about the WUO bombing of the Pentagon with his landlord, a man who had no idea that his tenants were directly responsible. Without any prompting, Ayers writes, the landlord praised the WUO for its actions.[45] The bombings expressed the frustration many felt but didn't know how to articulate. In *The Weather Eye*, Jonah Raskin notes that the WUO's 1973 ITT bombing about Chile spread "joy in segments of the movement," expressing the collective feeling of those who were "outraged by the coup and the criminal role this corporation played."[46]

Although isolated from sectors of the Left as a result of political differences coupled with sectarianism—its own and that of other radical organizations—the Weather Underground still had enough support to exist underground for six years with only a few serious security breaches. Even the group's harshest critics could be sympathetic. When SDS collapsed, former national officer Bob Pardun went to live on a commune in Arkansas for much of the '70s. Frustrated with the early Weatherman, Pardun still conceived of his commune as a potential safe space for Weather fugitives. "I disagreed with them politically," Pardun says in his memoir, "but I always cheered when they blew up another symbolic target and sent a communiqué explaining their reasons for choosing it. I didn't expect them to come to our farm, but it was always possible that some of them might need a place to hide in an emergency and I wanted to be able to protect them if necessary."[47]

Although the Weather Underground never had more than a few score members, it had hundreds, if not thousands, of supporters who gave material aid. There were no special effects here; as Bernardine Dohrn says in the film *Underground*, "It's not a trick; we don't exactly outwit the FBI. If people didn't support there being an underground, we wouldn't be here five years later."

The full network and range of the underground included not just those living clandestinely in the Weather Underground, the BLA, the George Jackson Brigade, the FALN, the United Freedom Front, the draft resisters, the clandestine abortion providers, the antiwar priests, and other such groups. It was much broader, including the many people who provided support in the form of money, houses, IDs, and information—the people who lived temporarily in safe houses to establish cover; those who provided cash, IDs, and cars; those who housed fugitives on the run; those who publicized, reprinted, and distributed communiqués and other documents emanating from the underground. All these people participated in forging an underground. Some participated for years, others for a short time. But there was a world beneath the surface of daily life in the United States, one committed to mutual support networks and not just flashy actions.[48] It was an ominous message for the government, which had always relied on white support for its legitimacy.

"Contrary to the spy movie mystifications that are all about sophisticated techniques and technology," Gilbert notes, "our survival underground was based on popular support from radical youth and the antiwar movement.... There were moments when the FBI hunt was breathing down our necks, but popular support meant that information was kept from the state and instead flowed to the guerrillas."[49]

INTERNAL DYNAMICS: DEMOCRACY AND GROUP PROCESS

LIKE MANY LEFT groups at the time—underground and otherwise—the WUO was built on the Leninist model of democratic centralism.[50] The anarchism-inspired participatory democracy of SDS was viewed as too loose and undisciplined for revolutionary struggle. Under democratic centralism, members are encouraged to discuss and debate, but once a decision has been reached, everyone is expected to follow along and defend the policy. This structure ultimately encouraged what Gilbert calls "commandism" and made it difficult to question decisions once they had been made. Having joined the organization in its last two years, Suzanne Ross says that "democratic centralism, as practiced by the WUO (and, no doubt, others) makes smart people turn stupid by accepting top-down positions without much questioning." The centralism, many activists now say, won out over the democratic, in practice if not in theory.

That the WUO and other Left groups would turn to democratic centralism in the 1970s should not be surprising.[51] The overly loose structure of SDS, it seemed, had enabled PL to wreak such havoc—a mistake no one was eager to repeat. And in a revolutionary moment, discipline was highly valued as a necessary trait. This was all the more true for the WUO as a clandestine group, where full democratic debate was impossible given that the group was being hunted by the state. Indeed, many ex-Weather members are quick to separate the value of discipline from their criticisms of the WUO's democratic centralist structure.

There was an added layer to the appeal of this organizational form: democratic centralism was the chosen method of structure for most of the Third World groups, including the victorious Vietnamese. In addition to politically fighting alongside the national liberation movements, it was understandable that the WUO would apply the organizational forms from struggles that seemed to be winning. Further, those groups in the United States who avoided discussions of discipline and democratic centralism often prided internal democracy over anti-imperialist political practice. Thus, democratic centralism was a political choice—one made based on what looked like a strategy to win.

Still, within the WUO and other groups who relied on this structure, democratic centralism proved disastrous. It cemented the power of those already in leadership and built a culture where questioning authority within the organization put one at risk of being ostracized while a fugitive.[52]

The centralized command structure excluded lower ranking members from knowledge of how the leadership related to other organizations, making accountability more difficult. The organizational hierarchy consisted of the national leaders on top, local and collective leaders in the middle, and (the biggest group), rank-and-file members at the bottom. For security purposes, communication between collectives was filtered through the national leadership. In practice, this meant that discussion became stymied, leading to an overly acrimonious split when criticisms began to emerge. Indeed, Laura Whitehorn says, it took years for her to find out that others in the WUO were raising some of the same criticisms that she was.

Being underground complicated notions of democracy; discipline and secrecy were necessary, but all agree today that debate and discussion suffered. And then there were the Cadre Schools, which were focused more on political indoctrination than dialogue and mutual engagement. This was quite an irony for an organization built on questioning, challenging, and fighting authority. "There were some moments that were better than others," Donna Willmott says. "But I think overall, it wasn't an organizational culture that valued democratic, deep discussion and critical thought and engagement."

WEATHERMAN RECONSIDERED:
GENDER, SEXUALITY, AND FEMINISM

EVEN THOUGH WOMEN like Bernardine Dohrn, Naomi Jaffe, Cathy Wilkerson, and others were pioneers of women's liberation within SDS, the Weather Underground had little in the way of internal programs dealing with women's and lesbian or gay liberation.[53] Although the organization took steps to counter the notion among some feminists that militancy is inherently patriarchal, the way in which the Weather Underground approached its actions was still marred by sexism and machismo, especially in the group's early months. Indeed, the only known time the organization was infiltrated by the state (prior to the split) was, according to Naomi Jaffe, due to patriarchal mindsets. Larry Grathwohl, an FBI agent posing as a disgruntled Vietnam vet, was able to join the group, for a short time, based on his enthusiastic celebration of armed struggle and self-proclaimed military skills.

Before joining the organization, Cathy Wilkerson wrote an article for *New Left Notes* critical of SDS/Weatherman for failing to incorporate the struggle against patriarchy into its analysis and program.[54] But when she decided to join a Weatherman collective in 1969, she had to do a two-day self-criticism of her feminist politics. "I basically had to renounce everything that I stood for," she remembers.[55] Having to repress one's feminist politics is an issue several former Weatherwomen raised in reflecting on their experiences with the group. "The things you allow yourself to *un-know* in order to do what you think you need to do!" Naomi Jaffe now says.

In an attempt to shatter sexually repressive social norms, Weatherman encouraged non-monogamous relationships; the organization even had a couple of group orgies early in its formation, though this practice was not nearly as prevalent as some outsiders have since suggested.[56] Although sexual experimentation was widespread in youth culture during this period, Weather initially raised it to a political principle. The efforts to "smash monogamy" often played out in typically sexist ways, in which women were expected to be sexually available to men and sex could be used in a manipulative, controlling way. And the WUO didn't understand or support lesbian and gay liberation as either a political principle or as a form of sexual and identity expression to be protected and nourished. "Smashing monogamy" frightened many away from the organization, including some who were already associated with it but didn't appreciate being told what to do sexually.[57] This practice faded as Weatherman became the Weather Underground, although it was already too late for some.

Once underground, women in the group still faced opposition from their male comrades. "Male culture and a resistance to the politics of feminism pervaded Weather from the beginning," says Robert Roth, noting that men in the organization were afforded a lot of "protection" from criticism. Women did challenge some sexism from men in the group—male supremacy was a common critique in criticism/self-criticism sessions—and there were examples of women building unity and working on projects together: internal retreats, a pamphlet of women's poetry, and three armed actions (two in relation to Vietnam and one against the Health, Education, and Welfare Department). Still, few men in the organization viewed the struggle against patriarchy as important, and women's initiatives did not change the overall culture of the WUO.[58]

Hostility to feminism characterized the organization from the beginning, even though many of the members—including many of those most committed to the politics—were women and feminists. Indeed, one Weathermember estimated that as of March 1970, almost three-quarters of the people in the group were women, which testifies to the solid anti-imperialism many women activists felt and the commitment many women had to the organization despite misgivings over some of the politics.[59] But the strains from sexism and the leading male minority found expression early on.

One vivid example was the fate of the Pittsburgh women's collective. A militant demonstration by Weatherwomen in Pittsburgh in the summer of 1969 ended in the arrests of more than two dozen. Stuck in the steel town awaiting trial, they decided to use the time to develop a women's collective, with its own leadership, to engage in political work and study. But Weatherman leadership viewed the women's group as a threat and worked to dismantle it, Naomi Jaffe remembers. One of the leaders of the women's collective was "accused of having no other motivation than to usurp" the power of the Weather Bureau (the name of the leadership body at the time), and the collective was dismantled.[60] It was a defining moment for Weatherman, says Jaffe, whose own analytical strengths were neither valued nor adequately utilized in almost nine years underground. Despite having been a Marxist long before it became fashionable in SDS, Jaffe was not included in a Weather study group on Marx's *Capital*, even though, she remembers wryly, she was among the few in the group who had already read the book.

In an unpublished article written after the organization broke up, Jaffe wrote that the WUO "set itself up against the women's movement as the only legitimate revolutionary course for women, and set anti-imperialism up against feminism.... The Weather ideology did push the women's movement on the crucial issues of racism and national oppression, but since its politics could only do that at the expense of feminism and the development of feminist theory, it weakened more than it strengthened the women's movement."[61] Today, Jaffe is careful to note that such problems weren't the sole province of men in the group. Women in the organization were also involved in attacking the women's movement, exhibited macho tendencies, and participated in creating the male chauvinist environment they challenged. "We were not just victims; we brought the baggage of sexism with us into the underground, and so our struggles against it were both valiant and inconsistent," she says.

Because Weather did not have a feminist internal culture, the leadership often viewed outspoken women in the organization as separatist or divisive threats. For many women, joining the group was a choice between patriarchal anti-imperialism or racist feminism. Jaffe, for instance, was convinced of the need for an anti-imperialist underground after talking with white feminists who dismissed the murders at Attica as not being a feminist issue. To her, the Weather Underground was "the most vital show in town." But, as historian Becky Thompson notes in *A Promise and a Way of Life: White Antiracist Activism*, Jaffe's decision to go underground meant "never being treated as a first-class citizen or as a leader within the Weather Underground and devoting herself to a movement, a politic, and a way of life that asked her to work against herself as a woman."[62] Jaffe recalls never being trusted by the leadership because she was a feminist and a "bit of a thorn in their side." Likewise, former Weatherwoman Donna Willmott says it was difficult to spend six years in an organization whose strengths were so weakened by sexism.

Of course, there were women's communities that were both feminist and anti-racist. Laura Whitehorn suggests that sexism within the organization would have been much worse if women hadn't been doing some of the best and most serious anti-imperialist organizing across the country. Judith Mirkinson makes the same point, saying it's not a question of the feminist movement versus the anti-imperialist movement, but that the two overlapped, coexisted, and challenged each other politically.

In addition to maintaining the strong anti-racist and internationalist standpoint developed in the Weather Underground, most former members have a commitment to women's and lesbian, gay, bisexual, and transgender liberation today. But such issues were largely absent from the WUO's program, even as they were being raised sharply in society at large and as some members came out of the closet while underground. Indeed, two clandestine groups that emerged after Weather dissolved (the Revolutionary Committee and a group that became known as the Resistance Conspiracy) included former WUO members; both had significant lesbian leadership.[63] Many former Weatherpeople now include the struggles for the liberation of lesbian, gay, bisexual, and transgender people in their political work.

PART II:

THE WEATHER UNDERGROUND IN TODAY'S WORLD

Along with other activists of the 1960s and 1970s, the Weather Underground helped make anti-imperialism a viable political framework again. Not since the U.S. Anti-Imperialist League, which emerged with the Spanish-American War (and U.S. occupation of the Philippines) in 1898, had such a broad critique of U.S. empire been posited from within. Former members of the Weather Underground are still involved in progressive activism, struggling to build a more just and equitable world. They may not agree on their past or challenges, but all have retained a lifelong commitment to social justice. They are, in other words, part of ongoing movements, most of them spearheaded by a new generation of activists and organizers. The world Left is generally engaged in organizing, educating, and mobilizing—not armed struggle. But the anti-imperialist paradigm Weather (and others) championed finds much current expression.

The U.S. invasion and ongoing occupation of Iraq has brought the term *imperialism* back into public consciousness. For the WUO, imperialism was a much broader phenomenon than overseas military conquest, however, even if that is a central component of it. What does anti-imperialism mean in a global economy and unending "wars on/of terrorism"?[64] What does it mean today to build movements that are militant in the best sense of the word—that is, uncompromising, visionary, creative, and rooted in the progressive aspirations of the world's oppressed majority? The absence of a clear strategy emanating from the Third World—together with the presence of non-state terrorism and insurgent right-wing forces—increases the difficulty of these queries, but the questions remain. What does it mean today to, in Robert Roth's words, "generate an independent political momentum that's not just tied to who wins the next election" but to fundamental social change?

In the 1960s and 1970s, the revolutionary context was established by the Third World: Ho Chi Minh and the National Liberation Front, Che Guevara and Castro in Cuba, Amilcar Cabral and Frantz Fanon and the movements in Africa, together with Malcolm X and the Panthers (among others) in the United States. They put forth a vision of a better world, with a strategy for getting there. Today, the context is still emerging from people of color, from Porto Alegre to Port-au-Prince, from Caracas to Chiapas, Durban to Detroit, Buenos Aires to Brooklyn, the West Bank to Washington. With the decline and destruction of many national liberation movements and the ascendancy of non-state terrorism and transnational capitalism, today's movements tend to be openly critical of state power as a *concept* for self-determination, and not just as it currently exists.[65] Marxist analyses of class coexist with anarchist insistence on participatory democracy in the new grassroots internationalism celebrated at popular mobilizations such as the World Social Forum, the World Conference Against Racism, and the global protests against institutions such as the International Monetary Fund.

Despite the differences between this historical period and the one that gave rise to the WUO, there are many ways in which the same questions—about race and U.S. power, about war and repression—still animate the political landscape. Movements for social justice are varied and plenty: from housing rights to reparations, immigrant justice to sexual and reproductive health and freedom, and beyond. Here, I want to focus on two movements, arguably the ones that most directly inherit the legacy of the Weather Underground, PFOC, and May 19th: the movement against the prison industrial complex and the global justice movement.

PRISONS AND POLITICAL PRISONERS

MUCH TO ITS credit, the WUO was a prescient observer of the role prisons played not just in U.S. society but globally. Communiqués and actions by the WUO, along with the publications and political work of PFOC and May 19th, consistently drew attention to those held in captivity, whether they were political prisoners such as George Jackson, the insurgent prisoners of Attica, or the 200,000 held in South Vietnamese prisons by the U.S.-backed Thieu regime. Weather recognized prisons as a crucial site of U.S. power against (potentially) rebellious classes of people—namely, poor, urban Black and Latino/a people in this country and the opponents of occupation abroad. "The prisons are part of a strategy of colonial warfare being waged against the Black population," Weather wrote in a 1971 communiqué on domestic incarceration, connecting it to U.S. foreign policy.[66] And the WUO didn't just *recognize* prisons as a site of racist oppression—it acted on that realization, making anti-racist opposition to prisons central to its work, and encouraging others to do the same. The same communiqué noted that the "history of Black people in this country has been one of passionate resistance to the slave masters.... Black and Brown people inside the jails are doing all they can; must they fight alone even now?"[67]

In the years since the WUO came and went, an incarceration binge has been in full effect. The United States now has the world's highest rate of imprisonment; indeed, the highest in all world history. More than 2.1 million Americans now find themselves behind bars (six times more than it was in 1970), and another 4.8 million are under state supervision (on parole or probation).[68] Five percent of the world's population, the United States now claims twenty-five percent of the world's prison population. More than half of those locked up are people of color, predominantly African American (with Black women being the fastest growing group of prisoners), as prisons have become a racially coded site of class and gender discourse.[69] In response, a prison movement is on the rise, with friends and families of the incarcerated playing a leading role in challenging the politics of prison and the austere laws giving rise to the prison industrial complex.[70] A new dialogue about crime and reconciliation slowly emerges, as more communities join together to oppose increased prison construction, the state's post-industrial version of public housing. It is not an overstatement to say that the movement against the prison industrial complex is at the cutting edge of domestic anti-racist political work, as indeed it must be.

Political prisoners, if largely unacknowledged, are at the crux of debates over incarceration. Their presence testifies to the ongoing legacy of social problems, which in itself is central to the cycle of crime and punishment. As the prison movement continues to grow in strength and stature, the question of political prisoners moves to front and center, precisely because these veterans of Sixties-era movements remain part of current endeavors for social justice. Their lengthy incarceration—many have life sentences—speaks to the vengeful mindset governing imprisonment in the United States. Supporting and working for their release is at the heart of building movements where activists look after one another and accept collective responsibility. "Political prisoners are incarcerated as testament to our successes and not just our failures," Naomi Jaffe says. "They're in there as our spokespeople."[71] They are serving collective prison time, for all those who participated in the movements from which they emerged.

Regarding political prisoners, the United States stands out in the world not so much for having them, as for being so vengeful in continuing their incarceration while denying their very existence. Even without a "Truth and Reconciliation Commission," most governments routinely release political prisoners every decade or so, and political internees are often held together or allowed increased family visits, in tacit recognition of the political nature of their "crimes." Not so in the United States, where amnesty is a forbidden term. Here, the political prisoner movement is banished to the margins of even the Left, rather than found at its heart, where it belongs. It was hard to be an activist in the United States in 1969 and not know about Huey Newton, George Jackson, or "the Attica Brothers." Today, political prisoners languish largely outside the movement's consciousness.

And yet, the prisoners remain; the past three decades have seen both victories and defeats in this movement. Merle Africa of the MOVE organization died of cancer in prison in 1998, after twenty years of incarceration. Mumia Abu-Jamal is still on death row, even though his death sentence has been stayed. Former Panther and BLA member Teddy Jah Heath died in prison on January 21, 2001.[72] After nearly thirty years of incarceration and despite documented illegalities at his trial, Albert Nuh Washington died of cancer alone in prison on April 28, 2000.[73] Jalil Muntaqim, one of Washington's codefendants, was denied parole in August 2001; Herman Bell, the third person from that case, was denied parole in February 2004. Former Panther Robert Seth Hayes has been denied parole four times, despite a clean disciplinary record. And while the 1999–2000 amnesty campaign was successful in getting pardons for white anti-imperialists Linda Evans and Susan Rosenberg (coming on the heels of a successful campaign for the release of eleven Puerto Rican Nationalist political prisoners), the campaign had centered on Native political prisoner Leonard Peltier and the many former Panthers currently locked up—none of whom were freed by Clinton.

Even though the U.S. Senate investigating committee called the FBI's COINTELPRO activities "little more than a sophisticated vigilante operation" that violated "even the most minimal standards of official conduct within a democratic society," no FBI agent has been imprisoned for his or her participation in the repression of legal movements.[74] (The only two FBI officials convicted of wrongdoing were quickly pardoned.) And it has been an uphill and thankless task securing freedom for those political prisoners who have been released. Former Panther Dhoruba bin Wahad was released after nineteen years, when it was shown that the prosecution withheld exculpatory evidence. Fellow Panther Geronimo ji Jagga Pratt served twenty-seven years in prison for crimes that FBI surveillance documents prove he did not commit. The political incarceration of people who became active in the 1960s is inextricably tied to state repression. Even when they committed illegal acts or acts of which they themselves are highly self-critical, their continuing incarceration cannot be separated from the legacy of COINTELPRO.

Because they were targets themselves, former WUO members and their allies have been among the most stalwart supporters of political prisoners. "Any radical movement is going to have political prisoners," says ex-PFOC leader Judith Mirkinson. "That's true all over the world. You have to support political prisoners and continue to do so, even when it's not popular, even when it's hard, even as they get old, even when you're tired and the situation seems so frustrating." The continued incarceration of political prisoners captured as a result of movement work that arose out of the 1960s proves that, as former Panther leader-turned-lawyer Kathleen Cleaver says, "it's not 30 years later." Today is not the same as 1975, but there are important similarities—many of the same people are still in jail. "When I look back I see that the penalty for the crimes of the state is not being paid by any of these perpetrators.... We're paying for their crimes."[75]

When I started to learn more about the Weather Underground, I was disappointed to find that David Gilbert was neither a founder nor a national leader of the organization, despite the ideological influence he had through his political writings. I naturally assumed that anyone in prison would surely have been among the top leaders. Instead, like countless other radicals, he was a foot soldier, willing to do what he felt it took to make a revolution. It is a problem, a weakness of today's movement, that he and others like him—Jaan Laaman, Leonard Peltier, Janet Africa, Oscar Lopez Rivera, Ed Poindexter, Sekou Odinga, Sundiata Acoli, and so many others—are not well-known. These are the people who risked everything to make progressive change in the world, who have lengthy sentences for their involvement in what were mass movements.

Above all, the existence of Sixties-era political prisoners is important because they are a direct connection between the movements of yesterday and those of today. "I don't think the story is fully done, even if the work of that period has ended," says Susan Rosenberg, who served more than fifteen years herself. "As long as there are still people in U.S. prisons as a result of that period, the story can never be done—the very specific story. The story of social struggle, of anti-racism—that's never done."

GLOBALIZATION, WAR, AND INTERNATIONALISM

THE 2004 U.S. presidential election—billed by some as the most important election in U.S. history—has come and gone, leaving many of those organizations activated around defeating Bush now settled into an enervated stupor, plotting for victory in the next election. But the history of the anti-imperialist Left presents a call for mass movements, which may use electoral politics as a tactic but are not beholden to it as a strategy for fundamental change. The Weather Underground saw itself as intimately connected and accountable to the world's people. Its strategic decisions were based on both domestic and global considerations. The seeming widespread success of national liberation movements made possible such feelings of global accountability, of participation in a world Left.

What does it mean to be accountable to the world's people today, especially in the absence of a clear global strategy and the presence of insurgent right-wing and fundamentalist elements? What are today's political alternatives to white supremacy and empire? They are difficult questions, ones that continually present themselves. The necessity to comprehend the role of the United States in relation to the rest of the world, to situate this country in a global context, has become all the more urgent since the use of commercial airplanes as weapons one fall day in 2001.

Even before 9-11, however—and prior to the subsequent wars in and occupations of Afghanistan and Iraq—the power and reach of U.S. corporate and state power was on the international agenda. Resistance to such policies has been ongoing; among the more notable examples being the Zapatista movement originating among indigenous people in southern Mexico and establishing global ties.[76] Globalization became a buzzword in the United States following the massive demonstrations that shut down the World Trade Organization ministerial in Seattle in 1999, inspiring subsequent mass mobilizations against the meetings of transnational economic consortiums throughout the globe.[77] Militant street tactics have been defining features of these protests, which led to World Social Forum calls for a liberating alternative globalization.[78]

The run-up to the war in Iraq saw the most massive global protest in world history, with upward of eleven million participants on February 15, 2003. Building off years of activism in the Global South, the worldwide opposition to the war underscored a new internationalism and cross-border solidarity. Many were demoralized that the mass demonstrations prior to the war didn't stop it, but the outpouring was an unprecedented showing of solidarity. (That the war-turned-occupation has failed in all the ways the antiwar movement predicted should serve to strengthen anti-imperialist action.) Together, the antiwar and global justice movements are developing a new challenge of power and privilege in the twenty-first century.

Not surprisingly, criticisms of U.S. hegemony remain central. "Speaking for myself," Indian writer Arundhati Roy said in a 2003 talk, "I'm no flag-waver, no patriot, and am fully aware that venality, brutality, and hypocrisy are imprinted on the leaden soul of every state. But when a country ceases to be merely a country and becomes an empire, then the scale of operations changes dramatically. So may I clarify that tonight I speak as a subject of the American Empire? I speak as a slave who presumes to criticize her king."[79]

The WUO, to its credit, constantly raised the issue of civilian casualties and massacres, whether caused by the U.S. military in Vietnam or European colonialism in Angola or Guinea-Bissau. Such an accounting is needed today, when the official term "collateral damage" conceals the fact that today's high-tech warfare—much like the non-state terrorism it is said to oppose—by design targets civilians. It is a high-intensity, cost-effective (low military casualty rate) warfare that targets civilian infrastructure—and with Iraq, is done in a country whose ability to fight back was destroyed through more than a decade of sanctions. And yet mainstream discourse and even segments of the antiwar movement have focused exclusive attention on the deaths of U.S. soldiers without mourning or even mentioning the tens of thousands of Iraqi civilians killed in the Pentagon's "shock and awe" campaign or the more than 1 million killed through U.S.-led sanctions between the first and second Gulf Wars.[80]

Perhaps more than ever before, women are central to today's political economy—the hardest hit by both corporate globalization and war. As feminist scholar Zillah Eisenstein notes, "the new working class of global capitalism is disproportionately girls and women of color." It is a class, she says, that can be found in "the sex/gendered structuring of the slave trade and racial apartheid, or the sexual terrorism of the trafficking of women, or their exploitation in the global factory." As a result, women are in the lead, "challenging global capital with its racialized patriarchal structures of domination and exploitation while also embracing a democratized gender agenda which will destabilize local/cultural misogynies."[81] Women's power remains central; for instance, it is the Revolutionary Association of the Women of Afghanistan that for years led opposition to the Taliban and continues to oppose the patriarchy of the Northern Alliance government and the U.S. occupation that upholds it. The organization mobilizes under the slogan that fundamentalism in any form is "the enemy of all civilization."[82]

THE POLITICS OF SOLIDARITY IN THE TWENTY-FIRST CENTURY

PRISONS AND GLOBALIZATION are increasingly interrelated. The prison population has increased with the de-industrialization of the U.S. economy, as prison becomes an important element in U.S. military control overseas. This is most visibly manifested in the scandals at U.S.-run military prisons in Abu Ghraib and Guantánamo, as well as the "preventive detention" of hundreds of Muslims, Arabs, and South Asians in the United States following 9-11.[83] The United States now stands accused of operating the twenty-first century gulag.[84]

Given the centrality of prisons and globalization to the current world, solidarity remains a central tenet—especially for those located in what is alternately referred to as the West, the Global North, or the One-Third World.[85] At its best, the Weather Underground recognized that one cannot isolate the foreign aggression of wars from the domestic aggression of prisons, used to control the "internally imprisoned colonized nations." White supremacy and patriarchy propel both the international and the national contexts; any movement for justice must tackle these structures of domination as central to a system of imperialism. Empire has both a domestic front and an international one, operating with some similarity on both sides of the borders. The Weather Underground offered passionate insistence that both merited attention and solidarity.

The legacy of the Weather Underground has helped shape the racial justice initiatives of white activists today, in the burgeoning critique of U.S. global military hegemony and in the growing Left opposition to transnational corporate crime and pillaging. At the same time, this legacy is positively amended and altered by the queer and transgender movement, by the strength of women's leadership in activist projects the world over, by the passion for transparent democracy in movement organizations as well as political structures. Even when they falter, most modern U.S. social movements recognize that they must in some way confront racism. While such considerations have sometimes gotten mired in discussions of group dynamics without sufficient attention to developing an anti-racist program, the Black Power and white anti-imperialist movements have successfully raised the issue of white supremacy as one the Left—and society—must deal with.[86]

The ongoing emphasis on racial justice and sexual and gender freedom is not the narrow parochialism of a much-maligned "identity politics," but the strategic and dynamic centerpiece of Left momentum today.[87] The task for people in the United States is, for example, to unite the democratic possibilities of the World Social Forum with the anti-racist militancy of the prison movement; to join women's activism against fundamentalism with the emerging networks of transgender health and safety; to connect support for the popular rebellions in Latin America with support for Africans fighting the AIDS crisis; to link opposition to the wars in and occupations of Afghanistan and Iraq with the ongoing struggles for justice led by people of color within this country. Bernardine Dohrn identifies this challenge as "how to be internationalist and yet grounded here in organizing work with a real radical critique of American power and inequality."

The specifics of what such solidarity will mean in the new millennium are still developing and taking shape. The practical lessons are emerging in the student-worker alliances of Florida's Coalition of Immokalee Workers (a farmworker union comprised primarily of Latino/a and Haitian workers); the cross-border solidarity modeled in organizations such as the International Solidarity Movement in Palestine, School of the Americas Watch, and projects focused on conflict zones like Haiti or the Philippines; and in the local relationships being built in cities and towns across the country, centered on building organizations and coalitions committed to racial, economic, environmental, gender, and sexual justice. Talk of dismantling "intersecting and interlocking systems of oppression" has replaced talk of fighting "the system." Yet solidarity remains at the root of movements for social justice, as they build toward a unified and global mass movement. They are movements united under the slogan "another world is possible," with networks of resisters who have set out to bring such a world into being.

What is the contemporary context set by the most oppressed—communities of color in America and people of the Third World/Global South/Two-Thirds World—today?[88] What are appropriate responses to systemic oppression? How can movements simultaneously exist in and relate to contexts that are local, regional, national, and global? Who are the leading progressive forces in the struggles of the twenty-first century? How can the various forms of privilege and oppression be confronted? What is the creative range of political responses possible and necessary? The Weather Underground and others from the U.S. anti-imperialist Left of the 1960s and 1970s don't offer the answers or provide an instruction manual. But they do present a legacy of constantly raising and grappling with these questions, a toolkit that new generations can use to develop both a vision of a better society and the means of creating it. Therein lies the future of the Weather Underground—and of the world.

Still an activist: David Gilbert in prison, 1998.
Photo courtesy of Claude Marks.

EPILOGUE

> *Being a political prisoner is not just a status designation; it's a lifelong commitment to fight against injustice.*
>
> *—David Gilbert*[1]

W E SIT, SMILING AND CHATTING OVER BAD COFFEE, *starchy food, and the watchful eyes of guards, first at Attica and then at Clinton Correctional Facility, where David was transferred in 2004 after a period of harassment at Attica. Clinton is in Dannemora, another small prison town, this one on the New York-Canada border. Another medieval prison, though this one manages to be more decrepit than Attica, the visiting room more stiff (albeit with more natural light).*

The conversation, however, still radiates. The 2004 presidential election, the debacle in Iraq, the global justice movement, sexual violence, terrorism—all the major political issues that I would discuss with most anyone are fair game for our conversation, mixed with other chatting about life and school. David even sneaks in the occasional sports reference.

With a few exceptions—when his son won a Rhodes Scholarship, when his partner and ex-wife Kathy Boudin was paroled, and after an event celebrating the release of a collection of his writings (in the winter of 2002, the summer of 2003, and the spring of 2004, respectively)—Gilbert's name hasn't appeared in the media. That suits him fine, though it does speak to how political prisoners, once incarcerated, are largely hidden from public view.

A voracious reader, David remains an activist and an intellectual, though prison imposes harsh restrictions on his ability to interact with broader social movements. Gilbert has tried to model what Turkish poet and former political prisoner Nazim Hikmet said about prison: "Being captured is besides the point. The point is not to surrender."[2] When I first sat down to write about David's life since being incarcerated, I was tempted to write about how he has "missed" the past twenty-plus years. Upon further reflection, and after rereading his letters and writings, I realize this is not the case. David Gilbert has not "missed" the past twenty-plus years, like someone who was cryogenically frozen in 1981, although he has experienced the past two decades from a notably different social as well as geographic location than most people. Just like other political prisoners.

Since being in prison, he has been able to maintain his values and commitment. When his best friend and codefendant Kuwasi Balagoon died of AIDS in 1986 after being diagnosed less than a month previously, Gilbert committed himself to AIDS activism.[3] Since that time, he has helped start participatory peer education groups on AIDS at different prisons in New York state, fighting an uphill battle against a prison bureaucracy afraid of prisoner organizing (even around health issues) and widespread "AIDS-phobia."[4] Part of Gilbert's organizing has included challenging conspiracy theories about the origin of AIDS, both in face-to-face communication and through writings.[5] From 1994 to 1998, he was able to work in an AIDS education office he created at Comstock prison—a position that paid him $7.75 a week.[6]

Besides his AIDS work, David has been active in the movement to free Black journalist and death row political prisoner Mumia Abu-Jamal. Since 2002, he has worked with ex-Panthers and current political prisoners Herman Bell and Robert Seth Hayes (along with a progressive organization in Canada) to put out radical calendars as a fundraiser for political causes. He has also mentored young activists—continuing to do all the things that compelled a sixteen-year-old kid in Florida to ply him with questions starting in 1998.

"To me, the most significant issue isn't really what happened to me individually—I don't mean to be cavalier. I feel it, my family feels it," he says. "But the most significant issue is, what are we doing to turn around the greater suffering?"[7] David has worked to maintain a lasting connection with progressive activism. At the height of the anti-apartheid and Central America solidarity movements of the 1980s, Gilbert sent public messages to teach-ins and civil disobedience actions at Columbia University and elsewhere.[8] With the rise of the global justice movement following the successful protests against the World Trade Organization in 1999—and the antiwar

---

movement that has blossomed during George Bush's so-called War on Ter-ror—he has written for several alternative newspapers to share lessons from his history with a new generation that is just beginning to cope with the issues of race, empire, and social change. And there's David, perennially urging that any social movement be anti-racist, pro-feminist, and self-reflective at its very base.[9]

As a way to both understand his own history and to help current movements (especially younger activists) find their political bearings, Gilbert has reflected con-siderably on the mistakes and accomplishments of the movements and organiza-tions he has been a part of. While prison has not removed him from the world, it has afforded him (or forced upon him) the opportunity to engage in a self-critical evaluation of his more than forty years as an organizer and activist. His lessons, published in book reviews, interviews, and historical and theoretical articles, engage in dialogue with those eager to avoid the pitfalls of egoism and oppression within movements. These actions—writing, AIDS education and organizing, commu-nicating with young activists—are extensions of, not deviations from, his lifelong commitment to social justice.

Politically, David Gilbert has spent the past twenty-some years trying to strike a balance between resisting pressures to renounce his past on the one hand, and, on the other hand, doing in-depth and honest self-criticism of the various groups and acts he has been associated with.[10] *In other words, he has tried to both take responsibility for and draw out the lessons from those parts of his own history that may have been "politically or humanly backward," without renouncing the "valid principle of staunch and militant solidarity with Third World struggles."*[11]

More basically, he has just tried to be himself—an intelligent, humble, and soft-spoken man trying to live his convictions in the most difficult of condi-tions. He has been a father to his son, seeing him as often as possible and writing frequently. He's had to mourn the loss of both parents without being allowed to attend either of their funerals. Through it all, he has been able to persevere with remarkable clarity, never losing sight of the larger struggle for social justice. His faith in the power of people to make change is unshakable. It shines through in our discussions of history, the present, and hopes for the future.

"But as terrible as things are," he says, "and without any guarantees that it's all going to work out okay, I think you do have to have a vision that people can have the potential to live together in a more decent and humane way…a view of people's creativity, of people's ability to love, of people's abil-ity to be cooperative, of people's ability to learn from each other. I think it's important to maintain that vision."[12]

★ ★ ★

Leaving the prison is a totally different experience from going in. When the guard yells "Visiting hours up!" at exactly 3:05 p.m., I feel the urge to squeeze everything I can into the last few seconds. Out of the corner of my eye, I see others also taking their time in finishing up conversation, rising, and exchanging farewells. David and I smile quietly at each other as we rise. He gives me a hug. I assure him that I'll be back soon. I then start to make my way diagonally across the room to the door, passing tearful goodbyes between parents and children, husbands and wives. I look periodically back at David, who stands alone, watching as I leave, a gentle smile on his lips. As I approach the door leading out of the visiting room, I turn a final time, wave, and close my hand into a clenched fist briefly before leaving—a small expression of solidarity and hope in these difficult circumstances.

The hallways seem shorter, less foreboding. As I leave with the friends and loved ones of other prisoners, complete with a guard to escort us, I once again notice how few white people and how few men are among the visitors. We all submit our hands under a black light for verification of the invisible ink stamp. We wait again for the gates to open, spitting us back into the bleacher-filled front room we entered this morning. It feels like it's been much longer than five hours. With the other visitors, I walk out into the fresh air and take a deep breath. A little girl who had been visiting her father is bawling as she steps outside with her mother.

I wonder where David is right now—getting searched? In his cell? Still waiting in the visiting room to endure the hassles associated with leaving a visit? I marvel at all I learned from him today, at the thought of prison being the quintessential place to learn about history—and the future. I want to go back inside for further discussion. I look up at the high walls looming over me. A guard yells down, telling me to get away from the prison and into my car. I'm outside the walls, and he's still ordering me around. It hits me how fully trapped the legacy of the Sixties remains behind these prison walls and other such walls across the country. I want to scream, organize, cry, shout, agitate, yell, laugh, march, stomp, write the walls down. For the history of the Sixties cannot be told, let alone understood, without unlocking the prison doors.

BIOGRAPHIES OF INTERVIEWEES

VICENTE ALBA, commonly known as Panama, has been a revolutionary and an activist for the past 35 years. His initial political activity was against the Vietnam War in the late Sixties. In 1970 he became a member of the Young Lords Party, and he became a political prisoner in 1977 as the first person arrested in the United States with alleged ties to *Fuerzas Armadas de Liberación Nacional* (FALN). He was acquitted after six months in jail and waiting five years for a trial. Panama is cofounder and coordinator of the David Sanes Rodriguez Brigade for Peace and Justice in Vieques (NYC), which initiated peaceful disobedience against and education about the U.S. bombing of Vieques, Puerto Rico. A founding member of the National Congress of Puerto Rican Rights, he has been involved in an ongoing campaign against police, racial violence, and murder of the poor and people of color. He has been involved in two takeovers of the Statue of Liberty, one to free the Puerto Rican Nationalist Prisoners and the other in support of the struggle of the people of Vieques. He has also worked for environmental justice in the Bronx, promoted racial justice in the media nationally, fought against the HIV/AIDS epidemic throughout New York City, and organized immigrant workers with the Laborers' Local 108, AFL/CIO.

ASHANTI ALSTON grew up in New Jersey and is a former member of the Black Panther Party and the Black Liberation Army. Captured in Connecticut in the mid-1970s for BLA activity, he was a prisoner of war for more than a decade. He is currently a board member of the Institute for Anarchist Studies and organizes with the New York branch of Critical Resistance and Estacion Libre, a people of color support group for the Zapatistas. He also produces a 'zine entitled *Anarchist Panther* and is now writing a memoir.

BILL AYERS joined Students for a Democratic Society in Ann Arbor, Michigan, in 1965, served as education secretary from 1969 to 1970, and was a founding member of the Weather Underground. He is still a member of both organizations, living in happy, active opposition to war, empire, and the culture of materialism. He is also distinguished professor of education and senior university scholar at the University of Illinois at Chicago, author of a memoir, *Fugitive Days*, and several books on teaching social justice, most recently *Teaching Toward Freedom: Moral Commitment and Ethical Action in the Classroom.*

SCOTT BRALEY grew up in a Republican family in Midland, Michigan, Dow Chemical's company town. He joined the Michigan State SDS chapter in 1967 and was a regional organizer in 1968 and 1969 with then-partner Linda Evans, Bill Ayers, and Diana Oughton. He was a member of the WUO until its breakup in 1977. Braley surfaced in San Francisco and worked with the Prairie Fire Organizing Committee until its end in 1995. He has been an offset printer and a silk-screen printer, and is now a photographer working with nonprofits and social justice organizations. He lives with his sweetie in Oakland, CA, and worked on the 2005 Attica to Abu Ghraib conference to oppose U.S. torture, illegal detention, and other human rights abuses.

LYNDON COMSTOCK joined SDS in 1968 during his first year at the University of Michigan and was a member of Weather during its aboveground period, which ended in early 1970. He subsequently participated in two autonomous political collectives in 1970, followed by working on an underground newspaper while also contending with legal problems arising from his time in Weather. He was a grand jury resister in 1972–73. Since then he has worked at, and/or helped to start, several cooperative businesses, a cooperative housing group, two nonprofits that initiate workforce and other programs, and two community-development banks. He became a Buddhist in 1978. He lives in northern California.

BERNARDINE DOHRN, activist, academic and director of the Children and Family Justice Center, is a former leader of Students for a Democratic Society (SDS) and the Weather Underground and was a fugitive on the FBI's Ten Most Wanted List for a decade. She grew up in Chicago and Milwaukee and attended college and law school at the University of Chicago—where she first began working with Dr. Martin Luther King, Jr. and the Southern Christian Leadership Conference when they came to the West Side of Chicago in 1965 to challenge segregated and non-habitable housing. She was the first law student organizer for the National Lawyers Guild, organizing against the war in Vietnam and in solidarity with the Black Freedom movement. She writes, teaches at Northwestern University School of Law, and speaks on international human rights law, children in conflict with the law, children's rights, and issues of global justice. Dohrn has three sons and a granddaughter, and she lives in Chicago with her husband Bill Ayers and her 90-year-old father-in-law.

DAVID GILBERT, born in 1944, was awakened and inspired by the Civil Rights Movement when he was 15 and went on his first picket line at 17. In 1965, he started the Independent Committee Against the War in Vietnam at Columbia University and became a charter member of the SDS chapter there. David wrote the first national SDS pamphlet that named the system "U.S. Imperialism" in 1967, and he participated in the Columbia strike of 1968. He joined the Weather Underground Organization when it formed in 1970 in response to the murderous government assaults on the Black Liberation Movement and the incessant, massive bombing of Vietnam. After a decade of underground resistance, David was captured on October 20, 1981, when a unit of the Black Liberation Army and allied white revolutionaries tried to take funds from a Brink's truck, with the tragic result of a shootout in which a guard and two policemen were killed. David was sentenced to 75 years to life, which means parole can't even be considered until 2056. David has received strong, consistent support from a community of family and friends throughout these years. In prison, he pioneered peer education programs on AIDS and has done a lot of political writing. A collection of his essays, *No Surrender*, was published by Abraham Guillen Press in 2004. David and Kathy Boudin have a thoughtful and loving, now grown-up, son.

NAOMI JAFFE grew up on a chicken farm in the Catskill Mountains. She participated in the anti-Vietnam War movement, SDS, and the women's liberation movement before joining the Weather Underground in 1969. After surfacing in 1978, she moved back to upstate New York and has been active in the anti-apartheid movement, the Central America solidarity movement, the movement to free Mumia Abu-Jamal, and a number of antiwar, anti-racist, feminist, and LGBT rights organizations. In 1991, she became executive director of Holding Our Own Women's Foundation in Albany, NY. She commuted from Albany to the Catskills to care for her parents and uncle until they died and now divides her time between maintaining the farm where she grew up and her work in Albany. She has a longtime life partner, a son, and an extended family/community.

JEFF JONES joined SDS in October 1965 after participating in the first International Days of Protest Against the Vietnam War. He left Antioch College in April 1967 to run the SDS New York City regional office. A founding member of the Weather Underground, he was a fugitive until his arrest in October 1981. His experiences in the movement have recently been told in the book *A Radical Line,* written by his eldest son, Thai Jones. Jeff believes that fighting the impacts and consequences of inequitable distribution and exploitation of the world's resources—as was discussed in the original Weatherman paper—on poor, developing nations and people of color, is the responsibility of all progressives in the 21st century. He remains politically active in New York, now working as the communications director of a statewide environmental organization.

ESPERANZA MARTELL is a human rights activist, educator, community organizer, trainer, counselor, mother, and poet/artist. She is a cofounder of Casa Atabex Ache, a board member and teacher at the Brecht Forum, and one of the coordinators of the ProLibertad Campaign to Free Puerto Rican Political Prisoners/POW's and end U.S. colonialism in Puerto Rico. She teaches community organizing and advises at Hunter College School of Social Work, and is a consultant who specializes in organizational development, team building, leadership skills, conflict resolution, diversity training, and alternative healing. She facilitates healing circles and support groups using culturally based techniques for emotional self-healing and empowerment. She holds a B.A. from City University of New York and an M.S.W. from Hunter College School of Social Work. In 2004 she received the Revson Fellowship at Columbia University. Esperanza has published essays and poetry, including in *The Puerto Rican Movement: Voices from the Diaspora* (Temple University Press, 1998). She has been honored with many awards for her work in New York and Puerto Rico, including the 2002 Peace & Social Justice Award from the Puerto Rican Working Women's Organization. Esperanza lives in Washington Heights, NYC, with her son, Amilcar Loi Alfaro-Martell.

JUDITH MIRKINSON is a legal and human rights worker. A longtime political activist, she got her start in the movements of the Sixties working in support of political prisoners, against the war and for women's liberation (all of which she continues to this day). It was also during this period that she lived in Okinawa, Japan, as a GI organizer. She was a member of PFOC and was on the editorial board of its journal, *Breakthrough*. She is a founding member of GABRIELA Network, a U.S.-Philippine women's solidarity organization, and San Francisco Women in Black. A feminist and anti-imperialist, she hopes activists will always include both viewpoints when they analyze the world.

MICHAEL NOVICK was born in a working class immigrant Orthodox Jewish family in Brooklyn, NY. In 1967, he joined SDS at Brooklyn College, where he was elected student body president and then expelled for sitting in for open admissions to the City University of New York for Black and Puerto Rican high school graduates. He was briefly underground with the WUO in 1970. Later he founded and edited *Brother: A Forum for Men Against Sexism*. As a member of PFOC, he helped start the John Brown Anti-Klan Committee. He's now a member of Anti-Racist Action-Los Angeles, author of *White Lies White Power*, and editor of *Turning the Tide: Journal of Anti-Racist Action, Research & Education* (contact c/o ARA, PO Box 1055, Culver City, CA 90232). He's a school teacher and teacher's union activist and is also involved in counter-recruitment work and political prisoner/POW solidarity. He's the elected chair of the Program Council for KPFK-FM.

SUSAN ROSENBERG, born in 1955 in NYC, was formerly a doctor of acupuncture and traditional Chinese medicine trained at Lincoln Hospital and the Montreal Institute of Chinese Medicine. She became an activist in the early 1970s, working as a feminist in support of Black political prisoners, against COINTELPRO, and in support of national liberation movements in Africa and Latin America. Targeted by the FBI, Susan went underground in 1982 rather than face a biased community in federal RICO conspiracy charges. Arrested and charged with weapons possession in New Jersey in November 1984, she was sentenced to fifty-eight years in federal prison, the longest sentence in U.S. history (at the time) for the charge. The judge cited her political ideology as the reason for the lengthy prison term. Charges against her for the Brink's robbery and escape of Assata Shakur were dropped for lack of evidence. Charges were also dropped in the 1988

"Resistance Conspiracy" case (for conspiring to oppose U.S. foreign and domestic policy through violence). Susan was one of three women political prisoners placed in the Lexington High Security Unit in 1986. They successfully fought against the psychological torture of this experimental unit. In over ten years of isolation and maximum-security conditions, Susan continued to organize, teach, and write. She obtained her master's degree in writing from Antioch in 2000 and worked as an HIV/AIDS prisoner peer-educator. She was pardoned by President Clinton in 2001. An international human- and prisoner-rights activist since her release, she is completing a memoir and has taught literature at John Jay School of Criminal Justice, City University of New York.

SUZANNE ROSS was born in Nazi Europe, escaped with her parents and brother to Mozambique for three years, then to a pre-1947 leftist kibbutz in Palestine, and ultimately to the U.S. In the sixties, she became immersed in anti-racist work as a psychologist and educator. She actively opposed the war in Vietnam, defined herself as an anti-imperialist, and supported the Vietnamese revolution. By 1970 she began working with the Weather Underground and went underground in 1974. When she surfaced in 1979, Suzanne resumed her solidarity work with Vietnam, Central America, Cuba, and Southern Africa. She was part of a multiracial International Working Women's Day collective, and participated in numerous other efforts to create people of color–led multiracial coalitions. More than a decade ago, she joined the Free Mumia movement, working closely with "amazing warriors" Safiya Bukhari and Pam Africa. Suzanne continues to be part of the Free Mumia movement, supports numerous other political prisoners, and recently began work with some prisoners who became politically conscious after their incarceration. She lives in Washington Heights, NYC, and enjoys her daughter, her three-year-old granddaughter, a close circle of friends and comrades, and a warm extended family. She spends as much time as she can at her cabin in the Catskills.

ROBERT ROTH is a high school social studies teacher and community activist. After the WUO ended, he moved to San Francisco and joined Prairie Fire Organizing Committee. In the 1980s, he worked with the Pledge of Resistance and the movement to end U.S. intervention in Central America. Since 1992, he has worked with the Haiti Action Committee to support the democratic movement in Haiti and, most recently, to oppose the U.S.-

orchestrated coup against President Jean-Bertrand Aristide. He is the co-author of the pamphlets *Hidden From the Headlines: The U.S. War Against Haiti* and *We Will Not Forget: The Achievements of Lavalas in Haiti.*

As a freshman at Columbia University in 1965, **MARK RUDD** was recruited to SDS by David Gilbert. He spent the next three years learning about the nature of imperialism from David and other SDS members and helping to organize against the Vietnam War and racism. He traveled to Cuba in February 1968, during the Tet Offensive in Vietnam. That spring, he was chairman of Columbia SDS when SDS led an uprising against the university's complicity with the war and racism. Thrown out of college, he became a regional and national traveler for SDS. Mark was elected the last national secretary of SDS in June 1969, when the Weatherman faction took over the SDS National Office. He helped found the Weather Underground in early 1970 but left the organization by the end of that year due to changes in his thinking about revolutionary warfare. He remained a fugitive until 1977, when he turned himself in and nothing happened. He now teaches developmental math at the local community college in Albuquerque, NM, and has been active over the years in the anti-nuclear, Indian solidarity, Central America solidarity, environmental, and union movements, among others. He still believes in anti-imperialism, though of a nonviolent variety.

JUDY SIFF became politically active in the Seattle area in 1968 and joined the Weather Underground in 1971. She spent four years in federal and state prison from 1977 to 1981 as a result of her political activity. She has remained an activist in the San Francisco Bay Area and Atlanta, Georgia, since her release. Judy and her partner of 23 years (also named Judy) are the parents of two teenagers.

MICHAEL W. TARIF WARREN grew up in Indianapolis and attended Central State University in Wilberforce, Ohio, and Duquesne University School of Law in Pittsburgh, Pennsylvania. As a college student he led an organization called Unity For Unity, which was a Student Nonviolent Coordinating Committee (SNCC) affiliate. Graduating from law school in 1973, he worked for five years in Washington, D.C., before coming to New York. He is currently in private practice in Brooklyn, specializing in criminal, police misconduct, and human rights cases. He has represented numerous political prisoners—including Mumia Abu Jamal—and currently represents Dr. Mutulu Shakur, a former member of the Black Liberation Army. He also served on the defense team in the 2002 capital murder trial of Jamil Abdullah Al-Amin (formerly H. Rap Brown) in Atlanta. He represented rapper Tupac Shakur in 1994, served as lead counsel in the 1998 Million Youth March case in Harlem, and was lead counsel in the "Central Park Five" case in which convictions of five young men wrongfully convicted of raping the "Central Park Jogger" were set aside. In December 2003, he served on the prosecution team at the International Criminal Tribunal for Afghanistan in Tokyo, where evidence was presented against George W. Bush and the U.S. government for the illegal bombing and use of depleted uranium weapons in Afghanistan.

LAURA WHITEHORN, an anti-imperialist activist, served nearly 15 years in prison for militant actions against U.S. policies during the 1980s. For many years before that, she was active in a variety of radical organizations, including the Weather Underground and the John Brown Anti-Klan Committee. Released from prison in 1999, she lives in New York City with her partner, Susie Day. Whitehorn is an editor at *POZ* magazine, a national source of information and news about HIV, and works with other activists in the New York State Taskforce for the Release of Political Prisoners.

CATHY WILKERSON worked in SDS from 1963 until 1970, during which time she was a community organizer and also an editor for *New Left Notes*, the weekly newspaper of SDS. She was in Weatherman until it ended and surfaced in 1980. She remains politically active, and is now an urban math educator.

DONNA WILLMOTT is an anti-imperialist activist who was part of the Weather Underground Organization. She was incarcerated in the mid-1990s for her activities in support of the Puerto Rican independence movement. She works at Legal Services for Prisoners with Children as a community organizer for the rights of prisoners and their families, and continues to do work in support of political prisoners. She makes her home in San Francisco with her life-partner, her teenage daughter and members of her extended family.

TIMELINE

Major sources for this timeline: Max Elbaum, www.revolutionintheair.com; Harold Jacobs, *Weatherman*; Ron Jacobs, *The Way the Wind Blew: A History of the Weather Underground*; Mahmood Mamdani, *Good Muslim, Bad Muslim: America, the Cold War, and the Roots of Terror*; and Jonah Raskin, ed., *Weather Eye: Communiqués from the Weather Underground*.

1949	**October 1:** Communists take control of China after more than twenty years of civil war.
1954	**March 1:** Lolita Lebrón, Rafael Cancel Miranda, Andrés Figueroa Cordero, and Irving Flores, members of the Puerto Rican Nationalist Party, unfurl a Puerto Rican flag and fire weapons from the gallery of the House of Representatives, wounding five Congressmen, protesting the law that made Puerto Ricans U.S. citizens. The four are imprisoned with lengthy sentences, along with Oscar Collazo, shot while trying to attack President Truman in Washington in 1950.
	May 7–8: French forces surrender in Dien Bien Phu, marking the end of French colonial presence in Vietnam.
	May 17: Supreme Court rules in Brown vs. Board of Education that separate is inherently unequal, helping launch a national movement against Jim Crow segregation.
1955	**December 1:** Rosa Parks is arrested for refusing to give up her seat on a Montgomery, Alabama, bus to a white passenger. The ensuing one-year bus boycott helps launch Dr. Martin Luther King, Jr., as a national civil rights leader.

| 1957 | **March 6:** Under the leadership of Kwame Nkrumah and using Ghandian nonviolence, Ghana becomes the first sub-Saharan African country to win its independence from a European colonial power (England). In the next 20 years, more than 30 African countries will liberate themselves from European colonialism, through both nonviolent and armed struggle. |

| 1959 | **January:** Cuba becomes the first socialist state in the Western hemisphere after a successful revolution led by Fidel Castro and Che Guevara. |

| 1960 | **January:** The Student League for Industrial Democracy changes its name to Students for a Democratic Society. The League for Industrial Democracy remains its parent group, for the time being.

February 1: Student sit-ins at lunch counters in Greensboro, North Carolina, launch a nonviolent direct action movement to challenge segregation.

March 21: Police murder sixty-nine people in Sharpeville, South Africa, during a protest against apartheid pass laws. The government shortly afterward bans the African National Congress and the Pan-African Congress, both of which then turn to clandestinity.

April 16–17: The Student Nonviolent Coordinating Committee (SNCC) forms as a Black-led multiracial group based primarily in the South. SNCC's community organizing, sit-ins, voter registration, nonviolent direct action, and other political work earn it the title "shock troops of the revolution."

June 30: Congo achieves independence from Belgium, under the leadership of leftist Patrice Lumumba. It is one of ten African nations that will secure independence from colonial regimes this year alone. Lumumba is assassinated months later by Belgian mercenaries, aided by the CIA.

August 27: A racist mob attacks demonstrators in Monroe, North Carolina, where armed self-defense advocate Robert F. Williams heads the National Association for the Advancement of Colored People (NAACP) chapter. Williams, charged with kidnapping a white couple, flees |

to Cuba, where he continues to influence the Civil Rights Movement through his writings and radio broadcasts, advocating for Black Power and self-defense.

December 20: The National Liberation Front (NLF) of Vietnam is officially formed, led by Ho Chi Minh. It is a leading organization in the anti-colonial efforts against the United States and in reunifying the country.

1961   **May:** The Congress of Racial Equality (CORE) joins with SNCC and other civil rights activists to organize the Freedom Rides, buses filled with white and Black activists intentionally disobeying the segregated interstate transportation system. Racist mobs attack the Freedom Riders and destroy buses.

1962   **June:** SDS issues its founding statement, the 60-page *Port Huron Statement*. Drafted mainly by Tom Hayden, *Port Huron* defines the vision of early SDS, including a liberal agenda for civil rights and against nuclear weapons.

1963   **Summer:** In what will become commonplace in the years to come, riots by Black citizens against police and racist violence erupt in Birmingham, Alabama; Lexington, North Carolina; Savannah, Georgia; Charleston, South Carolina; and Cambridge, Maryland. National Guard troops called into Cambridge will not be withdrawn until 1964.

June 12: Civil rights leader Medgar Evers is assassinated by Byron de la Beckwith in Mississippi.

September 15: Another riot erupts in Birmingham, following the murder of four young Black girls in a Klan bombing of the 16th Street Baptist Church.

November 23: President John F. Kennedy assassinated.

December: SDS forms the Education Research Action Project, a community organizing project sending white students to organize in poor white and African American neighborhoods in ten northern cities.

1964   **March:** Malcolm X publicly splits from the Nation of Islam (NOI), as a result both of his shift to the Left and of his belief that the NOI is corrupt. In June, he forms the Organization of Afro-American Unity, based on the Organization of African Unity, which he learned about during his trip to the continent and meetings with nationalist leaders there.

Summer: Riots erupt in Harlem; Rochester, New York; Jersey City, Paterson, and Elizabeth, New Jersey; Chicago; Philadelphia; Jacksonville and St. Augustine, Florida; Natchez, McComb, and Jackson, Mississippi; Henderson, North Carolina; Princess Anne, Maryland; Bogalusa, Louisiana; and Cambridge, Maryland (again). In the Philadelphia riot, almost 2,500 rioters are arrested and more than 1,000 stores destroyed.

August 3: U.S. Naval ships "fired on" by North Vietnamese boats in the Gulf of Tonkin. President Johnson responds by bombing North Vietnam, escalating the Vietnam War. Years later, it is revealed that the incident was made up.

1965   **February:** The United States intensifies the bombing of Vietnam.

February 21: Malcolm X is assassinated at the Audubon Ballroom in Harlem by members of the Nation of Islam.

April 17: SDS organizes the first national anti-Vietnam War march in Washington, drawing more than 20,000. As a result, SDS grows to several thousand members and more than 100 campus chapters.

August 11: The Watts neighborhood of Los Angeles erupts in riots following an incident of police brutality. More than 30,000 participate in the events of the ensuing five days; 4,000 are arrested and thirty-five killed.

November: At a national antiwar march in Washington, D.C., SDS leader Carl Oglesby gives a speech naming the system "corporate liberalism."

1966   **January:** Cuba hosts the Tricontinental Congress of 100 revolutionary organizations from around the world, founding the Organization of Solidarity with the People of Asia, Africa, and Latin America. In a message to this meeting, Che Guevara defines a strategy for defeating imperialism, urging revolutionaries to "create two, three, many Vietnams."

January 21: *New Left Notes*, the weekly newspaper for SDS, begins publishing.

June 5: James Meredith, the Black student who was the first to integrate the University of Mississippi in 1962, begins a 220-mile march from Memphis, Tennessee, to Jackson, Mississippi, to encourage voter registration and protest racist violence. On the second day of the march, Meredith is shot three times by a racist sniper, though he survives. National civil rights leaders join forces to continue the march, renamed the "Meredith March Against Fear."

October: Merritt College students Huey Newton and Bobby Seale form the Black Panther Party for Self-Defense in Oakland.

December: At its National Council meeting, SDS adopts "from protest to resistance" as its slogan. SDS is enjoying the influx of new members from outside the northeast, where it had thus far been based.

1967   **April 4:** The Reverend Dr. Martin Luther King, Jr., leader of the Civil Rights Movement, breaks his silence on the Vietnam War in a speech calling the United States the "greatest purveyor of violence in the world today."

Summer: Riots erupt in more than 120 cities across the country, including major ones in Newark and Detroit.

August 25: An internal memo launches the FBI's Counter Intelligence Program, known as COINTELPRO, "to expose, disrupt, misdirect, discredit or otherwise neutralize the activities of black nationalists." The Black Panther Party is especially targeted.

October 8: While in Bolivia trying to help spark a guerrilla movement and revolution, as he had done in Cuba with Fidel Castro, Ernesto Che Guevara is murdered by government troops, in concert with the CIA.

October 20: "Stop the Draft Week" begins in Oakland, California. Thousands of antiwar militants take the streets in a week of pitched battles with police.

October 21: Thousands demonstrate at the Pentagon against the Vietnam War. Military Police and National Guard beat the protesters, who respond by placing flowers in the gun-barrels of the state.

November 14: Thousands demonstrate against Secretary of State Dean Rusk, speaking in New York City. Roving bands of protesters trash midtown; police respond violently.

1968   **January 30:** On the third day of the Vietnamese New Year, the National Liberation Front launches the Tet Offensive, a coordinated attack in more than 100 cities, with thirty-six uprisings in provincial capitals alone. The U.S. embassy in Saigon is (temporarily) overrun. The rebellions show that the U.S. is losing the war and inspire the antiwar movement.

February 7: Police open fire on a demonstration by Black students at South Carolina State College in Orangeburg, killing three and wounding thirty-three.

March: The Republic of New Afrika forms with 500 people in Detroit. The Black Nationalist group declares its independence from the United States and its intention to establish a Black nation in the South (specifically the "Black belt South" of Alabama, Georgia, Louisiana, Mississippi, and South Carolina).

March 31: President Lyndon B. Johnson announces that he will not run for re-election. There is dancing in the streets.

April 4: Civil rights leader Martin Luther King is assassinated in Memphis, Tennessee, while supporting striking sanitation workers. Riots erupt in 125 cities across the nation.

April 6: Bobby Hutton, the first and, at 16, youngest member of the Black Panther Party, is shot and killed by Oakland police.

April 23: A demonstration at Columbia University erupts into an impromptu student strike against the construction of a gym in Harlem and against the university's ties to Defense Department research. Students occupy five buildings for five days, with Black students holding one building by themselves. National attention is fixed on the strike, as activists and Harlem community residents bring in food and other supplies to the strikers.

April 28: Columbia University calls in the police against the strike. More than 700 are arrested, as police beat everyone in sight.

May: Workers and students in Paris, France, bring the city to a near-standstill with a general strike.

May 21: Columbia is temporarily re-occupied in a more militant strike. Police brutally clear the campus. Some students fight back.

July: The American Indian Movement (AIM) forms. Its

daring actions will raise the issue of indigenous sovereignty to national debate and make the group a primary target of COINTELPRO.

August 8: Six Black people are killed in riots outside the Republican National Convention in Miami, Florida. Richard Nixon is nominated.

August 20: Half a million Soviet bloc troops invade Czechoslovakia to crush a popular reform movement—proof to many in the New Left that Old Left communism is corrupt.

August 28: Mass police violence confronts protests outside the Democratic National Convention. Hundreds are arrested and beaten without cause as the city of Chicago is turned into a military zone. Authorities investigating the incident will later call it a "police riot."

October 4: With student protests reaching a fever pitch, the Mexican government massacres at least 300 at the Plaza de las Tres Culturas in Mexico City.

October 18: U.S. Olympic runners Tommie Smith and John Carlos give the Black Power salute when receiving their Olympic medals in Mexico City.

November: Richard Nixon is elected president, promising to end the Vietnam War.

1969

January 17: After an FBI-orchestrated series of hostile exchanges, members of "United Slaves" (US) murder Black Panthers Alprentice "Bunchy" Carter and John Huggins at UCLA in Los Angeles.

March 20: Attorney General John Mitchell brings conspiracy to riot charges against eight organizers involved with the 1968 Chicago protests: Rennie Davis, Dave Dellinger, John Froines, Tom Hayden, Abbie Hoffman, Jerry Rubin, Bobby Seale, and Lee Weiner. The case becomes a major rallying point for the movement.

April 2: Fifteen New York City Black Panthers are arrested on charges of conspiring to blow up various landmarks, including the Statue of Liberty and the Botanical Gardens. Six other Panthers are indicted. The spurious Panther 21 case is part of the FBI's effort to crush the Black Panther Party.

June 18–22: In Chicago, SDS splits during its annual convention. A New Left coalition calling itself the Revolutionary Youth Movement (RYM) expels the Old Left Progressive Labor faction. RYM will soon split into Weatherman and RYM II.

Summer: The Weatherman faction of SDS moves to cities nationwide: building collectives, holding militant street protests, trying to organize white working class youth, and preparing to go underground.

August 29–September 1: Weatherman holds a conference in Cleveland to prepare for its National Action in Chicago that October. Bill Ayers gives a major speech.

September 24: Weatherman leads a militant demonstration in Chicago at the start of the Chicago 8 trial.

October 5: Weatherman blows up a police memorial statue in Haymarket Square in Chicago. Police rebuild the statue, which commemorates police officers who died in a melee surrounding a labor struggle in the city in 1886, for which eight anarchist organizers were arrested (four of them were executed; one committed suicide in jail).

October 8–11: So-called Days of Rage protests in Chicago, led by Weatherman—the group's first mass action and the decade's first planned street fight. Only a few hundred people show up, rather than the thousands expected. The group takes the streets, smashing the windows of hundreds of cars and businesses in Chicago's Gold Coast neighborhood. Battles with police ensue, in which eight people are shot and nearly 300 arrested. Also at this time, a Black Panther–RYM II coalition hosts a series of nonviolent protests.

October 29: Judge Julius Hoffman orders Black Panther Party leader Bobby Seale bound and gagged after Seale's repeated demands to represent himself during the Chicago 8 conspiracy trial. Seale's case is soon separated from the others.

November 15: During an antiwar march in Washington, D.C., 10,000 demonstrators break away from the main protest and lead a militant march against the U.S. Justice Department and the South Vietnamese embassy. Weatherman is among the crew, but not necessarily leading it.

December: A Cook County grand jury indicts sixty-four Weatherman activists on thirty-seven counts arising from the Days of Rage.

December 4: Chicago Black Panthers Fred Hampton and Mark Clark are assassinated by Chicago police in a pre-dawn raid. Hampton, 21, was a dynamic and respected leader. In response, Weatherman bombs empty Chicago police cars.

December 8: The Los Angeles chapter of the Black Panthers withstands an unprovoked pre-dawn military raid by police on its headquarters. The Panthers defend themselves from the police attack, without injuring anyone. After five hours, the Panthers successfully negotiate their surrender.

December 27–30: Weatherman holds its final conference— the "War Council"—in Flint, Michigan. The apocalyptic tone of the conference makes clear that the group is going underground.

1970

February: Weatherman firebombs the New York City home of John Murtagh, the judge presiding over the Panther 21 case.

February 20–21: Militant demonstrations erupt immediately following the conviction of the Chicago 7, in nationally coordinated "The Day After" (TDA) protests. The convictions will be overturned in 1972.

March 6: An accidental explosion at a Greenwich Village townhouse kills Weather members Ted Gold, Diana Oughton, and Terry Robbins. Kathy Boudin and Cathy Wilkerson escape. The entire organization goes underground.

March 9: A car bomb kills SNCC activists Ralph Featherstone and William "Che" Payne in Maryland.

April 2: Federal indictments are issued against twelve Weather members for Days of Rage. Besides Terry Robbins, everyone indicted is already underground.

April 15: Blowing the cover of its only infiltrator inside a Weather collective, the FBI arrests Weatherwomen Linda Evans, recently indicted, and Diane Donghi.

May 4: Four students are killed, nine injured, when the National Guard opens fire on an antiwar protest at Kent State

University in Ohio following the invasion of Cambodia. Protests shut down campuses across the nation.

May 10: Weatherman bombs National Guard Headquarters in Washington, D.C.

May 11: Police kill six Black people at an anti-police brutality demonstration in Augusta, Georgia.

May 14: Police kill two and wound twelve Black students at Jackson State University in Mississippi during a protest.

May 21: Weatherman Underground issues its first communiqué: "A Declaration of a State of War."

June 10: The Weatherman Underground bombs New York City Police headquarters, releasing a communiqué claiming credit for the action.

July 23: Thirteen Weatherpeople are indicted in Detroit on "conspiracy to commit terrorism."

July 25: The Weather Underground bombs Presidio Army Base and Military Police Station in San Francisco, to celebrate the eleventh anniversary of the Cuban Revolution. The same day, the group releases a defiant communiqué in response to the Justice Department indictments.

August 8: Three days before his capture and arrest for destroying draft records, underground Jesuit priest and pacifist radical Daniel Berrigan issues a constructive criticism of Weather from underground on the use of violence. The Weather Underground responds in October affirming its solidarity with Berrigan.

August 13: Jonathan Jackson, 17, enters the Marin County, California, Courthouse with arms in an effort to free his brother, George Jackson, and other political prisoners. He distributes weapons to the prisoners in court (William Christmas, Ruchell Magee, James McClain) and takes the judge, the district attorney, and several jurors hostage. Jackson, Christmas, McClain and several of the hostages are killed when police open fire. [Magee is still in prison today.]

August 24: A clandestine group calling itself the New Year's Gang bombs an Army research facility at the University of Wisconsin-Madison, inadvertently killing a graduate student working late. The institute had long been a target of antiwar activism in Madison.

August 29: The National Chicano Moratorium holds a march of more than 20,000 against the Vietnam War. It is the largest-ever march in Los Angeles at this point and the largest antiwar march initiated and led by organizations of color. Police attack the demonstration, killing three (including a popular Chicano journalist, who is sitting at a nearby bar). The murders spark riots.

September 15: The Weather Underground helps Timothy Leary escape from the California Men's Colony—where he is serving ten years for possession of several joints—and reach Algeria.

October 5–9: The Weather Underground's Fall Offensive: It again blows up the police statue in Haymarket Square, Chicago. (Police rebuild it yet again, this time inside a building.) The group also bombs the Long Island City Courthouse in Queens, in solidarity with prison revolts in New York City, and the Marin County Hall of Justice in response to the murders of Jonathan Jackson, William Christmas, and James McClain.

October 15: The "Proud Eagle Tribe" of the Weather Underground bombs the Harvard War Research Center for International Affairs. This is the first action by the unit that will eventually call itself the Women's Brigade of the Weather Underground.

December 6: The Weather Underground issues its "New Morning, Changing Weather" communiqué, which criticizes its own "militarist" errors and celebrates the counterculture.

1971   **January:** The Panther 21 issue a constructive criticism of the Weather Underground, following the release of the "New Morning" statement. The criticism goes unanswered.

February 28: The Weather Underground bombs the U.S. Capitol in response to the expansion of the Vietnam War into Laos. Richard Nixon calls it "the most dastardly act in U.S. history."

March: An acrimonious phone call between Black Panther leaders Huey Newton and Eldridge Cleaver is publicized, dramatically illustrating the split in the group, which is encouraged and welcomed by the FBI.

March 8: The Citizen's Commission to Investigate the FBI breaks into the bureau's Media, Pennsylvania, office, stealing thousands of pages of documents proving the existence of a secret program against the Left (COINTELPRO).

May 1: The Weather Underground addresses an open letter to the mother of a woman wrongfully arrested for the Capitol bombing.

May 1–5: Half a million antiwar demonstrators attempt to shut down Washington, D.C., through civil disobedience, resulting in more than 12,000 arrests. This demonstration comes days after the Vietnam Veterans Against the War hold a protest of almost 1,000 veterans throwing their medals over the Capitol steps.

May: The Panther 21 are acquitted on all charges, after twenty-six months. Several of those freed go underground to carry on the struggle in a new capacity, thus forming the Black Liberation Army.

June 13: The *New York Times* begins publishing the Pentagon Papers, showing years of lying and corruption by successive presidential administrations in the Vietnam War. A court order temporarily halts publication, though the Supreme Court eventually decides on the *Times*' behalf. The documents were leaked by former Defense Department insider Daniel Ellsberg, who was indicted for the leak. Charges are dropped when it is discovered that Nixon's "plumbers" broke into Ellsberg's psychiatrist's office looking for ways to discredit him.

August 21: Black Panther Party Field Marshal George Jackson is killed by guards as he allegedly tries to escape from San Quentin prison.

August 30: The Weather Underground bombs the California Department of Corrections in San Francisco and Sacramento, responding to the murder of George Jackson. The bombs go off hours before his funeral.

September 9: Attica prison rebellion starts when thousands of men take over the D-yard of the prison in response to racism, religious persecution, and cruel and unusual punishment.

September 13: After Governor Nelson Rockefeller orders them to retake Attica prison by force, NY state troopers kill 39 people—ten guards and twenty-nine prisoners. Surviving prisoners are stripped and beaten before being returned to their cells.

September 17: The Weather Underground bombs the New York Department of Corrections in Albany in response to the murders at Attica.

October: The "Proud Eagle Tribe" of the Weather Underground bombs an office at a Massachusetts Institute of Technology (MIT) center for war research. The bombing targets the offices of William Bundy, an ex-CIA agent who advised presidents Kennedy and Johnson about the Vietnam War.

1972

May 19: The Weather Underground bombs the Pentagon, in response to the bombing of Hanoi and the mining of harbors in North Vietnam. This action causes tens of thousands of dollars in damage.

June 17: Five men are arrested trying to break into Democratic National Committee headquarters at the Watergate Hotel in Washington, D.C. Over the coming years, the Nixon administration will be found to have ordered the break-in and other illegal acts, resulting in Nixon's resignation in 1974 to avoid impeachment.

1973

February 23: Weather Underground releases "Common Victories" communiqué following the ceasefire agreement between the U.S. and Vietnam. The statement analyzes the antiwar movement.

February 27: American Indian Movement activists occupy the hamlet of Wounded Knee, South Dakota, after giving a press conference there denouncing repression of Native activism. Two months later, the government will end its siege by force, leaving two AIM members dead, fourteen wounded, and twelve more missing and presumed dead.

May 3: Former Black Panthers and Black Liberation Army members Sundiata Acoli, Assata Shakur, and Zayd Shakur are stopped on the New Jersey Turnpike. A shootout erupts, during which Zayd Shakur and a state trooper are killed. Assata is shot, wounded, and arrested; Sundiata escapes but is captured days later.

May 18: The Weather Underground bombs the 103rd Precinct of the New York City police, after cops kill unarmed Clifford Glover, a 10-year-old Black child.

May: Jane Alpert publishes an open letter to women of the Weather Underground in the feminist journal *off our backs*. In it, Alpert sharply criticizes the Weather Underground and renounces the mixed-gender Left, opting instead for a biologically deterministic brand of feminist politics.

July: Women in the Weather Underground release an open letter to the women's movement, partly in response to Alpert.

September 28: The Weather Underground bombs the ITT Latin America Headquarters in New York City, in response to the company's support for the military coup in Chile.

October: The Justice Department drops its Detroit indictments against WUO members.

1974   **January:** The Justice Department drops its Chicago indictments against WUO members.

February 4: The Symbionese Liberation Army (SLA) kidnaps newspaper heiress Patricia Hearst, demanding that her wealthy father feed Oakland's poor. Hearst later joins the SLA. The group has already gained notoriety through the killing of Oakland's school superintendent. The Weather Underground critically engages with the group, writing several open letters about it.

March 6: The Women's Brigade of the Weather Underground bombs the federal offices of Health, Education and Welfare (HEW) in San Francisco. Their communiqué demands women's control of daycare, healthcare, and birth control, and denounces the forced sterilization by HEW of women of color.

March 14: In protest of his draconian drug laws, the Weather Underground stink-bombs a dinner at a New York City hotel honoring Governor Nelson Rockefeller.

April: The Weather Underground issues a detailed analysis of the Vietnam War and the antiwar movement; the statement is an excerpted chapter of *Prairie Fire*.

May 17: Police, FBI, and U.S. Treasury agents first use tear gas, then fire bullets, and finally unleash an incendiary device upon a house in South Central Los Angeles, where members of the SLA are holed up. Six members of the group, including its founder, are killed. The entire incident is broadcast live on TV.

May 31: The Weather Underground bombs the office of the California attorney general in response to the murder of the six SLA members.

June 13: The Weather Underground bombs Gulf Oil's headquarters in Pittsburgh for its involvement in the colonization of Angola. The bombing causes approximately $350,000 in damage. The communiqué also contains an excerpt from *Prairie Fire*.

July 24: The Weather Underground Organization releases *Prairie Fire: The Politics of Revolutionary Anti-Imperialism*. The book is written, published, and distributed from underground. Thousands of copies are distributed the first night. Aboveground groups reprint it; more than 40,000 copies are soon printed.

September 11: The Weather Underground bombs the Anaconda copper company's headquarters in Oakland on the anniversary of the coup in Chile.

October 26: In its first action, the *Fuerzas Armadas de Liberación Nacional* (FALN; Armed Forces for National Liberation) bombs several corporations in New York City, calling for Puerto Rican independence and the freeing of the five Puerto Rican nationalist prisoners. Over the next six years, the group will carry out more than 100 other bombings or incendiary attacks in the United States.

October 27: More than 18,000 people fill Madison Square Garden for a National Day of Solidarity with the Independence of Puerto Rico.

1975 **January 28:** The Weather Underground bombs the Vietnam section of the Agency for International Development (AID) in Washington, D.C., for the government's continued aggression in Vietnam, two years after the signing of peace agreements. A bomb placed at the Department of Defense Supply Agency in Oakland does not detonate.

Spring: The first issue of the Weather Underground Organization's quarterly newsmagazine, *Osawatomie*, appears. It is also written, published, and distributed from underground.

Spring: The Weather Underground publishes "Politics in Command," an essay affirming the role of the mass movement and legal, aboveground organization. While it supports the right of armed struggle, the essay's focus on building a communist party is believed by some to be part of attempts to forgo armed struggle and surface the entire organization.

June 16: The Weather Underground bombs a branch of the Banco de Ponce in solidarity with striking cement workers in Puerto Rico.

July 11–13: The first national conference of the Prairie Fire Organizing Committee (PFOC) is held in Boston.

Summer: *Underground* is released. Directed by Emile de Antonio with Mary Lampson and Haskell Wexler, the film features five members of the Weather Underground in a safe house talking about the group and politics.

September 4: The Weather Underground bombs the Kennecott Corporation in Salt Lake City, Utah, for its mining operations in Chile, which help prop up the Pinochet regime and aided in his seizure of power.

1976   **January 30–February 2:** The Prairie Fire Organizing Committee convenes the Hard Times Conference. More than 2,000 people attend; the idea and design for the conference comes from the Weather Underground. Although the conference is successful in bringing together a large and diverse mix of radical groups and people, it is denounced for being racist and sexist. The Weather Underground begins to splinter and disintegrate over the coming months.

February: The Bay Area PFOC chapter issues "Class and Revolutionary Politics," an essay refuting the political line put forth by the WUO at the Hard Times Conference and supporting the criticisms raised by people of color and women's groups. The essay is part of "rectification," a parallel process happening both underground and aboveground. For PFOC, rectification means severing ties with the WUO and charting its own course. Underground, the WUO will ultimately fracture over questions of race, class, gender, and internal democracy. Communiqués critical of the WUO leadership circulate in the underground and in PFOC.

April–May: *Osawatomie* goes bimonthly.

Summer–Fall: The Prairie Fire Organizing Committee splits during and after a national conference in San Francisco. The Bay Area chapter remains PFOC, while the New York chapter ultimately becomes the May 19th Communist Organization.

1977   **January:** It becomes publicly known that a group of WUO cadre calling itself the Revolutionary Committee of the Weather Underground has formed and has issued a communiqué expelling the Central Committee.

February 3: The Revolutionary Committee of the Weather Underground bombs the Immigration and Naturalization Services office in San Francisco in solidarity with Mexican workers and ongoing struggles against racist U.S. border policy.

February: PFOC publishes the first issue of its magazine, *Breakthrough*.

Spring: The John Brown Book Club, a PFOC project in Seattle, compiles various articles by PFOC and the Revolutionary Committee critical of the old WUO leadership; they're published in a pamphlet entitled *The Split of the Weather Underground Organization: Struggling Against White and Male Supremacy*.

September: Mark Rudd turns himself into New York City authorities.

November 20: Five members of the Revolutionary Committee of the Weather Underground are arrested, planning to blow up the offices of homophobic California state senator John Briggs.

1978	**April 10:** FBI top brass Mark Felt, Patrick Gray, and Edward Miller are indicted for COINTELPRO activities, specifically for illegal acts committed in the mid-1970s while trying to catch the Weather Underground. (Charges against Gray are later dropped, and Felt and Miller are pardoned by Ronald Reagan in 1981.
1979	**January 16:** A Left-Islamic coalition stages a revolution in Iran and deposes the Shah, although the leftists are soon removed from power. Also this year, Left movements take power in Grenada and Nicaragua.
	September 10: President Carter commutes the sentences of four Puerto Rican nationalist political prisoners: Lolita Lebrón, Rafael Cancel Miranda, Irving Flores, and Oscar Collazo. (The fifth, Andrés Figueroa Cordero, was released earlier for medical reasons, and died in March.)
	November 2: Assata Shakur escapes from a New Jersey prison. She will ultimately be granted political exile status in Cuba [where she still resides]. The Black Liberation Army releases a communiqué taking credit for helping her escape. Statements from Assata and the BLA are read at a Black Solidarity Day demonstration in New York City shortly after the escape.
1980	**April 4:** Eleven Puerto Ricans are arrested in Evanston, Illinois, and accused of membership in the FALN.
	July: Cathy Wilkerson, who survived the townhouse explosion, surrenders to authorities in New York City. She will serve more than a year in prison on charges of possession of explosives.
	December 3: In New York City, former Weather leaders Bill Ayers and Bernardine Dohrn turn themselves in. Charges against Ayers are dropped; Dohrn is placed on probation after it is revealed that the FBI had a plan to kidnap her nephew, among other dirty tricks.
1981	**May:** Two more suspected FALN members are arrested.
	October 20: Kathy Boudin, Sam Brown, Judy Clark, and David Gilbert are arrested in Nyack, New York, after a failed armored-car expropriation by the Black Liberation Army. One Brink's guard and two police officers are killed.

October 23: BLA member and former Black Panther Sekou Odinga is captured and Mtayari Sundiata is killed following a shootout with police in Queens.

October 25: Weather Underground members Jeff Jones and Eleanor Stein are arrested in an apartment in the Bronx.

1982

January 20: Kuwasi Balagoon of the BLA is arrested by the Joint Terrorism Task Force in the Bronx for the Brink's case. Like Odinga, Balagoon was part of the Panther 21 conspiracy case.

November 9: May 19th leader Silvia Baraldini is arrested in Manhattan and charged with federal conspiracy for helping Assata Shakur escape.

1983

September 3: Using laws designed to attack the Mafia, Sekou Odinga and Silvia Baraldini are convicted of "racketeering and racketeering conspiracy" and sentenced to 40 years each. Convicted as accessories, Jamal Joseph and Chui Ferguson are each sentenced to 12 years. Two others are acquitted.

September 15: Kuwasi Balagoon, Judy Clark, and David Gilbert are convicted of triple murder for the Brink's case. Claiming to be political prisoners, the three sat out their trial. All are sentenced to 75 years to life.

1984

April 26: Kathy Boudin pleads guilty to robbery and one count of murder in the Brink's case. She gets 20 years to life.

June 14: Although he cooperated with the prosecution after being tortured, Sam Brown is sentenced to 75 years to life. He is held in protective custody.

November 4: Five people are arrested in Ohio (two more will be arrested in April 1985) on charges of being part of the United Freedom Front, a group of white anti-imperialists that carried out a series of bombings (in which no one was injured) against U.S. government and corporate support for apartheid South Africa and death squads in Central America. Acquitted of seditious conspiracy, all seven will be convicted of other charges for alleged UFF activity. [Jaan Laaman, Tom Manning, and Richard Williams remain in prison today.]

November 29: Tim Blunk and Susan Rosenberg, members

of the May 19th Communist Organization, are arrested in Cherry Hill, New Jersey, at a storage facility housing a cache of explosives.

1985   **May 11:** Marilyn Buck, Linda Evans, and Laura Whitehorn are captured. In what will become known as the "Resistance Conspiracy case," the three are charged along with Dr. Alan Berkman, Tim Blunk, and Susan Rosenberg with conspiracy to resist the U.S. government by force.

1986   **November 3:** The first reports of the Iran-Contra affair are published. The United States sold weapons to Iran, to be used against Iraq, in exchange for U.S. hostages held in Iran and cash which was then funneled to the CIA-sponsored Contras who were engaging in a war of attrition against the democratically elected Sandinista government of Nicaragua.

December 13: Kuwasi Balagoon dies in prison of AIDS, less than a month after being diagnosed. David Gilbert begins a peer education program about AIDS in prison.

1989   **November:** The Berlin Wall comes down, in the most dramatic event of the months-long process marking the end of state socialist rule in Eastern Europe. The Soviet Union soon collapses.

1994   **January 1:** The Zapatista Army for National Liberation (EZLN) launches an attack in Chiapas on the day that the North Atlantic Free Trade Agreement (NAFTA) takes effect. The indigenous rebels hold five municipalities in southern Mexico in protest of NAFTA and the Mexican government's oppression of the indigenous population. The Zapatistas also mark the emergence of a global movement that challenges state power without directly seeking it.

April 27: The first multiracial vote is held in South Africa, marking the official end of apartheid. Nelson Mandela, former political prisoner and head of the African National Congress, is elected president.

1998   **March 27:** More than 5,000 people gather in Washington, D.C., for the Jericho March for the freedom of political prisoners. The march was called for by political prisoner Jalil Muntaqim.

1999	**August:** Laura Whitehorn is released after serving fourteen years in prison.
	September: President Clinton pardons eleven Puerto Rican Nationalist political prisoners. They were in prison since 1980.
	November 30: Approximately 50,000 people shut down the World Trade Organization ministerial in Seattle, helping bring the globalization movement to the forefront of public consciousness.
2000	**April 28:** Former Black Panther Albert Nuh Washington dies in prison of cancer. He was imprisoned for 29 years on questionable charges, along with Herman Bell and Jalil Muntaqim.
	December: On his last day in office, Bill Clinton pardons Linda Evans and Susan Rosenberg.
2001	**January 21:** Former Black Liberation Army member Teddy Jah Heath dies in prison, after a long struggle to get adequate healthcare.
	September 11: Nineteen men hijack four commercial airliners, crashing two of them into the twin towers of the World Trade Center and one into the Pentagon. The fourth is forced down in Pennsylvania. George Bush announces a War on Terror—and prompts the launch of what will become a global antiwar movement.
	October 7: "Operation Enduring Freedom" begins bombing Afghanistan.
2003	**February 15:** The largest protest in world history occurs against the impending war in Iraq. Approximately 11 million people worldwide participate.
	March 20: Ignoring both international law and opinion, the U.S. begins the invasion of Iraq, under the pretense of disarming what turns out to be an already disarmed country. Tens of thousands of Iraqis and thousands of U.S. soldiers will die in the months to come as a permanent occupation force is established.
	August 20: Kathy Boudin is granted parole after 22 years in prison.

INTRODUCTION
PAGES 1-13

[1] David Gilbert, "Message to Columbia Students," May 4, 1998, in author's files.

[2] The Attica rebellion and aftermath is thoroughly covered in Tom Wicker, *A Time to Die.*

[3] Committee to End the Marion Lockdown, ed., *Can't Jail the Spirit: Biographies of U.S. Political Prisoners.*

[4] This theme is developed throughout much of Freire's work, including his famous *Pedagogy of the Oppressed.*

[5] Assata Shakur, *Assata: An Autobiography*, p. 58.

[6] Gloria Anzaldúa, *Interviews/Entrevistas*, p. 279.

[7] David Gilbert and David Loud, *U.S. Imperialism*, Chicago: SDS, 1968 (third printing).

[8] Quoted in bell hooks, *Talking Back: Thinking Feminist, Thinking Black,* p. 10.

[9] In his unpublished memoir about Columbia SDS, Bob Feldman says, "I introduced Dave to the freshman as 'the Father of Columbia's New Left.' After the freshman went on his way...Dave said with a smile: 'It embarrasses me to be called "The Father of Columbia's New Left." It makes me feel like I'm an old man already.'" See *Sundial*, p. 149.

[10] For more, see Martin Duberman, *Stonewall*; Max Elbaum, *Revolution in the Air: Sixties Radicals Turn to Lenin, Che, and Mao*; and Ruth Rosen, *The World Split Open: How the Modern Women's Movement Changed America.*

[11] Bill Ayers calls being underground a "parallel universe" in *The Weather Underground*, Sam Green and Bill Siegel: 2003 (documentary).

[12] These figures come from a chart of "Guerrilla Acts of Sabotage and Terrorism in the U.S., 1965–1970" in *Scanlan's* vol. 1, number 8, January 1971, p. 12. The graph's origins are not credited, though it accompanies the editorial by *Scanlan's* publisher Warren Hinckle.

[13] This point is made elsewhere, most notably Elizabeth "Betita" Martinez, *De Colores Means All of Us*, pp. 21–30.

[14] Elbaum, *Revolution in the Air*, pp. 35–37.

[15] One of the best explanations of King's changing politics outside of King's later works themselves can be found in James Cone, *Martin and Malcolm and America: A Dream or a Nightmare?*

[16] King's purpose in Memphis is well reported; see, for instance, Michael Eric Dyson, *I May Not Get There with You: The True Martin Luther King, Jr.*, pp. 1–3. Attorney William Pepper doubts that James Earl Ray was the assassin. See Pepper, *An Act of State: The Execution of Martin Luther King*.

[17] The best description of these murders and other acts of repression that occurred in the Sixties can be found in *Agents of Repression: The FBI's Secret War Against the Black Panther Party and the American Indian Movement*, and *The COINTELPRO Papers: Documents from the FBI's Secret Wars Against Dissent in the United States*, both authored by Ward Churchill and Jim Vander Wall. To give but a sampling: Bobby Hutton, the first and youngest member of the Black Panther Party, was murdered by police after he surrendered to them in Oakland on April 6, 1968. Panthers Bunchy Carter and John Huggins were murdered in an FBI-orchestrated shooting on January 17, 1969, at UCLA. In Chicago, Panthers Fred Hampton and Mark Clark were murdered as they slept on December 4, 1969. Imprisoned intellectual and Panther leader George Jackson was murdered at San Quentin on August 21, 1971. On September 13, 1971, the state of New York moved to retake Attica Correctional Facility after a four-day rebellion; police killed thirty-nine people in the process. AIM member Anna Mae Aquash was found dead on February 24, 1976, after being threatened by the FBI several times for not cooperating with them following a standoff at the Pine Ridge reservation in South Dakota. She was one of dozens of AIM members to be murdered in this time period, many of them from Pine Ridge. These and similar incidents are discussed throughout this book, especially in chapter three.

[18] See the memorandum reprinted in Churchill and Vander Wall, *The COINTELPRO Papers*, p. 92.

[19] Mumia Abu-Jamal, *We Want Freedom: A Life in the Black Panther Party*, p.105.

[20] Robert Pardun, *Prairie Radical: A Journey Through the Sixties*, p. 236.

[21] Ibid., p. 253.

[22] Cited in Edward Morgan, *The Sixties Experience: Hard Lessons About Modern America*, p. 91. Morgan says 37 percent considered themselves Left or "far Left."

[23] Elbaum, *Revolution in the Air*, p. 18.

[24] Morgan, *The '60s Experience*, p. 354.

[25] Quoted in Elbaum, *Revolution in the Air*, pp. 18, 27.

[26] Roxanne Dunbar Ortiz, *Outlaw Woman: A Memoir of the War Years, 1960–1975*, p. 243. For more on the Kent State murders and aftermath, see James A. Michener, *Kent State: What Happened and Why*.

[27] Tim Spofford, *Lynch Street: The May 1970 Slayings at Jackson State*. For an excellent analysis of the movement response to the Kent State murders as compared to the Jackson State murders and, more recently, the murder of anti-capitalist Carlo Giuliani at a protest against the G8 in the summer of 2001, see Eugene Koveos and Nicole Solomon, "This Will Not Be Kent State: Fear, Loathing and Radical Movement: 1960s and the Present," in *ONWARD* 2 (Fall 2001) pp. 3, 8.

[28] George Katsiaficas, *The Imagination of the New Left: A Global Analysis of 1968*, p. 120.

[29] Elbaum, *Revolution in the Air*, p. 27.

[30] Robert Allen, *Black Awakening in Capitalist America*, p. 126.

[31] See Lance Hill, *The Deacons for Defense: Armed Resistance and the Civil Rights Movement*; and Timothy Tyson, *Radio Free Dixie: Robert F. Williams and the Roots of Black Power*.

[32] Morgan, *The Sixties Experience*, p. 298. More generally, see Tariq Ali and Susan Watkins, *1968: Marching in the Streets*.

[33] See, for instance, William Sales, Jr., *From Civil Rights to Black Liberation: Malcolm X and the Organization of Afro-American Unity*; George Breitman, ed., *Malcolm X Speaks: Selected Speeches and Statements*; Robin D.G. Kelley, *Freedom Dreams: The Black Radical Imagination*; and James Forman, *The Making of Black Revolutionaries*.

[34] Earl Caldwell, "Declining Black Panthers Gather New Support From Repeated Clashes with Police," *New York Times*, December 14, 1969, p. 64.

[35] See Greg Wells, "Infrastructure, Transience and the Death of Anarchist Organizing in Small Town America," in *ONWARD* vol. 2, iss. 2, p. 15. See also Churchill and Vander Wall, *The COINTELPRO Papers*, and Mumia Abu-Jamal, *We Want Freedom: A Life in the Black Panther Party*.

[36] See Martin Duberman, *Stonewall*; Fred Ho et al., eds., *Legacy to Liberation: Politics and Culture of Revolutionary Asian Pacific America*; Peter Matthiessen, *In the Spirit of Crazy Horse*; Miguel Melendez, *We Took the Streets: Fighting for Latino Rights with the Young Lords*; Ruth Rosen, *The World Split Open*; Ernesto B. Vigil, *The Crusade for Justice: Chicano Militancy and the Government's War on Dissent*.

[37] Memoirs include Bill Ayers, *Fugitive Days* (the only memoir by a former member of the Weather Underground so far in print), Mark Naison, *White Boy*; and Roxanne Dunbar Ortiz, *Outlaw Woman*. In *A Radical Line: From the Labor Movement to the Weather Underground, One Family's Century of Conscience*, Thai Jones tells his family story, including those of both his parents, who were in the Weather Underground, mix-

ing the memoir formula with scholarly research. Mumia Abu-Jamal also blends memoir and scholarly research in his book *We Want Freedom*. Recent more scholarly texts about the period include Max Elbaum, *Revolution in the Air*; Becky Thompson, *A Promise and a Way of Life: White Antiracist Activism*; and Jeremy Varon, *Bringing the War Home: the Weather Underground, the Red Army Faction, and Revolutionary Violence of the Sixties and Seventies*. Recent films about the period include Helen Garvy, *Rebels with a Cause*; Sam Green and Bill Siegel, *The Weather Underground*; and Errol Morris, *The Fog of War*. Fiction about or involving the Weather Underground includes Jay Cantor, *Great Neck*; Neil Gordon, *The Company You Keep*; and Robert C. Moore Jr., *Weathermen*.

[38] Perhaps the best example of this is Todd Gitlin, *The Sixties: Years of Hope, Days of Rage*. In a way, Gitlin argues both—the Weatherman "destroyed the Sixties" and do not deserve much attention (though he devotes considerable space to it) because the group was so misguided. He has elaborated this point in other works as well, including *Letters to a Young Activist: The Art of Mentoring*. From a different perspective, Max Elbaum says in his immensely useful *Revolution in the Air* that the group has received far more attention than it merits (pp. 35–36).

[39] For instance, in talking about political hijacking and the Left in the 1970s, Melani McAlister says in her *Epic Encounters: Culture, Media, and U.S. Interests in the Middle East, 1945–2000* that "Since 1968, a total of twenty-nine hijackings had been staged by Palestinian or pro-Palestinian groups [by 1976], while other groups, including several in Latin America as well as the Symbionese Liberation Army (SLA) and the Weathermen in the United States, had carried out kidnappings or assassinations," p. 182. While the SLA achieved notoriety for its kidnapping of newspaper heiress Patty Hearst, the Weather Underground never attempted or carried out a kidnapping, let alone an assassination. Similarly, in her history of the U.S. women's movement, Ruth Rosen says feminists operating underground—such as Susan Saxe or Jane Alpert—were members of the Weather Underground, when they were not. See Rosen, *The World Split Open*, pp. 248–249.

[40] Gitlin, *The Sixties*, presents a liberal-Left version of this perspective. For an arch right-wing approach, see Peter Collier and David Horowitz, *Destructive Generation: Second Thoughts About the '60s*, pp. 67–119.

CHAPTER ONE
PAGES 17-35

[1] David Gilbert, *No Surrender: Writings from an Anti-Imperialist Political Prisoner*, p. 17.

[2] Much of this description comes from David Gilbert, *A Lifetime of Struggle*, video by Freedom Archives.

[3] David Gilbert, interview for the Columbia Oral History Research office, pp. 6-8.

[4] Ibid., p. 20.

[5] Ibid., p. 23.

[6] Ibid., p. 5.

[7] Ibid., p. 24.

[8] Clayborne Carson, *In Struggle: SNCC and the Black Awakening of the 1960s*, p. 115. In 2005, former Klansman Edgar Ray Killen was sentenced to 60 years in prison for the murders. Michael Schwerner's brother Steven said in an interview that "I think you've heard me before say that we know that in 1964, if it was only Jim Chaney who was missing, it never would have made national news, and that there were many other identified and unidentified black bodies found in the search for the three young men, and the people who killed them have never been prosecuted, and indeed, those names and histories have never made national television." *Democracy Now!*, June 24, 2005. Transcript available online at http://www.democracynow.org/article.pl?sid=05/06/24/1348253&mode=thread&tid=25.

[9] Carson covers the struggle in Mississippi in detail. Carson, *In Struggle*, pp. 111-129.

[10] Robert Allen, *Black Awakening in Capitalist America*, p. 25.

[11] Gilbert, *No Surrender*, p. 19. Unless otherwise noted, the material in the next three paragraphs is quoted or paraphrased from this article.

[12] Ibid.

[13] Robert Pardun's memoir, *Prairie Radical: A Journey Through the Sixties*, for instance, goes through a similar revelation. In *SDS*, Kirkpatrick Sale details how the organization progressed to a more radical stance in ways that mirror Gilbert's experience, largely through its anti-poverty organizing with an SDS-initiated endeavor called the Economic Research and Action Project, ERAP.

[14] Gilbert, Columbia interview, p. 41.

[15] Gilbert, *No Surrender*, p. 20.

[16] Gilbert, in *A Lifetime of Struggle*, Freedom Archives: 2002 (documentary).

[17] James Cone, *Martin and Malcolm and America: A Dream or a Nightmare?* and William Sales, Jr., *From Civil Rights to Black Liberation: Malcolm X and the Organization of Afro-American Unity*.

[18] See George Breitman, ed., *Malcolm X Speaks: Selected Speeches and Documents*.

[19] William Sales, Jr., *From Civil Rights to Black Liberation: Malcolm X and the Organization of Afro-American Unity*.

[20] Lance Hill, *The Deacons for Defense: Armed Resistance and the Civil Rights Movement*. It is the only book-length study of the Deacons for Defense.

[21] Gilbert, Columbia interview, pp. 49-50.

[22] Unless otherwise noted, the rest of this paragraph comes from or is quoted in David Gilbert, Columbia interview, pp. 66-68.

---

23 Stanley Karnow, *Vietnam: A History*, p. 204.

24 Ibid, pp. 219-224.

25 David Gilbert, "Shadow Interview," [n.p.], in author's files.

26 David Gilbert, letter to the author, January 16, 2003. See also Mark Rudd, unpublished memoir in the author's files, p. 38.

27 James Miller, *Democracy is in the Streets: From Port Huron to the Siege of Chicago*, is largely built around the Port Huron Statement.

28 Kirkpatrick Sale covers the SDS/LID relationship in detail in *SDS*, pp. 15-77, 176-179, 237-240.

29 For more on SDS's non-exclusion policy, see Sale, *SDS*, pp. 56-57, 210-213, 237-239, 571-574.

30 Pardun, *Prairie Radical*, pp. 173-174.

31 For more on PL's bloc-voting and manipulative tactics in SDS, see Sale, *SDS* and Pardun, *Prairie Radical*. See also Todd Gitlin, *The Sixties: Years of Hope, Days of Rage*; Greg Calvert, *Democracy From the Heart: Spiritual Values, Decentralism, and Democratic Idealism in the Movement of the 1960s*; James Miller, *Democracy is in the Streets*; and Edward Morgan, *The 60s Experience: Hard Lessons About Modern America*, for more.

32 Pardun, *Prairie Radical*, p. 71.

33 For the number growth, see Sale, *SDS*, pp. 663-664. For the first march in D.C. against Vietnam and the attack on SDS by media and the state, see Sale, *SDS*, pp. 151-253 and Todd Gitlin, *The Whole World is Watching: Media in the Making and Unmaking of the New Left*, pp. 21, 40-59. For how the influx of new people changed the organization, see especially Pardun, *Prairie Radical*, and Sale, *SDS*.

34 Sale, *SDS*, pp. 204-210, 279-285.

35 Pardun, *Prairie Radical*, pp. 115-128; David Gilbert, letter to the author, January 16, 2003. Representations of these tendencies in SDS history varies. Robert Pardun's memoir, *Prairie Radical*, is probably the best explanation of the split. See pp. 122-123 and pp. 346-347 for how the Old Guard reacted to the first mailing after Prairie Power took over SDS National Office.

36 David Gilbert, Columbia interview, p. 61. For more on PL and the May 2nd Movement, see Sale, *SDS*, pp. 121-122, 160-191, 176-177, 196-197, 263-264.

37 David Gilbert, Columbia interview, pp. 70-74. Eduardo Galeano's *Open Veins of Latin America: Five Centuries of the Pillage of a Continent* is perhaps the best overall history in this regard. In the 1960s, John Gerassi's *The Great Fear in Latin America* was the classic reading about U.S.-Latin America relations, and it was one of the books Gilbert read in his studying this year.

38 Eduardo Galeano, *Open Veins of Latin America*, pp. 77-78; Pardun, *Prairie Radical*, p. 110.

39 David Gilbert, Columbia interview, p. 75.

[40] David Gilbert, "For the 20th anniversary of the Columbia Strike" message 1, [n.p.], in author's files. The emerging work on power structure analysis includes Stokely Carmichael (later Kwame Ture) and Charles Hamilton's *Black Power*; the work of Malcolm X; Che Guevara; Franz Fanon; James Forman, H. Rap Brown and others of the Student Nonviolent Coordinating Committee; and Huey Newton and the Black Panther Party.

[41] The foundational work on the subject was Stokely Carmichael and Charles Hamilton, *Black Power: The Politics of Liberation in America*. For more on Black Power, see also James Forman, *The Making of Black Revolutionaries*, and Stokely Carmichael (with Ekwueme Michael Thelwell), *Ready for Revolution: The Life and Struggles of Stokely Carmichael*. Author's conversations with Zoharah Simmons, a SNCC veteran instrumental in the Black Power shift, have also been instrumental.

[42] Kathleen Cleaver, interview with Sam Green and Bill Siegal, pp. [xix-xx].

[43] Mumia Abu Jamal, *We Want Freedom: A Life in the Black Panther Party*, pp. 31, 41.

[44] David Barber, "'A Fucking White Revolutionary Movement' and Other Fables of Whiteness," in *Race Traitor* number 12, p. 11; Robert Allen, *Black Awakening in Capitalist America*, p. 126.

[45] Robert Allen, *Reluctant Reformers: Racism and Social Reform Movements in the United States* offers a thorough history of this.

[46] Of the many books, both scholarly and memoir, to appear on the Black Panthers, perhaps the three most comprehensive are Mumia Abu Jamal, *We Want Freedom*; Kathleen Cleaver and George Katsiaficas, eds., *Liberation, Imagination, and the Black Panther Party*; and Charles Jones, ed., *The Black Panther Party Reconsidered*.

[47] Carson, *In Struggle*, pp. 183-189; Forman, *The Making of Black Revolutionaries*, pp. 444-446.

[48] Quoted in Carson, *In Struggle*, p. 188. For more on the murder of Younge, see also James Forman, *Sammy Younge Jr.*; and Mab Segrest, *Memoir of a Race Traitor*, pp. 25-27. Segrest is a longtime anti-racist lesbian feminist; it is her cousin who murdered Younge.

[49] Sale, *SDS*, pp. 303-304; Pardun, *Prairie Radical*, p. 200.

[50] David Gilbert, Columbia interview, pp. 99-100.

CHAPTER TWO
PAGES: 37-59

[1] David Gilbert, letter to the author, January 16, 2003.

[2] Greg Calvert, *Democracy from the Heart: Spiritual Values, Decentralism, and Democratic Idealism in the Movement of the 1960s*, p. 155.

[3] For more on corporate liberalism and attempts to "name the system," see Calvert, *Democracy from the Heart*, pp. 147–177 and Sale, *SDS*, pp. 170–196.

[4] Calvert, *Democracy from the Heart*, p. 160.

[5] Unless otherwise noted, the rest of the material in this paragraph comes from Calvert, *Democracy from the Heart*, pp. 160–164.

[6] See the Feb. 13, 1967, issue of *New Left Notes*.

[7] Feldman, *Sundial*, p. 99.

[8] "Praxis" supplement in *New Left Notes*, p. 5.

[9] Cathy Wilkerson, e-mail to the author, November 2, 2002.

[10] David Gilbert, letter to the author, October 2004 [no day]. See also Sale, *SDS*, p. 338.

[11] For more on the Revolutionary Youth Movement theories and factions in SDS, see chapters 4 and 5 of this text. More generally, see Elbaum, *Revolution in the Air*, pp. 1–40, and Sale, *SDS*, pp. 506–621.

[12] "Praxis and the New Left," *New Left Notes*, p. 5, and David Gilbert, letter to the author, January 16, 2003.

[13] Becky Thompson, *A Promise and a Way of Life: White Antiracist Activism*, p. 77.

[14] That Gilbert is known in history books only for his intellectual work on the New Working Class theory and, paradoxically, for being arrested in 1981 at a Black-led revolutionary action that resulted in deaths and prison sentences demonstrates a disconnect in the way the history of the Weather Underground is told, unable to reconcile intellectualism with militancy.

[15] David Gilbert, Columbia interview, p. 102.

[16] David Gilbert, letter to the author, October 2004 [no day].

[17] Jerry Farber, *Student as a Nigger* (no date given). This article not only makes a ridiculous comparison but makes invisible Black students; under Farber's logic, people are either "students" or "niggers." That the Port Authority Statement authors had more knowledge of Marxist theory is discussed in Calvert, *Democracy from the Heart*, p. 191, and Morgan, *The Sixties Experience*, p. 109.

[18] Calvert, *Democracy from the Heart*, pp. 190–191.

[19] Pardun, *Prairie Radical*, p. 182–183.

[20] David Gilbert, letter to the author, January 16, 2003.

[21] David Gilbert and David Loud, *U.S. Imperialism*, November 1968, p. 1.

[22] Gilbert, Columbia interview, p. 97.

[23] David Gilbert, letters to the author, October 4, 2002, and January 16, 2003. David Gilbert and David Loud, *U.S. Imperialism*, November 1968.

[24] David Gilbert, Columbia interview, p. 156.

[25] Quoted in Pardun, *Prairie Radical*, p. 175.

[26] Tanya Reinhart, *Israel/Palestine: How to End the War of 1948*, pp. 189–190.

[27] Quoted in ibid., p. 190.

[28] In his memoir, James Forman reprints a letter he wrote to others in SNCC in 1967, saying the organization needed to research the situation, take a stand, and be advised of how many American Jews felt about the issue. See Forman, *The Making of Black Revolutionaries*, pp. 492–497.

[29] Carson, *In Struggle*, pp. 268–269.

[30] Gilbert, *No Surrender*, p. 21.

[31] Carson, *In Struggle*, p. 249; Pardun, *Prairie Radical*, p. 198.

[32] Jim Fletcher, et al., *Still Black, Still Strong*, pp. 223–224; Churchill and Vander Wall, *The COINTELPRO Papers*.

[33] Fletcher et al., *Still Black, Still Strong: Survivors of the War Against Black Revolutionaries*, p. 224. Mumia Abu-Jamal, *We Want Freedom*, and David Hilliard, *This Side of Glory*, both discuss the "Free Huey" campaign.

[34] Katsiaficas, *The Imagination of the New Left*, p. 139. For more on VVAW, see Andrew E. Hunt, *The Turning: A History of Vietnam Veterans Against the War*. See also Nancy Zaroulis and Gerald Sullivan, *Who Spoke Up?* pp. 354–358, and New Yippie Book Collective, ed., *Blacklisted News, Secret History*, pp. 90–94. My knowledge of the VVAW comes in part from hearing VVAW leader Scott Camil speak half a dozen times in classrooms and public lectures at the University of Florida.

[35] Sale, *SDS*, pp. 369–374.

[36] Quoted in ibid., pp. 375–377.

[37] Ibid., pp. 377–379.

[38] Pardun, *Prairie Radical*, p. 201.

[39] See John Lee Anderson's exhaustive biography, *Che*.

[40] Lavan, ed., *Che Guevara Speaks*, p. 147.

[41] Ibid., pp. 158–159.

[42] Katsiaficas, *The Imagination of the New Left*, pp. 29–30.

[43] Elbaum, *Revolution in the Air*, p. 25.

[44] Katsiaficas, *The Imagination of the New Left*, pp. 33–34.

[45] Carson, *In Struggle*, pp. 249–250.

[46] Mumia Abu-Jamal, *We Want Freedom*, p. 114; David Hilliard, *This Side of Glory*, pp. 192–193; Jim Fletcher et al., *Still Black, Still Strong*, p. 226.

[47] Katsiaficas, *The Imagination of the New Left*, p. 41. More generally, see Daniel and Gabriel Cohn-Bendit, *Obsolete Communism: The Left-Wing Alternative*.

[48] For more, see Cohn-Bendit, *Obsolete Communism*.

[49] Pardun, *Prairie Radical*, p. 234.

[50] Bob Feldman presents a good sequence of events in his unpublished memoir, *Sundial*, pp. 248–288. More information can be found in Mark Rudd, unpublished manuscript, pp. 78–132; Kirkpatrick Sale, *SDS*, pp. 430–450; and Jerry Avorn et al., *Up Against the Ivy Wall: A History of the Columbia Crisis*.

[51] Freudenberg et al., *Why We Strike*, pp. 4–6.

[52] Rudd, unpublished manuscript, p. 80.

[53] Ibid., p. 98.

[54] Gilbert, Columbia interview, p. 136.

[55] Todd Gitlin, *The Sixties*, p. 307.

[56] Rudd, unpublished manuscript, p. 97.

[57] Ibid, pp. 107–108.

[58] Quoted in ibid, p. 93.

[59] Ibid., p. 144.

[60] Freudenberg et al., *Why We Strike*, p. 3.

[61] Rudd, unpublished manuscript, p. 116.

[62] For more on the Paris rebellion, see Cohn-Bendit, *Obsolete Communism*.

[63] Quoted in Rudd, unpublished manuscript, p. 120; Tom Hayden, *Reunion*, p. 282. The following school year, Columbia SDS engaged in another series of actions culminating in yet another building occupation. This time, the students left when arrest was imminent, although a handful of the top leaders had warrants put out for their arrest.

[64] For more on the specifics of the strike, see Avorn et al., *Up Against the Ivy Wall* and Freudenberg, et al., *Why We Strike*. For more on the strike's impact on the movement, see Sale, *SDS*, pp. 430–452.

[65] Quoted in Avorn, et al., *Up Against the Ivy Wall*, p. 220.

[66] Gilbert, *No Surrender*, p. 25.

[67] Ibid.

[68] Freudenberg, et al., *Why We Strike*, pp. 13–14.

[69] Gilbert, *No Surrender*, p. 25.

[70] Elbaum, *Revolution in the Air*, p. 69.

[71] Katsiaficas, *The Imagination of the New Left*, p. 80.

[72] Abbie Hoffman, *The Autobiography of Abbie Hoffman*, p. 161.

[73] Dave Dellinger, *More Power Than We Know*, p. 186. For more on the convention, see Sale, *SDS*, pp. 472–477. See also Hoffman, *The Autobiography of Abbie Hoffman*, pp. 137–164, 186–210; and Dellinger, *From Yale to Jail*, pp. 3–9, 319–409.

[74] Katsiaficas, *The Imagination of the New Left*, p. 80.

[75] Quoted in Pardun, *Prairie Radical*, 262. Although the mayor's words weren't audible, his lips were clearly visible as he cursed at Senator Ribicoff. In their respective memoirs, Ayers, Hoffman, and Pardun each make note of this point.

[76] Robert Allen, *Black Awakening in Capitalist America*, p. 126.

[77] Katsiaficas, *The Imagination of the New Left*, p. 203.

[78] Quoted in Sale, *SDS*, p. 451.

[79] Former Black Panther (and now political prisoner) Sundiata Acoli explains the use of the term "New Afrika" and why it is spelled with a 'k' instead of a 'c.' "We of the New Afrikan Independence Movement spell 'Afrikan' with a 'k' as an indicator of our cultural identification with the Afrikan continent and because Afrikan linguists originally used 'k' to indicate the [hard] 'c' sound in the English language. We use the term 'New Afrikan,' instead of Black, to define ourselves as Afrikan people who have been forcibly transplanted to a new land and formed into a 'new Afrikan nation' in North America." See Sundiata Acoli, "An Updated History of the New Afrikan Prison Struggle," in Joy James, ed., *Imprisoned Intellectuals: America's Political Prisoners Write on Life, Liberation, and Rebellion*, p. 138.

[80] For a fuller discussion of these issues, see Ward Churchill, ed., *Marxism and Native Americans*, and Peter Matthiessen, *In the Spirit of Crazy Horse.*

[81] See, for instance, Peter Matthiessen, *In The Spirit of Crazy Horse;* Elbaum, *Revolution in the Air*, pp. 41–90, Fred Ho, ed., *Legacy to Liberation.*

[82]For a sampling of these perspectives, see Stokely Charmichael and Charles Hamilton, *Black Power*; Mario Barrera et. al., "The Barrio as an Internal Colony;" and J. Sakai, *Settlers: The Mythology of the White Proletariat.*

[83] Marilyn Buck, David Gilbert, and Laura Whitehorn, *Enemies of the State: A frank discussion of past movements, their victories and errors, and the current political climate for revolutionary struggle within the USA*, p. 34.

[84] Scott Braley, interview with the author, June 9, 2004. Evans was an important figure in early Weatherman. In the 1980s, Evans again went underground with a white anti-imperialist group. Arrested in 1985, she was sentenced to forty years for housing a fugitive (Marilyn Buck) and possessing false identification. Along with Susan Rosenberg, she was pardoned by Bill Clinton on his last day in office.

[85] For a fuller discussion of the rise of the women's liberation movement, Ruth Rosen, *The World Split Open*. Becky Thompson also presents an interesting synopsis of feminism and anti-racism in *A Promise and a Way of Life*, pp. 113–227.

[86] Carson, *In Struggle*, pp. 147–148.

[87] Rosen, *The World Split Open*, pp. 181–185.

[88] Jo Freeman, "On the Origins of the Women's Liberation Movement from a Strictly Personal Perspective," in Rachel Blau DuPlessis and Snitow, eds., *The Feminist Memoir Project: Voices from Women's Liberation*, p. 180; Sale, *SDS*, p. 252.

[89] Naomi Jaffe, interview with the author, June 19, 2004.

[90] Rosen, *The World Split Open*, pp. 126–127.

[91] Gilbert, *No Surrender,* pp. 254–255. The jeering and catcalls directed at Buck in 1967 were repeated in a 1969 counter-inauguration rally against Richard Nixon. When longtime SDS activist Marilyn Salzman Webb spoke about women's oppression, men

responded angrily, yelling things like "Fuck her! Take her off the stage! Rape her in a back alley!" Quoted in Rosen, *The World Split Open*, p. 134.

CHAPTER THREE
PAGES: 61-73

[1] David Gilbert, *No Surrender*, p. 26.

[2] Ibid., p. 261.

[3] Herbert Marcuse, "Repressive Tolerance," available online at http://grace.evergreen.edu/~arunc/texts/frankfurt/marcuse/tolerance.pdf. Marcuse's notion of "repressive tolerance" said that governments allowed for such non-threatening opposition as a "safety valve" in order to cement its authority while appearing beneficent.

[4] Angus MacKenzie, *Secrets: The CIA's War at Home*, p. 61.

[5] Robert J. Glessing, *The Underground Press in America*, p. 17.

[6] Brian Glick, *War at Home: Covert Action Against U.S. Activists and What We Can Do About It*, p. 10.

[7] Ward Churchill and Jim Vander Wall, *Agents of Repression*, pp. 39–53.

[8] Ward Churchill, "'To Disrupt, Discredit and Destroy': The FBI's Secret War against the Black Panther Party," in Kathleen Cleaver and George Katsiaficas, eds., *Liberation, Imagination, and the Black Panther Party*, p. 109; Churchill and Vander Wall, *Agents of Repression*, p. 175.

[9] Churchill and Vander Wall, *Agents of Repression*, p. 42. Wesley Swearingen, an ex-FBI agent turned COINTELPRO whistleblower, said that the men who murdered Carter and Huggins were working for the FBI. See Swearingen, *FBI Secrets*, pp. 82, 160.

[10] Mumia Abu-Jamal, *We Want Freedom: A Life in the Black Panther Party*, p. 71.

[11] Ronald Fraser et al., *1968: A Student Generation in Revolt*, pp. 289–290.

[12] Ibid., p. 290.

[13] Churchill and Vander Wall, *Agents of Repression*, pp. 45–47. For more on RAM, see Kelley, *Freedom Dreams*, pp. 62–119.

[14] This memo is reprinted in Ward Churchill and Jim Vander Wall, *The COINTELPRO Papers: Documents from the FBI's Secret Wars Against Dissent in the United States*, p. 185.

[15] Churchill and Vander Wall, *Agents of Repression*, pp. 65–66; Churchill and Vander Wall, *The COINTELPRO Papers*, pp. 135–139, 210–211.

[16] Churchill and Vander Wall, *The COINTELPRO Papers*, pp. 210–213.

[17] Abu-Jamal, *We Want Freedom*, p. 122.

[18] See Churchill and Vander Wall, *The COINTELPRO Papers*.

[19] This memo is reprinted in Churchill and Vander Wall, *The COINTELPRO Papers*, pp. 92–93.

20 Earl Caldwell, "Declining Black Panthers Gather New Support From Repeated Clashes with Police," *New York Times*, December 14, 1969, p. 64.

21 This memo is reprinted in Churchill and Vander Wall, *The COINTELPRO Papers*, p. 177.

22 This memo is reprinted in ibid., p. 181.

23 This memo is reprinted in ibid., pp.183–184.

24 MacKenzie, *Secrets*, pp. 27–82.

25 Geoffrey Rips et al., *UnAmerican Activities: The Campaign Against the Underground Press*, pp. 139-151; Morton H. Halperin, et al., *The Lawless State: The Crimes of the U.S. Intelligence Agencies*, pp. 155–170; MacKenzie, *Secrets*, pp. 29–30.

26 Churchill and Vander Wall, *The COINTELPRO Papers*, pp. 207–208. See also MacKenzie, *Secrets*, pp. 3–4, 11, 22.

27 Cathy Wilkerson, interview with the author, July 16, 2004.

28 David Gilbert interview for Columbia Oral History Research Office, January 17, 1985, p. 208.

29 This memo is reprinted in Churchill and Vander Wall, *The COINTELPRO Papers*, p. 181.

30 This memo is reprinted in Rips, p. 61.

31 This memo is reprinted in Churchill and Vander Wall, *The COINTELPRO Papers*, p. 182.

32 Ibid, p. 183.

33 Clayborne Carson, *In Struggle: SNCC and the Black Awakening of the 1960s*, p. 258. More generally, see Christian Parenti, *Lockdown America: Police and Prisons in a Time of Crisis*.

34 Quoted in Abe Peck, *Uncovering the Sixties: The Life and Times of the Underground Press*, p. 144.

35 Robert Pardun, *Prairie Radical: A Journey Through the Sixties*, p. 255.

36 Ward Churchill, "A Person Who Struggles for Liberation: An Interview with Geronimo Pratt," in Ward Churchill and Jim Vander Wall, eds., *Cages of Steel: The Politics of Imprisonment*, p. 204.

37 Churchill and Vander Wall, *Agents of Repression*, pp. 77–94; Akinyele Omowale Umoja, "Set Our Warriors Free: The Legacy of the Black Panther Party and Political Prisoners," in Charles E. Jones, ed., *The Black Panther Party Reconsidered*, p. 422.

38 See CEML, ed., *Can't Jail the Spirit*, pp. 87–89.

39 Mackenzie, *Secrets*, p. 29.

40 Quoted in Rips, *UnAmerican Activities*, p. 94.

41 William Blum, *West Bloc Dissident*, p. 67.

42 David Armstrong, *A Trumpet to Arms: Alternative Media in America*, p. 158.

---

[43] Rodger Streitmatter, *Voices of Revolution: The Dissident Press in America*, p. 232.

[44] Cathy Wilkerson, e-mail to the author, November 2, 2002.

[45] Ibid., Glessing, *The Underground Press in America*, p. 124.

[46] Quoted in Streitmatter, *Voices of Revolution*, p. 215 and Peck, *Uncovering the Sixties*, 142.

[47] Quoted in Churchill and Vander Wall, *The COINELPRO Papers*, pp. 159, 161.

[48] Ibid., p. 212.

[49] Armstrong, *A Trumpet to Arms*, p. 148, Streitmatter, *Voices of Revolution*, p. 216.

[50] Peck, *Uncovering the Sixties*, p. 185; Churchill and Vander Wall, *The COINTELPRO Papers*, p. 163. The stink bomb plot was never carried out; Churchill and Vander Wall suggest that the plan was abandoned because the FBI could not gain access to the desired area, at least not without a burglary.

[51] Blum, *West-Bloc Dissident*, pp. .84- 85.

[52] Rodger Streitmatter, *Voices of Revolution: The Dissident Press in America*, pp. 215–217.

[53] Quoted in Peck, *Uncovering the Sixties*, p. 141.

[54] Ibid., p. 142.

[55] MacKenzie, *Secrets*, pp. 4–6, 27–31, 69–71. See also Blum, *West-Bloc Dissident* for more on Ferrera. Blum was close friends with Ferrera and the two worked on radical papers together, before Blum discovered his true identity.

[56] Mackenzie, *Secrets*, p. 33.

[57] This memo is reprinted in Rips, *UnAmerican Activities*, pp. 61–63.

[58] Rips, *UnAmerican Activities*, p. 104.

[59] Quoted in Peck, *Uncovering the Sixties*, p. 143.

[60] Glessing, *The Underground Press in America*, pp. 126-135.

[61] Mackenzie, *Secrets*, p. 30. See also Rips, *UnAmerican Activities*, pp. 139–151.

[62] Malcolm X, "At The Audubon, Dec., 13, 1964," in George Breitman, ed., *Malcolm X Speaks*, p. 93.

[63] This memo is reproduced in Rips, *UnAmerican Activities*, p. 65.

[64] Quoted in Abu-Jamal, *We Want Freedom*, p. 153.

[65] Berlet, "COINTELPRO Media Operations," from www.publiceye.org/huntred/Hunt_For_Red_Menace-02.html#TopOfPage

[66] Jeremy Varon, *Bringing the War Home*, p. 176.

[67] Quoted in Rips, *UnAmerican Activities*, p. 62.

[68] This memo is reprinted in Churchill and Vander Wall, *The COINTELPRO Papers*, p. 186.

[69] See, for instance, the internal FBI memo reprinted in Rips, *UnAmerican Activities*, pp. 61–63.

[70] James Forman, *The Making of Black Revolutionaries*, pp. 522–523.

[71] Todd Gitlin, *The Whole World is Watching*, p. 107.

[72] Glessing, *The Underground Press in America*, p. 12.

[73] The text of the entire letter is reproduced in Rips, *UnAmerican Activities*, p. 94–95. This quote is from p. 95; emphasis in original.

CHAPTER FOUR
PAGES: 75-91

[1] David Gilbert, *No Surrender*, p. 250.

[2] Robert Pardun, *Prairie Radical*, p. 208; Kirkpatrick Sale, *SDS*, pp. 455–460.

[3] For more on the Yippies, see Abbie Hoffman, *The Autobiography of Abbie Hoffman*; Jerry Rubin, *We Are Everywhere*; and Jonah Raskin, *Out of the Whale: Growing Up in the American Left*.

[4] Dave Dellinger, *From Yale to Jail*, pp. 321–404; Hoffman, *The Autobiography of Abbie Hoffman*, pp. 147–164, 186–209.

[5] Dellinger, *From Yale to Jail*, pp. 352–358.

[6] Ibid., pp. 377–380.

[7] Pardun, *Prairie Radical*, p. 264.

[8] Mike Klonsky, "Toward a Revolutionary Youth Movement," in Radical Education Project, ed., *Debate Within SDS: RYM II vs. Weatherman*, pp. 1–2.

[9] Rudd, unpublished manuscript, p. 182.

[10] Radical Education Project, ed., "Introduction," in *Debate Within SDS: RYM II vs. Weatherman*, p. ii.

[11] In addition to Sale (see following citation), a summation of the strike and the demands can be found online at a website maintained by San Francisco State University: http://www.library.sfsu.edu/strike/.

[12] Sale, *SDS*, p. 535.

[13] Rudd, unpublished manuscript, p. 185.

[14] See Churchill and Vander Wall, *Agents of Repression*, pp. 37–102, or *The COINTELPRO Papers*, pp. 91–164 for more on the Carter-Huggins murder as well as the overarching strategy.

[15] See Kuwasi Balagoon et al., *Look for Me in the Whirlwind: The Collective Autobiography of the New York 21*, p. 363; and Ward Churchill, "'To Disrupt, Discredit and Destroy': The FBI's Secret War against the Black Panther Party," in Kathleen Cleaver and George Katsiaficas, eds., *Liberation, Imagination, and the Black Panther Party*, pp. 102–103.

[16] Mumia Abu-Jamal, *We Want Freedom*, p. 106. For more on the international section of the party, see Kathleen Neal Cleaver, "Back to Africa: The Evolution of the

International Section of the Black Panther Pary (1969–1972)," in Charles E. Jones, ed., *The Black Panther Party Reconsidered*, pp. 211–254; and Michael L. Clemons and Charles E. Jones, "Global Solidarity: The Black Panther Party in the International Arena," in Kathleen Cleaver and George Katsiaficas, eds., *Liberation, Imagination and the Black Panther Party*, pp. 20–39.

[17] Balagoon et al., *Look for Me in the Whirlwind*, p. 364.

[18] *SDS Educational Packet. Imperialism: The Main Enemy of the People of the World*, newspaper from the Tamiment Collection at NYU's Bobst Library. No author, editor, or date given; circa May 1969.

[19] The "Weatherman" statement is reprinted in Harold Jacobs, *Weatherman*, pp. 51–90. The entire book is valuable in examining the differences between RYM I/SDS/Weatherman and PL.

[20] Unless otherwise noted, the rest of this paragraph comes from or is quoted in Karen Ashley et al., "You Don't Need a Weatherman to Know Which Way the Wind Blows," printed in Harold Jacobs, ed., *Weatherman*, pp. 51–90.

[21] Karen Ashley, et al., "You Don't Need a Weatherman," in Harold Jacobs, ed., *Weatherman*, p. 58.

[22] Sale, *SDS*, p. 557.

[23] Ibid., p. 564.

[24] Lyndon Comstock, e-mail to the author, June 11, 2005.

[25] Sale, *SDS*, p. 563.

[26] Jack Smith, "SDS ousts PLP," in *Guardian*, June 28, 1969, pp. 3, 11.

[27] Ibid.

[28] Sale, *SDS*, p. 566.

[29] Smith, "SDS ousts PLP," p. 11.

[30] Ibid. In a 2004 interview with the author, Jaffe said women's liberation was used as a political football regardless—and by all sides, given how none of the leading factions had an in-depth analysis about or program around women's liberation. PL saw the issue only as one of "male chauvinism," which relegated sexism to the realm of bad ideas alone. Although the RYM bloc viewed the problem as one of "male supremacy," and thereby involving a power structure, RYM had little understanding around what this meant and even less in the way of political practice.

[31] Quoted in Sale, *SDS*, p. 569.

[32] Sale, *SDS*, p. 569; Smith, "SDS ousts PLP," p. 11.

[33] Sale, pp. 570-571; Kopkind, *The Thirty Years' Wars: Dispatches and Diversions of a Radical Journalist*, p. 167.

[34] Robert Allen, *Reluctant Reformers: Racism and Social Reform Movements in the United States*. Allen presents a detailed history of how these and other white-led social

---

movements in the United States have ultimately sided with white supremacy against the demands of people of color, even where such movements had anti-racist roots.

[35] Carl Davidson, "Why SDS expelled the PLP," *Guardian*, July 5, 1969, p. 3.

[36] Andrew Kopkind, *The Thirty Years' Wars*, p. 167.

[37] Ibid.

[38] "SDS National Convention 1969" flyer, Tamiment Collection at New York University Bobst Library. No author or date given.

[39] Sale, *SDS*, p. 574.

[40] Rudd, unpublished manuscript, p. 195.

[41] Nancy Zaroulis and Gerald Sullivan, *Who Spoke Up? American Protest Against the War in Vietnam, 1963–1975*, p. 262.

[42] Kopkind, *The Thirty Years' Wars*, p. 168.

[43] David Gilbert, Columbia interview, p. 178.

[44] Mike Klonsky, et al., "Revolutionary Youth Movement II," in Radical Education Project, ed., *Debate Within SDS: RYM II vs. Weatherman*. This pamphlet contains several articles of interest in the RYM II split.

[45] Ibid.; Lyndon Comstock, e-mail interview with the author, June 6, 2005.

[46] Cathy Wilkerson, Columbia interview, p. 78.

[47] Steve Komm and Alan Smitow, "A True History of SDS Convention," *Convention Report*, July 1969, pp. 1–4.

[48] Finding much information on *Fire* is difficult. Sale (p. 453) only quotes from it—and only does so once—rather than discuss it. Gitlin merely mentions that the name was changed (*The Sixties*, p. 296).

[49] Quoted in Sale, *SDS*, p. 562.

[50] Kopkind, *The Thirty Years' Wars*, p. 164.

[51] See, for instance, Todd Gitlin, *The Sixties*; Tom Hayden, *Reunion*; and Nancy Zaroulis and Gerald Sullivan, *Who Spoke Up?* Better than most, Kirkpatrick Sale can also be said to engage in some of this in his book *SDS*.

[52] Quoted in Zaroulis and Sullivan, *Who Spoke Up?*, p. 262.

[53] Several people, including Scott Braley, Bernardine Dohrn, and David Gilbert, expressed this view in interviews with the author. An earlier such expression can be found in REP's introduction to the pamphlet *Debate Within SDS: RYM II vs. Weatherman*.

[54] Cathy Wilkerson, interview for Columbia Oral History Project, February 17, 1985, p. 56.

[55] Todd Gitlin in *The Weather Underground*, film by Sam Green and Bill Siegel.

[56] George Katsiaficas, *The Imagination of the New Left*, p. 144.

[57] Laura Whitehorn, interview with the author, March 21, 2004.

[58] David Gilbert, *SDS/WUO*, p. 15.

59 For more on the foundations of these principles, see V.I. Lenin, *The State and Revolution*. For a scholarly perspective, see Paul Le Blanc, *Lenin and the Revolutionary Party*.

60 Pardun, *Prairie Radical*, pp. 281–326.

61 For more on the response to Kent State, see Sale, *SDS*, pp. 636–637; and Urban Research Corporation, *On Strike... Shut it Down! A Report on the First National Student Strike in U.S. History*.

62 For more on the women's movement and the lesbian, gay, bisexual, and transgender movement, see Ruth Rosen, *The World Split Open*; Martin Duberman, *Stonewall*; Leslie Feinberg, *Trans Liberation: Beyond Pink or Blue*; and Karla Jay, *Tales of a Lavender Menace: A Memoir of Liberation*.

63 David Gilbert, *SDS/WUO*, p. 15.

CHAPTER FIVE
PAGES: 95-125

1 David Gilbert, *SDS/WUO*, p. 18.

2 See Shin'ya Ono, "A Weatherman: You Do Need a Weatherman to Know Which Way the Wind Blows," in Harold Jacobs, ed., *Weatherman*, pp. 227–274. This article originally appeared in *Leviathan*, December 1969.

3 Bill Ayers, "A Strategy to Win" in Jacobs, ed., *Weatherman* pp.185, 191–193. This article originally appeared in *New Left Notes*, September 12, 1969.

4 Ibid., p. 186.

5 Andrew Kopkind, "Going Down in Chicago," in Jacobs, ed., *Weatherman*, p. 288. This article originally appeared in *Hard Times*, October 20, 1969.

6 Ibid.

7 Jeremy Varon, *Bringing the War Home*, p. 160.

8 Mark Naison, *White Boy*, p. 124; more generally, see pp. 124–131.

9 Sale, *SDS*, p. 602.

10 Cathy Wilkerson, Columbia interview, p. 62.

11 Karen Ashley et al., "You Don't Need a Weatherman," in Jacobs, ed., *Weatherman*, p. 51–90. These quotes come from pp. 72–78.

12 Quoted in Feldman, *Sundial*, pp. 421–422.

13 Dave Dellinger, *More Power Than We Know: The People's Movement Toward Democracy*, p. 164.

14 "The Motor City 9," in Jacobs, ed., *Weatherman*, pp. 161–162. No author listed. This article originally appeared in *New Left Notes*, August 23, 1969.

15 Kopkind, "Going Down in Chicago," p. 288.

16 Cathy Wilkerson, Columbia interview, pp. 63–64.

[17] Quoted in Varon, *Bringing the War Home*, p. 57.

[18] Kopkind, "Going Down in Chicago," pp. 288–289.

[19] David Gilbert, Columbia interview, p. 271.

[20] Herb Dreyer, interview with the author, October 8, 2002.

[21] Mark Rudd, unpublished manuscript, pp. 61–66; Donna Willmott, interview with the author, June 4, 2004.

[22] Thai Jones, *A Radical Line: From the Labor Movement to the Weather Underground, One Family's Century of Conscience*, pp. 169–172; Varon, *Bringing the War Home*, p. 137. Author's respective interviews with Scott Braley, Lyndon Comstock, Bernardine Dohrn, and Donna Willmott were also instructive in this regard.

[23] Nicholas M. Horrock, "F.B.I. Asserts Cuba Aided Weathermen," in *New York Times*, October 9, 1977.

[24] David Gilbert, Columbia interview, pp. 265–267. For the dates, see John Castellucci's *The Big Dance: The Untold Story of Kathy Boudin and the Terrorist Family that Committed the Brink's Robbery Murder*, p. 173.

[25] Lyndon Comstock, e-mail to the author, June 6, 2005.

[26] Mark Rudd, unpublished manuscript, pp. 211–216. The goal in "smashing monogamy" was to smash boundaries and conventions, to erase jealousy and possessiveness. Not surprisingly, sexually transmitted infections were common.

[27] Ashley et al., "You Don't Need a Weatherman," pp. 86–87.

[28] Jones, *A Radical Line*, pp. 175–176.

[29] Rudd, unpublished manuscript, p. 236.

[30] Quoted in ibid, p. 225.

[31] The flyer was entitled "Off Rocky and His Friends," and can be found at the Tamiment Collection at the Bobst Library of New York University.

[32] The Young Lords Organization was a street gang that became a politically radical organization. It spawned another chapter in New York City, which ultimately became an independent organization calling itself the Young Lords Party and was from the beginning a revolutionary organization. The New York chapter related more closely to Weather, especially at the beginning. Eventually, this group changed its name to Puerto Rican Workers Party and joined the New Communist Movement sector of the Left. See Miguel Melendez, *We Took the Streets: Fighting for Latino Rights with the Young Lords*, and Andrés Torres and José E. Velázquez, eds., *The Puerto Rican Movement: Voices from the Diaspora*. Author's interviews with Esperanza Martell and Panama Alba were also helpful.

[33] Howard Zinn, *A People's History of the United States: 1492 to the Present*, pp. 263–266.

[34] Dellinger, *More Power Than We Know*, pp. 162–165.

[35] For more on militancy and the Black Panthers, see Mumia Abu-Jamal, *We Want Freedom*, and Charles E. Jones, *The Black Panther Party Reconsidered*. Hampton's criticisms can be heard in *The Weather Underground* documentary; they are also written about in Tom Thomas, "The Second Battle of Chicago," reprinted in Jacobs, ed., *Weatherman*, pp.196–226; Dave Dellinger, *More Power Than We Know*, pp. 162–165; and Thai Jones, *A Radical Line*, p. 204.

[36] Author's interviews with Robert Roth, Laura Whitehorn, and Donna Willmott were especially instructive in this regard.

[37] Varon, *Bringing the War Home*, p. 77.

[38] Ibid, p. 82.

[39] Tom Thomas, "The Second Battle of Chicago," in Jacobs, ed., *Weatherman*, p. 200.

[40] Quoted in ibid., p. 201.

[41] Jones, *A Radical Line*, pp. 178–179.

[42] Lyndon Comstock, "Days of Rage: October 8–11, 1969," unpublished article in author's files. I'm grateful to Lyndon Comstock for sharing with me this detailed and unpublished article chronicling the first night of the Days of Rage protests. The chronology presented here builds off Comstock's article, in addition to other sources cited below.

[43] *David Gilbert: A Lifetime of Struggle*, Freedom Archives: 2002 (documentary).

[44] David Gilbert, letter to the author, March 7, 2005.

[45] Thomas, "The Second Battle of Chicago," pp. 204–206.

[46] David Gilbert, letter to the author, March 7, 2005.

[47] Varon, *Bringing the War Home*, p. 81. For more on the Days of Rage, see Ayers, *Fugitive Days*, pp. 165–179; Jones, *A Radical Line*, pp. 173–180; Sale, *SDS*, pp. 579, 582, 586, 588–589, 591–592, 596, 600–615; Varon, *Bringing the War Home*, pp. 74–112; and Tom Thomas, *The Second Battle of Chicago, 1969* newspaper (also reprinted in Harold Jacobs, ed., *Weatherman*, pp. 196–225). For a variety of perspectives on it from outside of Weatherman, see Gitlin, *The Sixties*, pp. 393–395; and Dellinger, *More Power Than We Know*, pp. 135–197.

[48] Varon, *Bringing the War Home*, p. 82.

[49] Ibid; Ono, "A Weatherman," p. 271.

[50] Dellinger, *From Yale to Jail*, pp. 387–389.

[51] Varon, *Bringing the War Home*, p. 82. Varon also notes that some Mafia-owned property was damaged during the first night of the Days of Rage; in response, Mafia representatives surprised some Weatherman activists the following morning, and warned them to not let it happen again. Varon, *Bringing the War Home*, p. 81.

[52] Lyndon Comstock, e-mail to the author, June 15, 2005.

[53] Lyndon Comstock, "Days of Rage: October 8–11, 1969," unpublished article in author's files; Ayers, *Fugitive Days*, pp. 173–175.

[54] Tom Thomas, *The Second Battle of Chicago, 1969*, pp. 2, 18. A modified version of this paper is printed in Jacobs, *Weatherman*, though these quotes refer to the newspaper version.

[55] Sale, *SDS*, presents the best chronology of how SDS shifted politically. See especially pp. 317–403.

[56] Weatherman, *Two, Three, Many Vietnams*, pp. 13, 29, 62.

[57] See, for instance, Mark Naison, *White Boy*, and Bob Feldman, *Sundial* (unpublished memoir in author's files).

[58] *David Gilbert: Lifetime in Struggle*, Freedom Archives: 2002 (documentary).

[59] Rudd, from August 1, 1969, SDS memo, found at the Tamiment archives.

[60] Cathy Wilkerson, Columbia interview, pp. 64–65.

[61] Naomi Jaffe in *The Weather Underground*, Sam Green and Bill Siegel: 2003 (documentary).

[62] George Katsiaficas, *The Imagination of the New Left*, p. 123.

[63] See Sale, *SDS*, p. 632. Bill Ayers estimates as many as six a day during this time period; Ayers, *Fugitive Days*, p. 228.

[64] See the chart of "Guerrilla Acts of Sabotage and Terrorism in the U.S., 1965–1970," in *Scanlan's Monthly*, Vol. 1, Number 8, January 1971, p. 12. For how this issue of the magazine was censored, see David Armstrong, *A Trumpet to Arms: The Alternative Press in America*, p. 150.

[65] Pardun, *Prairie Radical*, p. 340.

[66] Varon, *Bringing the War Home*, pp. 117–118.

[67] Zaroulis and Sullivan, *Who Spoke Up?*, p. 262.

[68] Ron Jacobs, *The Way the Wind Blew: A History of the Weather Underground*, pp. 82–83; Varon, *Bringing the War Home*, pp. 125–129; Sale, *SDS*, p. 627.

[69] David Gilbert, Columbia interview, p. 198.

[70] Churchill and Vander Wall, *COINTELPRO Papers*, p. 140. O'Neal later killed himself; Mumia Abu-Jamal, *We Want Freedom*, pp. 148–150.

[71] For more on the Hampton-Clark assassinations, see Churchill and Vander Wall, *COINTELPRO Papers*, pp. 137–140, or Churchill and Vander Wall, *Agents of Repression*, pp. 17–103.

[72] Churchill and Vander Wall, *COINTELPRO Papers*, p. 140.

[73] David Hilliard and Lewis Cole, *This Side of Glory: The Autobiography of David Hilliard and the Story of the Black Panther Party*, p. 215.

[74] Churchill and Vander Wall, *COINTELPRO Papers*, pp. 135–141. See also Greg Wells, "COINTELPRO: Then and Now" in *ONWARD* vol. 1 iss. 3, pp. 13, 19, and Joy James, "Introduction," *Imprisoned Intellectuals*, p. xiii.

[75] Cathy Wilkerson, Columbia interview, p. 74.

[76] David Gilbert, Columbia interview, p. 201.

---

[77] David Gilbert, *No Surrender*, p. 256.

[78] *David Gilbert: A Lifetime of Struggle*, Freedom Archives: 2002 (documentary).

[79] Angela Davis provides an account of the police raid and resistance in her memoir, pp. 227–232.

[80] Varon, *Bringing the War Home*, p. 154. Max Elbaum, *Revolution in the Air*, p. 66.

[81] William Kunstler, *My Life as a Radical Lawyer*, p. 30; Jonah Raskin, *Out of the Whale: Growing Up in the American Left*, p. 122. David Gilbert has also raised this point with me several times.

[82] Laura Whitehorn in *OUT: The Making of a Revolutionary*, videotape, Sonja de Vries and Rhonda Collins, 2000 (documentary).

[83] Jonah Raskin, *Out of the Whale: Growing Up in the American Left*, p. 115.

[84] Ibid., pp. 118–119.

[85] Ibid., pp. 122–137.

[86] Weather Underground, *Prairie Fire: The Politics of Revolutionary Anti-Imperialism*, p. 4.

[87] Varon, *Bringing the War Home*, pp. 158–166.

[88] The flier is reprinted in Harold Jacobs, ed., *Weatherman*, p. 338.

[89] Sale, *SDS*, p. 627.

[90] Raskin, *Out of the Whale*, pp. 147–148.

[91] Varon, *Bringing the War Home*, p. 171.

[92] Pardun, *Prairie Radical*, p. 287; Rudd, conversation with the author, June 12, 2004.

CHAPTER SIX
PAGES: 127-151

[1] David Gilbert, *No Surrender*, pp. 256–257.

[2] Douglas Robinson, "Townhouse Razed by Blast and Fire; Man's Body Found," *New York Times*, March 7, 1970, p. 1.

[3] Kirkpatrick Sale describes the explosion in detail in *SDS*, pp. 3–6.

[4] John Neary, "The Two Girls From No. 18: Shock Troops on the Way to War at Home," *LIFE*, March 27, 1970, p. 27.

[5] Ibid.

[6] Bill Ayers, *Fugitive Days*, p. 192; Lyndon Comstock, e-mail interview with the author, June 6, 2005; Michael Novick, e-mail interview with the author, June 11, 2005.

[7] David Gilbert, in *The Weather Underground*, Sam Green and Bill Siegel: 2003 (documentary).

[8] Naomi Jaffe, interview with the author, June 19, 2004. See also Larry Grathwohl as told to Frank Reagan, *Bringing Down America: An FBI Informant with the Weatherman*.

[9] Naomi Jaffe, e-mail to the author, July 31, 2003.

[10] David Gilbert, in *Lifetime of Struggle*, Freedom Archives: 2002 (documentary). Sale, *SDS*, p. 3–6. Abbie Hoffman even went as far as to call the explosion a "blessing in disguise" because it once and for all steered the WUO away from carrying out any kind of violence directed against people. See *The Autobiography of Abbie Hoffman*, pp. 249–250. Author's interview with Naomi Jaffe (June 19, 2004) was also instructive in discussing the proposed action behind the townhouse explosion.

[11] For instance, Andrés Torres and José Velázquez, in the introduction to *The Puerto Rican Movement: Voices from the Diaspora*, identify the FALN and similar armed struggle groups as a specific strain of Puerto Rican activism in the broad spectrum of resistance to U.S. colonialism, whereas the white Left was much more divided (pp. 5–6). For the BLA, see Akinyele Omowale Umoja, "Repression Breeds Resistance: The Black Liberation Army and the Radical Legacy of the Black Panther Party," in Kathleen Cleaver and George Katsiaficas, eds., *Liberation, Imagination, and the Black Panther Party*, pp. 3–19. For more on the white Left's response to the WUO, which was admittedly wrapped up in far more sectarian disputes at the outset than these two groups, see Sale, *SDS*, pp. 600–657. Several essays from across the Left are also reprinted in Harold Jacobs, ed., *Weatherman*.

[12] Mark Rudd, unpublished manuscript, pp. 280–285. For the group's turn to more centralized structure, see Ayers, *Fugitive Days*, pp. 205–207. For JJ's death, see Jeremy Varon, *Bringing the War Home*, p. 182. Also, author's interview with Bernardine Dohrn, July 17, 2004, was instructive in this regard.

[13] Laura Whitehorn, interview with Nicole Keif, October 20, 2002, p. 24, in author's files.

[14] Clayborne Carson, *In Struggle: SNCC and the Black Awakening of the 1960s*, pp. 297–298. Brown was eventually caught after a shootout with police in 1971, and he was sentenced in 1973 to five-to-ten years in prison, where he became a Muslim and eventually changed his name to Jamil Al-Amin. Al-Amin is now serving life without parole for the shooting death of a Georgia police deputy in 2000. Al-Amin, a respected Imam in Atlanta prior to his arrest, maintains his innocence. For more on the case, see http://www.imamjamil.com/. More generally, see his memoir, H. Rap Brown, *Die, Nigger, Die! A Political Autobiography*.

[15] The Revolutionary Force 9 communiqué for this bombing is reprinted in the March 13, 1970, *New York Times* under the headline "Text of Terrorist Letter," p. 26. The group seemingly took its name from the Beatles song Revolution 9.

[16] Stanley Karnow, *Vietnam: A History*, pp. 604–612.

[17] Varon, *Bringing the War Home*, p. 176.

---

[18] Linda Evans, "Letter to the Movement," in Harold Jacobs, ed., *Weatherman*, pp. 462–463; Jonah Raskin, "Introduction," in *The Weather Eye: Communiqués from the Weather Underground*, pp. 13–14; Varon, *Bringing the War Home*, p. 176.

[19] Varon, *Bringing the War Home*, pp. 175–176. See also Evans, "Letter to the Movement," and Rudd, unpublished manuscript, pp. 263, 265.

[20] Quoted in Varon, *Bringing the War Home*, p. 178.

[21] No author, "9 Radicals Are on the Most-Wanted List," in *New York Times*, November 28, 1970, p. 13. Attorney William Kunstler said the expansion was to "stigmatize the movements to which they subscribe."

[22] Sale, *SDS*, pp. 636–637. See also Robert Pardun, *Prairie Radical*, pp. 287–288.

[23] Sale, *SDS*, pp. 635–638. See also James A. Michener, *Kent State: What Happened and Why*; Tim Spofford, *Lynch Street: The May 1970 Slayings at Jackson State*; and Eugene Koveos and Nicole Solomon, "This Will Not Be Kent State: Fear, Loathing, and Radical Movement" in *Onward* vol. 2 iss. 2, p. 3. For the Weatherman bombing of the National Guard headquarters, see John Herbers, "Big Capitol Rally Asks U.S. Pullout in Southeast Asia," in *New York Times*, May 10, 1970, p. 1. The group took credit for the National Guard bombing in *Prairie Fire*, p. 5.

[24] See, for instance, Susan Braudy, *Family Circle: The Boudins and the Aristocracy of the Left*; Todd Gitlin, *The Sixties: Years of Hope, Days of Rage*, and John Castellucci, *The Big Dance: The Untold Story of Kathy Boudin and the Terrorist Family that Committed the Brink's Murders*.

[25] David Gilbert quoted in Bob Feldman, "Beyond Brinks: David Gilbert Talks about the Robbery, the Underground, the Struggle," in, *Columbia Daily Spectator*, April 2, 1985, in author's files.

[26] In an interview in Ron Chepesiuk's *Sixties Radicals, Then and Now* (p. 81), Dellinger says: "Violence is a two-edged sword that turns back on the people who use it. But I do give a kind of critical support to some violent groups. Unlike some peace bureaucrats, I don't wash my hands of them when oppressed peoples think it is the only way to liberate themselves. I don't call myself a pacifist because a lot of pacifist organizations are interested only in their own purity, or, at least, they overvalue their own purity by condemning everyone who, in despair, feels the only hope is to act violently. They don't value the importance of working nonviolently with other people, whether they are violent or not, in order to get justice."

[27] I.F. Stone, "Where the Fuse on that Dynamite Leads," in Harold Jacobs, ed., *Weatherman*, p. 491.

[28] For more on the Red Army Faction, see Varon, *Bringing the War Home*. Red Army *Faction* is the common translation into English, rather than the original *fraction*, meant to emphasize that the group was only one segment of a large, international Marxist

struggle. For more on the Red Brigades, see Chris Aronson Beck et al., *"Strike One to Educate One Hundred": The Rise of the Red Brigades in Italy in the 1960s–1970s*.

[29] The rest of the information in this paragraph and the next is taken from or quoted in Bernardine Dohrn, "A Declaration of a State of War," in Raskin, ed., *Weather Eye*, pp. 16–18.

[30] In an internal report, the FBI claimed that the Weather Underground sent a letter (to whom is not specified, but presumably the bureau means the media) claiming credit for an attempted bombing of the San Francisco Hall of Justice on June 5, 1970. The bomb did not go off, though it was later found by workers in the building. It is, however, unclear whether Weatherman Underground was in any way connected with this attempt. See the Federal Bureau of Investigation, Freedom of Information Act archive, Weather Underground files, part 1c, p. 64.

[31] Jonah Raskin, "Introduction," in Raskin, ed., *Weather Eye: Communiqués from the Weather Underground*, p. 6.

[32] Michael Stern, "Mayor Vows 'Relentless' Drive to Track Down Police Bomber," in *New York Times*, June 11, 1970, p. 1.

[33] Ron Jacobs, *The Way The Wind Blew*, p. 109; Weatherman, "Communiqué No. 2," in Liberated Guardian Collective, ed., *Outlaws of Amerika: Communiqués from the Weather Underground*, p. 7.

[34] "Police Headquarters," a July 17, 1970, letter printed in the *New Morning, Changing Weather* pamphlet from Tamiment archives, p. 2.

[35] Varon, *Bringing the War Home*, p. 181; Sale, *SDS*, pp. 648–649.

[36] Ron Jacobs, *The Way the Wind Blew*, p. 109.

[37] Hoffman, *The Autobiography of Abbie Hoffman*, Jonah Raskin, *Out of the Whale: Growing Up in the American Left*, and Jerry Rubin, *We Are Everywhere*, all describe Yippie support for the Weather Underground.

[38] Unless otherwise noted, the rest of the information in this and the next paragraph comes from or is quoted in the two communiqués reprinted in Harold Jacobs, *Weatherman*, pp. 516–519. Weather's communiqué about the escape is on p. 516; Leary's letter is on pp. 517–519.

[39] Ayers, *Fugitive Days*, p. 247.

[40] Jones, *A Radical Line*, pp. 222, 225.

[41] Raskin, "Introduction," p. 6.

[42] This critique is most elaborated, if dogmatically, in the communiqués published in John Brown Book Club, ed., *The Split of the Weather Underground*.

[43] David Gilbert, interviews with the author, July 18 and July 19, 2002; see also Rudd, unpublished manuscript, p. 291.

[44] Weatherman, "Haymarket Square" communiqué, in *New Morning, Changing Weather*, p. 3.

[45] Bernardine Dohrn, Jeff Jones, and Bill Ayers, "Fall Offensive: Guard Your Children, Guard Your Doors," in Liberated Guardian, ed., *Outlaws of Amerika*, pp. 15–16.

[46] George Jackson, *Soledad Brother: The Prison Letters of George Jackson*; and Eric Mann, *Comrade George*.

[47] Angela Y. Davis, *Angela Davis: An Autobiography*, pp. 278–279.

[48] The Weatherman Underground, "Marin County," in Liberated Guardian, ed., *Outlaws of Amerika*, p. 19.

[49] Angela Y. Davis, ed., *If They Come in the Morning: Voices of Resistance*, and *Angela Davis: An Autobiography*.

[50] Wallace Turner, "Bombings Damage 3 Places in West," *New York Times*, October 9, 1970, p. 1. The other two bombings were not done by the Weather Underground. One was against an armory in Santa Barbara, the other against an ROTC at the University of Washington in Seattle. Another bomb in Berkeley was found by police before it went off.

[51] Weatherman, "Queens Courthouse communication," in *New Morning, Changing Weather*, p. 2.

[52] Alfred E. Clark, "FBI Investigates Bombing of Courthouse Here," *New York Times*, October 11, 1970, p. 11.

[53] Weatherman, "Queens Courthouse communication" in *New Morning, Changing Weather*, pp. 19–20.

[54] Stanley Karnow, *Vietnam: A History*, p. 255.

[55] Proud Eagle Tribe, "Boston," in Liberated Guardian, ed., *Outlaws of Amerika*, pp. 22–23; Naomi Jaffe, interview with the author, June 19, 2004.

[56] Hoffman, *Autobiography of Abbie Hoffman*, p. 257.

[57] Roxanne Dunbar-Ortiz, *Outlaw Woman*, p. 336. Dunbar-Ortiz details the decision to go underground as well as what underground life was like. Although her group never engaged in major illegal activities, it made serious preparations for possibly violent revolutionary acts. How many other 1960s activists went underground in the '70s is unknown, but Dunbar-Ortiz's work suggests that many people were at least quasi-underground. For more on her life underground as well as her decision to surface, see pp. 293–363.

[58] Weatherman Underground, "Declaration of a State of War," in Liberated Guardian, ed., *Outlaws of Amerika*, p. 3.

[59] Determining the exact number of actions that the Weatherman Underground did in 1970 is a bit tricky. At the time, communiqués went out for six actions: the police station, the Leary escape, the Haymarket statue, the Marin County Hall of Justice, the Queens courthouse, and the Harvard bombing. However, the women's brigade action at Harvard was claimed only by the Proud Eagle Tribe, which did not identify itself as a

section of the Weather Underground until later; the group as a whole did not claim this action until it was listed in *Prairie Fire*, along with the May 1970 bombing of National Guard headquarters in Washington, D.C., which occurred absent a communiqué. Same with the July 1970 bombing of the Presidio Army Base and MP station in San Francisco, which was claimed in *Prairie Fire* but not via a communiqué at the time. Similarly, a Bank of America bombing in New York City that occurred the same day as the police station bombing—June 9, 1970, in Weather's first claimed action as an independent group—was also not claimed in a communiqué. However, the FBI later contended that someone identifying himself as part of Weatherman claimed the action in a phone call to the press. The FBI also alleged that the bombing of a Santa Barbara National Guard office on October 8, 1970 (the major day of action for the Fall Offensive), was done by the Weather Underground. A communiqué at the time claimed the action by a group calling itself the "Park Home Grown Garden Society," and *Prairie Fire* makes no mention of this bombing. The basis for the FBI's claim comes from the fact that the communiqué announcing the Fall Offensive said actions would occur from Boston to Santa Barbara, and *Prairie Fire* claimed the Harvard action as a Weather one. However, the Fall Offensive communiqué also said resistance would spread not only from Boston to Santa Barbara but "back to Kent and Kansas," and there were no actions claimed in either place. So the FBI's logic is by no means foolproof here. The *Outlaws of Amerika* pamphlet, edited by the Liberated Guardian, reprints communiqués from several self-proclaimed "tribes," and there is no indication whether these groups had any connection to the Weather Underground. See the Federal Bureau of Investigation, Freedom of Information Act archive, Weather Underground files, part 1c, pp. 178–180.

[60] See the chart of guerrilla acts printed in *Scanlan's Monthly*, p. 12. George Katsiaficas presents an excellent overview of the movement in 1970 in *The Imagination of the New Left*, pp. 117–177.

[61] Almost immediately after it happened (and still today), the explosion at the West 11th Street townhouse became known simply as "the townhouse." Sometimes people use "the townhouse" to refer to the blast itself; other times it is used to refer to the set of militarist politics that resulted in the explosion.

[62] Bernardine Dohrn, *New Morning, Changing Weather*, p. 6. Unless otherwise noted, the rest of the information in this and the next paragraph comes from pp. 6–7 of this pamphlet.

[63] David Gilbert, letter to the author, October 13, 2004.

[64] "Open Letter to Weatherman Underground from Panther 21," in author's files. Unless otherwise noted, the rest of the information in this paragraph comes from this letter.

[65] The copy in my files was reprinted in an undated issue of *Breakthrough*, the magazine of the Prairie Fire Organizing Committee. PFOC didn't come into existence until

1974, and *Breakthrough* didn't start until 1977. For more on PFOC and its publication, see Ron Jacobs, *The Way the Wind Blew*, pp. 175–177. Author's interviews with Judith Mirkinson and Susan Rosenberg were also instructive about PFOC.

[66] David Hilliard and Lewis Cole, *This Side of Glory: The Autobiography of David Hilliard and the Story of the Black Panther Party*, p. 320.

[67] Weather Underground, *Prairie Fire*, p. 11.

[68] For more on Berrigan and the Catonsville 9, see Nancy Zaroulis and Gerald Sullivan, *Who Spoke Up?*, pp. 230–237. Prior to his capture, Berrigan showed up surreptitiously at several public antiwar events and spoke, managing to escape without being caught.

[69] Daniel Berrigan, "Letter to the Weatherman," in Joy James, ed., *Imprisoned Intellectuals*, pp. 242–247. Weatherman Underground, "Message to Brother Dan," in Liberated Guardian, ed., *Outlaws of Amerika*, p. 29.

[70] In addition to Ross, Naomi Jaffe, David Gilbert, and Laura Whitehorn in separate interviews with the author each spoke about the prevalence of political study in underground living. This did not translate as much for those members of the Weather Underground living a public life and active in the movement, who had too much political work to do (legal and covert) to study as intensively.

[71] David Gilbert, *SDS/WUO*, p. 22.

[72] Suzanne Ross, quoted in Becky Thompson, *A Promise and a Way of Life: White Antiracist Activism*, p. 98.

[73] David Gilbert, letter to the Resistance in Brooklyn Sixties Study Group, in which the author participated, June 15, 2004.

[74] Andrew Kopkind, "Going Down in Chicago," in Harold Jacobs, ed., *Weatherman*, p. 287.

[75] In the McCarthyist period, several members of the Communist Party went underground to escape repression, but this was a defensive rather than an offensive move. Its underground was to protect party members, not to carry out actions.

[76] This press conference is excerpted in *Underground*, Emile de Antonio, Mary Lampson and Haskell Wexler: 1975 (documentary).

[77] Bernardine Dohrn, Jeff Jones, and Bill Ayers, "Fall Offensive: Guard Your Children, Guard Your Doors," in Liberated Guardian, ed., *Outlaws of Amerika*, p. 16.

[78] Berrigan, "Letter to the Weatherman," pp. 245–247.

[79] Reprinted in David Gilbert, *SDS/WUO*, pp. 24–25.

[80] Quoted in Zaroulis and Sullivan, *Who Spoke Up?*, p. 262.

[81] Weatherman Underground, "Message to Brother Dan," in Liberated Guardian, ed., *Outlaws of Amerika*, p. 29.

[82] Berrigan, "Letter to the Weatherman," p. 243.

[83] Bernardine Dohrn, *New Morning, Changing Weather*, p. 6.

[84] David Gilbert, *SDS/WUO* p. 17.

CHAPTER SEVEN
PAGES: 153-181

[1] David Gilbert, interview for the Columbia University Oral History Research Office, p. 294.

[2] David Gilbert, Columbia interview, pp. 295–296; Mark Rudd, conversation with the author, June 12, 2004.

[3] For more on this incident, see Tom Bates, *Rads: The 1970 Bombing of the Army Math Research Center at the University of Wisconsin and Its Aftermath*.

[4] David Gilbert, interview with the author, July 18, 2002; Suzanne Ross, interview with the author, June 27, 2004. Sometimes the WUO would call media outlets and police agencies in several cities at one time to alert them to the bomb and ensure everyone would get out safely. The coordinated efforts underscored the seriousness of the call. Bill Ayers, conversation with author, October 2, 2003.

[5] William Worthy, "A Real Bomber's Chilling Reasons," in *LIFE*, March 27, 1970, p. 30. A *LIFE* magazine correspondent, Worthy interviewed an anonymous underground activist.

[6] Ibid. Geronimo ji Jaga Pratt and Ray Luc Levasseur were both veterans who joined the underground a few years after their return to this country. See, for example, Geronimo ji Jaga, "Every Nation Struggling to Be Free Has a Right to Struggle, a Duty to Struggle," in Cleaver and Katsiaficas, eds., *Liberation, Imagination, and the Black Panther Party*, pp. 71–77; and Ray Luc Levasseur, *The Trial Statements of Ray Luc Levasseur*.

[7] Naomi Jaffe, conversation with the author, May 23, 2004. For more on the average class background of New Leftists, see Robert Pardun, *Prairie Radical*; Kirkpatrick Sale, *SDS*; and Jeremy Varon, *Bringing the War Home*.

[8] Jeremy Varon, *Bringing the War Home*, p. 57.

[9] David Gilbert, interview with Sam Green and Bill Siegel for *Weather Underground*, part II, p. 7, n.d. [circa 1998]. Transcript in author's files.

[10] In his unpublished memoir, Mark Rudd recounts an early robbery attempt, done more for the experience than because the organization had to rely on such means of fundraising. Rudd, unpublished manuscript, p. 297.

[11] David Gilbert, letter to the author, September 20, 2003.

[12] David Gilbert, letter to the author, November 19, 2004. For more on the Newton-Cleaver call, see Mumia Abu-Jamal, *We Want Freedom*, pp. 215–219.

[13] Jones, *A Radical Line*, pp. 225–227.

[14] David Gilbert, letter to the author, November 19, 2004; Jones, *A Radical Line*, pp. 225–227.

[15] David Gilbert, Sam Green interview, part II, p. 2.

[16] David Gilbert, letter to the author, November 19, 2004.

[17] The FBI documents were initially published in the New Left journal *WIN*. There is little published about the Media, Pennsylvania, FBI break-in. Mumia Abu-Jamal covers it in *We Want Freedom*, pp. 155–158. See also Richard Gid Powers, *Secrecy and Power:*

The Life of J. Edgar Hoover, pp. 464–467. For more on the Pentagon Papers leak and aftermath, see Daniel Ellsberg, *Secrets: A Memoir of Vietnam and the Pentagon Papers*. Ellsberg was a former Department of Defense employee and RAND analyst. Although the papers were ultimately published in the *New York Times*, the "paper of record" was reluctant to do so for quite some time.

[18] Mark Rudd, unpublished manuscript, p. 339.

[19] Dan Berger, "Mark Felt's Other Legacy," http://www.thenation.com/doc.mhtml?i=2 0050704&s=berger, posted June 22, 2005. See also M. Wesley Swearingen, *FBI Secrets: An Agent's Expose*.

[20] Mark Rudd, unpublished manuscript, pp. 338–339. See also Swearingen, *FBI Secrets*.

[21] John Castellucci, *The Big Dance*, p. 124.

[22] Varon, *Bringing the War Home*, p. 296.

[23] Jennifer Dohrn spoke of this and other ways in which she was targeted by COIN-TELPRO in a June 2, 2005 edition of the radio program *Democracy Now!* with Amy Goodman. The program is available online at http://www.democracynow.org/article. pl?sid=05/06/02/1445253&mode=thread&tid=25.

[24] Varon, *Bringing the War Home*, p. 296.

[25] Raskin, ed., *Weather Eye*, p. 14.

[26] See Morton Halperin, et al., *The Lawless State*, pp. 209–219.

[27] Jonah Raskin, "Introduction," in *Weather Eye*, p. 6.

[28] For more on grand juries, see Morton Halperin, et al., *The Lawless State*, pp. 209-219. Author's interviews with Lyndon Comstock were also instrumental in this regard.

[29] For information on the current grand juries, see Jaxon Van Derbeken, "Former Black Panther Jailed for Not Testifying," in *San Francisco Chronicle*, September 1, 2005. See also www.fbiwitchhunt.com. For more on grand juries in the 1980s, see Bob Feldman, "Civil Liberties and the 1981 Brink's Case," and David Gilbert, "To the Berkshire Forum," July 19, 1989, articles in author's files; Ward Churchill and Jim Vander Wall, *The COINTELPRO Papers*, p. 310. Author's interviews with Esperanza Martell, Scott Braley, Bernardine Dohrn, and David Gilbert were also instructive in this regard.

[30] Akinyele Omowale Umoja, "Repression Breeds Resistance: The Black Liberation Army and the Radical Legacy of the Black Panther Party," in Kathleen Cleaver and George Katsiaficas, *Liberation, Imagination, and the Black Panther Party*, pp. 3–19.

[31] For more on the split, see Mumia Abu-Jamal, *We Want Freedom*, pp. 205–227.

[32] Umoja, "Repression Breeds Resistance," and Jalil Muntaqim, *On the Black Liberation Army*, pamphlet in author's files, published in 1997 by the Anarchist Black Cross Federation (originally written in 1979). For more on expropriations, see Eric Hobsbawm, *Bandits*, pp. 120–138.

[33] Black Liberation Army Coordinating Committee, *Message to the Black Movement: A Political Statement from the Black Underground*, pamphlet in author's files, published in 1997 by the Autonomous Zone (no date of original, though it likely appeared around 1975).

[34] Ashanti Alston, interview with the author, May 29, 2004.

[35] Weather Underground, "Clifford Glover, 103rd Precinct," communiqué in Jonah Raskin, ed., *Weather Eye*, p. 68.

[36] Stanley Karnow, *Vietnam*, pp. 593–596.

[37] Ibid., pp. 629–632. The bombing of Laos was the heaviest in any war in world history until that point.

[38] Ibid., pp. 631–633.

[39] Ron Jacobs, *The Way The Wind Blew*, p. 130.

[40] Weather Underground, "We Bombed the Capitol," in Liberated Guardian, ed., *Outlaws of Amerika*, p. 41.

[41] Weather Underground, "Dear Mrs. Bacon," in *Outlaws of Amerika*, p. 45.

[42] Pardun, *Prairie Radical*, p. 299.

[43] This was said by Judy Gumbo and can be seen in the film *Underground*, Emile de Antonio, Mary Lampson, and Haskell Wexler: 1975 (documentary).

[44] David Gilbert, Sam Green interview, part I, p. 12.

[45] Weather Underground, "We Bombed the Capitol," in Liberated Guardian, ed., *Outlaws of Amerika*, pp. 41–44.

[46] Ayers, *Fugitive Days*, p. 261. For more on the action, see pp. 256–261.

[47] Suzanne Ross, interview with the author, June 27, 2004.

[48] Angela Davis, *The Autobiography of Angela Davis*, p. 317. See also Eric Mann, *Comrade George: An Investigation into the Life, Political Thought, and Assassination of George Jackson*.

[49] Weather Underground, "George Jackson," in Raskin, ed., *Weather Eye*, pp. 42–47.

[50] Mann, *Comrade George*, p. 143.

[51] Weather Underground, "George Jackson," in Jonah Raskin, ed., *Weather Eye*, pp. 45–46. Hanrahan and Parks were each the public spokespeople after the Hampton and Jackson murders, respectively. Both men called the Panthers violent and denied any government malfeasance in the murders.

[52] Sam Melville, *Letters From Attica*, pp. viii-ix.

[53] The most thorough telling of Attica remains Tom Wicker, *A Time to Die*. John Cohen and Jane Alpert's respective introductions to Sam Melville's *Letters From Attica* also contain some useful information.

[54] This text is reprinted in Wicker, *A Time to Die*, pp. 401–402. It was read publicly and eloquently by Elliot L.D. Barkely, a 21-year-old Black man sent to Attica for driving

without a license (following an earlier charge of check forgery). Barkely was one of those murdered when police retook the prison.

[55] The full list of proposals is reprinted in Wicker, *A Time to Die*, pp. 403–404.

[56] The full list of supplemental demands is reprinted in ibid., pp. 401–402.

[57] See Wicker's chilling account, *A Time to Die*, pp. 343–364. The total death toll for the Attica rebellion was forty-three. Thirty-nine died from police gunfire in the September 13 retaking of the prison. One guard died as a result of beatings he received at the beginning of the rebellion. And three prisoners were killed at some point while the prisoners held control of D Yard, possibly as retaliation for a perceived betrayal. See Wicker, *A Time to Die*, pp. 216–217, 381. Bert Useem and Peter Kimball report that some troopers were so eager to crush the rebellion and punish the prisoners that they brought their deer hunting rifles from home rather than bother with getting state-issued weapons. See Useem and Kimball, *States of Siege: U.S. Prison Riots 1971–1986*, p. 52.

[58] Wicker, *A Time to Die*, pp. 370–371.

[59] Weather Underground, "Attica," in Raskin, ed., *Weather Eye*, pp. 46–49.

[60] Weather Underground, "Clifford Glover, 103rd Precinct," in Raskin, ed., *Weather Eye*, pp. 66–69.

[61] Quoted in William Blum, *Killing Hope: U.S. Military and C.I.A. Interventions Since World War II*, p. 209. Blum attributes this quote to a 1974 issue of *Newsweek*.

[62] For more on the coup and background, see Patricia Politzer, *Fear in Chile: Lives Under Pinochet*; William Blum, *Killing Hope*, pp. 206–215; and Eduardo Galeano, *Open Veins of Latin America*, pp. 270–273, 283.

[63] Quoted in Weather Underground, "The Bombing of ITT Headquarters for Latin America," in Raskin, ed., *Weather Eye*, p. 84.

[64] "On Structure," unpublished packet by Weatherwoman, January 1973, in author's files courtesy of Naomi Jaffe.

[65] "Mountain Moving Day," unpublished paper by Weatherwomen, n.d. [circa February 1973], in author's files courtesy of Naomi Jaffe.

[66] "After the Tempest," unpublished packet by Weatherwomen, n.d. [circa January 1975], p. 2, in author's files courtesy of Naomi Jaffe.

[67] See, for instance, those published in John Brown Book Club, ed., *The Split of the Weather Underground Organization: Struggling Against White and Male Supremacy*. Also, several internal articles written by women as the group was falling apart (in author's files) are instructive in this regard.

[68] One of the best articulations of this now-ubiquitous expression can be found in Patricia Hill Collins, *Black Feminist Thought: Knowledge, Consciousness, and the Politics of Empowerment*. Collins also uses the phrase "matrix of domination."

[69] "Six Sisters," unpublished packet by Weatherwomen, n.d. [circa September 1973], pp. [i–iii], in author's files courtesy of Naomi Jaffe.

[70] Jacobs, *The Way the Wind Blew*, pp. 151–154.

[71] Several women underscored this point in separate interviews with me, especially Naomi Jaffe and Donna Willmott.

[72] John Cohen, "Introduction," in Sam Melville, *Letters From Attica*, pp. 50–52.

[73] Jane Alpert, "Introduction," in Sam Melville, *Letters From Attica*, pp. 1–43.

[74] Quoted in Jane Alpert, *Growing Up Underground*, pp. 343–347; Roxanne Dunbar-Ortiz, *Outlaw Woman*, pp. 397–398. For the death toll, see Wicker, *A Time to Die*, p. 381.

[75] Alpert's letter can be found online through Duke University at: http://scriptorium. lib.duke.edu/wlm/mother/.

[76] Women of the Weather Underground, "A Collective Letter to the Women's Movement," in Raskin, ed., *Weather Eye*, pp. 68–79. The communiqué said that the Weather Underground was now a feminist organization, but there was no sense of what that meant in terms of the organization's politics or practice.

[77] This quote comes from an internal document written by an anonymous Weatherwoman or women, entitled "After the Tempest," p. 2. There is no date given, but it is circa fall 1973.

[78] Alpert, *Growing Up Underground*, p. 346, Rudd, unpublished manuscript, pp. 331–332.

[79] Rudd, unpublished manuscript, pp. 332–333.

[80] Moylan was older than most of the group, and her religious beliefs likely added a further troubling divide. She was underground for ten years, eventually surfacing and serving a year and a half in prison for the Catonsville action. According to a friend, she had apparently become an alcoholic while underground. She passed away in 1995. See Rosemary Radford Ruether, "To Mary Moylan, Another Casualty of War," in *National Catholic Reporter*, November 10, 1995. Available at http://www.findarticles.com/p/articles/mi_m1141/is_n4_v32/ai_17883936. Moylan's letter to Alpert is printed in Raskin, ed., *Weather Eye*, pp. 80–83.

[81] Weather Underground, "Dear Mrs. Bacon," in Liberated Guardian, ed., *Outlaws of Amerika*, pp. 45–46. This quote is from p. 46. Some now question the precedent established through writing and publishing such a letter. Scott Braley says that it was a bad idea, given that it could create the public impression that unless Weather wrote a letter each time the government harassed somebody, it could lead to the presumption of guilt.

[82] Unless otherwise noted, the rest of the information about this communiqué comes from Weather Underground, "Common Victories," printed in Raskin, ed., *Weather Eye*, pp. 54–66.

[83] Abbie Hoffman, *The Autobiography of Abbie Hoffman*, pp. 249–250.

[84] Raskin, "Introduction," p. 9.

[85] Howie Machtinger, "A Letter From Howard Machtinger," in Raskin, ed., *Weather Eye*, p. 90.

[86] Weather Underground, "The Symbionese Liberation Army: Patty Hearst Kidnapping," in Raskin, ed., *Weather Eye*, p. 96.

[87] Ibid., pp. 92, 94.

[88] Ibid., p. 92.

[89] Ibid., pp. 94–95. For a case study of how the mainstream media elevated the moderate alternative in the antiwar movement, see Todd Gitlin, *The Whole World is Watching: Mass Media in the Making and Unmaking of the New Left*, pp. 205–232.

[90] Roxanne Runbar-Ortiz, *Outlaw Woman*, p. 396.

[91] Raskin, "Chronology," in *Weather Eye*, p. 15.

[92] Unless otherwise noted, information in this and the next three paragraphs comes from or is quoted in the "Weather Underground Bombs Gulf Oil" communiqué, June 13, 1974. From Tamiment archives.

[93] Jacobs, *The Way the Wind Blew*, p. 158.

[94] Mahmood Mamdani, *Good Muslim, Bad Muslim: America, the Cold War, and the Roots of Terror*, pp. 77–94.

CHAPTER EIGHT
PAGES: 183-197

[1] David Gilbert, interview for the Columbia Oral History Research Office, pp. 349–350.

[2] Bill Ayers, *Fugitive Days*, p. 233.

[3] Ron Jacobs, *The Way The Wind Blew*, p. 160.

[4] Weather Underground, *Prairie Fire: The Politics of Revolutionary Anti-Imperialism*, p. [x].

[5] Thai Jones, *A Radical Line*, p. 238.

[6] Donna Willmott, interview with the author, June 4, 2004.

[7] Jones, *A Radical Line*, p. 249, gives the location of the school.

[8] Ayers, *Fugitive Days*, p. 232.

[9] Ibid.

[10] Ibid.; Scott Braley, interview with the author, June 7, 2004; Naomi Jaffe, interview with the author, June 19, 2004.

[11] Weather Underground, *Prairie Fire*, pp. [iii–iv].

[12] Ibid., pp. [v–vi].

[13] Ibid., p. [vi].

[14] Weather Underground, *Prairie Fire*, pp. 1, 4–5.

[15] Ibid., pp. 7–8. Some of the other books that view 1968 as a turning point include Tariq Ali and Susan Watkins, *1968: Marching in the Streets*; Max Elbaum, *Revolution in the Air*; and George Katsiaficas, *The Imagination of the New Left: A Global Analysis of 1968*.

[16] Weather Underground, *Prairie Fire*, p. 10.

[17] Ibid., p. 13.

[18] Ibid., p. 40; Mahmood Mamdani, *Good Muslim, Bad Muslim*; William Blum, *Killing Hope: U.S. Military and C.I.A. Interventions Since World War II*; David Gilbert, Columbia interview, p. 354.

[19] Maureen Dowd, "War Introduces a Tougher Bush to Nation," in *New York Times*, March 2, 1991, p. 2.

[20] David Gilbert, conversation with the author, March 19, 2005.

[21] Max Elbaum covers the impact of the Sino-Soviet split and its effect on the party-building groups in *Revolution in the Air*, pp. 53–54, 130–131, 208–211.

[22] Weather Underground, *Prairie Fire*, pp. 79–108.

[23] Ibid., pp. 109–138.

[24] Ibid., pp. 141–142.

[25] Ibid., p. 146.

[26] David Gilbert, conversation with the author, March 19, 2005.

[27] Jeremy Varon, e-mail to the author, August 11, 2002.

[28] Rudd, unpublished manuscript, pp. 343–344.

[29] Jones, *A Radical Line*, p. 238.

[30] Revolutionary Committee, "Criticism of the Central Committee," in John Brown Book Club, ed., *The Split of the Weather Underground*, p. 26.

[31] Weather Underground, "Rockefeller and the Drug Law," in Raskin, ed., *Weather Eye*, pp. 106–107.

[32] Raskin, "Introduction," in *Weather Eye*, pp. 10–11.

[33] Weather Underground, "The Symbionese Liberation Army: Patty Hearst Kidnapping," in Raskin, ed., *Weather Eye*, p. 92.

[34] Naomi Jaffe, "Criticism of Prairie Fire," unpublished paper in author's files.

[35] Several Weatherpeople raised this critique with me in interviews, including Scott Braley, Naomi Jaffe, and Donna Willmott.

[36] David Gilbert, letter to the author, May 14, 2004.

CHAPTER NINE
PAGES: 199-223

[1] David Gilbert, interview for the Columbia Oral History Research Office, p. 370.

[2] Unless otherwise noted, the rest of the information in this paragraph comes from or is quoted in the "Weather Underground Organization Bombs Anaconda, Oakland, California" communiqué. From Tamiment archives.

[3] See, for instance, Kevin Danaher, *Corporations Are Gonna Get Your Mama: Globalization and the Downsizing of the American Dream*, or Michael Hardt and Antonio Negri, *Empire*.

[4] Author's interviews with Judith Mirkinson and Susan Rosenberg were instructive on the transition from PFDC to PFOC. See also Laura Whitehorn, interview with Nicole Kief, p. 29.

[5] Sharon Martinas, conversation with the author, June 5, 2004.

[6] For more on the Steins, see Thai Jones, *A Radical Line*. Jones is the son of Eleanor Stein and Jeff Jones.

[7] Ron Jacobs, *The Way the Wind Blew*, pp. 174–176, 185. Judith Mirkinson, interview with the author, June 6, 2004; Laura Whitehorn, interview with the author, March 21, 2004.

[8] News of the bombing is printed as an announcement in *Osawatomie*, no. 1, spring 1975, p. 30. There is no headline or byline for this story.

[9] Quoted in Akinyele Omowale Umoja, "Repression Breeds Resistance," in Kathleen Cleaver and George Katsiaticas, eds., *Liberation, Imagination, and the Black Panther Party*, pp. 12–14.

[10] Peter Matthiessen, *In the Spirit of Crazy Horse: The Story of Leonard Peltier and the FBI's War on the American Indian Movement* covers AIM in detail. Of the four people indicted for the 1975 shootout, one was let go for lack of evidence, two were acquitted on the grounds of self-defense, and Peltier was convicted. Leonard Peltier went underground after the shootout but was captured in Canada and convicted under questionable circumstances.

[11] For more on the Puerto Rican movement in the 1970s, see Andrés Torres and José E. Velázquez, eds., *The Puerto Rican Movement: Voices from the Diaspora*; Ronald Fernandez, *Prisoners of Colonialism: The Struggle for Justice in Puerto Rico*; and the pamphlet edited by Movimiento de Liberacion Nacional, *Toward People's War for Independence and Socialism in Puerto Rico: In Defense of Armed Struggle*. For more on the BLA, see Akinyele Umoja, "Repression Breeds Resistance" in Kathleen Cleaver and George Katsiaficas, eds., *Liberation, Imagination, and the Black Panther Party*, pp. 3–19; and Jalil Muntaqim, *On the Black Liberation Army*.

[12] Becky Thompson, *A Promise and a Way of Life: White Antiracist Activism*, presents a useful summary of multiracial feminism, pp. 143–170. See also Ruth Rosen, *The World Split Wide Open: How the Modern Women's Movement Changed America*, pp. 263–290.

[13] Quoted in *Scanlan's*, January 1971, p. 12.

[14] Quoted in Resistance in Brooklyn, ed., *John Brown 2000: U.S. Political Prisoner/ POW Writings on the 200th Birthday of John Brown and Nat Turner*, p. 56.

[15] For more about John Brown, see W.E.B. Du Bois, *John Brown*; Dan Berger, "Refusing to Surrender: John Brown and White Anti-Racist Struggle" in *ONWARD* vol. 2, iss. 4, pp. 13, 20; and James Loewen, *Lies My Teacher Told Me: Everything Your American History Textbook Got Wrong*, pp. 171–200. Loewen says that Brown was labeled

mentally imbalanced only *after* he died. For racism in the abolitionist movement, see Robert Allen, *Reluctant Reformers: Racism and Social Reform Movements in the United States*, pp. 11–48.

[16] J.K. Hudson quoted in William Elsey Connelley, *John Brown,* p. 364.

[17] Weather Underground, *Prairie Fire*, p. 56.

[18] Jeff Jones and Cathy Wilkerson in *Underground,* Emile de Antonio, Mary Lampson, and Haskell Wexler: 1975 (documentary).

[19] See, for instance, the "Who We Are" box in *Osawatomie* no. 1, spring 1975, p. 2.

[20] See "Who We Are" box in *Osawatomie*, no. 1, spring 1975, p. 2.

[21] Rudd, unpublished manuscript, p. 350.

[22] All of the quotes in the rest of this paragraph come from *Osawatomie* no. 2, summer 1975, p. 2.

[23] See "Who We Are" box in *Osawatomie* vol. 2, no. 2, June–July 1976, p. 27.

[24] There were—in places such as California, Michigan, North Carolina, and Washington—confrontational struggles by workers in the 1970s. But a movement of U.S. workers as a whole was not unified politically or tactically, nor did such confrontations necessarily translate into building such a radical and unified labor movement.

[25] The rest of this paragraph comes from or is quoted in "Where We Stand: Don't Mourn, Organize!" in *Osawatomie* no. 1, spring 1975. Although the article goes from pp. 3–5, most of the information here comes from p. 5.

[26] See, for instance, the "Who We Are" box in *Osawatomie* no. 2, summer 1975, p. 2.

[27] For more on Lenin's view of the press, see Paul Le Blanc, *Lenin and the Revolutionary Party,* pp. 35–39, 68–76, 83–94. For more on the New Communist Movement's use of media, also in Leninist terms, see Max Elbaum, *Revolution in the Air.*

[28] No author, "A Mighty Army: An Investigation of Women Workers" in *Osawatomie* no. 2, summer 1975, pp. 6–13.

[29] No author, "The War Comes Home: Roots of the Economic Crisis," in *Osawatomie* no. 1, spring 1975, pp. 18–24.

[30] No author, "Break the Chains," in *Osawatomie* no. 3, autumn 1975, pp. 7–13.

[31] The six Puerto Rican political prisoners were Oscar Collazo, Lolita Lebrón, Irving Flores, Andrés Figueroa Cordero, Rafael Cancel Miranda, and Carlos Feliciano. Collazo was in prison for attempting to shoot Harry Truman. Lebron, Flores, Figueroa Cordero, and Miranda were arrested for shooting in the U.S. Congress. Feliciano was arrested on bombing charges but convicted on lesser charges. Popular movements succeeded in freeing these prisoners in 1979. See *Osawatomie* no. 1, spring 1975, pp. 16–17. For more on these prisoners, see Ronald Fernandez, *Prisoners of Colonialism: The Struggle for Justice in Puerto Rico.* The Douglass centerfold appears in *Osawatomie* vol. 2, no. 2, (June–July 1976), pp. 14–15.

[32] Quoted in Elbaum, *Revolution in the Air*, p. 203.

[33] Bernardine Dohrn, "An Open Letter to U.S. Workers," in *Osawatomie* vol. 2, no. 1 (April–May 1976), p. 11.

[34] For more on the PSP, see José E. Velázquez, "Coming Full Circle: The Puerto Rican Socialist Party, U.S. Branch," in Torres and Velázquez, eds., *The Puerto Rican Movement: Voices from the Diaspora*, pp. 48–68.

[35] No author, "Victory to the Ponce Cement Strike," in *Osawatomie* no. 2, summer 1975, p. 20.

[36] Bernardine Dohrn, "Armed Struggle and the SLA," in *Osawatomie* no. 4, winter 1975–1976, pp. 30–31. All other quotes in this paragraph come from this article.

[37] Celia Sojourn and Billy Ayers, *Politics in Command*, pamphlet from Tamiment archives. For a critique of the WUO's line of thinking, see E. Tani and Kae Sera, *False Nationalism, False Internationalism: Class Contradictions in the Armed Struggle*, pp. 137–161.

[38] David Gilbert, letter to the author, May 14, 2004.

[39] In retrospect, though, Braley says it shouldn't have been so shocking because by 1976, "we had spent two solid years moving in that direction.... It was also a gradual period of losing our bearings on the question of national liberation."

[40] Author's interviews and conversations with Max Elbaum, David Gilbert, Judith Mirkinson, and Laura Whitehorn all underscored this point.

[41] Mark Rudd, unpublished manuscript, p. 361.

[42] Jones, *A Radical Line*, pp. 247–252.

[43] Ronald P. Formisano, *Boston Against Busing: Race, Class, and Ethnicity in the 1960s and 1970s*.

[44] "The Battle of Boston: An Investigation of ROAR," *Osawatomie*, no. 1, spring 1975, p. 8.

[45] Laura Whitehorn, Kief interview, pp. 32–34.

[46] Elbaum, *Revolution in the Air*, p. 190. More generally, see pp. 187–191.

[47] Revolutionary Committee, "Criticism of the Central Committee," in John Brown Book Club, ed., *The Split of the Weather Underground*, pp. 28, 31; and Bernardine Dohrn statement in ibid., pp. 33–34.

[48] Celia Sojourn, "The Women's Question is a Class Question," in *Osawatomie* no. 4, winter 1975–1976, pp. 3–5.

[49] Several internal (and largely untitled) documents written by anonymous women members of the Weather Underground in the author's files courtesy of Naomi Jaffe testify to this point.

[50] Rosen, *The World Split Open*, pp. 182–183. See also Angela Davis, "JoAnne [*sic*] Little: The Dialectics of Rape," in Joy James, ed., *The Angela Y. Davis Reader*, pp. 149–160.

[51] Susan Saxe, "Statement of Susan Saxe at Her Guilty Plea in Federal Court in Philadelphia on June 9, 1975," in Barbara Deming, *Remembering Who We Are*, pp. 201–204. See also Rosen, *The World Split Open*, pp. 248–249; and Thompson, *A Promise and a Way of Life*, p. 132.

[52] Bernardine Dohrn, "Our Class Stand," in *Osawatomie*, no. 3, autumn 1975, pp. 3–6.

[53] Randolph Lewis, *Emile de Antonio: Radical Filmmaker in Cold War America*, pp. 181, 183.

[54] Lewis, *Emile de Antonio*, pp. 188–194. Lewis says that the faces were more visible before de Antonio and Lampson "reshot [*sic*] the negative using [a] painted-over print." See also *Underground*.

[55] Ibid., pp. 195–196; Haskell Wexler, forward to *Emile de Antonio: A Reader*, edited by Douglas Kellner and Dan Streible, p. xii.

[56] Unless otherwise noted, material on the subpoena and reactions to it come from Lewis, *Emile de Antonio*, pp. 197–201.

[57] Wexler, "Forward" in Kellner and Streible, eds., *Emile de Antonio*, p. xii.

[58] Lewis, *Emile de Antonio*, p. 199.

[59] For more on reactions to the film, see Lewis, *Emile de Antonio*, pp. 201–208.

[60] Emile de Antonio and Jeff Jones letters, printed under the headline "Fighting for our Film," in *Osawatomie* no. 3, autumn 1975, pp. 16–17.

[61] Rudd, unpublished manuscript, p. 355.

[62] Unless otherwise noted, the rest of this paragraph comes from or is quoted on the final page of an unnumbered insert of letters compiled by the John Brown Book Club and printed in their edition of *Osawatomie* vol. 2, no. 1 (April–May 1976).

[63] Ayers, *Fugitive Days*, p. 282.

[64] This is a recurring theme in the criticisms of the Revolutionary Committee of the WUO, printed in John Brown Book Club, ed., *The Split of the Weather Underground Organization*, pp. 18–32.

[65] Author interviews with Judy Siff, Naomi Jaffe, and Robert Roth, respectively. Other members I spoke with echoed these critiques.

[66] Rudd, unpublished manuscript, p. 353.

CHAPTER TEN
PAGES: 225-243

[1] David Gilbert, "Criticize to Advance: Review of *False Nationalism, False Internationalism*," unpublished review in author's files (written circa 1986).

[2] The bank was owned by the same company that owned the cement plant against which workers in Puerto Rico were striking.

[3] According to the *New York Times*, the Kennecott bombing caused an estimated $40,000 to $50,000 in damage. UPI, "None Hurt as Blast in Utah Damages Kennecott Offices," in *New York Times*, September 5, 1975, p. 15. Although the Banco de Ponce action was covered in the newspapers, there was no estimate given as to how much damage the bomb at Rockefeller Center caused.

[4] The list of committees is reprinted in Western Goals, *Outlaws of Amerika: The Weather Underground Organization*, p. 30.

[5] Ibid., pp. 30–32.

[6] Thai Jones, *A Radical Line*, p. 250.

[7] Quoted in Ron Jacobs, *The Way The Wind Blew*, p. 172.

[8] Ibid.

[9] Some of these are discussed in Western Goals, *Outlaws of Amerika*, p. 28, and in Jacobs, *The Way the Wind Blew*, p. 173.

[10] David Gilbert, letter to author, April 5, 2003.

[11] Unnamed, unpublished packet on the Hard Times conference and the Central Committee authored by members of the organization, n.p., n.d. [circa September 1976], in author's files.

[12] Laura Whitehorn, interview with Nicole Kief, October 20, 2002, p. 31. More generally, see pp. 28–32.

[13] Billy Ayers and Joe Reed, "*Osawatomie* Goes Bimonthly," in *Osawatomie* vol. 2, no. 1 (April–May 1976), p. 2. The rest of this paragraph comes from or is quoted in this editorial. Both Ayers and Reed were members of the Central Committee; Reed was a pseudonym.

[14] Central Committee, Weather Underground Organization, "Anti-imperialism vs. opportunism: self-criticism," *Osawatomie* vol. 2, no. 2, p. 16.

[15] Prairie Fire Organizing Committee, Bay Area, "Class and Revolutionary Politics," in John Brown Book Club, ed., *The Split of the Weather Underground Organization*, p. 5.

[16] George Jackson Brigade, *Creating a Movement with Teeth: Communiqués of the George Jackson Brigade*, p. 34.

[17] "Open Letter to the Revolutionary Committee," in John Brown Book Club, ed., *The Split of the Weather Underground Organization*, pp. 41–42. This open letter is simply signed by "some Native American warriors."

[18] I'm grateful to Naomi Jaffe, Suzanne Ross, and Judy Siff for explaining this process to me in separate interviews.

[19] A transcript of the letter appeared along with the Revolutionary Committee's criticism of the Central Committee. They were first published in the radical magazine *Takeover* and captured the attention of the *New York Times*, who covered the story. See John Kifner, "Weather Underground Splits Up Over Plan to Come Into the Open," in *New York Times*, January 18, 1977, p. 12.

[20] Revolutionary Committee, "Criticism of the Central Committee," in John Brown Book Club, ed., *The Split of the Weather Underground Organization*, pp. 25–32.

[21] Suzanne Ross, interview with the author, June 27, 2004; Judy Siff, interview with the author, June 7, 2004.

[22] David Gilbert, interviews with the author, July 18 and July 19, 2002. Most of the couples did get back together. In the tabloid and gossipy books to come out about the WUO since the Brink's arrests, reporters have twisted this story to say that all the men left all the women, perhaps as "proof" of their cold-heartedness. For examples of this, see Susan Braudy, *Family Circle: The Boudins and the Aristocracy of the Left*, p. 272; and John Castellucci, *The Big Dance: The Untold Story of Weatherman Kathy Boudin and the Terrorist Family that Committed the Brink's Robbery Murders*, pp. 126–133.

[23] Robert Roth, interview with the author, June 6, 2004. Scott Braley, David Gilbert, and Naomi Jaffe also repeated similar claims in interviews with me.

[24] This re-creation draws heavily from my interview with Judy Siff, June 7, 2004.

[25] Castellucci, *The Big Dance*, pp. 129–131; Judy Siff, interview with the author, June 7, 2004.

[26] Jacobs, *The Way the Wind Blew*, p. 179, and author's interviews with David Gilbert, July 18 and July 19, 2002, and Judy Siff, June 7, 2004.

[27] Revolutionary Committee, "Criticism of the Central Committee," in John Brown Book Club, ed., *The Split of the Weather Underground Organization*, pp. 31–32.

[28] Jeremy Varon, e-mail to the author, August 11, 2002.

[29] David Gilbert, letter to the author, January 16, 2003. Jeff Jones, whose leadership was particularly criticized in the pamphlet, said some of the criticisms (about the group's retreat from armed work, for instance) were based in fact, even if he thinks that decisions such as inversion, sharply criticized in the pamphlet, were not mistaken.

[30] John Brown Book Club, "Introduction," in John Brown Book Club, ed., *The Split of the Weather Underground Organization*, p. 4.

[31] Nancy Borman, "W.U.O. Blows Self Up!" in New Yippie Book Collective, ed., *Blacklisted News, Secret Histories: From Chicago to 1984*, pp. 115–116.

[32] Rob McBride, interview with the author, June 4, 2002.

[33] Author's interview with Susan Rosenberg, July 8, 2005, was particularly instructive in talking about the PFOC/May 19th split. Author's interviews with Judith Mirkinson and Robert Roth were also useful in this regard.

[34] Laura Whitehorn, interview with the author, March 21, 2004.

[35] May 19th Communist Organization, *Principles of the May 19th Communist Organization*, p. 12.

[36] Ward Churchill and Jim Vander Wall, *The COINTELPRO Papers*, pp. 315, 414.

[37] Judith Mirkinson, interview with the author, June 6, 2004. No book-length study of PFOC exists to date.

[38] My interviews with Scott Braley, David Gilbert, Suzanne Ross, Judy Siff, and Donna Willmott all underscored this point.

[39] Jacobs, *The Way the Wind Blew*, p. 201.

[40] Mark Rudd's unpublished manuscript presents a detailed view of his work after surfacing in 1977, pp. 384–392. My individual interviews with people such as Scott Braley, Suzanne Ross, and Robert Roth yielded similar information.

[41] Jacobs, *The Way the Wind Blew*, pp. 180–186.

[42] Ibid., p. 184; Cathy Wilkerson, interview with the author, July 16, 2004. Dohrn later served seven months for refusing to cooperate with a grand jury investigating the Brink's case.

[43] Rudd, unpublished manuscript, p. 391.

[44] Unless otherwise noted, the information in this paragraph about Gilbert's surfacing comes from the David Gilbert Columbia interview, pp. 386–389, 405–409.

[45] David Gilbert interview with Sam Green and Bill Siegel for *Weather Underground*, part I, p. 7, n.d. [circa 1998]. Transcript in author's files, courtesy of Sam Green.

CHAPTER ELEVEN
PAGES: 245-265

[1] David Gilbert, *No Surrender: Writings from an Anti-Imperialist Political Prisoner*, p. 27. The quote is from Gilbert's opening statement to court on September 13, 1982.

[2] Ronald Fernandez, *Prisoners of Colonialism: The Struggle for Justice in Puerto Rico*, p. 206. Communiqués from 1974 to 1978 are gathered in Movimiento de Liberacion Nacional et al., *Toward People's War for Independence and Socialism in Puerto Rico: In Defense of Armed Struggle*.

[3] Akinyele Omowale Umoja, "Repression Breeds Resistance: The Black Liberation Army and the Radical Legacy of the Black Panther Party," in Kathleen Cleaver and George Katsiaficas, eds., *Liberation, Imagination, and the Black Panther Party*, pp. 13–15.

[4] Jalil Muntaqim, *On the Black Liberation Army*, pp. 12–14.

[5] Robert Hanley, "Miss Chesimard Flees Jersey Prison, Helped by 3 Armed Visitors," in *New York Times*, November 3, 1979.

[6] Evelyn Williams, *Inadmissible Evidence: The Story of the African-American Trial Lawyer who Defended the Black Liberation Army*, p. 171. In addition to being her attorney, Williams is also Shakur's aunt.

[7] Michael L. Clemons and Charles E. Jones, "Global Solidarity: The Black Panther Party in the International Arena," in in Kathleen Cleaver and George Katsiaficas, eds., *Liberation, Imagination, and the Black Panther Party*, p. 38.

[8] Williams, *Inadmissible Evidence*, pp. 3–7.

[9] Umoja, "Repression Breeds Resistance," p. 13.

[10] Assata Shakur, *Assata: A Memoir*, describes the series of trials, as does Evelyn Williams, *Inadmissible Evidence*.

[11] Michael Ratner, "Immoral Bounty for Assata," in *Covert Action Quarterly* 65 (Fall 1998).

[12] Williams, *Inadmissible Evidence*, p. 179.

[13] Sheila Rule, "On Solidarity Day, Blacks Say 'We Are Still Slaves,'" in *New York Times*, November 6, 1981.

[14] Quoted in Umoja, "Repression Breeds Resistance," p. 15.

[15] Josh Barbanel, "3 Killed in Armored Car Holdup," *New York Times*, October 21, 1981.

[16] A BLA communiqué released on November 5, 1981, said the BLA has "never shot or killed anyone with their hands in the air surrendering." See BLA, "On the Strategic Alliance of the Armed Military Forces of the Revolutionary Nationalist and Anti-Imperialist Movement," in author's files. In his trial statements (see the following citation), Balagoon talks at length about how the BLA viewed armed robberies.

[17] Kuwasi Balagoon, *Kuwasi Balagoon: A Soldier's Story: Writings by a Revolutionary New Afrikan Anarchist*, pp. 59–60.

[18] John Castellucci, *The Big Dance: The Untold Story of Weatherman Kathy Boudin and the Terrorist Family that Committed the Brink's Robbery Murders*, pp. 18–21.

[19] Ibid., pp. 26–27.

[20] Ibid., pp. 1–3, 16–20.

[21] Ibid., p. 10.

[22] Colin Campbell, "Samuel Brown: A Past Defined By Police Files," in *New York Times*, October 23, 1981.

[23] Robert McFadden, "Man Killed in Queens Car Chase; Plate Tied to Armored Car Gang," in *New York Times*, October 24, 1981.

[24] Robert Service, *Joseph Stalin: A Biography*; Nelson Mandela, *Long Walk to Freedom: The Autobiography of Nelson Mandela*. More generally, see Eric Hobsbawm, *Bandits*, pp. 118–137.

[25] Bob Feldman, "Beyond Brinks: David Gilbert Talks About The Robbery, the Underground, the Struggle," *Columbia Daily Spectator*, April 2, 1985.

[26] Ibid.

[27] Castellucci, *The Big Dance*, pp. 222–224. See also Bob Feldman, "Beyond Brinks."

[28] Castellucci, *The Big Dance*, p. 223.

[29] Bob Feldman, "Civil Liberties and the 1981 Brink's Case," *Downtown*, October 23, 1991.

[30] New York State Task Force on Political Prisoners, "Clemency Petition," p. 19; Bob Feldman, "Beyond Brinks"; and Williams, *Inadmissible Evidence*, pp. 178–179.

[31] Umoja, "Repression Breeds Resistance," p. 17.

[32] Feldman, "Civil Liberties and the 1981 Brink's Case."

[33] J. Sakai, "A Few Words on the Brinks Trial," in Balagoon, *Kuwasi Balagoon: A Soldiers Story*, pp. 21–23. More generally, see the pamphlet *Sundiata Acoli's Testimony at the Brinks Trial*. My interview with Jeff Jones (June 25, 2004) was also helpful in this regard, as was Ward Churchill and Jim Vander Wall, *The COINTELPRO Papers*, pp. 309–312.

[34] Jeff Jones, interview with the author, June 25, 2004; Thai Jones, *A Radical Line: From the Labor Movement to the Weather Underground, One Family's Century of Conscience*, pp. 272–278.

[35] Fernandez, *Prisoners of Colonialism*, covers the FALN's founding and actions. Some primary materials are gathered in Movimiento de Liberacion Nacional et al., *Toward People's War for Independence and Socialism in Puerto Rico*.

[36] For more on *Los Macheteros*, see Fernandez, *Prisoners of Colonialism*, pp. 227–263. On September 23, 2005, the FBI shot the group's founder, Filiberto Ojeda Rios, 72, to death at his home in Puerto Rico; see Abby Goodnough, "Killing of Militant Raises Ire in Puerto Rico," *New York Times*, September 28, 2005. For more on the United Freedom Front and the other groups arrested, see Churchill and Vander Wall, *The COINTELPRO Papers*, pp. 313–318. See also Committee to Fight Repression, ed., *Build a Revolutionary Resistance Movement! Communiqués from the North American Armed Clandestine Movement, 1982–1985*.

[37] Churchill and Vander Wall, *The COINTELPRO Papers*, pp. 312–319; Ray Luc Levasseur, *Trial Statements of Ray Luc Levasseur*. (An excerpt of one of Levasseur's statements, "On Trial," can be found in Joy James, ed., *Imprisoned Intellectuals*, pp. 227–237.)

[38] Fernandez, *Prisoners of Colonialism*, pp. 227–263.

[39] In 2005, a Philadelphia jury awarded twenty-four homeowners whose homes were destroyed a $12 million settlement for the bombing and the poor reconstruction of the block by the city. Martha T. Moore, "1985 Bombing in Philadelphia Still Unsettled," in *USA Today*, May 12, 2005. For more on the bombing, see MOVE, *25 Years on the MOVE*.

[40] Mahmood Mamdani, *Good Muslim, Bad Muslim: America, the Cold War, and the Roots of Terror*, covers the 1980s U.S. foreign policy in detail. See also Noam Chomsky, *Hegemony or Survival: America's Quest for Global Dominance*, pp. 73–75; Howard Zinn, *A People's History of the United States*, pp. 551–600.

[41] Esperanza Martell, interview with the author, May 29, 2004. I am especially grateful to Martell for framing Brink's in the context of political arrests, trials, and prisoner support work of the time.

[42] Castellucci, *The Big Dance*, pp. 29–30.

[43] "Memorandum Opinion and Order," *United States v. Ferguson*, United States Court of Appeals for the Second Circuit, 758 F.2d 843, March 28, 1985.

[44] David Gilbert, interview with the author, August 1, 2003; Balagoon, *Kuwasi Balagoon*, pp. 27–28.

[45] Attorney Susan Tipograph, quoted in Feldman, "Civil Liberties and the 1981 Brinks Case." In the same article, Tipograph mentions receiving several death threats for her role as counsel in the case.

[46] Description of the security measures at the trial comes from James Feron, "Hearings Begin in Brink's Case Amid Protests," *New York Times*, September 14, 1982. Unless otherwise noted, the rest of this paragraph comes from this article.

[47] Report of the New York State Task Force on Political Prisoners, p. 30.

[48] Edward Hudson, "Miss Boudin and Miss Clark Refuse to Plead to Charges," *New York Times*, November 25, 1981.

[49] Feron, "Hearings Begin in Brink's Case Amid Protests," *New York Times*, September 14, 1982.

[50] Castellucci, *The Big Dance*, pp. 283–284.

[51] Joyce Wadler, "Brink's Holdup Hearing Becomes a Free-for-All," in *Washington Post*, September 21, 1982.

[52] David Gilbert, Sam Green interview part I, pp. 9–10.

[53] Balagoon's opening, closing, and sentencing statements are printed in *Kuwasi Balagoon: A Soldier's Story: Writings by a Revolutionary New Afrikan Anarchist.*

[54] This document may be found online at www.un.org/documents/ga/res/32/ares32r122.pdf.

[55] This document may be found online at http://www.ohchr.org/english/law/prisonerwar.htm.

[56] Marilyn Buck, "The Struggle for Status Under International Law: U.S. Political Prisoners and the Political Offense Exception to Extradition," in Joy James, ed., *Imprisoned Intellectuals*, pp. 203–204.

[57] Julio Rosado, "Political Prisoners in the United States," in Ward Churchill and Jim Vander Wall, eds., *Cages of Steel*, pp. 382–283.

[58] I.F. Stone, "Where the Fuse on that Dynamite Leads," in Harold Jacobs, ed., *Weatherman*, p. 491.

[59] Nelson Mandela has been involved in the African National Congress since 1942. In 1960, the apartheid rulers of South Africa outlawed the ANC, and Mandela became the commander in chief of its armed unit, Umkhonto we Sizwe. He was a political prisoner from 1962 until 1990 on Robben Island, a maximum-security prison on an island off

the coast of South Africa. He was given a life sentence for violating racist apartheid laws prohibiting travel or organizing by Africans. His release came after a long international campaign against apartheid. For more, see Nelson Mandela, *The Struggle is My Life* or *Long Walk to Freedom*.

[60] Resolution 32/122, adopted by the General Assembly 105th plenary meeting, December 16, 1977. Available from www.un.org/documents/ga/res/32/ares32r122.pdf.

[61] Ibid.

[62] James Forman, *The Making of Black Revolutionaries*, p. 524.

[63] Quoted in Abu-Jamal, *We Want Freedom*, p. 100.

[64] Umoja, "Repression Breeds Resistance," p. 14.

[65] Balagoon, *Kuwasi Balagoon*, p. 50.

[66] Ibid., p. 53.

[67] Ibid., p. 27.

[68] See, for example, Leslie Maitland, "Police Find History of Arrests," *New York Times*, October 24, 1981.

[69] Alan Finder and Richard Levine, "'War' Is Not a Defense, Brink's Jurors Decide," in *New York Times*, September 18, 1983.

[70] Castellucci, *The Big Dance*, p. 284.

[71] Gilbert was in the U-Haul truck which met the Black radicals at a different location than Nanuet Mall, where the expropriation attempt occurred.

[72] Robert Hanley, "State Jury Finds 3 Radicals Guilty in Brink's Killings," *New York Times*, September 15, 1983.

[73] Castellucci, *The Big Dance*, pp. 226–228. Castellucci attributes this not to racism per se but sloppy investigations and politicking by DA Gribetz, who had ambitions to run for office and needed to satisfy Nyack's call for blood.

[74] "Memorandum Opinion and Order," *Mutulu Shakur and Marilyn Buck v. United States of America*. U.S. District Court for the Southern District of New York, 32 F. Supp. 2d 651, January 13, 1999.

[75] Castellucci, *The Big Dance*, p. 273.

[76] It is worth noting that Odinga was found innocent of the more substantial parts of the indictment: those involving "bank robbery, armed bank robbery, and murder in the commission" of two robberies. He was convicted of RICO conspiracy and a general count of violating RICO laws. Baraldini was only indicted on these two counts. "Memorandum Opinion and Order," *United States v. Mutulu Shakur*, United States District Court for the Southern District of New York, 656 F. Supp. 241, February 20, 1987.

[77] Castellucci, *The Big Dance*, pp. 273–281.

[78] "Memorandum Opinion and Order," *Mutulu Shakur and Marilyn Buck v. United States of America*. U.S. District Court for the Southern District of New York, 32 F. Supp. 2d 651, January 13, 1999.

[79] Buck, "The Struggle for Status Under International Law," pp. 201–215.

[80] "Mutulu Shakur: New Afrikan Political Prisoner," in CEML, ed., *Can't Jail the Spirit*, pp. 106–109; "Marilyn Buck: Anti-Imperialist Political Prisoner," in CEML, ed., *Can't Jail the Spirit*, pp. 167–169.

[81] "Memorandum Opinion and Order," *United States of America v. Mutulu Shakur, Sekou Odinga, Cecil Ferguson, Edward Lawrence Joseph, William Johnson, Silvia Baraldini, Susan Rosenberg, Cheri Dalton, Iliana Robinson, Nilse Cobeo, and Alan Berkman*. United States District Court for the Southern District of New York, 565 F. Supp. 123, 560 F. Supp. 313, March 28, 1983. The court, however, did not describe Brown's treatment as torture, nor did they bar his testimony despite finding him untrustworthy and unpredictable.

[82] "Mutulu Shakur" in CEML, ed., *Can't Jail the Spirit*, pp. 106–107. Castellucci, *The Big Dance*, pp. 45–48.

[83] "Memorandum Opinion and Order," *United States of America v. Mutulu Shakur et al.* United States District Court for the Southern District of New York, 565 F. Supp. 123, June 21, 1983.

[84] "Memorandum Opinion and Order," *United States of America v. Mutulu Shakur et al.* United States District Court for the Southern District of New York, 560 F. Supp. 318, March 28, 1983.

[85] Castellucci, *The Big Dance*, p. 275.

[86] Ibid., pp. 264–265.

[87] Arnold H. Lubasch, "Brink's Defendant Questions Witness," *New York Times*, May 11, 1983.

[88] Arnold H. Lubasch, "Brink's Witness Tells of Robbery in Bronx in 1981," *New York Times*, May 5, 1983.

[89] Arnold H. Lubasch, "Killer Says He Helped in Chesimard's Escape," *New York Times*, December 2, 1987.

[90] Ibid.

[91] David Gilbert, "To the Berkshire Forum," July 19, 1989. In author's files courtesy of Bob Feldman.

[92] Quoted in Churchill and Vander Wall, *The COINTELPRO Papers*, p. 310.

[93] Christian Parenti, *Lockdown America: Police and Prisons in an Age of Crisis*.

[94] Although it is but one example of racism in the war on drugs, racism is especially apparent in the arrest and sentencing disparity. While whites account for approximately 76 percent of all drug users, African Americans are arrested, tried, and convicted on drug charges far

outside their proportion to drug users. Though crack (a drug used presumably more by people of color) and powdered cocaine (a drug used presumably more by whites) come from the same substance, the sentences for each differ drastically. Law professor Kenneth Nunn observes, "[a] person sentenced with intent to distribute a given amount of crack cocaine receives the same sentence as someone who possessed one hundred times as much powder cocaine." Kenneth Nunn, "Race, Crime and the Pool of Surplus Criminality: Or Why the 'War on Drugs' Was a 'War on Blacks,'" in *The Journal of Gender, Race, & Justice*, volume 6, no. 2, p. 396. It bears noting that in other industrialized countries, such as Canada, England, and the Netherlands, drug laws are much more liberalized than in the United States. See Eric Schlosser, "The World: Up in Smoke; The U.S. Bucks a Trend on Marijuana Laws," *New York Times*, June 1, 2003.

[95] Buck, "The Struggle for Status Under International Law," p. 203.

[96] For more information on these prisoners and their experiences in super-max prisons and control units, see their respective biographies in CEML, ed., *Can't Jail the Spirit: Biographies of U.S. Political Prisoners.*

[97] Susan Rosenberg, "Reflections on Being Buried Alive," in Churchill and Vander Wall, ed., *Cages of Steel*, p. 128.

[98] Ibid. Baraldini was a May 19th Communist Organization activist convicted in the first federal RICO trial after Brink's. She has since been transferred back to her native Italy, following a lengthy campaign for her return. She remains incarcerated there. Rosenberg was convicted in the mid-1980s for her role with the Armed Resistance Unit/Red Guerrilla Resistance, a white anti-imperialist underground group similar to the WUO in its targets and its restraint from injuring people. She was pardoned by President Clinton on his last day in office. Torres was convicted of seditious conspiracy for her alleged membership in the Puerto Rican underground group, the FALN. She was pardoned with ten of her codefendants in 1999.

[99] Korn, "Excerpts from—Report on the Effects of Confinement in the Lexington High Security Unit," in Churchill and Vander Wall, eds., *Cages of Steel*, pp. 123–127.

[100] Excerpts from the tribunal's findings are published in Churchill and Vander Wall, *Cages of Steel*, pp. 403–413. These specific incidents are covered on pp. 409–410.

[101] For more on this case, see Elbaum, *Revolution in the Air*, pp. 235–236 or Mab Segrest, *Memoir of a Race Traitor*, pp. 5–9, 12, 51, 75–76, 120–121. The Klansmen received significant support from local police in planning their assassinations—two police agents had infiltrated the group prior to the murders—which could account for the lack of convictions in the case.

[102] Whitehorn, "Preventive Detention: A Prevention of Human Rights?" in Churchill and Vander Wall, eds., *Cages of Steel*, p. 368.

[103] Julio Rosado, "Political Prisoners in the United States—the Puerto Rican Charade," in Churchill and Vander Wall, eds., *Cages of Steel*, pp. 382–385.

[104] Ibid., p. 385.

[105] Black Liberation Army, "On the Strategic Alliance of the Armed Military Forces of the Revolutionary Nationalist and Anti-Imperialist Movements," November 5, 1981, in author's files.

[106] M.A. Farber, "Changing Views of Brink's Case: Narcotics Allegations Emerge," in *New York Times*, March 7, 1983.

[107] David Gilbert, "*No Surrender* and the Losses of 10/20/81," November 25, 2004 statement in author's files.

[108] Marilyn Buck, David Gilbert, and Laura Whitehorn, *Enemies of the State: A Frank Discussion of Past Political Movements, Their Victories and Errors, and the Current Political Climate for Revolutionary Struggle Within the U.S.A.*, p. 35.

[109] Susan Braudy, *Family Circle: The Boudins and the Aristocracy of the Left*; John Castellucci, *The Big Dance: The Untold Story of Weatherman Kathy Boudin and the Terrorist Family that Committed the Brink's Robbery Murders*; Ellen Frankfort, *Kathy Boudin and the Dance of Death*. Each book has its own narrative format, but all follow the same formula. Braudy's book covers a wider time period than just the Brink's robbery and aftermath, though she does spend considerable time on it. Still, she does little more than repeat what Castellucci wrote almost two decades earlier. Frankfort's book is the least researched; it's a magazine journalist's attempts at psychoanalysis and capitalizing on the headlines. Castellucci's book has the most research, but he still conducts a pseudo-psychoanalysis in attempting to get into the heads of the people he writes about—most of whom he never interviewed. He thus presents his text as "the untold story," capturing the thoughts and feelings of those alleged to have participated. Yet he, for instance, details how Gilbert felt about parenting and other personal issues without ever having spoken to Gilbert or Boudin.

[110] Naomi Jaffe, letter to Chesa Boudin, August 21, 2003, in author's files, courtesy of Naomi Jaffe.

CHAPTER TWELVE
PAGES: 269-303

[1] David Gilbert, *SDS/WUO*, p. 23.

[2] See, for instance, Peter Blumberg and Dennis J. Opatrny. "S.F. Grand Jury Probing 1970s Police Murders," in *Daily Journal*, August 2, 2005; Sam Pazzano, "No Bail for '70s Fugitive; U.S. Wants Him in Cop Shooting," *Toronto Sun*, November 9, 2004, p. 26; Sam Stanton, "Olson Likely to Serve Longest SLA Sentence, Officials Say," *Sacramento Bee*, September 30, 2004, p. B2; Jeremy Varon, *Bringing The War Home*, p. 300. Author's conversation with Scott Braley, May 30, 2005, also underscored this point. See Abby Goodnough, "Killing of Militant Raises Ire in Puerto Rico," *New York Times*, September 28, 2005, for more on the FBI shooting death of *Los Macheteros* founder Filiberto Ojeda Rios.

[3] Immanuel Wallerstein, *The Decline of American Power*. For more on U.S. malfeasance in relating to these movements, see William Blum, *Killing Hope: U.S. Military and C.I.A. Interventions Since World War II*; and Mahmood Mamdani, *Good Muslim, Bad Muslim*. For the impact of global capitalism, see Kevin Danaher, *Fifty Years is Enough: The Case Against the World Bank and the International Monetary Fund*, or Michael Hardt and Antonio Negri, *Empire*.

[4] See Mamdani, *Good Muslim, Bad Muslim*; Tariq Ali, *Bush in Babylon: The Recolonisation of Iraq*; and Chip Berlet and Matthew Lyons, *Right-Wing Populism in America: Too Close for Comfort*. Violent right-wing movements include the World Church of the Creator, whose head, Matthew Hale, was recently imprisoned for conspiring to kill a judge; Eric Rudolph, who bombed the 1996 Olympics in Atlanta, populated abortion clinics, and gay nightclubs; and the Minutemen, an anti-immigrant vigilante group of whites in the U.S. Southwest.

[5] Lisa Duggan, *Twilight of Equality: Neoliberalism, Cultural Politics, and the Attack on Democracy*.

[6] Ibid. See also Thomas Frank, *What's the Matter with Kansas? How Conservatives Won the Heart of Middle America*; Christian Parenti, *Lockdown America: Police and Prisons in an Age of Crisis*; and Mamdani, *Good Muslim, Bad Muslim*.

[7] Research Unit on Political Economy, *Behind the Invasion of Iraq*, pp. 44–47.

[8] Blum, *Killing Hope*, details these and other interventions, military operations, and weapons contributions overseas.

[9] Theories and theorists of globalization are widespread. Among the more notable are Michael Hardt and Antonio Negri, *Empire*; Michael Hardt and Antonio Negri, *Multitude*; William K. Tabb, *The Amoral Elephant: Globalization and the Struggle for Social Justice in the Twenty-First Century*, and Immanuel Wallerstein, *The Decline of American Power*.

[10] For an explanation and analysis of these concepts (and why they have failed to solve the problem of racism in the United States) see Joel Olson, *The Abolition of White Democracy*, pp. 95–123.

[11] See, for instance, Ted Allen, *The Invention of the White Race* (two volumes); Karen Brodkin, *How Jews Became White Folks and What That Says About Race in America*; Joe Feagin, *Racist America: Roots, Current Realities, and Future Reparations*; Noel Ignatiev, *How the Irish Became White*; Louise Newman, *White Women's Rights: The Racial Origins of Feminism*; Michael Omi and Howard Winant, *Racial Formation in the United States: From the 1960s to the 1990s*; David Roediger, *The Wages of Whiteness: Race and the Making of the American Working Class*.

[12] The lackadaisical response to the crisis in New Orleans, a city that is two-thirds Black, is certainly a telling instance of racism (combined with the government's "free-

market" logic that disregards social welfare, leaving the city so ill prepared to begin with). But examples of white supremacy abound: racially biased mechanisms of policing, sentencing, imprisonment, and implementation of the death penalty; the Black disenfranchisement in the 2000 presidential elections; the anti-immigrant laws and vigilante groups; and the misallocation of resources for urban schools or to treat diseases, such as HIV/AIDS, that disproportionately impact people of color.

[13] I am grateful to Kenyon Farrow and Stephanie Guilloud for discussions of anti-racism among whites as a form of both leading and getting out of the way.

[14] See, for instance, David Roediger, *Toward the Abolition of Whiteness* or *Colored White: Transcending the Racial Past*; or Becky Thompson, *A Promise and a Way of Life: White Antiracist Activism*. Other writings about white privilege are collected in Paula Rothenberg, *White Privilege: Essential Readings on the Other Side of Racism*.

[15] Many historians and political scientists have detailed how whiteness as a political construct was created in opposition to those deemed non-white, to stave off solidarity among people. For a good overview, see Joel Olson, *The Abolition of White Democracy*.

[16] In its first communiqué, for instance, Weather said it could be found in "every tribe, commune, dormitory, farmhouse, barracks and townhouse where kids are making love, smoking dope and loading guns." Bernardine Dohrn, "A Declaration of a State of War," in Raskin, ed., *Weather Eye*, p. 18.

[17] Bill Ayers, *Fugitive Days*, p. 177.

[18] David Gilbert, Columbia interview, pp. 266–67.

[19] Quoted in Becky Thompson, *A Promise and a Way of Life*, p. 96.

[20] See, for instance, John Brown Book Club, ed., *The Split of the Weather Underground*; David Gilbert, *SDS/WUO*, pp. 19–20; and E. Tani and Kaé Sera, *False Nationalism, False Internationalism: Class Contradictions in the Armed Struggle*, pp. 132–162. Unpublished internal memos written by Naomi Jaffe, Suzanne Ross and others were also helpful in this regard. Some of the published and unpublished criticisms, written during or shortly following the heat of the split, are sectarian and overly harsh, as discussed in chapter 10. Thus, some allegations must be taken with a grain of salt.

[21] David Gilbert interview with Sam Green and Bill Siegel for *The Weather Underground*, part II, p. 3, n.d. [circa 1998]. Transcript in author's files, courtesy of Sam Green.

[22] Quoted in Sale, *SDS*, p. 590.

[23] Jalil Muntaqim, letters to the author, September 9, 2003, and June 1, 2004.

[24] For instance, in *Revolution in the Air*, Max Elbaum criticizes PFOC as a group that, "along with the Weather Underground continued to frame its outlook in Marxist-Leninist terms while rejecting the central role of the working class," (p. 123). Before Weatherman went underground, articles in the *Debate in SDS* pamphlet and many movement

discussions in the pages of radical newspapers criticized the group for dismissing or downplaying the centrality of class politics to revolutionary movements (among other criticisms). See REP, ed., *Debate Within SDS*, and Harold Jacobs, *Weatherman*. And in books such as *Letters to a Young Activist*, *The Sixties*, and *The Twilight of Common Dreams*, Todd Gitlin has criticized the Weather Underground and the Black Power movement in particular for detracting from attempts at building a universalistic Left.

[25] This theory has been developed more thoroughly in the years since the WUO. A foundational work in this regard is David Roediger, *The Wages of Whiteness*. An independent scholarly approach can be found in Ted Allen's two-volume *The Invention of the White Race*, and, from a somewhat different perspective, J. Sakai, *Settlers: Mythology of the White Proletariat*.

[26] See Karen Ashley et al., "You Don't Need a Weatherman to Know Which Way the Wind Blows," reprinted in Harold Jacobs, ed., *Weatherman*.

[27] Weather Underground, "Attica," in Raskin, ed., *Weather Eye*, p. 48.

[28] David Gilbert, letter to the Resistance in Brooklyn Sixties Study Group, in which the author participated, June 15, 2004.

[29] Mark Rudd in *The Weather Underground*, Sam Green and Bill Siegel: 2003 (documentary).

[30] Shin'ya Ono, "A Weatherman: You Do Need a Weatherman to Know Which Way the Wind Blows," in Harold Jacobs, ed., *Weatherman*, p. 230.

[31] Many people, of course, have written on these issues. To give a WUO-related example, David Gilbert published a lengthy essay in pamphlet form entitled *Looking at the White Working Class Historically*. The essay is also republished in his book, *No Surrender*, pp. 49–66.

[32] David Gilbert, letter to the Resistance in Brooklyn Sixties Study Group, June 15, 2004.

[33] Laura Whitehorn, Keif interview, p. 22.

[34] Bill Ayers, conversation with the author, July 29, 2004. For more on Bobby Sands and the IRA hunger strike in the early 1980s, see Tim Pat Coogan, *IRA* or David Beresford, *Ten Men Dead*.

[35] An excellent discussion of these issues in the African context can be found in Bill Sutherland and Matt Meyer, *Guns and Gandhi in Africa: Pan-African Insights on Nonviolence, Armed Struggle, and Liberation in Africa*.

[36] Quoted in Thompson, *A Promise and a Way of Life*, p. 96.

[37] Suzanne Ross, quoted in ibid, p. 97.

[38] Women of the Weather Underground, "A Collective Letter to the Women's Movement" in Raskin, ed., *Weather Eye*, p. 78.

[39] Mickey Ellinger, e-mail to the author, August 16, 2004.

[40] Caleb Carr, *Lessons of Terror: A History of Warfare Against Civilians: Why It Has Always Failed and Why It Will Fail Again*, p. 6.

[41] Eqbal Ahmad, *Confronting Empire: Interviews with David Barsamian*, pp. 94–98.

[42] Ayers, *Fugitive Days*, p. 263.

[43] Quoted in John Bryan, *This Soldier Still at War*, p. 3.

[44] Naomi Jaffe, conversation with the author, May 20, 2004.

[45] Ayers, *Fugitive Days*, pp. 261–262.

[46] Raskin, "Introduction," in *Weather Eye*, pp. 8–9.

[47] Pardun, *Prairie Radical*, p. 308.

[48] In their respective memoirs, both Mark Rudd and Bill Ayers cover the material support they personally and the organization received while living underground. Author's interview with Rob McBride (June 4, 2004) was also instructive in this regard.

[49] Gilbert, *SDS/WUO*, pp. 21–22.

[50] For more on democratic centralism, see Paul Le Blanc, *Lenin and the Revolutionary Party*, pp. 127–141.

[51] I'm grateful to Sharon Martinas for conversations about democratic centralism in theory and practice in the 1970s.

[52] David Gilbert, interview with the author, July 18, 2002.

[53] Few people, even in the gay movement, were addressing the needs of bisexual and transgender people. In order to provide a fair criticism of Weather, I analyze the group in relation to lesbian and gay liberation, which was more pronounced at the time than bisexual and transgender liberation struggles. For more, see Leslie Feinberg, *Trans Liberation: Beyond Pink or Blue.*

[54] Cathy Wilkerson, "Toward a Revolutionary Women's Militia" in Harold Jacobs, ed., *Weatherman*, pp. 91–96. The article originally appeared in the July 8, 1969, issue of *New Left Notes.*

[55] Cathy Wilkerson, Columbia interview, p. 66.

[56] Though sexual experimentation was a part of the Weatherman, popular history has blown this out of proportion, as if to suggest that all the Weather Underground did was have group sex and blow up buildings. This hedonistic portrayal is found particularly (but not only) in the tabloid-style books such as Susan Braudy's *Family Circle: The Boudins and the Aristocracy of the Left.* Braudy, for instance, incorrectly and without attribution says that the Weather Underground "strictly enforc[ed] group sex as well as homosexuality," p. 191.

[57] This is discussed, for instance, in Rudd, unpublished manuscript, p. 215.

[58] Donna Willmott, conversation with the author, April 5, 2003.

[59] "December, 1969: Weatherman Goes Underground," in *Scanlan's*, p. 15. This article is an anonymous interview with two anonymous people—a current and a former member of the Weather Underground.

[60] Naomi Jaffe, "Criticism of *Prairie Fire*," June 1977, unpublished article in author's files.

[61] Ibid.

[62] Thompson, *A Promise and a Way of Life*, pp. 121–122.

[63] The Resistance Conspiracy case involved Alan Berkman, Tim Blunk, Marilyn Buck, Linda Evans, Susan Rosenberg, and Laura Whitehorn. Evans, Rosenberg, and Whitehorn did an interview edited by Queers United In Support of Political Prisoners called *Dykes and Fags Want to Know: Interview With Lesbian Political Prisoners*.

[64] This expression comes from Zillah Eisenstein, *Against Empire: Feminisms, Racism, and the West*.

[65] See, for instance, Michael Hardt and Antonio Negri, *Multitude: War and Democracy in the Age of Empire*; Tom Hayden, ed., *The Zapatista Reader*; John Holloway, *Change the World Without Taking Power: The Meaning of Revolution Today*; and Immanuel Wallerstein, *The Decline of American Power*.

[66] Weather Underground, "George Jackson," in Raskin, ed., *Weather Eye*, p. 42.

[67] Ibid., pp. 45–46.

[68] Rachel Herzing, "American Gulag, Part 1: The U.S. Prison Industrial Complex," in *Left Turn*, no. 17, pp. 8–9. More generally, see Peter Wagner, *The Prison Index: Taking the Pulse of the Crime Control Industry*.

[69] See Sundiata Acoli, "A Brief History of the New Afrikan Prison Struggle," printed in Joy James, ed., *Imprisoned Intellectuals*, pp. 151–152. Acoli notes that at the beginning of 1970, 200,000 people were locked up, and that the 1970s were the first time the prison system grew by 100,000 people in a single decade. "The previous 100,000 [person] increase, from 100,000 to 200,000, had taken thirty-one years, from 1927 to 1958. The initial increase to 100,000 had taken hundreds of years, from America's original colonial times." The rapid growth of prisons continues; the prison population went from 2 million to 2.1 million in just three years. For more on the coded discourse of prisons, see Joy James, ed., *States of Confinement: Policing, Detention, and Prisons*; and Christian Parenti, *Lockdown America: Police and Prisons in an Age of Crisis*.

[70] See, for instance, Vijay Prashad, *Keeping Up with the Dow Joneses: Debt, Prison, Workfare*, pp. 69–132.

[71] Naomi Jaffe, conversation with the author, May 24, 2004.

[72] David Gilbert, letter to the author, February 18, 2001.

[73] Elizabeth Kaufman, "Jalil Abdul Muntaqim [biography]," in Joy James, ed., *Imprisoned Intellectuals*, pp. 105–106. See also the report of the New York Task Force on Political Prisoners, pp. 17–19.

---

[74] Ward Churchill, "A Person Who Struggles for Liberation: An Interview with Geronimo Pratt," in Churchill and Vander Wall, eds., *Cages of Steel*, p. 204.

[75] Kathleen Cleaver, interview with Sam Green and Bill Siegel, in author's files courtesy of Sam Green, n.p. [xxxii–xxxiii].

[76] There are several books about the Zapatistas and collections of its communiqués and written statements. See, for instance, Tom Hayden, *The Zapatista Reader*; and John Holloway, *Zapatista! Reinventing Revolution in Mexico*.

[77] A timeline, along with much useful analysis, of this movement, can be found in Eddie Yuen, Daniel Burton-Rose, and George Katsiaficas, eds., *Confronting Capitalism: Dispatches from a Global Movement*.

[78] See, for instance, Wallerstein, *The Decline of American Power*, pp. 259–296. See also Boaventura de Sousa Santos, "The World Social Forum: Towards a Counter-Hegemonic Globalization," and Francine Mestrum, "The World Social Forum: A Democratic Alternative," both in François Polet and CETRI, eds., *Globalizing Resistance: The State of Struggle*, pp. 165–187 and pp. 188–205, respectively.

[79] Arundhati Roy, *An Ordinary Person's Guide to Empire*, p. 42.

[80] See Tariq Ali, *Bush in Babylon: The Recolonisation of Iraq*, pp. 139–141; Tariq Ali and David Barsamian, *Speaking of Empire and Resistance*, pp. 215–216. More generally, see Research Unit for Political Economy, *Behind the Invasion of Iraq*. There is also a website dedicated to monitoring the number of reported civilian casualties in Iraq since the 2003 invasion began: www.iraqbodycount.net. As of July 2005, the civilian death toll had surpassed 23,000.

[81] Zillah Eisenstein, *Against Empire: Feminisms, Racism, and the West*, pp. 141, 182, 190.

[82] Quoted in ibid., pp. 167–168. More generally, see Anne E. Brodsky, *With All Our Strength: The Revolutionary Association of the Women of Afghanistan*.

[83] See David Cole, *Enemy Aliens: Double Standards and Constitutional Freedoms in the War on Terrorism*.

[84] Alan Cowell, "U.S. 'Thumbs its Nose at Rights,' Amnesty Says," in *New York Times*, May 26, 2005, p. A10.

[85] For an explanation of these terms, see Chandra Talpade Mohanty, *Feminism Without Borders: Decolonizing Theory, Practicing Solidarity*, pp. 29–30, 143–144, 226–227.

[86] For a history of this development since the 1960s, see Becky Thompson, *A Promise and a Way of Life: White Antiracist Activism*. Anti-racist commentary and critique emanating from the global justice movement can be found online at the Colours of Resistance website, www.colours.mahost.org.

[87] Duggan, *The Twilight of Equality*, pp. 67–88. See also Robin D.G. Kelley, *Yo Mama's Dysfunktional! Fighting the Culture Wars in Urban America*, pp. 103–124.

[88] The terms Global South/Global North and Two-Thirds World/One-Third World have gained currency instead of the First World/Third World formulation. Functionally, however, they mean very similar things: that the centers of the world economy are numerically small but economically well-off and politically united in ways that would not be possible were it not for the poverty of the more numerous countries.

EPILOGUE
PAGES: 305-309

[1] Marilyn Buck, David Gilbert, and Laura Whitehorn, *Enemies of the State: A Frank Discussion of Past Political Movements, Their Victories and Errors, and the Current Political Climate for Revolutionary Struggle Within the U.S.A.*, p. 45.

[2] The title of Gilbert's book, *No Surrender*, is taken from this poem, which is called "It's This Way." Hikmet spent thirteen years in prison in Turkey for charges of inciting the military to riot through his poems. He died after thirteen years in exile. For more, see Randy Blasing and Mutlu Konuk, eds., *Poems of Nazim Hikmet*. The editors/translators give a biographical overview of Hikmet on pp. xiii-xviii. "It's This Way" is on p. 135.

[3] David Gilbert, "Getting to Know Nuh," in Nuh Washington, *All Power to the People*, p. 88. Gilbert's father died within three months of Balagoon.

[4] Becky Thompson, *A Promise and a Way of Life: White Antiracist Activism*, pp. 270, 270–276.

[5] David Gilbert, "AIDS Conspiracy Theories: Tracking the Real Genocide."

[6] David Gilbert, letter to the author, August 28, 2000.

[7] *David Gilbert: A Lifetime of Struggle*, Freedom Archives: 2002 (documentary).

[8] See, for instance, his "Statement to the [Columbia] Student Activist Forum," November 1986; "To Columbia Students," May 1998; and "To the Berkshire Forum," July 1989. All these statements are in the author's files.

[9] See, for instance, his *SDS/WUO* pamphlet and his article "The Terrorism that Terrorism Wrought," in *No Surrender*. The essays on SDS/WUO were originally published in two consecutive issues of *ONWARD*, a newspaper that emerged out of the global justice movement. In the late 1980s and early 1990s, Gilbert regularly wrote book reviews for a New York City magazine.

[10] Quoted in Thompson, *A Promise and a Way of Life*, pp. 271–273, 290.

[11] David Gilbert, letter to the author, May 30, 2004.

[12] David Gilbert, interview with Ron Grele for the Columbia University Oral History Research Office, pp. 448, 451.

BIBLIOGRAPHY

INTERVIEWS

Unless otherwise noted, all interviews were conducted in person with the author.

Vicente "Panama" Alba. New York, NY, June 26, 2004

Ashanti Alston. New York, NY, May 29, 2004

Bill Ayers. Chicago, IL, May 3, 2004

_____. Philadelphia, PA, July 27, 2004

Terry Bisson. San Francisco, CA, June 7, 2004

Scott Braley. Oakland, CA, June 7, 2004

_____. Emeryville, CA, April 24, 2005

Kathleen Cleaver. interview with Sam Green and Bill Siegel, n.d.; circa 1999, in author's files

Lyndon Comstock. E-mail interview with the author. June 6, 2005

_____. E-mail interview with the author. June 11, 2005

Bernardine Dohrn. Chicago, IL, May 3, 2004

_____. New York, NY, July 17, 2004

Herb Dreyer. Telephone interview with the author. October 7, 2002

_____. Telephone interview with the author. October 15, 2002

David Gilbert. Attica, NY, July 18, 2002

_____. Attica, NY, July 19, 2002

_____. Attica, NY, July 31, 2003

_____. Attica, NY, August 1, 2003

_____. Attica, NY, February 6, 2004

_____. Dannemora, NY, June 13, 2004

_____. Dannemora, NY, March 8, 2005

_____. Interview with the Columbia University Oral History Research Office, January 16 and 17, 1985, and June 18 and 19, 1985

_____. Interview with Sam Green and Bill Siegel, n.d.; circa 1998, in author's files

396

Naomi Jaffe. Glen Wild, NY, June 19, 2004
Jeff Jones. Princeton, NJ, June 25, 2004
Claude Marks. San Francisco, CA, June 5, 2004
Esperanza Martell. New York, NY, May 29, 2004
Rob McBride. San Francisco, CA, June 4, 2004
Judith Mirkinson. San Francisco, CA, June 6, 2004
Michael Novick. E-mail interview with the author, June 3, 2005
Susan Rosenberg. New York, NY, July 8, 2005
Suzanne Ross. Glen Wild, NY, June 19
_____. New York, NY, June 27, 2004
_____. New York, NY, July 16, 2004
Robert Roth. San Francisco, CA, June 6, 2004
_____. San Francisco, CA, May 31, 2005
Mark Rudd. Interview with the Columbia Oral History Research Office, March 20, 1987
_____. Philadelphia, PA, June 11, 2004
Judy Siff. San Francisco, CA, June 7, 2004
_____. San Francisco, CA, April 25, 2005
Michael Tarif Warren. Brooklyn, NY, July 18, 2004
Laura Whitehorn. New York, NY, March 21, 2004
_____. Interview with Nicole Keif, October 20, 2002, in author's files
Cathy Wilkerson. E-mail interview with the author, November 11, 2002
_____. Interview with the Columbia Oral History Research Office, February 17, 1985
_____. New York, NY, July 16, 2004
Donna Willmott. San Francisco, CA, June 4, 2004

ARCHIVES

Butler Library, Columbia University
      Oral History Research Office, "Student Movements of the 1960s."
Freedom of Information Act Online Archive, Federal Bureau of Investigation
      Weather Underground Organization Files
Naomi Jaffe—Personal Archive
Matt Meyer—Personal Archive
Tamiment Collection at the Bobst Library, New York University
      Christian Dykema Collection
      Michael Padwee Collection
      Black Panther Party Vertical File
      Black Liberation Army Vertical File
      May 19th Communist Organization Vertical File

Prairie Fire Organizing Committee Vertical File

Student Nonviolent Coordinating Committee Vertical File

Students for a Democratic Society Vertical File

Weather Underground Vertical File

Roz Payne—Personal Archive

NEWSPAPERS AND PERIODICALS

Black Panther (1967–1970)

Convention Report (1969)

Insurgent (1986–1989)

Movement (1968–1970)

Movement for a Democratic Society Newsletter (1966–1968)

New Left Notes (1966–1969)

New York Times (1969–2005)

Osawatomie (1975–1976)

Resistance (1982–1986)

RYM II (1969)

Second Battle of Chicago (1969)

Scanlan's (1971)

Washington Post (1981–1985).

ARTICLES AND PAMPHLETS

Acoli, Sundiata. *A Brief History of the New Afrikan Prison Struggle.* Harlem: Sundiata Acoli Freedom Campaign, 1992.

_____. *Sundiata Acoli's Brink's Trial Testimony.* Paterson, N.J.: Paterson Anarchist Collective, 1994.

Alpert, Jane. "Mother Right: A New Feminist Theory." Available online at http://scriptorium.lib.duke.edu/wlm/mother/

Alston, Ashanti. "Beyond Nationalism But Not Without It," in *ONWARD* vol. 2, iss. 4 (spring 2002), p. 11.

Arce, Rose Marie. "David Gilbert: A CU Activist Goes From Protest to Violence," in *Columbia Daily Spectator*, April 2, 1985.

Barber, David. "'A Fucking White Revolutionary Mass Movement' and Other Fables of Whiteness" in *Race Traitor* no. 12, spring 2001 pp. 4–90.

Barrera, Mario, Carlos Munoz and Charles Ornelas. "The Barrio as an Internal Colony," In Harlan Hahn, ed., *Urban Affairs Annual Review vol. 6: People and Politics in Urban Society*, pp. 465–498. Beverly Hills: Sage, 1972.

Berger, Dan. "Mark Felt's Other Legacy." Available online at
    http://www.thenation.com/doc.mhtml?i=20050704&s=berger, posted June
22, 2005.

_____. "Refusing to Surrender: John Brown and White Anti-Racist Struggle," in
    ONWARD vol. 2, iss. 4 (spring 2002).

Black Liberation Army Coordinating Committee. *Message to the Black Movement: A
    Political Statement from the Black Underground.* Chicago: Autonomous Zone
    Distribution, 1997.

Blumberg, Peter and Dennis J. Opatrny. "S.F. Grand Jury Probing 1970s Police
    Murders," in *Daily Journal*, August 2, 2005.

Buck, Marilyn, David Gilbert, and Laura Whitehorn. *Enemies of the State: A Frank
    Discussion of Past Political Movements, Their Victories and Errors, and the
    Current Political Climate for Revolutionary Struggle Within the USA.* Montreal:
    Abraham Guillen Press and Arm the Spirit, 2002.

Bukhari-Alston, Safiya, ed. *Panther Sisters on Women's Liberation.* California: Black
    Panther Newspaper Publishing, 1994.

Committee to Fight Repression, ed. *Build a Revolutionary Resistance Movement!
    Communiqués from the North American Armed Clandestine Movement, 1982–
    1985.* New York: Committee to Fight Repression, n.d. [circa 1985].

Comstock, Lyndon. "Days of Rage: October 8–11, 1969." Unpublished article in
    author's files.

Davidson, Carl. "Why SDS expelled the PLP," in *Guardian*, July 5, 1969, p. 3.

Feldman, Bob. "Anti-War Movements Now and Then: David Gilbert Interview," in
    Shadow, June/July 1991. Article in author's files.

_____. "Beyond Brinks: David Gilbert Talks About The Robbery, the
    Underground, the Struggle," in *Columbia Daily Spectator*, April 2, 1985.
    Article in author's files.

_____. "Civil Liberties and the 1981 Brinks Case" in *Downtown*, October 23,
    1991. Article in author's files.

Freudenberg, Nick, Ted Gold, Bob Tomashevsky, Mike Klare, Paul Rockwell, Art
    Leaderman, Judith Kopecky, and Steve Goldfield. *Why We Strike.* New York:
    Columbia Students for a Democratic Society, 1968.

George Jackson Brigade. *The Power of the People is the Force of Life: The Political
    Statement of the George Jackson Brigade.* Montreal: Abraham Guillen Press and
    Arm the Spirit, 2002.

_____. *Creating a Movement with Teeth: Communiqués of the George Jackson
    Brigade.* Montreal: Abraham Guillen Press and Arm the Spirit, 2003.

Gilbert, David. *Consumption: Domestic Imperialism. A New Left Introduction to the Political Economy of American Capitalism.* New York: Movement for a Democratic Society, circa 1968.

_____. "Criticize to Advance: Review of *False Nationalism, False Internationalism.*" Unpublished review in author's files (written circa 1986).

_____. "For the 20th Anniversary of the Columbia Strike," message dated April 1988.

_____. *SDS/WUO.* Montreal: Solidarity and Arm the Spirit, 2002, in author's files.

_____. "To the Berkshire Forum," message dated July 19, 1989, in author's files.

_____. "To Columbia Students," message dated May 4, 1998, in author's files.

_____. "Message to The Blockade Against Apartheid: From A Political Prisoner," message dated April 1985, in author's files.

_____. "Statement to the [Columbia] Student Activist Forum," message dated November 1986, in author's files.

Gilbert, David and David Loud. *U.S. Imperialism.* New York: Students for a Democratic Society, 1967.

Herzing, Rachel. "American Gulag, part 1: The U.S. Prison Industrial Complex," in *Left Turn* no. 17 (August–September 2005), pp. 8–9.

Jacobs, Ron. "Thinking About the Weather (Underground)." Available online at http://www.counterpunch.org/jacobs0726.html

John Brown Book Club, ed. *The Split of the Weather Underground Organization: Struggling Against White and Male Supremacy.* Seattle: John Brown Book Club, 1977.

Koveos, Eugene and Nicole Solomon. "This Will Not Be Kent State: Fear, Loathing, and Radical Movement: 1960s and the Present," in *ONWARD* vol. 2, iss. 2 (Fall 2001), pp. 3, 8.

Levasseur, Ray Luc. *The Trial Statements of Ray Luc Levasseur.* Montreal: Solidarity and Arm the Spirit, 2002.

Liberated Guardian Collective, ed., *Outlaws of Amerika: Communiqués from the Weather Underground.* New York: Liberated Guardian Collective, 1971.

May 19th Communist Organization. *Liberation in Our Lifetime: A Call to Build a Revolutionary Anti-Imperialist Women's Liberation Movement.* New York: May 19th Communist Organization, 1981.

_____. *Principles of Unity.* New York: May 19th Communist Organization, circa 1979 (no date listed).

Moore, Martha T. "1985 bombing in Philadelphia still unsettled," in *USA Today*, May 12, 2005.

MOVE. *25 Years on the MOVE.* N.p., 1997.

Movimiento de Liberacion Nacional, with Committee in Solidarity with Puerto Rican

Independence, May 19th Communist Organization, October 30th Committee, Prairie Fire Organizing Committee, and Sojourner Truth Organization. *Toward People's War for Independence and Socialism in Puerto Rico: In Defense of Armed Struggle. Documents and Communiqués from the Revolutionary Public Independence Movement and the Armed Clandestine Movement.* No city or publisher listed, 1979.

Muntaqim, Jalil. *On the Black Liberation Army.* Paterson, N.J.: Anarchist Black Cross Federation, 1997.

Neary, John. "The Two Girls From No. 18: Shock Troops on the Way to War at Home," in *LIFE*, March 27, 1970, pp. 26–29.

New York State Task Force on Political Prisoners. "Clemency Petition." Unpublished report in author's files [circa 2002].

Nunn, Kenneth. "Race, Crime and the Pool of Surplus Criminality: Or Why the 'War on Drugs' Was a 'War on Blacks.'" *The Journal of Gender, Race, and Justice*, vol. 6, no. 2 (Fall 2002).

Oglesby, Carl. *Trapped in a System.* Chicago: Students for a Democratic Society, 1965.

Pazzano, Sam. "No Bail for '70s Fugitive; U.S. Wants Him in Cop Shooting," in *Toronto Sun*, November 9, 2004, p. 26.

Potter, Paul. *March on Washington.* Chicago: Students for a Democratic Society, 1965.

Prairie Fire Organizing Committee. *Women's Liberation and Imperialism.* San Francisco: PFOC, 1977.

Queens 2 Defense. *The Queens Two Black Political Prisoners.* Queens, New York: Queens 2 Defense [n.d., circa 1998].

Queers United in Support of Political Prisoners. *Dykes and Fags Want to Know: Interview with Lesbian Political Prisoners.* Toronto: Arm the Spirit 1995.

Radical Education Project, ed. *Debate Within SDS: RYM II vs. Weatherman.* Ann Arbor, Michigan: Radical Education Project, 1969.

Ratner, Michael. "Immoral Bounty for Assata," in *Covert Action Quarterly* 65 (Fall 1998).

Resistance in Brooklyn, ed. *John Brown 2000: U.S. Political Prisoner/POW Writings on the 200th Birthday of John Brown and Nat Turner.* New York: Jericho Movement and RnB Publication, 2000.

Ruether, Rosemary Radford. "To Mary Moylan, Another Casualty of War," in *National Catholic Reporter*, November 10, 1995. Available online at http://www.findarticles.com/p/articles/mi_m1141/is_n4_v32/ai_17883936.

Smith, Jack, "SDS ousts PLP," in *Guardian*, June 28, 1969, pp. 3, 11.

Sojourn, Celia and Billy Ayers. *Politics in Command.* [no city or date listed]. Red Dragon Print Collective [circa 1975]. In author's files.

Stanton, Sam. "Olson likely to serve longest SLA sentence, officials say," in *Sacramento Bee,* September 30, 2004.

Students for a Democratic Society. *Occupation Troops Out!* Chicago: Students for a Democratic Society, 1969.

Weatherman. *Two, Three, Many Vietnams.* [No publisher, city, or date listed; circa 1970]. In author's files.

Wells, Greg. "COINTELPRO: Then and Now part II" in *ONWARD* vol. 1, iss. 3 (winter 2001), pp. 5, 13, 19.

_____. "Infrastructure, Transience and the Death of Small-Town Anarchist Organizing" in *ONWARD* vol. 2, iss. 1 (summer 2001), p. 14.

Western Goals. *Outlaws of Amerika: The Weather Underground Organization.* Alexandria, VA: Western Goals, 1982.

Worthy, William. "A Real Bomber's Chilling Reasons," in *LIFE*, March 27, 1970, p. 30.

BOOKS

Abu-Jamal, Mumia. *We Want Freedom: A Life in the Black Panther Party.* Cambridge: South End Press, 2004.

Achcar, Gilbert. *Clash of Barbarisms: September 11 and the Making of the New World Disorder.* New York: Monthly Review Press, 2002.

Ahmad, Eqbal. *Confronting Empire: Interviews with David Barsamian.* Cambridge: South End Press, 2000.

Albert, Stew and Judith Clavir, eds. *The Sixties Papers: Documents of a Rebellious Decade.* New York: Praeger Publishers, 1984.

Ali, Tariq. *Bush in Babylon: The Recolonisation of Iraq.* London: Verso, 2004.

Ali, Tariq and David Barsamian. *Speaking of Empire and Resistance.* New York: The New Press, 2005.

Ali, Tariq and Susan Watkins. *1968: Marching in the Streets.* New York: The Free Press, 1998.

Allen, Robert. *Black Awakening in Capitalist America.* Trenton, New Jersey: Africa World Press, 1992.

_____. *Reluctant Reformers: Racism and Social Reform Movements in the United States.* Washington, D.C.: Howard University Press, 1974.

Alpert, Jane. *Growing Up Underground.* New York: Citadel, 1990.

Anzaldúa, Gloria. *Interviews/Entrevistas.* New York: Routledge, 2000.

Armstrong, David. *A Trumpet to Arms: The Alternative Press in America.* Boston: South End Press, 1981.

Avorn, Jerry et al. *Up Against the Ivy Wall: A History of the Columbia Crisis.* New York: McClelland and Steward Ltd., 1968.

Ayers, Bill. *Fugitive Days: A Memoir*. Boston: Beacon, 2001.

Balagoon, Kuwasi. *Kuwasi Balagoon: A Soldier's Story: Writings by a Revolutionary New Afrikan Anarchist*. Montreal: Solidarity, 2001.

_____ et al., eds. *Look for Me in the Whirlwind: The Collective Autobiography of the New York Twenty-One*. New York: Vintage Books, 1971.

Baldwin, James. *The Fire Next Time*. New York: Dial Press, 1963.

Beck, Chris Aronson, Reggie Emilia, Lee Morris, and Ollie Patterson. *"Strike One to Educate One Hundred": The Rise of the Red Brigades in Italy in the 1960s–1970s*. Chicago: Seeds Beneath the Snow, 1986.

Bell, Derrick. *Faces at the Bottom of the Well: The Permanence of Racism*. New York: Basic Books, 1992.

Beresford, David. *Ten Men Dead: The Story of the 1981 Irish Hunger Strike*. New York: Atlantic Monthly Press, 1987.

Berlet, Chip and Matthew Lyons. *Right-Wing Populism in America: Too Close for Comfort*. New York: Guilford, 2000.

Blum, William. *Killing Hope: U.S. Military and C.I.A. Interventions Since World War II*. Monroe, Maine: Common Courage, 2004.

_____. *West-Bloc Dissident*. New York: Soft Skull Press, 2002.

Blunk, Tim and Ray Luc Levasseur, eds. *Hauling Up the Morning. Izando la Mañana*. Trenton, New Jersey: Red Sea Press, 1990.

Braudy, Susan. *Family Circle: The Boudins and the Aristocracy of the Left*. New York: Alfred Knopf, 2003.

Breitman, George, ed. *Malcolm X Speaks: Selected Speeches and Documents*. New York: Pathfinder Press, 1989.

Bryan, John. *This Soldier Still at War*. New York: Harcourt, Brace, Jovanovich, 1975.

Calvert, Greg. *Democracy from the Heart: Spiritual Values, Decentralism, and Democratic Idealism in the Movement of the 1960s*. Eugene: Communitas Press, 1991.

Carmichael, Stokely, with Ekwueme Michael Thelwell. *Ready for Revolution: The Life and Struggles of Stokely Carmichael (Kwame Ture)*. New York: Scribner, 2003.

Carr, Caleb. *Lessons of Terror: A History of Warfare Against Civilians: Why It Has Always Failed and Why It Will Fail Again*. New York: Random House, 2002.

Carson, Clayborne. *In Struggle: SNCC and the Black Awakening of the 1960s*. Cambridge, Mass.: Harvard University Press, 1995.

Castellucci, John. *The Big Dance: The Untold Story of Weatherman Kathy Boudin and the Terrorist Family that Committed the Brink's Robbery Murder*. New York: Dodd, Mead & Company, 1986.

Chepesiuk, Ron. *Sixties Radicals: Then and Now*. Jefferson, North Carolina: MacFarland & Company, 1995.

Chomsky, Noam. *Hegemony or Survival: America's Quest for Global Dominance*. New York: Owl Books, 2004.

Churchill, Ward and Jim Vander Wall. *Agents of Repression: The FBI's Secret War Against the Black Panther Party and the American Indian Movement*. Boston: South End Press, 1988.

_____, eds. *Cages of Steel: The Politics of Imprisonment*. Washington DC: Maisonneuve Press, 1992.

_____. *The COINTELPRO Papers: Documents from the FBI's Secret Wars Against Dissent in the United States*. Boston: South End Press, 1990.

Cleaver, Kathleen and George Katsiaficas, eds. *Liberation, Imagination, and the Black Panther Party: A New Look at the Panthers and Their Legacy*. New York: Routledge, 2001.

Cohn-Bendit, Daniel and Gabriel. *Obsolete Communism: The Left-Wing Alternative*. San Francisco: AK Press, 2000.

Cole, David. *Enemy Aliens: Double Standards and Constitutional Freedoms in the War on Terrorism*, New York: The New Press, 2003.

Collier, Peter and David Horowitz. *Destructive Generation: Second Thoughts About the '60s*. New York: Summit Books, 1990.

Collins, Patricia Hill. *Black Feminist Thought: Knowledge, Consciousness, and the Politics of Empowerment*. New York: Routledge, 2000.

Committee to End the Marion Lockdown, ed. *Can't Jail the Spirit: Political Prisoners in the U.S.* Chicago: Editorial Coqui Publishers, 1998.

Cone, James. *Martin and Malcolm and America: A Dream or a Nightmare?* Maryknoll, New York: Orbis, 2000.

Connelley, William Elsey. *John Brown*. New York: Books for Libraries Press. 1900.

Danaher, Kevin. *Corporations Are Gonna Get Your Mama: Globalization and the Downsizing of the American Dream*. Monroe, Maine: Common Courage, 1997.

Davis, Angela Y. *Angela Davis: An Autobiography*. New York: International Publishers, 1988.

_____. *Are Prisons Obsolete?* New York: Seven Stories, 2003.

_____. *If They Come in the Morning: Voices of Resistance*. New York: Signet, 1971.

Debray, Régis. *Revolution in the Revolution?* New York: Grove Press, 1967.

Dellinger, Dave. *From Yale to Jail: The Life of a Moral Dissenter*. Marion, South Dakota: Rose Hill Books, 1993.

_____. *More Power Than We Know: The People's Movement Toward Democracy*. New York: Anchor Press/Doubleday, 1975.

Deming, Barbara. *Remembering Who We Are*. Tallahassee, Florida: Pagoda, 1981.

Dray, Philip. *At the Hands of Persons Unknown: The Lynching of Black America*. New York: Modern Library, 2002.

Duberman, Martin. *Stonewall*. New York: Plume, 1993.

Duggan, Lisa. *The Twilight of Equality: Neoliberalism, Cultural Politics, and the Attack on Democracy*. Boston: Beacon, 2003.

DuPlessis, Rachel Blau and Ann Snitow, eds. *The Feminist Memoir Project: Voices from Women's Liberation*. New York: Three Rivers Press, 1998.

Eisenstein, Zillah. *Against Empire: Feminisms, Racism and the West*. London: Zed, 2004.

Elbaum, Max. *Revolution in the Air: Sixties Radicals Turn to Lenin, Che and Mao*. London: Verso, 2002.

Ellsberg, Daniel. *Secrets: A Memoir of Vietnam and the Pentagon Papers*. New York: Penguin, 2002.

Feagin, Joe, Hernán Vera, and Pinar Batur. *White Racism: The Basics*. New York: Routledge, 2000.

Feinberg, Leslie. *Trans Liberation: Beyond Pink or Blue*. Boston: Beacon, 1999.

Feldman, Bob. *Sundial: Columbia SDS Memories*. Unpublished memoir in author's files.

Fernandez, Ronald. *Prisoners of Colonialism: The Struggle for Justice in Puerto Rico*. Monroe, Maine: Common Courage Press, 1994.

Fletcher, Jim, Tanaquil Jones, and Sylvére Lotringer, eds. *Still Black, Still Strong: Survivors of the War Against Black Revolutionaries*. New York: Semiotext(e), 1993.

Forman, James. *The Making of Black Revolutionaries*. Seattle: University of Washington Press, 2000.

Formisano, Ronald P. *Boston Against Busing: Race, Class, and Ethnicity in the 1960s and 1970s*. Chapel Hill: University of North Carolina, 1991.

Frankfort, Ellen. *Kathy Boudin and the Dance of Death*. New York: Stein and Day, 1984.

Fraser, Ronald et al., eds. *1968: A Student Generation in Revolt*. New York: Pantheon Books, 1988.

Freire, Paulo. *Pedagogy of the Oppressed*. New York: Continuum, 1993.

Galeano, Eduardo. *Open Veins of Latin America: Five Centuries of the Pillage of a Continent*. New York: Monthly Review Press, 1997

Gilbert, David. *No Surrender: Writings from an Anti-Imperialist Political Prisoner*. Montreal: Abraham Guillen Press and Arm the Spirit, 2004.

Gitlin, Todd. *The Sixties: Years of Hope, Days of Rage*. New York: Bantam, 1993.

_____. *The Whole World is Watching: Mass Media in the Making and Unmaking of the New Left*. Berkeley: University of California Press, 1980.

Glessing, Robert J. *The Underground Press in America*. Bloomington: Indiana University Press, 1970.

Glick, Brian. *War at Home: Covert Action Against U.S. Activists and What We Can Do About It*. Cambridge: South End Press, 1989.

Halperin, Morton H., Jerry J. Berman, Robert L. Borosage, and Christine M. Marwick. *The Lawless State: The Crimes of the U.S. Intelligence Agencies*. New York: Penguin, 1976.

Hardt, Michael and Antonio Negri. *Empire*. Cambridge: Harvard University Press, 2000.

Hayden, Tom. *Reunion: A Memoir*. New York: Random House, 1988.

_____, ed. *The Zapatista Reader*. New York: Nation Books, 2002.

Hill, Lance. *The Deacons for Defense: Armed Resistance and the Civil Rights Movement*. Chapel Hill: University of North Carolina, 2004.

Hilliard, David and Lewis Cole. *This Side of Glory: The Autobiography of David Hilliard and the Story of the Black Panther Party*. Boston: Little Brown, 1993.

Ho, Fred, ed., with Carolyn Antonio, Diane Fujino, and Steve Yip. *Legacy to Liberation: Politics and Culture of Revolutionary Asian Pacific America*. San Francisco: AK Press, 2000.

Hobsbawm, Eric. *Bandits*. New York: New Press, 2000.

Hoffman, Abbie. *The Autobiography of Abbie Hoffman*. New York: Four Walls Eight Windows, 2000.

hooks, bell. *Talking Back: Thinking Feminist, Thinking Black*. Boston: South End Press, 1989.

Andrew E. Hunt. *The Turning: A History of Vietnam Veterans Against the War*. New York: New York University Press, 2001.

Jackson, George. *Soledad Brother: The Prison Letters of George Jackson*. Chicago: Lawrence Hill Books, 1994.

Jacobs, Harold, ed. *Weatherman*. Berkeley, California: Ramparts Press, 1970.

Jacobs, Ron. *The Way the Wind Blew: A History of the Weather Underground*. New York: Verso, 1997.

James, Joy, ed. *The Angela Y. Davis Reader*. Malden, Mass.: Blackwell, 1998.

_____, ed. *Imprisoned Intellectuals: America's Political Prisoners Write on Life, Liberation, and Rebellion*. Lanham, Maryland: Rowman and Littlefield, 2003.

_____, ed. *States of Confinement: Policing, Detention, and Prisons*. New York: Palgrave Macmillan, 2000.

Jay, Karla. *Tales of a Lavender Menace: A Memoir of Liberation*. New York: Basic Books, 1999.

Jones, Charles E., ed. *The Black Panther Party Reconsidered*. Baltimore: Black Classics Press, 1998.

Jones, Thai. *A Radical Line: From the Labor Movement to the Weather Underground, One Family's Century of Conscience*. New York: Free Press, 2004.

Karnow, Stanley. *Vietnam: A History*. New York: Penguin, 1983.

Katsiaficas, George. *The Imagination of the New Left: A Global Analysis of 1968*. Boston: South End Press, 1988.

Kelley, Robin D.G. *Freedom Dreams: The Black Radical Imagination*. Boston: Beacon, 2002.

_____. *Yo Mama's Dysfunktional! Fighting the Culture Wars in Urban America*. Boston: Beacon, 1998.

Kellner, Douglas and Dan Streible, eds. *Emile de Antonio: A Reader*. Minneapolis: University of Minnesota Press, 2000.

Kopkind, Andrew. *The Thirty Years' Wars: Dispatches and Diversions of a Radical Journalist, 1965–1994.* New York: Verso, 1995.

Kunstler, William with Sheila Isenberg. *My Life as a Radical Lawyer.* New York: Citadel, 1994.

Lavan, George, ed. *Che Guevara Speaks.* New York: Pathfinder Books, 1997.

Le Blanc, Paul. *Lenin and the Revolutionary Party.* Atlantic Highlands, New Jersey: Humanities Press International, 1993.

Lewis, Randolph. *Emile de Antonio: Radical Filmmaker in Cold War America.* Madison: University of Wisconsin Press, 2000.

Loewen, James. *Lies My Teacher Told Me: Everything Your American History Textbook Got Wrong.* New York: Touchstone, 1995.

Mackenzie, Angus. *Secrets: The CIA's War at Home.* Berkeley: University of California, 1997.

Mamdani, Mahmood, *Good Muslim, Bad Muslim: America, the Cold War, and the Roots of Terror.* New York: Pantheon, 2004.

Mandela, Nelson. *The Struggle Is My Life.* New York: Pathfinder Press, 1986.

Mann, Eric. *Comrade George: An Investigation into the Life, Political Thought, and Assassination of George Jackson.* New York: Perennial Library, 1974.

_____. *Dispatches from Durban: Firsthand Commentaries on the World Conference Against Racism and Post-September 11 Movement Strategies.* Los Angeles: Frontline Press, 2002.

Martinez, Elizabeth "Betita." *De Colores Means All of Us: Latina Views for a Multi-Colored Century.* Boston: South End Press, 1998.

Matthiessen, Peter. *In the Spirit of Crazy Horse: The Story of Leonard Peltier and the FBI's War on the American Indian Movement.* New York: Penguin, 1991.

McAlister, Melani. *Epic Encounters: Culture, Media, and U.S. Interests in the Middle East, 1945–2000.* Berkeley: University of California Press, 2001.

Melendez, Miguel "Mickey." *We Took the Streets: Fighting for Latino Rights with the Young Lords.* New York: St. Martin's Press, 2003.

Melville, Sam. *Letters from Attica.* New York: William Morrow & Company, 1972.

Michener, James A. *Kent State: What Happened and Why.* New York: Ballantine, 1982.

Miller, James. *"Democracy is in the Streets": From Port Huron to the Siege of Chicago.* Cambridge: Harvard University Press, 1994.

Mohanty, Chandra Talpade. *Feminism Without Borders: Decolonizing Theory, Practicing Solidarity.* Durham, North Carolina: Duke University Press, 2003.

Morgan, Edward. *The Sixties Experience: Hard Lessons About Modern America.* Philadelphia: Temple University Press, 1991.

Morgan, Robin. *Going too Far: The Personal Chronicle of a Feminist.* New York: Vintage Books, 1978.

Muntaqim, Jalil. *We Are Our Own Liberators! Selected Prison Writings.* Montreal: Abraham Guillen Press and Arm the Spirit, 2003.

Naison, Mark D. *White Boy: A Memoir.* Philadelphia: Temple University Press, 2002.

The New Yippie Book Collective. *Blacklisted News, Secret Histories: From Chicago to 1984.* Berkeley: Bleecker Publishing, 1983.

Olson, Joel. *The Abolition of White Democracy.* Minneapolis: University of Minnesota, 2004.

Ortiz, Roxanne Dunbar. *Outlaw Woman: A Memoir of the War Years, 1960-1975.* San Francisco: City Lights, 2001.

Pardun, Robert. *Prairie Radical: A Journey Through the Sixties.* Los Gatos, California: Shire, 2001.

Parenti, Christian. *Lockdown America: Police and Prisons in an Age of Crisis.* London: Verso, 1999.

Payne, Charles M. *I've Got the Light of Freedom: The Organizing Tradition and the Mississippi Freedom Struggle.* Berkeley: University of California Press, 1995.

Peck, Abe. *Uncovering the Sixties: The Life and Times of the Underground Press.* New York: Citadel, 1991.

Polet, François and CETRI. *Globalizing Resistance: The State of Struggle.* London: Pluto, 2004.

Politzer, Patricia. *Fear in Chile: Lives Under Pinochet.* New York: Pantheon, 1989.

Powers, Richard Gid. *Secrecy and Power: The Life of J. Edgar Hoover.* New York: Free Press, 1987.

Prashad, Vijay. *Keeping Up with the Dow Joneses: Debt, Prison, Workfare.* Cambridge: South End Press, 2004

Raskin, Jonah. *Out of the Whale: Growing Up in the American Left.* New York: Links Books, 1974.

_____, ed. *The Weather Eye: Communiqués from the Weather Underground.* New York: Union Square Press, 1974.

Ratner, Michael and Ellen Ray. *Guantánamo: What the World Should Know.* White River Junction, Vermont: Chelsea Green Publishing, 2004.

Reinhart, Tanya. *Israel/Palestine: How To End the War of 1948.* New York: Seven Stories, 2002.

Research Unit for Political Economy, *Behind the Invasion of Iraq.* New York: Monthly Review, 2003.

Rips, Geoffrey, with comments by Allen Ginsberg, Todd Gitlin, and Angus McKenzie. *UnAmerican Activities: The Campaign Against the Underground Press.* San Francisco: City Lights, 1981.

Roediger, David. *Toward the Abolition of Whiteness.* London: Verso, 1994.

_____. *The Wages of Whiteness: Race and the Making of the American Working Class.* London: Verso, 1991.

Rosen, Ruth. *The World Split Open: How the Modern Women's Movement Changed America.* New York: Penguin, 2000.

Roy, Arundhati. *An Ordinary Person's Guide to Empire.* Cambridge: South End Press, 2004.

Rubin, Jerry. *We Are Everywhere.* New York: Harper and Row, 1971.

Rudd, Mark. Unpublished memoir in the author's files.

Sakai, J. *Settlers: Mythology of the White Proletariat.* Chicago: Morningstar, 1989.

Sale, Kirkpatrick. *SDS.* New York: Vintage, 1974.

Sales, William W., Jr. *From Civil Rights to Black Liberation: Malcolm X and the Organization of Afro-American Unity.* Boston: South End Press, 1994.

Segrest, Mab. *Memoir of a Race Traitor.* Boston: South End Press, 1994.

Shakur, Assata. *Assata: An Autobiography.* Chicago: Lawrence Hill Books, 1987.

Spofford, Tim. *Lynch Street: The May 1970 Slayings at Jackson State.* Kent, Ohio: Kent State University Press, 1988.

Streitmatter, Rodger. *Voices of Revolution: The Dissident Press in America.* New York: Columbia University Press, 2001.

Sutherland, Bill and Matt Meyer. *Guns and Gandhi in Africa: Pan-African Insights on Nonviolence, Armed Struggle, and Liberation in Africa.* Trenton, New Jersey: Africa World Press, 2000.

Swearingen, M. Wesley. *FBI Secrets: An Agent's Expose.* Boston: South End Press, 1995.

Tabb, William K. *The Amoral Elephant: Globalization and the Struggle for Social Justice in the Twenty-First Century.* New York: Monthly Review, 2001.

Tani, E. & Kaé Sera. *False Nationalism, False Internationalism: Class Contradictions in the Armed Struggle.* Seeds Beneath the Snow (no city given), 1985.

Thompson, Becky. *A Promise and a Way of Life: White Antiracist Activism.* Minneapolis: University of Minnesota: 2001.

Torres, Andrés and José E. Velázquez, eds. *The Puerto Rican Movement: Voices from the Diaspora.* Philadelphia: Temple University Press, 1998.

Ture, Kwame, and Charles V. Hamilton. *Black Power: The Politics of Liberation.* New York: Vintage Books, 1992.

Tyson, Timothy. *Radio Free Dixie: Robert F. Williams and the Roots of Black Power.* Chapel Hill: University of North Carolina Press, 1999.

Urban Research Corporation. *On Strike... Shut it Down! A Report on the First National Student Strike in U.S. History.* Chicago: Urban Research Corporation, 1972.

Useem, Bert and Peter Kimball. *States of Siege: U.S. Prison Riots 1971–1986.* New York: Oxford University Press, 1991.

Varon, Jeremy. *Bringing the War Home: The Weather Underground, the Red Army Faction, and Revolutionary Violence of the Sixties and Seventies*. Berkeley: University of California, 2004.

Vigil, Ernesto B. *The Crusade for Justice: Chicano Militancy and the Government's War on Dissent*. Madison, Wisconsin: The University of Wisconsin Press, 1999.

Wagner, Peter. *The Prison Index: Taking the Pulse of the Crime Control Industry*. Springfield, Massachusetts: Prison Policy Initiative/Western Prison Project, 2003.

Wallerstein, Immanuel. *The Decline of American Power*. New York: New Press, 2003.

Washington, Albert Nuh. *All Power to the People*. Montreal: Arm the Spirit and Solidarity, 2002.

Weather Underground. *Prairie Fire: The Politics of Revolutionary Anti-Imperialism*. San Francisco: Communications Co., 1974.

Wicker, Tom. *A Time to Die*. New York: Ballantine Press, 1975.

Williams, Evelyn. *Inadmissible Evidence: The Story of the African-American Trial Lawyer Who Defended the Black Liberation Army*. Lincoln, Nebraska: Universe.com, Inc., 2000.

X, Malcolm and Alex Haley. *The Autobiography of Malcolm X*. New York: Ballantine Books, 1965.

Yuen, Eddie, Daniel Burton-Rose, and George Katsiaficas. *Confronting Capitalism: Dispatches from a Global Movement*. Brooklyn: Soft Skull Press, 2004.

Zaroulis, Nancy and Gerald Sullivan. *Who Spoke Up? American Protest Against The War in Vietnam 1963–1975*. New York: Holt, Rinehart and Winston, 1984.

Zinn, Howard. *A People's History of the United States: 1492 to the Present*. New York: HarperPerennial, 1980.

VIDEOTAPES

David Gilbert: A Lifetime of Struggle. Produced and directed by Freedom Archives. 29 minutes, 2002.

The End of SDS. Produced and directed by Helen Garvy. 94 minutes, 2003.

Freedom is Contagious. Produced and directed by Helen Garvy. 40 minutes, 2003.

Jalil Muntaqim: Voice of Liberation. Produced and directed by Freedom Archives. 20 minutes, 2003.

OUT: The Making of a Revolutionary. Produced and directed by Sonja de Vries and Rhonda Collins. 60 minutes, 2000.

Rebels With a Cause. Produced and directed by Helen Garvy. 110 minutes, 2001.

Resistance Conspiracy. Produced and directed by PCTV. 40 minutes, 1988.

Underground. Produced and directed by Emile de Antonio with Mary Lampson and Haskell Wexler. 88 minutes, 1976.

The Weather Underground. Produced and directed by Sam Green and Bill Siegel. 92 minutes, 2003.

INDEX

Boudin, Leonard, 222

BPP. *See* Black Panther Party

Braley, Scott, 33, 106, 135, 168, 273; and aboveground allies, 372n.81; biography of, 311; and bombings, 108; and criticism/self criticism, 105; and Flint War Council, 122, 123; going underground, 56; and Hampton-Clark murders, 121; and inversion, 216, 377n.39; and PL, 78; and protests, 54, 109; and Red Dragon Collective, 185; and SDS, 45, 83, 84, 86, 91; surfacing of, 241; and townhouse explosion, 129, 131; and WUO, 114, 116, 130, 205, 278; and WUO publications, 81, 186, 194

Braudy, Susan, 388n.109, 392n.55

Bray, Michael Donald, 261

Breakthrough (journal), 240, 366n.64

Briggs, John, 236

"bringing the war home" slogan, 129, 146

Brink's robbery, 141, 247–48; aftermath, 251; arrests, 248–49; conspiracy trials, 249, 252, 257, 262; criticism of, 262–63; grand juries, 258–59, 381n.42; and political prisoners, 252–56; security, 384n.46; state violence, 248–49; testimony at, 252. *See also* conspiracy trials; grand juries; political prisoners; specific individuals

Brooklyn College, 103

Brooks, Mel, 222

Brotherhood of Eternal Love, 138–39

Brown, H. Rap, 131, 136, 139. *See also* Al-Amin, Jamil

Brown, John, 186, 205–206, 375n.15

Brown, Sam, 248; testimony of, 257, 386n.81; torture of, 248–49; trial of, 252, 256

Brown, Waverly, 248

Brown Berets, 11, 55, 83–84

Bryn Mawr College, 128

Buck, Marilyn, 58, 257, 260

Bundy, William, 187

Bureau of Indian Affairs, 171

Bush, George, 189

Bush, George W., 270, 272, 307

C

Cabral, Amilcar, 180, 294

Cadre Schools, WUO: and class struggle, 194–95, 220; and democratic centralism, 290; and *Prairie Fire*, 184

California Department of Corrections, 166, 187

California State Capitol, 43

Calvert, Greg, 40

Cambodia: civil war, 131; invasion of, 117, 132, 164, 285; and Lon Nol, 202; and Nixon, 76

capitalism, 37. *See also* globalization

Capitol, United States, 164–65

car bombs, 122, 131

Carr, Caleb, 286

Carter, Bunchy, 63, 79

CASA, 226

Castellucci, John, 388n.109

Castro, Fidel, 45, 183

casualties of war, 76, 301

Catholics, radical, 148, 174–75. *See also* Catonsville 9

Catonsville 9, 148, 174

censorship, 68, 115. *See also* Federal Bureau of Investigation media program

Center for International Affairs, 100, 142, 187. *See also* Harvard University

Central Committee of WUO, 130, 210; criticism of, 232–33, 237–38; expulsion from WUO, 235; and FBI, 236; and Hard Times, 225, 229; and inversion, 208, 215; self criticism, 230, 231; and WUO publications, 184, 212. *See also* Weather Bureau

Central Intelligence Agency (CIA), 37, 40, 62, 65

Chaney, James, 19

Chase Manhattan, 117

chemical warfare. *See* tear gas

Chesimard, Joanne. *See* Assata Shakur

Chicago 8: conviction of, 117; defense attorneys, 76; trial of, 107, 109, 115, 242; and WUO protest, 119. *See also* Chicago Democratic Convention

Chicago Armed Forces Induction Center, 111

Chicago Democratic Convention (1968), 53–54, 75, 99

Chicano Moratorium protest, 134

Chile: coup, 169, 225, 287; and political prisoners, 261; support of, by US activists, 199, 227; and trade embargoes, 169

China, 188, 190, 241. *See also* Red Guard, the

Christian Right, 270

and WUO, 99, 104, 112, 124; and WUO publications, 89

Comstock prison, 306

Congressional Record, 71

Congress of Racial Equality (CORE), 18, 24, 64

conspiracy trials, 76, 115; and Angela Davis, 141; and Brink's case, 250, 252, 257, 262; charges against WUO members, 138, 156, 242; and Chicago 7, 107, 109; and Chicago DNC arrests, 53, 75–76; and Panther 20, 79, 115, 147, 162

Convention Report (newspaper), 89. *See also New Left Notes*

Coordinating Committee of the Black Liberation Army, 245

CORE. *See* Congress of Racial Equality

corporations: and colonialism, 190; destruction of property, 245, 250, 284; and globalization, 271, 301; as WUO targets, 169–70, 180–81, 199–200, 225

counterculture, 28, 66, 139; political limits of, 204; and racism, 147; and SDS, 52, 79; and WUO, 80, 137, 138, 146. *See also* drugs

counterinsurgency research, 48, 100, 143

courthouse bombings, 117, 141, 142. *See also* bombings

criticism/self criticism: and feminism, 291; softening of, 130; and townhouse explosion, 129; and WUO, 105, 113, 118, 231, 234

Cronkite, Walter, 47

Cuba: and Assata Shakur, 246; and clandestinity, 135; and *foco* theory, 46; revolution, 10, 45, 183, 294; support of Vietnam, 104; and WUO, 104, 128

culture, 138

D

Daley, Richard, 53, 54, 112

Dannemora, town of, 305

D'Aubisson, Robert, 261

Davidson, Carl, 85

Davis, Angela, 7; and George Jackson, 166; and Jonathan Jackson, 141–42; and WUO, 139, 143

Davis, Rennie, 75–76

Days of Rage, 109–14, 359n.46; buildup to, 103–107; indictments, 132; WUO recruitment for, 99. *See also* Weatherman

Deacons for Defense and Justice, 23

de Antonio, Emile, 222–23

death penalty, 236, 251, 389n.12

Debray, Régis, 45, 46, 101. *See also foco* theory

Deep Throat. *See* Mark Felt

defeatism, 96–97

Defense Department Supply Agency (Oakland), 202. *See also* Department of Defense

Delgado, Marion, 110

Dellinger, Dave, 75–76, 101, 108, 121, 134

democracy: in activist groups, 301; participatory, 76, 289, 295; in WUO, 184, 231, 233, 289–290

democratic centralism, 289–290

Democratic Party, 19, 20, 26. *See also* Atlanta Democratic Convention; Chicago Democratic Convention

Department of Corrections (California), 166, 187

Department of Defense (DOD), 47–48, 202

Department of Health, Education and Welfare (HEW), 171, 172, 187, 291

Der Spiegel (magazine), 41

desegregation, 7, 18, 217. *See also* Boston busing crisis

Detroit *Sun,* 70

Diem regime, 25. *See also* Vietnam War

discipline, 289

DOD (Department of Defense), 47–48, 202

Dohrn, Bernardine, 121, 150, 302; biography of, 311–12; and Brink's grand jury, 259, 381n.42; and clandestinity, 153, 242; and conferences, 84–86, 123, 226; and elitism, 113, 189; family of, 160; and FBI, 132, 156, 159, 236; and FBI encirclement of WUO, 157; and nationalist movements, 54–56; and political theory, 237; at protests, 50, 111; and SDS, 54, 79, 84, 85; self criticism, 234; and *Underground,* 221, 223; and US defeat in Vietnam, 202–203; and white activists, 277–78; and white privilege, 273, 280; and Women's Liberation, 57, 290; and WUO, 101, 220, 228, 288; and WUO legacy, 217, 286; and WUO publications, 136, 145, 176, 186, 194, 209, 213

Dohrn, Jennifer, 201, 226, 369n.23

Dominica, 261

Dominican Republic, 29

Donghi, Dianne, 132

Douglass, Frederick, 213

Dow Chemical, 44

draft: lottery, 122; protests, 44, 148; resisters, 7, 288

Drake Hotel, Chicago, 110

Dreyer, Herb, 102

drugs: arrests, 70, 193; and BLA, 163, 262–63; and people of color, 147; and racism in legal system, 259, 386n.94; and revolution, 139, 146; and WUO, 106, 136. *See also* counterculture

Drumgo, Fleeta, 141

Dunbar-Ortiz, Roxanne, 143, 179, 365n.57

Dutschke, Rudi, 41

Dylan, Bob, 80, 145

E

Eastern bloc, 270

Economic Research and Action Project (ERAP), 27, 28, 344n.13

Egypt, 42

Eisenstein, Zillah, 300

Elbaum, Max, 9, 52, 176, 218

El Comité, 11, 55

electoral politics, 53, 163, 186–87, 294, 298–299

elitism, 96, 102, 113, 223. *See also* exceptionalism

Ellinger, Mickey, 285

Ellsberg, Daniel, 159, 222, 368n.17

Elrod, Richard, 112

El Salvador, 251, 261

environmentalism, 270

ERAP (Economic Research and Action Project), 27, 28, 344n.13

Evans, Linda, 57, 132, 297, 350n.84

exceptionalism, 188–89. *See also* elitism

exemplary action strategy, 98–99, 114. *See also foco* theory

expropriations. *See* robberies

F

factionalism, 90, 232. *See also* sectarianism

factories, 99

FALN. *See Fuerzas Armadas de Liberacion Nacional*

Fanon, Frantz, 45, 294

Farber, Jerry, 40

farm workers, 210, 212, 302. *See also* working class

FBI. *See* Federal Bureau of Investigation

fear, and clandestine living, 135

Featherstone, Ralph, death of, 131

Federal Bureau of Investigation (FBI), 62; accountability of, 297; attacks on revolutionary groups, 119, 179; and Brink's investigation, 249; and grand juries, 161–62; harassment, 222; infiltration, 129, 172, 235–36, 290; informers, 174, 258; and media, 68–72, 208; Most Wanted List, 132, 142, 156, 160; and state repression, 8, 43; and WUO, 159–60, 242, 274, 288, 365n.59; and WUO encirclement, 157–59, 192. *See also* COINTELPRO

Feldman, Bob, 38, 101, 340n.9

Felt, Mark, 159, 240

feminism, 203, 229, 307; and activist groups, 238, 239, 240; anti-Left, 173; and SDS, 57–58; and women's self-defense, 219; and WUO, 170–72, 290–93, 372n.76

feminist movement. *See* Women's Liberation Movement

Ferrera, Sal, 69

Field, Sally, 222

Fight the People, 96

Fire! (The Fire Next Time), 88, 356n.48. *See also New Left Notes*

flags, NLF, 100, 101, 111, 114

Flint War Council, 122–24, 131, 138, 146

foco theory, 46–47, 214; and WUO, 98, 101, 146. *See also* Régis Debray

Foerster, Werner, 246

Forcade, Tom, 68, 72

Foreign Policy Association, 44–45

Forman, James, 72, 254–55

Foster, Marcus, 178

Frankfort, Ellen, 388n.109

Freedom Rides. *See* Congress of Racial Equality

Freire, Paulo, 5

FRELIMO (Front for the Liberation of Mozambique), 180

Frey, John, 43

Froines, John, 75–76

Fromm, Erich, 51

Front for the Liberation of Mozambique (FRELIMO), 180

Fuerzas Armadas de Liberacion Nacional (FALN), 215, 245, 250, 260, 288

G

Gamachi, Phil, 235

Garcia, Inez, 219

gay liberation movement, 357n.61; and John Briggs, 236; and the Left, 91, 227, 240, 293; rise of, 11, 270, 301; and WUO, 208, 210, 290, 291

gender oppression, 57, 170–72, 291; and women of color, 203. *See also* male supremacy; sexism

General Motors, 117

General Telephone and Electronics, 131

Geneva Accords, 24–25

Geneva Convention, 253–54

George Jackson Brigade, 288

Germany, 41, 135, 260

Gilbert, David: and aboveground support of WUO, 288; and antiracism, 134, 306–307; biography of, 312; and Brink's robbery, 247, 248, 385n.71; in Castellucci account, 388n.109; and Columbia, 17–24, 51, 52; and Days of Rage, 110, 111; and democratic centralism, 289; departure from pacifism, 30, 56; early years, 4, 38; family of, 259, 307; and FBI encirclement, 157–58; going underground, 129, 131; and Hampton-Clark murders, 120; and inversion, 215; and militancy, 283; and New Working Class, 38–40; and prison, 305–308; remorse, 262, 263, 307; and RYM, 87; and SDS, 6, 28, 87; status in WUO, 298; surfacing of, 243; trial of, 252–56; and US government, 90, 285; and white privilege, 274–76; and WUO, 91, 101, 102, 104, 114, 149, 287; and WUO Cadre Schools, 184; and WUO publications, 38, 40, 146, 191, 196; and WUO split, 234, 237

GI organizing, 99, 102, 201, 280

Gitlin, Todd, 7, 12n.38, 72, 90, 390n.24

Giuliani, Carlo, 342n.27

Glick, Brian, 62

globalization, 271, 298–300, 299, 389n.9

global justice. *See* social justice movements

Global North, 301, 394n.88

Global South, 302, 394n.88. *See also* Third World

Gold, Ted, 172, 186; death of, 128, 136; and WUO, 101, 102, 129

Gold Coast neighborhood, Chicago, 110

Goodman, Andrew, 19

Goodwin, Guy, 160

Gorz, Andre, 40

Gottlieb, Bob, 38

grand juries, 160–62, 220, 235, 258, 369n.28, 369n.29; and Brink's investigation, 250, 252, 258–59; in ongoing investigations, 269; persecution of activists, 75; and WUO, 138, 222. *See also* specific individuals

Grathwohl, Larry, 132, 290

Great Depression, 190

Grenada, 189, 251, 271

Gribetz, Kenneth, 256, 385n.73

Guantánamo prison, 254, 301

Guardian, 85. *See also* Liberated Guardian

guerilla war, 116, 135; and abolition movement, 205; and Geneva Convention, 253–54; and WUO, 165, 187, 287

Guevara, Che, 5, 45–47, 82, 294; and clandestinity, 155; murder of, 107; "two, three, many Vietnams," 46, 97, 201, 270

Guinea-Bissau, 180, 190

Gulf Oil Corporation, 180

Gulf War, 189

Gumbo, Judy, 370n.43

gun control, 43

H

Haiti, 271, 302

Hale, Matthew, 389n.4

Hameed, Bashir, 249

Hamilton Hall, Columbia, 48, 49

Hampton, Fred, 71, 123; criticism of WUO, 108; murder of, 119–20, 166, 187, 274; response to murder of, 120–22

Hanrahan, Edward, 119, 166

harassment, 106–107, 174; by FBI, 159–60, 222

Hard Times Conference, 225–28, 238

Harlem, New York, 247; and Columbia, 20, 48–49; and racism, 19–21

Harvard University, 34–35. *See also* Center for International Affairs

Hayden, Casey, 57

Hayden, Tom, 26, 75–76, 109

Hayes, Robert Seth, 297, 306

Haymarket Riots statue, 108, 139. *See also* police

Hearst, Patty, 178, 179

Hearst, William Randolph, 179

Heath, Teddy Jah, 297

HEW (Department of Health, Education and Welfare), 171, 172, 187, 291

high schools, 70, 97, 100–101, 104, 176

Hikmet, Nazim, 306, 395n.2

Hilton Hotel, 193

hippies, 146. *See also* Brotherhood of Eternal Love; counterculture; drugs

Hirsch, Phoebe, 241

HIV/AIDS, 270, 302, 306, 389n.12

Ho Chi Minh, 17, 239, 294; as a slogan, 83, 86, 100, 110, 122; and WUO, 177

Hoffman, Abbie, 53, 155; indictment of, 75–76; support of WUO, 143, 177, 362n.10

Hoffman, Dustin, 127

Hoffman, Julius, 76, 110

Hollywood, 222, 223

Holocaust, 42

homosexuality, 105, 291. *See also* gay liberation; lesbian liberation

Hoover, J. Edgar, 144; and FBI, 33, 62, 71; and WUO, 132

House Un-American Activities Committee (HUAC), 75, 235

Huggins, John, 63, 79

human rights, 22

Human Rights Commission, 21

human targets, 129

Humphrey, Hubert, 53

hunger strikes, 284, 391n.34

Hurricane Katrina, 272, 389n.12

Hutton, Bobby, 47

I

IBM Corporation, 131, 250

ICV. See Independent Committee on Vietnam

IDA (Institute for Defense Analysis), 48

identification, fake, 157

identity politics, 270, 301

IMF (International Monetary Fund), 295

imperialism, 37, 50, 85, 123, 287; in Africa, 180–81; and Brink's defense, 252; and Third World, 40, 281; US, 11, 34, 40, 190–91, 270–71, 294, 299–300; and Vietnam War, 164; white and male supremacy, 58, 301; and WUO, 97, 131, 137, 207, 281; and WUO legacy, 272; and WUO publications, 81, 140, 149. *See also*

anti-imperialism

Independent Committee on Vietnam (ICV), 24, 25, 61

Indiana University, 69

indigenous people, 163, 190, 203; and WUO imagery, 142, 145, 146; and Zapatistas, 299. *See also* American Indian Movement

Industrial Workers of the World (IWW), 190

infiltration: by COINTELPRO, 63; by FBI, 129, 172, 235–36, 240; of radical media, 69

Institute for Defense Analysis (IDA), 48. *See also* counterinsurgency research

integration. *See* desegregation

internal colonies. *See* colonialism

Internal Revenue Service (IRS), 62, 65

internationalism, 50, 293, 295, 302; and Women's Liberation, 170; and working class, 204; and WUO, 103, 135, 137, 280–81, 299; and WUO publications, 89

International Monetary Fund (IMF), 295

International Solidarity Movement (Palestine), 302

International Telephone and Telegraph (ITT): bombing of, 177, 187, 287; and Chilean coup, 169, 200

International Tribunal on Political Prisoners and Prisoners of War in the United States, 261

International Women's Day, 172, 207

interracial couples, 249

interracial organizing, 27. *See also* coalitions, multiracial

inversion strategy, 215–17. *See also* clandestine living; surfacing; WUO

Inwood project of SDS, 98

IRA. *See* Irish Republican Army

Iran, 243

Iraq: and collateral damage, 300; and US imperialism, 189, 294; US involvement in, 299, 305; and US sanctions, 271, 300

Ireland, 260, 261

Irish Republican Army (IRA), 202, 284, 391n.34

IRS (Internal Revenue Service), 62, 65

Israel, 42, 156

Israel, Jared, 89

Italy, 135, 387n.98

ITT (International Telephone and Telegraph), 169, 177, 187, 200, 287

militancy, 40, 117, 130, 136, 188; and BPP, 108, 359n.35; and Days of Rage, 109–14; decline of, 192, 203, 216; rise of, 8, 10, 34–35, 43–47, 116, 143; in twenty-first century, 294; veterans training activists, 155; and women, 219–20, 290; in WUO, 95, 99, 101, 144; and WUO publications, 82, 186; as WUO strategy, 283–88

militarism, 283, 284

military, 62, 70, 100; bases and, 102, 129, 138; induction centers for the, 111, 117, 172; manuals of the, 155; prisons, 301; propaganda, 189; resistance within, 9, 65

Miller, Edward, 240

Minutemen, 389n.4

Mirkinson, Judith, 227, 289, 298; biography of, 314; and feminism, 219, 293; and PFOC, 201, 238

Mississippi Freedom Democratic Party, 20

Mississippi Freedom Summer, 19

Mitchell, John, 75–76, 117, 132, 138

MIT (Massachusetts Institute of Technology), 187

Mobe. See Mobilization to End the War in Vietnam

Mobilization to End the War in Vietnam, 113

Mobil Oil Company, 131

moderation, 179, 373n.89

monogamy, 105, 106, 291

Moses, Robert, 34

Motor City 8, 101

Motorola, 250

"Mountain Moving Day," 170–71

Movement for a Democratic Society, 40

MOVE Organization, 251, 297, 383n.39

Movimiento de Liberación Nacional, 281

Moylan, Mary, 174, 175, 372n.80

Mozambique, 180

MPLA (People's Movement for the Liberation of Angola), 180

Ms. magazine, 173

Muntaqim, Jalil, 277, 297

Murtagh, John, 142

N

Naison, Mark, 100

National Action. *See* Days of Rage

National Bisexual Liberation Movement, 203. *See also* bisexual liberation

National Black Feminist Organization, 203

National Collective. *See* Revolutionary Youth Movement

National Conference of Black Lawyers, 259

National Gay Task Force, 203. *See also* gay liberation

National Guard, 10, 112; bombing of headquarters by WUO, 134, 187, 363n.23; Kent State murders, 9, 117, 133, 357n.61

National Interim Committee. *See* Revolutionary Youth Movement

nationalism. *See* Black nationalism; national liberation movements

National Lawyers Guild, 161

National Liberation Front of Vietnam (NLF), 135, 164, 165, 294; Cuban support of, 104; flags, 100, 101, 111, 113; and Operation Phoenix, 144; and Tet Offensive, 8; and US activists, 45, 77, 113, 201; and WUO, 99, 103–104. *See also* Vietnam War

national liberation movements, 5, 55; in 2005, 270; Angolan, 210; and communists, 232; decline of, 294; and defeatism, 96; and democratic centralism, 289; and Geneva Convention, 253–54; and internationalism, 299; and white activists, 235, 238, 239, 241, 243, 273; and working class, 279; and WUO, 95, 194, 289; WUO neglect of, 204, 211, 275; and WUO publications, 80–81, 185, 190; WUO support of, 135–36, 180–81, 195, 200. *See* Black Power; revolutionary movements; specific groups

National March Against Racism, 218

National Student Association, 65

National Task Force for COINTELPRO Litigation and Research, 239–40

National Union for Total Independence of Angola (UNITA), 180

National War Council. *See* Flint War Council

Nation of Islam, 22

Native American movement. *See* American Indian Movement

neocolonialism, 190. *See also* colonialism

neo-Nazis, 240, 261. *See also* activists, Right wing; white supremacy

Neruda, Pablo, 177

Neutrality Act, 261

Paris rebellion, 47, 188

Park Home Grown Garden Society, 365n.59

Parks, James, 166, 370n.51

party-building. *See* communist parties

patriarchy. *See* Women's Liberation Movement

Payne, William "Che," 131

Peace Corps veterans, 128

Peltier, Leonard, 203, 260, 297, 298, 375n.10

Pentagon, 165, 287

Pentagon Papers, 159, 222, 368n.17

people of color, 11, 116, 150, 202; access to universities, 56; and armed struggle, 130, 362n.11; and class, 281; in George W. Bush administration, 272; as leaders for white activists, 177, 273, 284, 294; and police violence, 137; and prison system, 259, 296; as revolutionaries, 89, 276; and state repression, 203; and Women's Liberation, 172, 219. *See also* communities of color; self-determination; women of color; specific groups or individuals

People's Movement for the Liberation of Angola (MPLA), 180

People's War strategy, 46, 80, 144

petty crime, 106

PFDC. *See* Prairie Fire Distribution Committee. *See also* Prairie Fire Organizing Committee

PFOC. *See* Prairie Fire Organizing Committee

Philippines, 294, 302

Pine Ridge reservation, 203

Pinochet, Augusto, 169; and political prisoners, 261; supporters, 199, 225. *See also* Chile

PL. *See* Progressive Labor Party

Plumbers. *See* Watergate

Poindexter, Ed, 298

police, 41, 115; attacks on radical groups, 120, 179, 251, 383n.39; at Attica revolt, 168; and BLA, 163, 245; bombing of police stations, 129, 137, 138; brutality, 9, 98, 133, 248–49; and Clayton Van Lydegraf, 235; community control of, 276; Haymarket statue, 108, 140; and imperialism, 50; and John Brown Anti-Klan Committee, 240; and Klan murders, 261, 387n.101; murder by, 9, 119, 133, 169, 203; murder of, 132; at protests, 50–51, 53, 110–11, 115; and racism, 274;

and state repression, 62; and Stonewall, 91; at student protests, 9, 24, 43, 47; and WUO, 100, 106, 109, 154, 187, 368n.4. *See also* state violence

Police Sergeant's Association, 140

political prisoners, 260–63, 305–308; amnesty for, 167, 261, 298; and Brink's case, 252–56; criticism of *Underground,* 223; murders of, 166; and prison movement, 296–98; and radical groups, 203, 239, 240; in the 1980s, 251; solidarity with prisoners of war, 255–57; treatment of, 246; tried as criminals, 254, 257; and WUO publications, 139, 141, 186, 192, 213, 376n.31. *See also* prisoners of war; specific individuals

Political Research Associates (PRA), 71

Pol Pot, 241

poor people, organizing, 27

Port Authority Statement, 38–40

Port Huron Statement, 26

Portugal, 180

Potter, Paul, 37

Power, Kathy, 132

Prairie Fire (book), 183–96, 234, 365n.59; and aboveground allies, 207, 226; and other WUO publications, 180, 208; and Panther criticism, 147

Prairie Fire Distribution Committee (PFDC), 193, 201

Prairie Fire Organizing Committee (PFOC), 193, 201–202, 234, 366n.65; and Boston busing crisis, 218; and Hard Times, 225–28, 232; and prisons, 295; public support for, 287; and Puerto Rican independence movement, 213; separation from underground, 229, 238; and split within, 239; and WUO, 216, 285; and WUO publications, 207

Prairie Power, 28

PRA (Political Research Associates), 71

Pratt, Geronimo, 67, 155, 297

Praxis. See New Left Notes

Prensa Latina (news service), 46

Presidio Army Base, 138, 187

press, underground: aboveground support for, 288; Red Dragon Print Collective, 185; and WUO publications, 137, 175–76, 195, 208. *See also* media, radical

preventive detention, 301

primary contradiction, 194, 237

prisoners, political. *See* political prisoners

316–17

Washington, Albert Nuh, 297

Washington Free Press (newspaper), 69

Washington Post (newspaper), 159

Washington Square Church, New York, 193

Watergate scandal, 159, 162

weapons, 114

Weather Bureau of WUO, 108, 292; name change, 130; and relocation of WUO members, 105, 118. *See also* Central Committee

Weatherman, 5, 12, 91; bombings, 5, 122; and Days of Rage, 103–107, 109–14; elitism in, 113–14; going underground, 118, 120, 122–24, 129, 135; "jailbreaks," 99–100; and karate, 100, 101; and Midwest National Action conference, 96–98; organizing whites, 98–99; predecessors of, 79; and revolution, 113; sexism in, 291–92; as a symbol, 12; and townhouse explosion, 127–31, 136, 146. *See also* collectives; Weather Underground

Weatherman statement, 80–82, 100, 210, 355n.19; and class, 87, 278–89; and SDS split, 88; and state repression, 106–107

The Weather Underground (film), 90, 115

Weather Underground Organization (WUO): aboveground allies, 143–44, 153–56; accountability of, 275–78, 390n.20; "A Declaration of War," 136–37; bombings, 151, 164–65, 166, 168–69, 169, 199; and Boston busing crisis, 217; and Catholic Left, 175; changes in, 214–15; and class, 155, 204–205, 210–12, 219, 278–82; communiqués, 136–37, 175–78; encirclement by FBI, 157–59; funding of, 156; and Hard Times Conference, 225–29; inversion strategy, 215–217; and John Brown as symbol, 205–206; and Leary escape, 138–39; legacy of, 13, 272–78; name change, 145, 199; "New Morning, New Weather," 145; ongoing investigation of, 269; opposition to, 102–103; and *Osawatomie,* 207–209, 230; and party-building, 186–87, 194, 200, 211, 215; and *Prairie Fire,* 183–96; and prisons, 295–96; promiscuity in, 106, 291, 358n.26, 392n.56; recruitment, 98–99; and rectification, 232; response to criticism, 147–48, 148, 173–74; as retaliatory force, 149; and SLA, 178–80, 214; solidarity with Third World, 12–13, 149, 278; and split, 231–38; and strategy of militancy, 283–86; support of BLA, 163–64, 276–77; surfacing of members,

241–43; and Women's Brigade, 142, 172; and Women's Liberation, 170–72, 219–20, 377n.49. *See also* militancy; Weatherman; specific bombings; specific individuals

Webb, Marilyn Salzman, 350n.91

Weinberger, Casper, 172

Weiner, Lee, 75–76

welfare rights, 270

Wells Fargo Bank, 250

Western Union, 157

Wexler, Haskell, 221, 222

white activists. *See* activists, white

white guilt: and antiracist work, 13, 134, 206; in popular press, 263

Whitehall Induction Center. *See* military induction centers

Whitehorn, Laura, 121, 129, 130, 134, 283, 290; biography of, 317; and Boston busing crisis, 218; and Brink's robbery, 263–64; and feminist anti-imperialism, 293; and *Osawatomie,* 213; and PFDC, 193; and WUO, 229

whiteness. *See* race

white privilege, 81, 232, 273–74; and ability to surface, 242; and clandestinity, 274–75; and FBI tactics, 159; and working class, 278; and WUO, 96, 150, 156, 210–11, 228; and WUO legacy, 272–78

white supremacy, 232, 252; as an American value, 150; and BLA, 163; and Boston busing crisis, 209, 218; and class, 194, 282; and prison system, 169, 246; and social justice movements, 54, 190, 355n.34; in twenty-first century, 272, 389n.12; and WUO, 195, 204, 210–11; and WUO legacy, 273, 301. *See also* Ku Klux Klan; racism

Wicker, Tom, 167

Wilkerson, Cathy, 65, 88, 115, 119–20; biography of, 317; and machismo in WUO, 100; *New Left Notes,* 38; surfacing of, 242; and townhouse explosion, 128, 131; and *Underground,* 221, 223; and Women's Liberation, 290; and WUO publications, 147, 194, 207; and WUO split, 233, 234

Wilkerson, James, 128

Williams, Evelyn, 381n.6

Williams, Robert, 10, 23

Willmott, Donna, 273; and aboveground allies, 226; biography of, 317; and changes in WUO, 203, 205; and Cuba, 103; departure from pacifism, 121; and Leary escape, 139; and self-determination, 136; and sexism in WUO, 293; and white privilege, 242, 274, 275; and WUO, 220, 223, 229, 290; and WUO propaganda, 151; and WUO publications, 191, 208, 214; and WUO split, 232

WITCH. *See* Women's International Terrorist Conspiracy from Hell

women, 213; in BLA, 246; and Hard Times, 229; and self-determination, 227; in WUO, 291, 292. *See also* sexism; Women's Liberation Movement

Women of All Red Nations, 203

women of color, 203, 276, 296, 300. *See also* people of color

women-only actions: bombings, 142, 172; and WUO, 97, 101

Women's Brigade of WUO, 142, 172. *See also* Proud Eagle Tribe

Women's International Terrorist Conspiracy from Hell (WITCH), 57

Women's Liberation Movement, 57–58, 84, 188, 241; and class struggle, 219; and Flint War Council, 123; and Hard Times, 227; PFOC involvement in, 202; and *Prairie Fire*, 190, 191; racism in, 113; and Revolutionary Committee, 235; and SDS, 91, 357n.62; at 1969 SDS Convention, 83; and WUO, 103, 113, 146, 174, 290; WUO commitment to, 170–72; WUO criticism of, 113, 195. *See also* feminism; male supremacy

Woodward, Bob, 159

workers, Black, 77, 78

Worker-Student Alliance, 77

Workers World Party (WWP), 226

working class, 212, 226; in Puerto Rico, 213; and state repression, 376n.24; and students, 38–39, 77; and women of color, 300; and WUO, 200, 204; WUO neglect of, 278, 390n.24; and WUO publications, 195, 230

working class, multinational, 211, 227; lack of unity in, 281; and WUO, 204–205, 220; WUO as leaders of, 215, 229; and WUO publications, 207, 219

working class, white: and Boston busing crisis, 217; and privilege, 278, 279, 391n.25; and Weatherman statement, 80; and WUO, 95–96, 220, 282, 391n.31; WUO members, 155; and WUO recruitment, 98

World Church of the Creator, 389n.4

World Conference Against Racism, 295

World Social Forum, 295, 299, 302

World Trade Organization (WTO), 299, 306

Wounded Knee shoot-out, 203, 276

WTO (World Trade Organization), 299–306

WUO. *See* Weatherman; Weather Underground Organization

WWP (Workers World Party), 226

X

X, Malcolm, 22–24, 82, 206, 221, 239, 294; and BPP, 32–33; and the media, 70

Y

Yellow Peril, 11

Yippies, 75, 138, 238

The YIPster Times (newspaper), 238

Younge, Sammy, 34

Young Lords Party, 11, 55, 115, 242; and Attica revolt, 167; and Days of Rage, 108, 358n.32; and revolution, 97, 281; at 1969 SDS Convention, 83–84; and WUO, 277. *See also* Puerto Rican independence movement

youth activists. *See* activists, student; activists, youth

Youth Against War and Fascism, 226

youth culture. *See* counterculture

Z

Zapatista movement, 299, 394n.76

Zedong, Mao, 183

Zimbabwe, 226, 243

Zinn, Howard, 226